A WORLD IN REVOLUTION

Books by *Herbert L. Matthews*

HERBERT L. MATTHEWS

A
WORLD IN
REVOLUTION

A Newspaperman's Memoir

Charles Scribner's Sons, New York

ACKNOWLEDGMENTS

I wish to express my thanks to *The New York Times* for permission to reprint the many passages from my articles quoted in this book. The work has been greatly improved by the patient and expert editing of Norbert M. Slepyan of Charles Scribner's Sons, and the encouragement and advice of Charles Scribner, Jr. Neither, of course, is responsible for my opinions or narrative.

720068

TO THOSE WHOM I HAVE ALWAYS
HELD MOST DEAR: *Nancie, Eric,*
AND *Priscilla*

CONTENTS

A WORLD IN
REVOLUTION

Chapter 1

BEGINNING

A revered friend of mine, the late Maharaj Rana of Dholpur in India, once told me that Mercury is the planet that rules over journalists and journalism. He was not being critical. I myself never believed that newspapermen had any tutelary planet or guardian angel. They are on their own.

My story—insofar as it means anything—is a newspaper story. My life has no other significance to the world outside the circle of my family and friends. If it has any interest, it is not as a life but as a career. I have been places and seen things and met people, but always as a professional. This is therefore an empirical book, a process of induction from my experiences as secretary, reporter, cable editor, foreign correspondent, war correspondent, bureau chief, and editorial writer. I am not a philosopher, sociologist, scholar, or historian. I am a newspaperman, which has always been my proudest boast.

Today meant infinitely more to me as I went along than all my yesterdays—so long as I was working on *The Times*, which was from July 10, 1922 to October 1, 1967. A man of my age, looking back, seeks for meanings, trends, causes—something that can help to explain this disordered, frantic, revolutionary, changing world of the 1970's.

The day I was born—January 10, 1900—seems to have been deceptively quiet so far as news was concerned. All that I could find in the *Annual Register*, which at that time was England's most authoritative chronicle of events, was that "the first through train from Cairo to Khartoum reached its destination." To be sure, there were the Boer War in South Africa and the Boxer "Rebellion" in China. McKinley was re-elected in November. It was a period of some senseless assassinations, and McKinley himself was to be a victim in September 1901.

His Vice-President, Theodore Roosevelt, could not have been more remote from me as a one-year-old baby in New York City, but a newspaperman's roots have a thousand branches. "Teddy" Roosevelt had been chosen as a vice-presidential candidate in 1900 because of his swashbuckling role in the Spanish-American War. That war changed the history of Cuba and started the island on a path that was to lead to the Cuban Revolution. When Roosevelt died on January 6, 1919, I stood at parade rest in our Tank Corps base near Langres, France, for twenty-one interminable minutes in a heavy, slashing rain, which the wind drove straight into our faces. As the cannon salutes went on, our feet sank deeper and deeper into the mud of a France that I could hardly wait to leave.

The stage was being set for World War I when I was born, and I was barely able to get into it and over to France, since I was only eighteen when the war ended. It was the last war that young Americans, as a whole, were eager to join. I concede that we did not have as much sense as our children in World War II, or our grandchildren in the Vietnam War. But we were that way perhaps because we, who were just soldiers and not generals or statesmen, had no idea what the first global conflict was about.

I still do not know any sensible reasons for it. I was later to read all about it with a feeling of despair. The utter senselessness of the massive slaughter of young men in trench warfare and the criminal stupidity of the generals on both sides made—and still make—almost unbearable reading.

Anyone born in 1900 ushered in a century of murderous irrationality, although the United States, having won the "Splendid Little War" of 1898, was complacent, peaceful, prosperous, and still lulled by Thomas Jefferson's admonition to avoid "entangling alliances" with the wicked, predatory European nations.

The Britain that I learned about in the still heavily dominated Irish-American atmosphere of New York City was "perfidious Albion." France was a romantic perennial ally who had supposedly helped the American colonies to win their War of Independence out of altruism, not in the course of power politics. China and Japan, William Randolph Hearst kept telling us, represented "the Yellow Peril."

When I was nine years old, my mother gave me for my birthday a copy of Richard Harding Davis' *Soldiers of Fortune*. It was a book about some of the men who had played a role in his time and his career. Davis was one of the greatest war correspondents in American journalistic history. He covered Cuba at the beginning of her second War of Independence, then the Spanish-American War (for the *New York Herald*, *The Times* of London and Scribners), the Boer War, the Russo-Japanese War, and World War I from 1914 to 1916 when he died of illness at fifty-three —in bed, after so many adventures and dangers.

He was very brave, serious, accurate, and honest. In a letter from Cuba to his brother, Charles, on June 26, 1898, he wrote disgustedly: "Fortunately, the survival of the fittest is the test and only the best men in every sense get to the front. There are fifty others at the base [in sight of Santiago de Cuba] who keep the wire loaded with rumors, so when after great difficulties we get the correct news back to Daiquire [sic] at Siboney there is no room for it. . . . Generals fight to have us on their staffs and all that sort of thing, so I really can't complain, except about the fact that our real news is crowded out by the faker in the rear." (This is the enduring complaint of all war correspondents worth their salt.)

The quality of American war corresponding deteriorated. It was rather poor in World War I. The work of correspondents such as Edwin L. James of *The New York Times* or Floyd Gibbons of the *Chicago Tribune* in World War I would be quite unacceptable to editors today—I mean qualitatively and not through any lack of courage or effort.

I am not suggesting that my parents had me tagged for a future newspaperman, or that my mother could have foreseen what my career would be. The copy of *Soldiers of Fortune,* which I still possess, is nevertheless a symbol to me—or if I wanted to believe it, a freakish sign from Mercury that I was to be under his rule.

I entered journalism by the back door when I answered a want ad signed "Publisher," hoping that it was a book publisher. Instead, I found myself a secretary in the Business Department of *The New York Times.* This was on graduating from Columbia in 1922. In those days it was still considered highly desirable for a newspaperman to serve an apprenticeship in the mechanics of his trade—to know something of printing; how the type is set; how newsprint is made; how a press works; what happens to advertising. Adolph S. Ochs, the publisher during my first thirteen years on *The Times,* had begun his career as a "printer's devil."

The journalist is now a specialist. All-around experience is no longer valuable. In fact, I would be hard put to explain precisely what good my long apprenticeship did for me. And yet I am sure that it gave me a "feel," an understanding, a greater involvement. I became absorbed in the work as if I were drawn into, and became a part of, *The New York Times* by a process of osmosis. It was *my* newspaper in a way that I cannot help feeling it is not to those employees of the last few decades working on *The Times.*

Being a journalist is, in one respect, like being a doctor. For a doctor any human being is a patient whose ills or wounds must be treated even if he be a murderer. For a journalist the worst monster on earth—let us say Stalin in his most cruelly paranoiac period—is a wonderful subject to write about. In such cases, the treatment should be as clinical as possible, but at that stage we journalists diverge from the doctors. Their treatment is technical, physical, almost mechanical. The journalist deals in ideas and other intangibles. He is undermined by his emotions. Bias is an inescapable ingredient for the newspaperman.

His eyewitness reports can be the most illuminating of historical material, but there is the temptation and danger of overinvolvement. The important thing is to write the truth, favorable or unfavorable, and all the truth that a correspondent can obtain. I am pro-French, pro-British, pro-Italian, anti-German, and so on around the globe. Who isn't one thing or another?

I believe that I was generally correct in saying we journalists merely provide "the material for history." But I discovered when I published my interview with Fidel Castro in the Sierra Maestra in 1957 that a journalist can *make* history. This was also true in writing editorials. *The New York Times* has great influence, and not only in Washington. It was extraordinary—and frightening—how greatly our editorials could affect government policies or statesmen in many countries where American opinion was important. This is not true of powerful democracies like Britain, France, or Germany, nor of the Communist nations which discounted *The Times'* editorials as naturally anti-Communist. But in the case of a Latin American country, the effects of our editorials were often profound. My Latin American friends were sure that our critical editorials on Perón in Argentina, Pérez Jiménez in Venezuela, Rojas Pinilla in Colombia, and Trujillo in the Dominican Republic contributed to the downfall of those dictators. There seems little doubt that *The Times* played a role in building up public opinion against escalating the Vietnam War or continuing on its tragic, hopeless course. In so doing, it seems clear, we helped to persuade President Johnson to give up and President Nixon to go through with his "Vietnamization."

So we really do make history sometimes, as well as simply describing events as they happen. I am speaking here of the individual journalist, not the mass media of communications as a whole, which obviously can affect public opinion on certain issues and thus influence the government. When the mass media do that, they are much more likely to be reflecting an already formed public opinion than creating and moulding it.

A more difficult problem for the journalist is whether, or to what extent, he should let moral judgments influence his work. Is it honest to have private beliefs without forming positive public judgments, or without taking action? Cynicism and inaction, or an assumed objectivity, provide easy escapes. I would always opt for honest, open bias. A newspaperman should work with his heart as well as his mind. Any journalist whose ideas and opinions were the same in 1970 as they were, let us say, in 1930 or 1940 is an ossified fool, a Bourbon who has learned nothing and forgotten nothing.

The philosopher Santayana once said to me that personally he had no feeling, either of opposition or approval, concerning Communism or Fascism. "Doubtless there are good things in both," he added. "I think it is right that there should be new movements, suitable to new generations and periods. They shock and disturb those who are attached to old institutions, but they are not meant for such persons."

I now find myself agreeing with him to a considerable extent. There should be "new movements suitable to new generations and periods," and if they take the forms of Black Power or student power or social revolution in nations that are ripe for them, I can understand and even sympathize with their motives while usually disapproving of their actions.

Santayana felt a detachment that was suitable to a philosopher who could truly say, as he did to me, "I live in the eternal." A journalist, of all people, lives in the present.

Of course, there is another school of thought with champions quite as eminent as Santayana. For them, moral judgment is the highest function of the historian. Benedetto Croce, the Italian philosopher, argued in the last half of his long life that all history is a study of the history of liberty.

How many words have I written in half a century? Five million words? Ten million? It is appalling to think now of that vast flow of which so little could have been worth keeping for posterity. But, of course, this is beside the point for any writer. One poem, one song—and a man or woman will have lived a precious life. History and posterity are kindly judges in that respect. Their criteria are qualitative, not quantitative. I wrote some stories, articles, and editorials that I am willing to put up for judgment.

I do not expect to live long enough to see my writings on Cuba generally accepted, as they are now accepted by most Latin Americanists and by most impartial students of Cuban affairs.

One day in October 1963, when my wife and I were with Fidel Castro and Celia Sánchez in her house in Havana, Fidel said earnestly to me: "You will be vindicated some day. People will see that you told the truth and are telling the truth now about the Cuban Revolution."

"I'm afraid I'll be dead by that time," I answered.

He agreed. In time the truth—or enough of it—gets sorted out by unemotional historians and students. I took comfort in this belief during and after the Spanish Civil War and I have lived long enough to find myself in the main stream of the historiography of that conflict.

"The trouble about contemporary history," the British historian E. H. Carr wrote in *What Is* History?, "is that people remember the time when all the options were still open, and find it difficult to adopt the attitude of the historian for whom they have been closed by 'the *fait accompli.*' " This is exactly the problem of the newspaperman who describes what is happening or has happened—and then is blamed for being responsible for the events he writes about, or for agreeing with something that he is merely describing. No professional is swept along faster by the powerful and chaotic forces at work in the world today than the correspondent, but fortunately he is not required to provide solutions for the historic developments that he describes. He need only try to understand, explain, and interpret what is happening.

The newspaperman works with what is in front of him; deals with the immediate present; approaches an event with a fresh outlook. But unless he is a reporter covering a fire, he must add something. For a correspondent dealing with a political situation, or a national or international development, freshness, zest, interest are all invaluable, but they are not guides to accuracy. Experience, background, and knowledge are what make the difference between a competent reporter and the true correspondent, or chronicler, whose work will be as valuable to future historians and students as it is to the daily, contemporary reader. Get a story right on a given day and it will always be right.

Professor Arthur Schlesinger, Jr., after serving President Kennedy as a White House assistant, told a meeting of the American Historical Association that newspaper and magazine articles "are sometimes worse than useless." He had decided, he said, never again to take them seriously, for "their relation to reality is often less than the shadows in Plato's cave." This is going to be his loss. Anyway, historians in glass houses should not throw stones. My own experiences with life, with the reality of events, taught me that history is pretty much what Napoleon called it: *"une fable convenue."*

I am convinced that there is far more invention in history books than in newspapers. Schlesinger, if taken at his word, does not know how properly to use newspaper despatches, memoranda, and diaries. If he cannot distinguish good journalism from bad, or trustworthy newspapermen from phonies, he should not try to write contemporary history. After his experiences in the White House, I cannot believe he would rely on official documents or military communiqués. His own famous White Paper on the Cuban Revolution, written in preparation for the Bay of Pigs invasion, was an excellent polemical document, but I would feel sorry for the historian who relied on its supposed accuracy.

The historian is a judge, a critic, a compiler, an interpreter working on all available material of which the most valuable, with all due respect, will be the eyewitness accounts of reliable journalists. They will make mistakes, but so will Arthur Schlesinger and other historians.

One newspaperman, even in a long and unusual career, can see only a small part of the unfolding drama. But I saw much of war, worked in many countries, and met some of the men who made the history of the twentieth century. I believe that men make history, that every event is the result of some action taken or initiated by an individual.

I see the past—my past included—as a prelude to the present. The continuity is there. I cannot divorce the France of the early 1930's from the "Revolution of 1968"; or the Abyssinian War from the survival of Fascism; or the Spanish Civil War from the world war that it ushered in, or from the Spain in travail today. History is a kaleidoscope of the same pieces of glass, changing but changeless. My yesterdays brought to pass your today. My world was not old, and your world is a part of it.

I graduated from Columbia in 1922. The student rebels of 1968 in that same institution were revolting against a larger and more developed university in many respects, but not against a different one or a different world—or let us say, the differences were superficial. For a variety of reasons we did not rebel in my time, although looking back I would say we had just as much reason to do so in that aftermath of World War I, with Harding as President, an economic depression, a stupid isolationism, the idiocy of Prohibition, and a university with all the faults ascribed to Columbia in 1968. After I graduated the years brought changes in the attitude of students, in social sentiments, in racial affairs. Perhaps each event—the depression, the Abyssinian War, the Spanish Civil War, World War II, the cold war, Korea, Vietnam, the population explosion—was building up pressures that are now exploding in so many countries.

The world is no worse than in 1922 when I joined *The New York Times*, but the young and the underprivileged now will not put up with social injustice without protest—and in a minority of cases, violent protest. The result, whichever side one takes, is a world in revolution. It will be generations or perhaps centuries before humanity can hope to settle down again—always supposing some madman does not press the nuclear button.

Meanwhile, we must make the best of the world we have. My work brought me into contact with events that broke down a more ordered society and brought us today's danger and chaos. I saw forty-five crucial years of *The New York Times'* history. I have ideas and feelings about journalism that I want to get out of my system. Events, *The New York Times,* and journalism are going to go on. I am not, which is why I am writing a book. And now, as W. B. Yeats asked: "When all that story's finished, what's the news?"

Chapter 2

SPAIN

Do we all need roads to Damascus? The Spanish Civil War of 1936–1939 was a political and moral conversion for me. It was this for a great many people in many countries, but especially for the relatively few foreigners who lived through the war in Spain on the Republican side. As Carlos Baker's biography shows, Ernest Hemingway came of age, politically, in the Spanish Civil War. George Orwell, whose book, *Homage to Catalonia*, was such a potent weapon for years against the Loyalists, was to write long after: "The Spanish war and other events in 1936–1937 turned the scale and thereafter I knew where I stood." Where he stood was the antitotalitarian position that produced the nightmarish, but fortunately misleading, *Animal Farm* and *1984*. Orwell's dire predictions of a world turned into police states is no longer to be feared.

All of us who *lived* the Spanish Civil War felt deeply emotional about it. There was nothing comparable to it in that respect until the Vietnam War. Vietnam has moved the youth all over the world, and especially in the United States, as did the Spanish Civil War before today's youngsters were born.

"I can no longer pretend to be objective," Arthur Koestler

wrote in his *Spanish Testament.* "Anyone who has lived through the hell of Madrid with his eyes, his nerves, his heart, his stomach—and then pretends to be objective, is a liar." I agree; I always felt the falseness and hypocrisy of those who claimed to be unbiased, and the foolishness, if not rank stupidity, of editors and readers who demanded "objectivity" or "impartiality" of correspondents writing about the war. Spain was the setting for one of my two great battles with *The New York Times.* Cuba was the other. Both struggles created a good deal of interest, especially in the newspaper world, and I am pleased to be able, at last, to write about them frankly and without holding back names or incidents.

The sustained interest in the Civil War in the American academic world has been a source of great satisfaction to me. No year passed that I did not have a half dozen or more university students or professors visiting me in my office at *The Times* to seek information or advice for a term paper, a master's thesis, a doctoral dissertation, or a book on some aspect of the Spanish Civil War. And there were many letters. Almost invariably, sympathies were with the Republicans, which I, of course, also found gratifying.

History keeps trying to judge—a bit too soon, I would say. I have always liked something that the English historian G. M. Trevelyan said in one of his last lectures in 1945: "It is still too early to form a final judgment on the French Revolution, and opinion about it (my opinion certainly) is constantly oscillating."

We were so sure of our judgments back in 1936! I agree that we oversimplified a very complex situation. Historians tell us that nothing is ever all black or white, good or bad, right or wrong. They are correct, but as a result, too many of them become the purveyors of anticlimax and of uncertainty. They take the heart out of events and give us the lifeless skin and bones. The Spanish Civil War still lives in minds and hearts, not only in Spain but abroad. Why else would students and professors be writing theses and books on the war, year after year, as they are still doing? I have just (June 1971), myself, completed a reappraisal of the Civil War on request.

One's opinions, as Trevelyan put it, oscillate, if only within limits. Every belief needs periodic re-examination if it be based on reason and not on faith. There are few modern events more controversial than the Spanish Civil War. How do I describe that war, more than thirty years later, after other wars and other revolutions, much reading, much talking, visits to Franco's Spain, and the noise of "battles long ago" grown faint, and the world changed, and I am old?

I made up my mind years ago that we were all wrong to see the conflict simply in ideological terms. It was not merely a struggle for democracy against Fascism, for national freedom against Communism, for left against right, Christianity against Marxist atheism, East against West, radicalism against reaction. It could be argued that it was all of those things and a great deal more.

All modern conflicts are "world wars"—Spain, Korea, Vietnam, Cambodia, Laos, Biafra, the Middle East, the Great Wars. A revolution like Cuba's becomes a global struggle, as it did in the missile crisis of 1962. The Spanish Civil War directly involved Spain, Portugal, Germany, Italy, and the Soviet Union. Indirectly, Britain, France, and the United States were caught up in the struggle. From the beginning, it was a rehearsal for World War II. Ironically, that great conflict began with Nazi Germany and the Soviet Union as allies, which, in itself, made our simplifications of 1936–1939 ridiculous.

Nevertheless, it was, most certainly and—as I realized later—more than anything, a *civil* war, a Spanish war, a conflict whose primary causes and manifestations were to be found in Spanish history. In this, again, there were extraordinary complications—class conflict, religious strife, liberalism versus reaction, land hunger, republicanism against monarchism, the profound regional rivalries and differences, militarism against civilian rule, left against right, with factionalism seeming to pit every Spaniard against every other.

But men do not fight for complications. All the contending forces played their roles, but in different ways with different individuals, classes, regions, ambitions, emotions, and necessities. Yet for each man and woman it was simple. I calculated during the war that roughly 10 percent on each side felt a deep enough hatred or conviction to want to fight it out to a finish. The remaining 80 percent would have liked to live in peace, but were caught up in the struggle. The main thing, as in the French Revolution, was to survive.

Franco was supported almost from the beginning by Nazi Germany and Fascist Italy, which desired to see the Rebels win for the political and strategic designs of the Axis. The reactionary Salazar dictatorship in Portugal backstopped for them and Franco. After the war started, the Republicans were supported, in half-hearted fashion by Communist Russia, which was hoping to see the Loyalists win but was unwilling to pay the price or to risk a European war by pushing its designs too aggressively. France and, to a much lesser extent, Britain would have liked to see the Loyalists win, but were vigorously pursuing the appeasement policy. London therefore insisted on maintaining the hypocritical policy of "nonintervention," which was primarily instrumental in handing victory to the Rebels. The United States went along by imposing an arms embargo although, as Gallup Polls throughout the war showed, American public opinion favored the Loyalists.

The Loyalist regime had been fairly elected early in 1936 and was the legitimate government of Spain. As such, it should have had the backing of the democracies and the League of Nations and been able, at the very least, to purchase arms to defend itself. The Nationalists, as they euphemistically came to be called, were nothing but rebels against a constitutional government.

The religious factor, unfortunately and unfairly, played a vital role. Spain had a historic record, long antedating the Civil War, of fierce and bitter anticlericalism leading to church burning and to terrible violence against the clergy. The two principal reasons for this were that the Church hierarchy in Spain had always sided with the ruling classes—aristocracy, landowners, monarchy, and the army—against the people, and that the Church was extremely, almost medievally, orthodox. The Roman Catholic hierarchy in Spain (until the younger priests of the last few decades came along) was more papist than the Pope. As a correspondent in Rome, I learned how embarrassed the Holy See was at times over the bigoted, nationalistic extremism of the Spanish Church. It was no accident of history that the Holy Office of the Inquisition was such a cruel and terrible mechanism in Spain. Most people simply think in terms of the *Spanish* Inquisition. The Grand Inquisitor in Dostoevsky's *The Brothers Karamazov* could only have been Spanish, and he was so frighteningly believable because he was Spanish.

None of this excuses the terrible excesses of church burning and killing of priests and nuns by Loyalists at the outbreak of the Civil War. However, these crimes were committed spontaneously by an aroused and embittered populace. The Republican government not only did not instigate or condone the excesses, but set to work to stop them, which it did in a matter of weeks. The religious outrages were not Communist policy, if only for tactical and practical reasons. I know how earnestly Premier Juan Negrín later tried to induce the Vatican to allow Spanish priests to come back and perform their offices. His and previous governments looked away as hundreds of priests quietly carried on their religious work in civilian clothes behind the scenes all through the war. Generalissimo Franco, be it noted, had Basque priests executed for political reasons.

In a similar way the question of atrocities was used with revolting hypocrisy against the Loyalists, while greater atrocities all through the war were hushed up or condoned on the Insurgent side. Yet, as with the anticlericalism, the crimes on the Republican side were due to a popular, uncontrolled explosion of hatred against an oppressive ruling class. As soon as it could, the Madrid government restored law and order. The atrocities on the Franco side were carried out systematically, in cold blood, as a policy of terrorism and revenge. They did not stop until years after the war ended.

It is hard at this distance in time for non-Spaniards to comprehend why the Civil War was unavoidable in 1936 and why it aroused such a murderous hatred between Spaniards. After King Alfonso XIII was forced to abdicate in April 1931, a republic was formed by well-intentioned, moderate, liberal, and democratic forces. There was only a tiny Communist element, but the Anarcho-Syndicalists were powerful in Catalonia and Andalusia. Their trade unions and those of the Socialists in Castile and the north controlled most of the organized peasants and industrial workers.

Not only anarchism and socialism, but liberalism was anathema to the traditional ruling classes of landowners, industrialists, aristocracy, army, and Church. A fascistoid movement called the Falange indulged in deliberately destructive terrorism. So did the extreme leftists. The worldwide economic crisis was a disaster for Spain and the Republican governments. The rise of Nazism and the attraction of Italian Fascism were strong. The army generals were alienated by economy measures and unending disorder. The Church hierarchy was embittered by property confiscation and above all by the attempt to separate Church and state and take away the Church's virtual monopoly of education.

Thus the stage was set for a constant stream of strikes, sabotage, terrorism, and political crises. The Republican governments were weak and timid, but in 1934 the government called in General Francisco Franco to repress an uprising of miners at Oviedo in Asturias. Franco sent to Morocco for the brutal Foreign Legion, with which he had served, and Moorish troops whose savagery was proverbial. The uprising was crushed speedily and followed by a horrible repression. Asturias left an enduring mark on all Spanish workers.

When the Left and Center parties, organized in a Popular Front, won a general election in February 1936, the disorder in the country got completely out of hand. A group of generals began plotting a military coup to restore order and return Spain's traditional ruling classes to power. They struck on July 17, 1936, at a time when the atmosphere in Spain was so heated that no outcome was possible except the destruction of one side by the other.

There was little talk of Communism at the beginning of the war because the party was small and there were only 16 Communist deputies in the Cortes of 473 members. After Italy and Germany had saved the Rebels from defeat in July, Stalin reluctantly sent aid that reached Madrid in mid-October. This, in its turn, saved the Loyalists. The war took on the semblance of democracy against Fascism, and it was this aspect, more than anything, that aroused liberals everywhere in the world to champion the Republican cause. The spontaneous outburst of church burning and the killing of priests and nuns by enraged mobs of people turned the Vatican and American Roman Catholics into permanently bitter enemies of the Loyalists. The Franco cause was given the appearance of a Christian crusade against godless Communism.

The true and complete picture was enormously complicated, but emotions (mine included) were swayed by simple ideas. Yet, throughout the war, Spaniards fought Spaniards with little regard to foreign ideologies or foreign troops on their soil.

This rough compilation of the factors involved and the pros and cons may be branded as personal and biased. It will never be possible, even a century from now, for a historian to make an assessment of the Spanish Civil War that is not personal and biased. However, with later historians, unless religion twists their judgment, it will be a case of "all passion spent." It cannot be that now for anyone alive and adult in 1936–1939.

My feelings long ago ceased to be intensely emotional. My judgment is not as clouded as it was, and I know a great deal about the war that I could not have known at the time, especially features derogatory to the Loyalists and to the Internationals, including the Lincoln Battalion. I have grown old and, if not wiser, at least much more experienced in the ways of statesmen and the functioning of ideologies and power politics.

What I am sure will be my final, reasoned judgment on the Spanish Civil War is that those of us who championed the cause of the Republican government against the Franco Nationalists were right. It was, on balance, the cause of justice, legality, morality, decency. It was, as we thought, a tragedy that the Loyalists lost. This goes for the practical, international, political aspect, for if the Madrid government had won or held its own, the democratic world would have been stronger in the European war that Hitlerite Germany was willing to risk.

This judgment is, of course, based on a conviction that I held at the time and never changed—that a victory for the Republican government would not have led to a Communist Spain. No one can prove what did not happen, but I knew Premier Juan Negrín, his cabinet, the political and military leaders, the temper of the people, and the strength of the Spanish and Russian Communists. Later, the world saw that Nazi Germany and Fascist Italy could not dictate to the Franco regime. It was equally true that if the Loyalists had won, Stalin would not have been able to dictate to a Negrín government.

Life's might-have-beens gnaw at the mind in old age. Throughout all these years since 1936 that plump little rebel general who started in the Canary Islands has been on top in Madrid. Have those who fought, and we who believed in them, really lost out? The lives, the passions, the hopes—have they all been in vain?

Haunting questions for me so many years after the Spanish Civil War ended. I still say that the Loyalists wrote a glorious page of Spanish history, but I have lived to see new generations of Spaniards come along who think that their parents and grand-parents were mad. They do not know what happened, because of censorship during and after the war, lack of communications since, and the distortions of the Franco regime's account of the war. When Franco and his generation are dead and gone, when there is freedom to publish and read and think, Spaniards will learn the truth about the traumatic experience through which their nation passed in the 1930's—but not before.

My experience as a war correspondent in Spain was, among many other things, a lesson in journalism. It showed how difficult it is to make readers believe truths to which they have shut their minds. I was at all times baffled by the fact that I was describing at firsthand what I saw and heard as honestly and completely as I knew how, and yet my copy was often doubted or disbelieved, not only by Roman Catholic readers, which could be understood, but by my own editors on *The New York Times.*

Every newspaperman makes mistakes, and I made my share, but my despatches on the Spanish Civil War have proved to be basically correct. It has always been my contention that a journalist who writes truthfully what he sees and knows on a given day is writing for posterity. The skepticism and criticisms that I met in some quarters during the Spanish conflict made me feel at times that I was working more for the historical record than for the daily reader.

In an address he made at Chapel Hill, North Carolina, on January 20, 1938 (the war still had fourteen months to go), Arthur Hays Sulzberger, then publisher of *The New York Times,* said:

"*The Times'* coverage of the Spanish conflict. . . . seems to me an outstanding case history for students of journalism. Strangely enough, it is not the censors on either side in Spain who cause most of the difficulties—even though they cause plenty. It is the folks on the sidelines, the partisans of one side or the other who create the trouble. Their excited denunciation is nothing short of amazing. When I told the editor who is responsible for our 'Letters' column that I planned to make reference to this Spanish situation in what I had to say here today, he wrote me the following line: 'One point, I think, should be emphasized: No matter who writes the despatch, the other side will accuse him of broadcasting propaganda or downright lying. In all my ten or twelve years' experience with letters to the editor, I have never encountered a situation in which so much absolutely rabid partisanship was manifested. It is partisanship that cannot be reasoned with and which, consequently, gets nowhere.' "

So far, so good, But the publisher went on at great length to argue that *The Times* was as fair *and accurate* as any newspaper could have been. It was nothing of the sort.

The intentions of the organization and its editors were of the best. I did not impugn the good faith or sincerity and honest beliefs of the editors, nor did I feel when the war was over that there was any deliberate vindictiveness or animosity toward me personally. I also believe that the publisher and his managing editor, Edwin L. (Jimmy) James, were seriously, carelessly, and thoughtlessly mistaken. To me, it is beyond question that the bull pen (the night editors who made up the news columns and controlled its policies), the night cable editors, and one or two of the copyreaders (most were my champions) allowed their sincere and natural partisanship to influence the way they handled my copy.

All four of the editors who worked in the bull pen throughout the war were Roman Catholics: Raymond McCaw, the assistant managing editor in charge; Neil MacNeill, the second man; Clarence Howell, a convert who was almost fanatically religious; and Harvey Getzloe.

The Civil War, as I said earlier, aroused passionate religious feelings in the United States because of the killing of priests and nuns and church burnings by the populace. The Roman Church as a whole—the Vatican and the hierarchies in every country—immediately and understandably came out in the strongest terms against the Loyalists. This continued throughout the war. It meant that anyone like myself, writing with sympathy and understanding about the war from the Republican side, became anathema—almost in the literal sense of being cursed of God and the Church. This was the way that American Catholics felt. (In the European democracies, majority sentiment, even among Catholics, favored the Loyalists.)

It stood to reason that *The Times'* editors would have treated my copy with suspicion, anger, and, at times, disbelief. They could not, although I must presume they tried, handle my despatches objectively and dispassionately for their news value and technical proficiency. Although my stories held up as basically correct, and *The Times'* correspondent's on the Franco side did not, the bull pen could never bring itself to an acceptance of the facts.

The conditions for coverage on the Loyalist side were unique in this century. They were like the open facilities American war correspondents found in the War between the States and the Spanish-American War. At least chronologically, we set the pattern in Spain for the coverage of World War II, Korea, and Vietnam.

On the Nationalist side war correspondents were greatly restricted in their movements and in what they could be told, and they were under heavy censorship. On the Republican side there were virtually no restrictions on where we went or what we did. Censorship was not strict. Spanish and International Brigade officers at the front, even commanders, were always accessible. A correspondent could go to the front lines, watch a battle, join an advance, or fall back with the troops in a retreat. He became a military observer and a chronicler of history, for there were no official historians during the conflict.

Neither side was equipped for transmission from the front. A correspondent on the Republican side had to return to Madrid, Valencia, or Barcelona to cable or telephone his despatches. This cut down on the number of stories one could write and the continuity of a particular coverage. It also meant that despatches were often written under conditions of extreme fatigue.

When the Spanish Civil War began I was back in the Paris bureau following a vacation in New York after the end of the Abyssinian War. I had reminded Edwin James that I spoke Spanish and would be glad to go to Spain, but at that time our regular correspondent, William P. Carney, was still in Madrid. Carney was a Roman Catholic. He felt strongly about the church burnings and persecution of the clergy—as everyone did whatever his religion—but in Carney's case it blinded him to any other aspect of the rebellion. His copy from Madrid was consistently hostile to the Republican government.

On October 27 I received a cable from James: "Article we've asked Carney to write may make him persona non grata. It may not. In any event during his absence would like you to go to

Spain. Please proceed to Valencia. Don't go to Madrid without consulting office."

The war was going badly for the Loyalists. Franco—by then the supreme rebel commander—was concentrating his main forces on Madrid, where the Rebel advance had been checked. The world expected the capital to fall quickly and the war to end, which explains James' warning not to go to Madrid without permission. When I got to Valencia and talked to the government people and soldiers there, I realized that Madrid was in no immediate danger and advised New York that it would be safe to go there. McCaw replied: "Sulzberger advises use your own judgment regarding Madrid trip avoiding much as possible danger zones."

The advice about avoiding danger was well meant, but a war correspondent who avoids danger had better be doing other things. Madrid held out, helped by the small International Brigade, which was soon to get its baptism of fire, and by the planes and tanks that had finally arrived from Russia. However, the Insurgents were still attacking the capital, and the fall of the city seemed so certain to the Franco command and to the American correspondents with the Rebels that four or five of them—some famous names—sent despatches back from Toledo to Hendaye on the French side of the frontier saying that the city had fallen. One of the men actually described the enthusiasm of the Madrileños as the Nationalist troops entered the capital in triumph. This was the first and worst of the many bloopers from the Rebel side due to misinformation and, especially, a failure to understand the Loyalist situation.

In Madrid we did not believe at any time that the city was going to fall and I said so in my despatches. However, the government had gone to Valencia and from New York the situation looked bad. I was dismayed to receive a telegram from Paris on December 11 reading: "James cables he considers you best leave Madrid as Apee [Associated Press] now covering us on spot news there." This made no sense to me, and I was suspicious, so I asked Percy J. Philip, head of the Paris bureau, to give me the full text of the New York message. It read: "James's full telegram reads quote since if heavy attack starts and is successful you wont be able to send out anything think you should leave Madrid now. Apee covering us on spot news there."

This was, as I suspected, not an order to leave but an argument and suggestion. Philip resented my staying in Spain and wanted me back in Paris. I staked my credibility by replying to James that Madrid was not going to fall and that I should remain. He cabled back: "Alright but expect you to leave when big show starts." When I thanked him he replied: "Wish you luck." Madrid did not fall until the end of the war, two and a half years later.

I was left unhampered for a few exciting months. There were bitter and costly battles on the Jarama River, and in the Casa de Campo on the edge of the capital. Madrid was being bombed and shelled daily, while the Madrileños showed heartbreaking heroism. *No Pasarán!* was the motto, and they did not pass. It was terrible and wonderful—and there were remarkable stories to write. "Ernest's euphoria surpassed even that of Matthews," Carlos Baker wrote of Hemingway's first visit to Madrid, made at that time.

My memories of Spain are inextricably and happily mingled with thoughts of Ernest Hemingway. I met him for the first time in Madrid and we were friends—as my wife, Nancie, was, too—until he died. The picture drawn of him in Carlos Baker's biography is not my picture, for all its massive accuracy of detail. The seemingly endless chain of quarrels, the pugnaciousness, the fits of bullying and brutality, the ingratitude and suspiciousness that almost monopolize Baker's account simply had no part in our relationship.

Ernest had been reading my despatches to *The Times* before he reached Madrid in March 1937, and he was nice about them. We worked closely together on all his trips to Spain, along with Martha Gellhorn, for this was the period in his life when he fell in love with her. The later story of their tempestuous marriage and divorce belongs to a time when I was in other parts of the world. In Spain they were happy together. In many ways I am sure it was one of the happiest periods of Hemingway's life.

Cuba was to be, too, with Mary Welsh who became his fourth wife, until his final illness and breakdown.

Perhaps I was lucky to have known him principally in good times. Whatever the reasons, my picture of Ernest Hemingway would be of a warm, generous, brave, and always friendly companion, hypersensitive and hot-tempered, to be sure, and moody now and then. He was like an overgrown boy; it was as if he never grew up inside of him to match his big, powerful body.

I do not question the accuracy of Carlos Baker's meticulous study, but for me the character he draws lacks the qualities that made Hemingway a grand human being. He would do anything for a friend. I had bought a monster of a car to use in Spain, an ancient, secondhand Belgian Minerva with a very tricky old-fashioned gear box. On one vacation during the Civil War, I managed to drive it to Paris where Nancie was waiting. Ernest joined us, and when he learned of my problems with "Old Minnie" and that I was going to drive her back to Spain, he could not bear the idea. I suppose he was afraid that I would not get there alive. So he insisted that I let him drive me down to the Spanish border—a two-day journey—showing me all the tricks of my huge Minerva. It was an act of kindness and thoughtfulness that was extraordinary in my life—but it was typical of him.

He was a wizard with a car. I remember once when we were caught in a nasty bombing and strafing attack near Tortosa how he took the wheel away from me and in two seconds shot the car off the road and had it parked within no more than a few inches of a barn wall.

An episode in the war that I thought well worth publishing, but the Cable Desk in New York cut out of my story, was a moment when Ernest saved the lives of Henry Buckley of the *London Daily Telegraph* and myself—and I suppose his own life. It was during the Ebro battle in 1938; we had to take a rowboat to get over from the west to the east bank because the bridges had been bombed down. The current was swift and there were some nasty rapids a few hundred yards down the river, so the boat was being partly pulled across by a rope, which snapped.

We started drifting swiftly toward the rapids. Hemingway quickly took the oars; Buckley acted as coxswain to pace his strokes with shouts, and by an extraordinary exhibition of strength, Ernest got us safely across. He was a good man in a pinch.

I was careful never to ask him for anything, not even autographed copies of his books. He did, however, send me *For Whom the Bell Tolls* when it came out, inscribed: "To Herbert with love from Martha and Scrooby."

"Scrooby" was Martha Gellhorn's pet name for Ernest which I, Bob Capa the photographer, and a few other intimates used during the Civil War. It is one of the few details that Carlos Baker seems to have missed.

In March 1937 the largest Insurgent force yet assembled struck downward and westward toward Guadalajara, north of Madrid. Success would have meant the end of the war. The news —and the lines—were too fluid for us to know where to go at first. Then word came that the Rebel force had been stopped well short of Guadalajara.

I dashed up there the next morning to find that the attacking divisions had been Italian. They had been routed and were fleeing back, but they left many prisoners, many dead, and an immense number of rifles, machine guns, ammunition, and some disabled tanks. I talked to prisoners—in Italian. I examined the arms (with which I was familiar from Abyssinia). I watched the dead being buried.

The story was a very big one. This was the first positive evidence that Mussolini had not merely sent planes, cannons, tanks, technicians, and advisers—he had sent an expeditionary force. I was naturally excited when I got back to Madrid and wrote my story. I told just what I had done and what I had seen —the men, the bodies, the weapons. To emphasize the outstanding point, I said that "they were Italian and nothing but Italian."

The next day I received a cable which started an exchange with the office that became known quickly around New York and then took its place in books on the Civil War. As I learned later, the assistant managing editor, Raymond McCaw, had ordered the copyreaders to substitute the word "Insurgent" wherever I had sent "Italian." Whoever edited the story on the Cable Desk had his tongue in his cheek. When he came to my phrase saying "they were Italian and nothing but Italian," he dutifully changed it to: "They were Insurgent and nothing but Insurgent."

Here are the texts of the messages sent up and back between March 10 and 20, 1937.

> Matthews
> American Embassy Madrid
> None here wants you do anything other than send spot news rather than handout stuff. Your handicaps realized but we cannot print obvious propaganda for either side even under bylines. You've virtually been alone in emphasizing Italian angle. Only others so doing being Moscow papers.
>
> McCaw.

> Times
> New York
> James deeply resent McCaw's insinuations about propaganda. Ive never done any for anybody and never will. Ive sent straight news and I know what Im writing about. If you dont like my stuff please recall me. Moreover if I dont receive some explanation Im taking this up with Mister Sulzberger.
>
> Matthews.

I sent two more indignant cables giving a list of the names of other newspapers and agency correspondents who had sent the same information about the Italians. I also pointed out that I had visited the Guadalajara front three times in eight days and was using my own eyewitness accounts and not handouts.

I regret that I have lost the first few sentences of Managing Editor James' reply to my barrage, but the main body of his message was as follows:

Neither McCaw nor anyone else here thinks youre sending propaganda in sense that you created it. Ever since thereve been wars and war correspondents propaganda has been handed out and sent. Remember World War. Thats true now from both sides in Spain. Take alleged Mussolini letter which Loyalists handed out there. Authenticity denied from every source except Madrid. Even if authentic we must take cognizance of these denials. Furthermore Franco headquarters say Civil Guard and Moors well as Italians fighting Guadalajara. We must print that and other statements from other side. Messages sent only to help you not hinder. Not slightest doubt your sincerity honesty.

James.

I was still burning. In fact, I still am more than three decades later. James' weaseling, extraneous reply was hardly satisfactory, so I sent off a parting shot by letter, after I received a clipping of the story in question from New York.

Madrid, April 11 (1937)

Dear Mr. James:

A clipping of my big Guadalajara story just reached me, and much as I hate to stir up the ashes again, I feel I must insist on a hearing. Here it is, roughly worked out in the attached sheets, which speak for themselves. [I pasted up the clipping and made marginal notes about the changes in my copy.]

Your cable, if I may say so, was somewhat beside the point. There is, of course, no question involved of *The Times*'s policy of printing both sides, or its natural aversion to propaganda in the form of handouts. The question is solely that when an accredited correspondent says he saw something with his own eyes, you *must* believe him—or else discharge him. To give just one instance in this story: I said an officer approached with a stack of *Italian* documents under his arm (it being quite obvious that he showed them to me and I examined them all finding them to be genuine Italian stuff), and it was changed in *The Times* to *Insurgent* documents. That, in short, is nothing but a refusal to trust your own correspondent— a deliberate lack of faith which you surely must realize is intolerable. You cannot ask any self-respecting correspondent who is trying to give you straight stuff to continue under such an attitude.

That is why I am writing you now. I shall be on vacation when you receive it, and I want you to feel quite free, if you do not agree with me, to send someone else back to Madrid.

As a matter of fact, I honestly believe that this whole thing involves a principle of the utmost importance to *The Times* as a whole, and all its correspondents, which is one reason why I am bringing it up again. I could offer you clippings of other stories about the Italians, showing deliberate refusal to accept my word for *first-hand* information, but it would only labor the point, which is either that you trust your correspondent more than you do his competitors or his editors 3,000 miles away, or else you ask for your correspondent's resignation. You cannot expect the staff to keep their faith in the organization when their loyalty is met by lack of loyalty in New York.

In December 1937 the Loyalists attacked and occupied the important town of Teruel. It was to be their greatest military victory of the war, except for Guadalajara. Franco threw all he had into counterattack after counterattack until he finally recaptured the city. Hemingway, Sefton Delmer of the *London Daily*

Express, Robert Capa, finest of war photographers and finest of men, and I made a number of trips to Teruel under difficult, dangerous, and exhausting conditions. The battle and siege provided me with some of my best stories of the war. They also were a source of bitterness and anger toward *The Times.*

My printed despatches could give only a faint idea of the difficulties and danger of covering the Teruel battle, especially as the stories were being ruthlessly cut by the Cable Desk.

In the first twelve days, Hemingway, Delmer, and I drove nearly 3,000 miles. On four occasions we drove, worked, and wrote for more than twenty-four hours (once for forty-four) at a stretch. I have never in my life experienced such cold. We rarely got a square meal. Because it was firsthand copy, we were beating the other correspondents by as much as four days, and since Delmer worked for a London newspaper and Hemingway for the North American Newspaper Alliance, this meant that I was giving *The Times* scoops with every story.

On December 17, 1937, the three of us "took" Teruel along with the Spanish *dinamiteros* in one of the greatest days of my life. Then we drove back to Valencia and after twenty hours on the go, I sat down at midnight, writing until four in the morning. It was the best story I got in the Spanish Civil War. In New York it was cut to less than half its length and buried in the inside of the paper under another Spanish item. I received a sharp cable saying that my story was too long. Such was life on the Loyalist side in Spain. What the editors could not take away from me was the memory of one of the most thrilling days of my life, shared with Ernest Hemingway whom I liked and admired so much.

The Rebel counterattacks met stubborn resistance, but the Nationalists were so confident that they issued a communique one day announcing the recapture of Teruel. Bill Carney, our correspondent on the Franco side who was nowhere near the front, not only sent the handout but gave a vivid description of how the citizens of Teruel joyfully received the Insurgent troops, giving them the Fascist salute.

The Times printed his despatch. On that day I was making a difficult, two-day journey with Bob Capa through snow and ice to Teruel, where I got a humdinger of a story. I cabled it in all innocence and no malice to New York when I got back to Barcelona. The details were so obviously based on personal experience that *The Times* had to print the story, with what editorial embarrassment I could only guess at when I learned what had happened. I heard that Jimmy James, the managing editor, was mildly annoyed with Carney and chided him gently.

Hemingway was phoning me from Paris every other day at that stage of the battle. He told me that he knew my despatches were being cut drastically in New York—"even maliciously." I was bitter enough at the time to believe in malice and deliberate sabotage.

I learned early in January 1938 that a Catholic history professor in the United States, Joseph Thorning, had made an address before the American Catholic History Association calling me "a rabid Red partisan," which was rather amusing to me, but I thought might annoy *The Times.* The office really was annoyed, as I discovered from a letter Arthur Sulzberger wrote me on January 11, 1938. I did not keep the clipping he sent, but the contents can easily be imagined.

"We published a letter this morning," the publisher wrote, "which calls you every name under the sun. I am enclosing a clipping of it. It was published against the will of everyone here and on my authority, because the Reverend Dr. Thorning of Mount Saint Mary's College has been waging a constant war on our news from Spain, and I thought it might be wise to let him have his full say, at least once. This morning I received another letter from him, indicating that it is impossible to satisfy him, which brings me to the conviction that I was wrong in allowing this morning's letter to appear.

"I trust that the praise from your friends, however, offsets the criticism of your enemies these days and that the knowledge of the high regard in which your work is held here in the office will assuage any wounds for which I may have been responsible."

The copy of the letter that the publisher wrote to Dr. Thorning read as follows:

"We published your letter this morning. I have also today written an apology to Mr. Matthews for having done so.

"I note with regret from your communication of January 8th that you are unable to retain your view as to my freedom from bias and further, are unable to trust other members of this staff. I am afraid there is nothing more to be said."

(Arthur Sulzberger's action in this case was typical of his invariable fairness, loyalty to his employees, and thoughtfulness. I would never want it to be thought that anything I wrote, or am writing, on the Spanish Civil War and *The Times* is a criticism of him. I disagreed with the way he carried out his understandable policy of trying to hold a fair balance on the war and to give both sides, in Ochs' famous phrase, "without fear or favor." My quarrels were with the top echelons of the News Department.)

Father Thorning was, in 1937, just beginning a very long career of attacks on me which continued until my retirement from *The Times* in October 1967. Aside from my books and signed articles on Franco Spain, he sensed or knew that when an editorial—almost invariably hostile to Franco—appeared in *The New York Times*, I would have written it. The unfailing result would be an indignant letter to the editor taking me and *The Times* to task. While the letters always evoked groans of weary resignation from the editors in charge, most were printed as a matter of fairness in presenting a contrary point of view.

I expect Father Thorning to pursue me into my grave, and I know he is sure where I will end up in the hereafter. Personally, I always found him ill-informed and boring, a rather extreme example of the American Roman Catholic's attitude toward Spain during and after the Civil War. For Catholics, the Republicans were all "Reds"; the Nationalists were crusaders fighting for God and righteousness against the forces of evil. This was a minority opinion since there were three Protestants in the United States for every Roman Catholic and majority opinion in America favored the Loyalists. However, the Catholic community was organized, united, and very vocal. *The Times* would often get a batch of protest letters saying the same things, which indicated that a parish priest or bishop had told his whole flock what to write.

The Catholic sensibilities of the bull pen led to another sharp and bitter quarrel between me and the editors. It concerned the bishop of Teruel, Anselmo Polanca Fonseca, who was one of the last inhabitants of Teruel to surrender. I saw him being led out of the town, grim, weary, white-faced but composed. He would naturally have expected to be executed, but that period of the war had long passed. He was taken to Mora de Rubielos where he issued a statement saying he had been "treated with every sort of consideration" and was "heartily grateful therefore." At the end of the war, Anarchists who had been ordered to conduct the bishop safely into France, treacherously murdered him.

I had mentioned the bishop of Teruel several times in despatches, and our Barcelona correspondent, Lawrence Farnsworth, had written a despatch about the respectful way the prelate was being treated as a prisoner. The bull pen was so touchy about religious matters that they cut out the references in my stories and suppressed Farnsworth's. When something about the bishop came up in April 1938, the managing editor asked me for his whereabouts. I replied that he was in Barcelona but did not mention the fact that he was a prisoner since I took it for granted that this was well known in New York. James then sent me a stern and reproachful letter because I had not said in my message that the bishop was a prisoner. I did not get his letter for a month, as mail contacts to Spain during the war were slow and chancy.

It was one of many occasions in which I was furious with the New York office. Since it happened to be an incident where the bull pen had stuck out its neck, I was in a position to raise hell —with great satisfaction. I even brought the publisher into the affair and was pleased to see him reproach the desk for "sloppiness."

I mention the incident because it was a good example of the

mutual sensitivity of the editors and myself—theirs because of excessive touchiness over religious issues and mine because it showed the extent to which I was on edge. As I wrote Arthur Sulzberger—perhaps with a bit of exaggeration—the Spanish assignment was "more dangerous and nerve-wracking than any which newspapermen have had."

The strain of the Civil War coverage became greater as the war dragged on. We on the Loyalist side were covering a wide-open retreat in Aragon in the first quarter of 1938. There is nothing more dangerous in war corresponding. Again and again, out in the front lines, I would learn that the unit I was with was being flanked on one side or both, and it was always a tricky business getting back before being cut off or caught in a rout.

"If you really want to be helpful in New York," I wrote James petulantly, "you would give me credit for doing my best as honestly as I know how and save complaints for after the war is over."

The fact that parts of despatches (in this case about the bishop of Teruel) had been cut out and not printed would have been normal and expected for space reasons at all times. My complaints were based on *what* was being cut out. The deletions were too often a form of censorship. Moreover, my despatches were also being cut to make them quantitatively equal to the despatches of Bill Carney.

As the Thorning affair has indicated, one of the minor irritations during the war was the policy followed in the Letters to the Editor columns. The editor in charge was ordered to balance the letters—one pro-Loyalist with one pro-Rebel, one praising me with one praising Carney and so forth. It did not matter if letters favoring the Republicans on a particular issue or incident outnumbered letters against them—we still published one for one. I argued in vain that it was dishonest to give the impression that *The Times* was receiving equal numbers of letters from both sides. Our readers' opinions should be respected, whichever way the chips fell.

I mention these things to show, on the one hand, the strains and stresses—and sensitivity—to which a war correspondent is exposed, and, on the other, the inability of editors, sitting safely at their desks, to understand the correspondent's problems. In the world war that followed Spain, I was more philosophical. It took a Cuban Revolution to make me and *The Times* get embroiled with each other again.

To give an idea of how I felt in the spring of 1938 when the Loyalist forces were being routed and the Rebels were driving down to the sea and cutting Republican Spain in two, I will cite a paragraph from a letter to my father, written on April 7. The Abraham Lincoln Battalion had just been broken up in a battle on the west bank of the Ebro River.

"Hemingway arrived last Friday," I wrote, "and made the last five trips with Delmer and me—and, of course, he will be with us from now on. It is certainly grand to have him here, although this is a far cry from the happy days of Madrid and Teruel. So many of our friends in the Brigade are gone. I never had a sadder story to write than the smashing of the Lincoln-Washington. It made me positively sick. I knew all those men very well and they were some of the finest chaps I ever hope to meet. I would have given a year's salary not to have had to write that story."

But, of course, one does have to write such stories, and there is consolation in the thought that they are written by someone with understanding and feeling. The so-called objectivity of an outsider would give a false picture.

The last period of the war was a personally discouraging one for me, aside from the unhappiness with which I experienced the gradual crushing of Loyalist strength and hopes. In a letter to my wife, written from Barcelona on November 18, 1938, with the end in sight, I discussed the possibility of working for a magazine instead of a daily paper. I had had some tempting offers.

"Last night I sent a full, rounded story of [Spanish General] Lister's account of the retreat from the Ebro," I wrote. "Now, that had a considerable historical value; it was interesting, and it came out well in the writing. I polished it off with a bit about Napoleon which was effective—but only if the despatch has been correctly transmitted and printed in full—and I *know* it has not. . . .

"*The Times,* after all, won't print my stories as I write them, and in other words won't let me do my work as I want to, and can do it. Maybe a magazine would. It won't—incidentally—do any harm for you to hint around as much, casually. *The Times* might as well know how dissatisfied I am, and if they would be sorry to lose me (about which I am not too sure) it would be a warning that might prove salutary. . . .

"However, under any circumstances, dead or alive, I'm going to see this war through, unless the paper made it quite impossible for me to stay. But next year ought surely to see the end of it."

In answer to a letter I received, I wrote my wife again on December 2, from Bourg-Madame. "Young [Eugene Young, *New York Times'* cable editor] is an old fool who thinks he knows all about Europe and has never been there. He is the most dangerous type of editor. He showed his complete ignorance by not believing that Italian story, which is not only true, but very logical and obvious. You can say what you please, but I got a batch of *Times* pages in the same mail and I see, first, that my Ebro story [mentioned in the letter above] was murdered and all reference to Ernest [Hemingway] saving our lives (which he really did and which *was* news) cut out. I see two Hendaye AP stories front-paged, both utterly false, and it shows their refusal to realize the stupidity of using Hendaye AP. You only see the paper. You don't see what I write and you don't know what the stories could be like under more intelligent and courageous editing."

The reference to "the Italian story" was to a despatch I sent on Election Day giving the figures on men, war matériel, planes, tanks, and technical advisers—very high figures—that Mussolini had sent to Rebel Spain for the final stage of a war that was being lost by the Loyalists. My wife, Nancie, had stopped off at the news room on the way to a cocktail party being given by the publisher, to ask for news of me. Eugene Young came out and mentioned with complete skepticism the despatch I had sent about the Italian intervention, which had come from official Republican intelligence sources.

"We are printing it," Young said, "but of course, Mussolini would not do anything so ridiculous."

After the war, when I was head of the Rome bureau, I got a news scoop on an article that Count Ciano wrote giving figures on the Italian military intervention in Spain. The numbers surpassed what the Republican intelligence had gathered. James had the grace to send me a cable, both to congratulate me on the scoop and to confess that I had been right from the beginning.

In my last letter to Nancie, written on January 30, 1939, from Perpignan, France, after the Spanish forces—and I— had been driven out of Spain, I said: "Won't *The Times* ever learn that the only system now is to have correspondents friendly to the regime they work in, *but honest?* [My emphasis in the original letter.] It's the only combination that can work, aside from having spineless or brainless types, or the James type of unprincipled, unfeeling reporters—and they don't do a good job."

My ideas on coverage never extended to a belief that a correspondent in Fascist Italy had to be pro-Fascist, or in Nazi Germany pro-Nazi, or in Russia pro-Communist. When I worked in Rome after the Spanish Civil War I was bitterly anti-Fascist, but at least nine out of ten Italians were also anti-Fascist and so were all our Italian friends. This did not prevent me from sending every newsworthy story favorable to the Fascist regime.

A correspondent in Berlin during Hitler's regime could be pro-German and anti-Nazi in his personal feelings. A Moscow correspondent could—and should—feel sympathy and liking for the Russian people however anti-Communist he might be. The problem in these three cases is to make and keep the maximum number of official contacts without becoming an apologist for a criminal policy like Hitler's racism or the sadistic paranoia of a Stalin. The correspondent must understand and explain such horrors; he does not need to approve of them. Honestly, thoroughness, understanding—these are the three keys to good journalism, and the hardest and most important is understanding.

In the worst of circumstances—and I would rate Hitlerite Germany and Stalinist Russia as about the worst—it is possible to find enough in the environment to develop sympathy for the people and the country, as contrasted with the political regime. Totalitarian regimes, in any case, have censorship. A correspondent showing hostility in despatches to Mussolini, Hitler, or Stalin would not have lasted long. Experience teaches a journalist how far he can go and, in some cases, how to trick the censors. During the retreat in Catalonia, when my military news was ahead of the censors, since I would just have returned from the front, I would telephone my story to Paris at a time when I knew the censor was out to lunch.

The Greeks had a word for what is required: *empatheia*—empathy in English. The Oxford dictionary defines it as "the power of projecting one's personality into (and so fully comprehending) the object of contemplation." This is a primary requirement for a newspaperman.

I went back to New York for a vacation in March 1939, after completing the tragic and disagreeable story of the Spanish refugees in their French concentration camps. There had been another sharp exchange between me and James over my despatches on the inexcusably hard-hearted treatment of the refugees by the French officials. (Hugh Thomas, in his *History of the Spanish Civil War*, writes: "Callousness was shown by persons comfortable in America or England. Mr. Herbert Matthews, for example, was told by the editor of *The New York Times* not to send emotional reports of the conditions of the camp.")

All things considered, I did not know whether I would be welcome in the New York office, and I actually paid my own fare on the ship, second class, much to the surprise of James who expected me back first class at *The Times'* expense. On reaching New York I was upset that none of the editors—all of whom I had known for years—got in touch with me to say hello.

No one could realize the strain I had been under, physically and mentally, in the last very dangerous and nerve-wracking months of the war. During the desperate weeks of fighting between the launching of the Insurgent offensive against Catalonia on December 23, 1938, and the fall of Barcelona on January 26, I went from one sector of the front to another every day. The stories I sent, although many were cut and some unpublished, provided a unique contribution to the history of the war, for no other correspondent had the opportunity, time, or personal contacts to do what I did. I had the equivalent of a mild kind of shell shock at the end, as I realized better in World War II, watching men under prolonged stress. I had no right to expect anyone in New York to understand this when I did not quite understand it myself.

I made the mistake of going to see Arthur Sulzberger a few weeks after arriving in New York, and while I do not remember the details, I know that I did say what I thought of the way my copy had been handled and gave my opinions of *The Times'* coverage of the Spanish Civil War. The conversation with the publisher must have been a hot one. I wrote him a long letter after sleeping on the matter. It summed up all my grievances against *The Times*—not one of which I would withdraw today.

The principal points I made were that I did not quarrel with *The Times'* ideals, intentions, and policies, nor about the integrity of any member of the editing or publishing staffs in trying to interpret and carry them out. I argued that if I showed an unconscious bias in sending the news, there was an unconscious bias in the editing by the night staff. *The Times,* I said, "cannot claim for the Spanish Civil War to have provided a history of such documentary value as the paper's traditions would ordinarily call for."

One example I gave of *The Times* losing the full documentary value of my coverage was the story I sent of the Loyalist withdrawal from the Ebro bridgehead on November 17, 1938. This was a full account by none other than the Spanish commanding officer, Enrique Lister, of the end of one of the major battles of the war. It was an exclusive, historical document—and it was cut in two by the desk.

I especially took strong exception to the fact that in the effort to be "impartial," *The Times* had throughout alternately featured mine, and Carney's, and the Associated Press' Hendaye's copy from the Franco side, regardless of news values, accuracy, and honesty.

Poor Arthur Sulzberger! He had his problems with me in my time, but he was always fair and loyal and understanding. So were his successors, Orvil Dryfoos and Arthur Ochs (Punch) Sulzberger. I disagreed, sometimes mildly, sometimes violently, and always vocally. They knew what I thought and so did everybody else. But I never had doubts about the high ideals and quality of *The New York Times.* This was something that many outsiders could not understand in the cases of the Spanish Civil War and the Cuban Revolution. Both led to the equivalent of family quarrels, not basic differences or loss of faith.

I understood *The Times'* problems at least as much as I disagreed, at times, with their handling of them. During the Spanish War the emotions of our Catholic readers were so fervid that *The Times* could not have afforded to alienate them, even had it wanted to. For practical and news reasons we had to have a correspondent on the Franco side. I never questioned that. It was *The Times'* misfortune (and this was by no means only my opinion) to have had a poor and unreliable correspondent stationed in Burgos, Franco's capital, and Hendaye on the French border.

However, William P. Carney, from the beginning, became identified with the pro-Franco–anti-Republican side, as I did with the opposite. In his case it meant that he was a paladin of good and virtue to our Catholic readers. He could not be changed without *The Times* paying a high price in circulation and advertising. I could not be removed without a great outcry from the liberal, pro-Loyalist readers—a great majority.

The publisher laid down a mechanical, theoretically impartial, plan of operation—print both sides, equal prominence, equal length, equal treatment. This often meant equality for the bad with the good—the official handouts hundreds of miles from the front lines with the eyewitness stories, the tricky with the honest, the wrong with the right.

I say that not only I, but the truth suffered. No student can today go back to the files of *The New York Times* from July 1936 to April 1939 and get a competent, balanced, complete *journalistic* picture of the Spanish Civil War. *The Times* failed its readership and posterity because although it gave them much, it could have given more and better.

So far as my own despatches are concerned, I saved carbon copies of all of them. They are now in the Journalism Library of Columbia University, bound, listed, and catalogued. I want my work on the Spanish Civil War to be judged by them, not by what was printed under my by-line in *The New York Times*.

The best histories of the Civil War are now being written by non-Spaniards. For us who lived through the war, a vital dimension is missing—the personal, firsthand knowledge, which puts its imprint of truth, however limited or one-sided, on any historic event. When I read even so splendid a work of scholarship as the young Briton, Hugh Thomas', history of the Spanish Civil War, I know where he has gone astray on this or that detail, where he is guessing, where he is using unreliable sources, or where he has misjudged a man or an incident because he had to choose between conflicting opinions. Most of all, the striving for "impartiality" and "objectivity" has tripped up Thomas, as it has every scholar who has written about the Spanish conflict. In spite of himself, Thomas' bias in favor of the Republicans comes clearly through the pages of his book.

This reminds me of a history of Europe written by Professor Carlton Hayes of Columbia University, which was a textbook used during my years in Columbia. Hayes was an ardent Roman Catholic (I believe a convert), and the Catholic bias was evident in his work. During World War II he was the American ambassador in Madrid and he wrote a book about Franco Spain which I reviewed for *The Times Book Review*. Although he was an eminent historian who, at the very least, should have got his facts straight, the book was so full of palpable mistakes that much as I liked the charming old man, I felt constrained—and was able —to fault it heavily.

At the other extreme was the book that our ambassador to Spain, Claude Bowers, wrote after his experiences in the Civil War. As ambassador, he was heart and soul with the Republicans, but because of his unique and firsthand knowledge, he could have written a very valuable book. Instead, he half-filled it with his prejudices and pro-Loyalist–anti-Franco mistakes. Again, in reviewing his book, I had to attack it, though with regrets. The Spanish Republican cause did not—and does not —need anything but the truth.

There were many books written by former combatants in the International Brigade. Those who kept to their personal experiences did valuable work, but beyond that they harmed the Loyalist cause by emotional distortions and Communist propaganda.

The best—and worst—example of this was the compilation of writings on the war done by Alvah Bessie in 1952 called *The Heart of Spain.* Bessie had written what to me was one of the best novels on the war, *Men in Battle.* I liked it in some ways as much as Ernest Hemingway's *For Whom the Bell Tolls,* the most famous work on the Spanish Civil War. Hemingway was the best, most helpful, and most influential friend the Americans of the Abraham Lincoln Battalion had. Yet because, in his novel, he depicted André Marty, the French Communist commander of the International Brigade, as the sadistic, twisted fanatic that he was, and had a vivid chapter on Loyalist atrocities, the American Communists turned on Hemingway and vilified him. He had also written some splendid journalistic pieces for the North American Newspaper Alliance. Nothing by Hemingway (or, for that matter, Arthur Koestler, George Orwell, and André Malraux) was included in Bessie's anthology.

"It was felt," Bessie wrote in his introduction, "that Hemingway's talent and the personal support he rendered to many phases of the Loyalist cause were shockingly betrayed in his work *For Whom the Bell Tolls* in which the Spanish people were cruelly misrepresented and leaders of the International Brigade maliciously slandered." As a piece of black ingratitude this would be hard to beat. Bessie and other Communist members of the Abraham Lincoln Battalion propagated what was to me a specious exaggeration—that orthodox Communists deserved all the credit for the great role played in the war by the International Brigade. I calculated—and wrote in *The New York Times*— that 80 percent of the Americans in the Brigade were or became Communist. The original concept was Communist and the leadership was nearly all Communist. In the British, French, German, and some other contingents, the proportion of Communists was smaller. What gave the International Brigade its unique aura of self-sacrificing heroism and idealism was partly the number of non-Communist volunteers it attracted—an estimated 40 percent—but also the fact that most of the Party members were volunteers who fought for idealistic, not communistic reasons. The amalgam was anti-Fascism and all that it meant in those years to liberals and leftists everywhere and to exiles from Nazi Germany and Fascist Italy. It was a passionate conviction that they were fighting for good against evil, for democracy against Fascism, for liberty against tyranny.

The International Brigade was a unique phenomenon in the modern world. The volunteers left precious memories for those of us who knew them and watched them fight and saw so many of them die or be wounded. We, as well as the survivors, are richer for the experience. There was nothing comparable on the Insurgent side—only a very small and almost useless Irish Catholic contingent. Not a single American, so far as is known, volunteered to fight for Franco.

The International Brigade gave to the Spanish war a cachet and an atmosphere of exaltation that helped to make the conflict uniquely great in our century. The record was later blurred and smeared by the hysterical form that anti-Communism took in the United States after World War II, but that record will be set straight one of these days. Some young historians (like Prof. Cecil Eby of the University of Michigan) are shocked when they read and hear of the bungling, partisan, bloody, and brutal aspects that accompanied the idealism and glory. The International Brigade was not a baseball club. The task was desperate; the men had to be tough as well as brave.

I once wrote of the Brigaders as "the finest group of men I ever knew or hope to know in my life." They were that.

The International Brigade was something that seemed so rich and precious that most of us could not believe it would die—or, worse, betray its ideals. This, alas, was romanticism. The climate, the conjuncture of events, mass emotions, an almost religious, crusading urge, had all combined to bring about the formation of a body of men from all over the world to fight and die for Republican Spain. The Spanish Civil War ended in April 1939; in August of that same year Hitler and Stalin made the pact that permitted Germany to start World War II. Consequently, there could be no International Brigade in that war— nor in Korea, since anti-Communism was not a fighting cause for any but Americans and South Koreans. There could be no International Brigade in the cold war, for obvious reasons. Vietnam was a possibility—on the side of Hanoi—but by then the concept of an International Brigade had gone into history. The youth of today know virtually nothing about the International Brigade.

Of all the famous men writing about the Spanish Civil War, George Orwell was, to me, the most intriguing. His *Homage to Catalonia*, written in 1938, was reprinted in the United States in 1952 when it had already become a minor classic. The book did more to blacken the Loyalist cause than any work written by enemies of the Second Republic—a result that Orwell did not intend, as some things he wrote later proved.

In *Homage* Orwell was writing in white heat about a confused, unimportant, and obscure incident in a war he did not understand. All he saw, from December 1936 to May 1937, was a little stretch of the "phony front" at Huesca, and a bloody clash between Communists and Anarchists in Barcelona. He had volunteered in London through the leftist Independent Labor party, which had links to the Spanish POUM (*Partido Obrero de Unificación Marxista*). This was a dissident, very Marxist, not treacherous, but somewhat subversive revolutionary group that was proving dangerous to the Republican government. As Dr. Negrín wrote me in a letter I reproduced in *The Nation*, the POUM was "certainly controlled by elements very allergic. . . . to anything that meant a united and supreme direction of the struggle under a common discipline."

The POUM, and Orwell with them, were fighting for a social revolution; the Largo Caballero government was fighting desperately to win the war. Orwell was bitter when he discovered that the Communists in Spain were—like all post-Lenin Communists—counterrevolutionary. Their policy, and the government's, was to win the war first and worry about a revolution, if any, afterward. In the end Orwell was severely wounded and pursued by the police. He barely succeeded in fleeing to France. The honest result from that very brave, decent, and fair-minded man was, as I indicated, the document most damning for the Republicans that anyone had written on the war, but as later historians noted, it was a misleading book.

I should think that very few people have read the bits and pieces—essays, reviews, letters—that Orwell wrote about Spain in later years. They show a far better understanding of events than he had when he was in Spain. Even in *Homage to Catalonia*, he wrote at the end: "It sounds like lunacy, but the thing that both of us wanted [his wife was with him] was to be back in Spain. . . . Curiously enough, the whole experience has left me with not less but more belief in the decency of human beings. And I hope the account I have given is not too misleading."

In July 1937, two months after he had fled from Spain, Orwell wrote that "the International Brigade is in some sense fighting for all of us—a thin line of suffering and often ill-armed human beings standing between barbarism and at least comparative decency."

On April 27, 1938, writing to Cyril Connolly, who had just

been in Spain,* Orwell said: "The game's up, I'm afraid. I wish I were there. The ghastly thing is that if the war is lost, it will simply lead to an intensification of the policy that caused the Spanish Government to be let down, and before we know where we are we shall be in the middle of another war to save democracy."

I remembered that Don Juan Negrín had mentioned Orwell to me, so I wrote him in 1952 and asked him to tell me what he recalled. The reply is the letter I reproduced, in part, in a review of the book for *The Nation*.

> After we got acquainted, Negrín wrote me of Orwell, we met several times, and I venture to say that a reciprocal current of esteem, sympathy, and even friendship, was established. . . .
>
> "After reading his book I did not change my opinion about Orwell—a decent and righteous gentleman, biased by a too rigid, puritanical frame, gifted with a candor bordering on naiveté, highly critical but blindly credulous, morbidly individualistic (an Englishman!) but submitting lazily and without discernment to the atmosphere of the gregarious community in which he voluntarily and instinctively anchors himself, and so supremely honest and self-denying that he would not hesitate to change his mind once he perceived himself to be wrong."

That is as fair and acute a picture of George Orwell as I have seen. Don Juan Negrín was a shrewd judge of character, but his own character has been as greatly misjudged as that of any man I knew. The Spanish Republican exiles quarreled bitterly among themselves as exiles in a lost cause always do (*vide* the anti-Castro Cuban exiles). There was much ado about finances,

---

*This and some other references to Spain can be found in *The Collected Essays, Journalism and Letters of George Orwell* (London: Secker and Warburg, 1968).

which I never got to the bottom of. Certainly, Don Juan lived in very handsome style, with homes in Paris and outside of London. I know that Dr. Negrín considered himself entitled, as the premier when the Spanish Civil War ended, to the emoluments of that office, but he resigned in 1945. He was accused by his enemies of appropriating Republican funds for his private benefit. He was quite well-to-do when the war started. I knew Juan Negrín well and cannot conceive of him doing anything underhand or dishonest. He made his mistakes, as he confessed to me on several occasions—and to others—but I see him as a morally unblemished character.

The popular myth, propagated by his enemies and by the *Franquistas,* that he was a puppet of the Spanish Communists and/or of the Russians is ridiculous to anyone who knew him or watched him in operation. It is a weakness of the Communist system internationally that it cannot control strong leaders who are unwilling to accept discipline, or who are not ideologically committed to Communist dogma, Moscow style.

Negrín was neither a Communist nor a revolutionary. "Spaniards have a bias for liberty," he once said to me, "and they will die with that bias." I do not believe that Negrín gave the idea of a social revolution any thought before the Civil War. This was a weakness of all the Republican leaders in a country that desperately needed (it still does) drastic social reforms. Negrín retained all his life a certain indifference and blindness to social issues. Paradoxically, this put him in agreement with the Communists in the Civil War.

He was equally blind in an ideological sense. He was a prewar Socialist in name only. Russia was the only nation that helped Republican Spain; the Spanish Communists were among the best and most disciplined soldiers; the International Brigade, with its Communist leadership, was invaluable. Therefore, Premier Negrín worked with the Russians, but never succumbed to or took orders from them.

I know he was sharply critical of the Soviet Union during the 1939–1941 period when the Russians were allies of the Nazis. He was quarreling with the Russians (I do not know why) in

1943 and 1944, but he remained on friendly terms with Russian statesmen until he died. This was political sophistication and detachment, not a case of ideological affinity.

Negrín was always conscious of history and wanted to leave a good record on behalf of Republican Spain. Unfortunately, the ruthlessness and skullduggery of the Spanish Communists, and the high-handed cruelty and cold calculation of the Russian Stalinist envoys working behind the scenes, are what left the deepest mark on the historic record. There were occasions when Dr. Negrín protested privately against Communist machinations, but he was too dependent on Russian help to do so openly or effectively. As a rule he was faced with *faits accomplis,* which could not be reversed.

Russia was not prepared for a world war and Stalin did not want to see Spain spark the great conflict that was looming on the horizon. Russian aid was cut down to almost nothing in the final six or eight months of the Civil War. Diplomatic feelers were already out between Stalin and Hitler. Only historians— and, I should add, we journalists—know the extent to which the Spanish Loyalists were fighting on their own in the last stage of the war, while Germany and Italy stepped up the aid by which Franco won.

The last year of fighting was a miracle of dogged, hopeless courage, made possible solely by the tenacity and indomitable spirit of Negrín. However, this astonishing display of leadership was the most bitterly criticized feature among Spaniards of Dr. Negrín's career. The fight was hopeless, his critics said, and all that "unnecessary" destruction, all those extra lives lost, all the intensified hatred of Spaniard for Spaniard, could have been avoided. It is certain, on the other hand, that the Loyalists could have held out longer had it not been for treachery, and that World War II could have saved Republican Spain.

The bitterness and even hatred toward Juan Negrín of so many Spanish contemporaries on both sides after the Civil War make a balanced judgment still impossible. In my opinion, Don Juan's aims were consistent, patriotic, and honorable. He stood for a fight to the finish, first to save the Second Republic and—

when that became impossible—to get the best terms for those who had remained loyal. In the process, he had to rely heavily on Stalinist Russia, and then almost exclusively on the Spanish Communists. He was left with no other choice, thanks to the misnamed "nonintervention" policy of the Western democracies and Franco's insistence on unconditional surrender.

Spain was betrayed—but not by Juan Negrín. The worst that could be said of him was that he was quixotic and unreasonable —two qualities that are not uncommon to the Spanish character. For a species of epitaph, I would repeat today the judgment that I put in my book, *The Yoke and the Arrows,* which was written in 1956, just after he died. It is a final judgment on him that I cannot conceive myself ever changing.

"He was a great Spaniard, and he fought for all that was best in the contemporary aspirations of Spain. The battle he lost will be resumed, and because he fought it so well, it may be resumed without civil strife—and sooner or later it will be won. Those who fight for freedom never fight in vain."

It has been an undying prejudice among us *aficionados* of the Spanish Civil War that all the best people were on the Loyalist side or sympathetic with it. I still have that prejudice.

One of the best of all has been Pablo Casals, the cellist, who came down to Barcelona once at a desperate time in 1938 and gave a concert. The whole government was there, as well as those lucky individuals who could beg or scrounge a ticket. I had listened to Casals play often in New York. (I once asked him in San Juan when he had first played in New York City. "It seems to me," I said, "that I have been hearing you all my life." "1903," he replied.) Of all the Casals concerts I have heard, the Barcelona one was the most thrilling. I felt sure he had never played better in his life. Of course, my emotion was subjective, but he confessed to me years later that he was deeply moved that day and had played with all his heart.

Pablo (Pau) Casals is a Catalan, a Spaniard, a consummate musician and, best of all, a great soul. He refused to go to Spain after the Civil War, making an exception only once to attend the funeral of his brother. He refused to play for years in the United

States because of Washington's military pact with the Franco regime. He is as sweet and kindly a human being as ever lived, but he hated Franco and all he stood for. I know of no greater criticism that one can make of Franco Spain than that a man like Pablo Casals considers it unfit for Spaniards like himself.

All the Spaniards who fought in the Civil War are now old and in exile or dead. Young Spaniards think of the conflict as ancient history, a crazy, baffling episode that they brush aside impatiently. The widespread opposition to the Franco regime is a heritage of the Civil War, echoing down the decades, but the youth do not see it as such. The protests take the form of student riots and illegal strikes. Republicans, Socialists, Communists, Anarchists are underground, waiting for Franco to die.

I, too, am waiting for Franco to die. I want to live to see Spain a free country again, as it will be. Spaniards really do have "a bias for liberty." It can be granted that Generalissimo Francisco Franco will always be one of the towering figures of Spanish history, but after he dies it will be seen that the mark he made was not enduring, for it had no vision; it did not represent modern Spain; there is no such thing as "Francoism." It is a historical anachronism and a piece of trickery to have named Prince Don Juan Carlos of Bourbon as the future king of Spain, which Franco did in July 1969. Juan Carlos was not the legitimate heir; his father, Don Juan, was. The son is dominated by a strong-willed Greek wife and a ruthless mother-in-law, Queen Frederika. He has no competence to rule a government, no experience, no real popularity, and he will have, in Spain, one of the most unruly countries in Europe.

In naming him, Franco was putting the future power mainly in the hands of two or three strong, reactionary military leaders who can sit on a lid for a while—until the pressure blows them and Don Juan Carlos sky-high. The explosion will be delayed because of the powerful, new moneyed interests, which have grown during the Franco interregnum—industrialists, bankers, new landowners, plus the entrenched bureaucracy of the trade union leadership.

There are no competent biographies either of Franco or Negrín. The Generalissimo, who was born in 1892, cannot have many more years to rule. That he should still be the dictator of Spain—the *Caudillo*—more than thirty years after the Civil War ended shows how shrewd, tough, and cautious he is, and how shell-shocked the whole nation was after the orgy of self-destruction. We noted those three qualities of his during the Civil War—plus his cruelty and ruthlessness.

He was not religious—until it paid him to become so. He was not a confirmed monarchist nor was he anti-Republican—until he saw where his personal and national interests seemed to lie. Because he was a soldier all his life and came from a long line of naval officers, he did passionately believe in "law and order." This, in my opinion, is by far the most important reason why he joined the rebellion. Once in, he schemed to head it because of ambition and a genuine belief that he, alone, was qualified to lead the Insurgents to victory and then to "save" the nation in World War II and the postwar period.

The concept that we in the Loyalist zone had of him in the Civil War was, at least partly, a caricature. The Spanish artist Luis Quintanilla published many acidly brilliant pictures of the short, tubby, vacuous-looking General. (There is, incidentally, more Republican history in Quintanilla's drawings than in a library of books.)

Nothing was—or is—easier than to criticize this narrow, barren man, but the rocklike qualities that gave him victory in war and a long dictatorship in peace were suited to the times. Character, not generalship, was his strong point. He never commanded his troops in any battle or campaign in the Civil War. He took little or no advice on strategy from the Germans or Italians who gave him the men and matériel to win the war. He went his own steady, inflexible way.

The fears entertained during the conflict that Spain would be run by the Nazis and Fascists proved false. Franco got them out quickly, and in World War II performed his greatest service for

Spain by keeping the nation out of the conflict. He wanted the Axis to win and helped in what ways he could, but he drove Hitler into stamping fits of rage with his refusal to do more.

A less cautious and stubborn man might have won the Civil War quicker. In the same way Spain's postwar progress in economy has been far slower than necessary. In politics the country has hardly budged since 1945. There has been a sort of enforced civic peace. Anyway, no Spaniard has wanted another civil war. This is a typical Spanish period of apathy after an exhausting national effort. It will end.

I have visited Spain a half dozen times since the end of World War II, but Franco would never agree to see me. I talked to every foreign minister and Cabinet minister whom I wanted to see, and invariably met the courtesy and even friendliness for which Spaniards are justly famous. All the same, it has been made clear enough that, journalistically speaking, I am Public Enemy No. 1. My record in the Civil War has never been forgotten. It was well known in Madrid that I wrote *The New York Times'* hostile editorials on the Franco regime. My books on Spain and my biography of Fidel Castro are on the blacklist and cannot be imported or sold in Spain. That is a situation that will also come to an end one of these days.

The meaning, the intensity of feeling, the realization of the heroism, the glory, the tragedy of the Spanish Civil War, the heart-warming sense of camaraderie among us who were there —these will die when we who experienced them die. Those of us who lived through the Spanish War could say to the world, as King Henry IV did for all men in all times: "Hang yourself, brave Crillon, we have fought at Arques and you were not there."

André Malraux, who has changed so much since he flew in an old crate of a plane for the Loyalists at the beginning of the Civil War, has not changed about Spain. "Thirty years ago," he told the Paris correspondent of *The New York Times*, Henry Tanner, in an interview in October 1968, "the only important thing was the Spanish Civil War. I attached a very great importance to it, not only as a struggle, but also because it was a most profound experience of brotherhood."

I did what I could, during and after the Spanish war, to convey what it meant and how men felt. When I dedicated my book, *The Education of a Correspondent,* to my nephew, Lieut. Robert Alan Matthews, killed in action on his twenty-second birthday in World War II, I used a quotation about Spain.

At the time when the Internationals were ending their service in Spain, the father of a volunteer named John Cookson, who was adjutant of the Transmissions Company of the 15th Brigade, wrote his son a letter which read, in part: "My health is bad, my heart is playing out. If I am not here any more when you return, always remember that I am glad you went over. *A man may as well die young, having died for a purpose, than live a whole life without one.*" The sentence in italics was the one I used in my dedication. Cookson was killed in the Ebro battle before the letter arrived.

That is how men felt about the Spanish Civil War. Here is how I felt, as the war ended and as I expressed it in the same book. I think of it as my unchanging and unchangeable valedictory to a wonderful and terrible experience.

"I was sick at heart that night when I wrote my last despatch on the Spanish Civil War, but at least I, in a humble way, felt vindicated. 'Countries do not live by victories only,' Negrín had said, 'but by the examples which their people have known how to give, in tragic times.' The Spanish people had, indeed, given a glorious example, and that night in Perpignan, exhausted as I was, I knew that the fight had not been in vain.

"But what of my reputation as a journalist? The hopes that I had so confidently expressed had been belied by the swift pace of events. The story that I told—of bravery, of tenacity, of discipline and constant decency, of optimism that came from courage and high ideals—had been scoffed at by many. The despatches describing the callousness of the French and the cynicism of the British had been objected to and denied.

"I, too, was beaten and sick at heart and somewhat shell-shocked, as any person must be under the nerve strain of seven weeks of incessant danger, coming at the end of two years' campaigning. . . . So I was depressed, physically and mentally and morally. I felt as if I were crawling home to New York and to my wife and children, a little of a stranger to my family and a little of a failure to my newspaper.

"But the lessons I had learned! They seemed worth a great deal. Even then, heartsick and discouraged as I was, something sang inside of me. I, like the Spaniards, had fought my war and lost, but I could not be persuaded that I had set too bad an example.

" 'Open thy arms,' cried Sancho Panza, 'and receive thy son Don Quixote too, who, though he got the worst on't with another, he ne'ertheless got the better of himself, and that's the best kind of victory one can wish for.' "

Chapter 3

FRANCE

France is an acquired taste. There is no more rewarding one in the world. It was far from a case of love at first sight when I and my Tank Corps unit debarked in Le Havre at the beginning of November 1918. We were racing against time, for the war was clearly approaching its end, and my "buddies" and I had enlisted to fight.

World War I, as I said before, was the last one in which a great section of American youth were eager to join up. By present-day standards we were simple-minded. I, for instance, had no idea what that first global war was about. Making the world safe for democracy was not a satisfactory explanation. I swallowed all the propaganda about the Germans—and so hated them passionately—but without valid reasons such as we had in World War II. I was patriotic in the primitive, enduring, nationalistic, "my-country-right-or-wrong" sense. In France, I am now ashamed to remember, I kept longing for "God's country," meaning, of course, the United States.

I was eighteen—just old enough to enlist—and since tanks were something new, romantic, dashing, and dangerous, I chose the Tank Corps. The medical examiners almost rejected me because of flat feet. In those days doctors had the ridiculous idea that a man with flat feet could not make long marches. I indignantly pointed out that I was regularly playing as much as ten or twelve sets of tennis a day.

As I trained in the tank center at Gettysburg, the problem was how to get over to France. I made it because I had become a specialist for an experiment in radio communication in battle. The idea was that on the battlefield, an operator, standing behind the driver of a French whippet tank, would receive messages in Morse code from the commanders in the rear. I don't remember how we were supposed to convey the orders to the gun-bearing (37-millimeter) tanks in action, and I am sure the whole idea was impractical, but it was good enough to get me and my detachment urgently assigned to the Tank Corps center of the American Expeditionary Force in France.

Our whole Corps in World War I had fewer tanks and less fire and manpower than one tank battalion today. The United States Army itself had no tanks, but used French ones—the light whippets with a turret and the "heavy" slanted, rectangular ones with guns pointing every which way.

Even in the American army we were not pampered. On the passage over, we slept in hammocks down below deck, the food was always ghastly; on land there were no overflowing canteens to buy everything from chewing gum to cameras at cost prices; and my pay as a private was thirty dollars a month, of which I only got ten dollars in cash, the rest going to insurance and I don't know what else.

The day we landed in Le Havre I had one of the migraine headaches from which I have suffered since the age of six. I was in Le Havre for the "false armistice" of November 7 when everyone else went wild with joy, while I, with youthful selfishness, was in despair thinking that I had missed the war after all. When that most famous of false journalistic scoops was corrected, and we were ordered to get to the Tank Corps center from which we would be moved immediately to the front, my hopes rose again. However, it took so long to reach our destination in the old *Huits Chevaux Quarante Hommes* (8 horses 40 men) freight cars, that we arrived on November 11, as the firing stopped.

The Tank Corps was in and around a hamlet called Bourg, five miles from the lovely old walled town of Langres. We had to be kept busy despite the peace, so our training continued in lackluster fashion. Meanwhile, there was the chance to meet Frenchmen and Frenchwomen and learn a little about the country—a chance that everybody passed up. This was even more true early in 1919 when we were moved south to Castellon on the Dordogne River, 60 miles or so from Bordeaux. There was nothing to do but march around a bit each day in the lovely *Midi* countryside while we waited with burning impatience to be shipped back home.

We grumbled that after all we had done for France—God save the mark! France which had suffered more than any nation in that war—the French were ungrateful and greedy for our money.

Toward the end of April 1919, we embarked for "God's country."

In 1926 I returned to France as a graduate student on a Bayard Cutting Taylor fellowship from Columbia University. (I had spent eight months of the allotted twelve in Italy.) I was on leave from *The New York Times,* whose business office I had joined three years before. This time I *was* interested in the French people and captivated by Paris—once and forever. Paris has been for me what it was for Ernest Hemingway, "a moveable feast." She will never cease to be the "City of Light"—*La Ville Lumière.* As its motto says, *fluctuat nec mergitur* (it floats but does not sink). It was the most beautiful of all cities until a plague of automobiles swarmed over its boulevards, streets, and squares, and even on the fringes of the parks.

I rented a room across from the Odéon Theatre, close to the Luxembourg and within walking distance of the Sorbonne where I often attended lectures and classes. My fellowship was for a year's study of Dante and medieval Italian literature, which were major subjects for me at Columbia under the greatest scholar and teacher I ever knew, Dino Bigongiari.

French politics and economics were of no interest, except that changing dollars into dizzily gyrating francs was fun and games for me and very distressing for forty million Frenchmen. Although I paid no attention, 1926 was a time of financial and political crisis in France, but it was not a revolutionary period.

I could be unaware of politics in 1926 because they did not affect daily life. The right wing had won in the general election of November 1919, and it controlled the National Assembly in fourteen out of the next twenty years. The veteran politician, Raymond Poincaré, headed a government of "National Union" in 1926. Two years later, he succeeded in stabilizing the franc and creating a moderate government of center groups. In so doing he saved France for the bourgeoisie, or at least saved the middle class from ruin. Revolution was a threat—it always is in France—but the people were war-weary, and the nation had been drained white by the tremendous losses of World War I.

The only active revolutionaries, at least in principle, were the Communists, but they were to win only fourteen seats in the 1928 election. Votes for the Communists, then as now, were to a considerable extent a form of protest, but the Party was under the control of the Kremlin and the Comintern, and it really was ideologically revolutionary.

A process of osmosis was at work for me. Instinctively, I was absorbing French civilization and learning to understand the complex, sometimes abrasive, but much more often warm and friendly character of the French people.

Edwin L. James, who later became managing editor of *The Times*, was head of the Paris bureau, then on the Rue de la Paix. Jimmy James was a character out of another, and, to me, better, age on the paper. He was Adolph S. Ochs' fair-haired boy although he was not a good foreign correspondent or war correspondent. He rarely let a day go by without a two-column dispatch, loosely and poorly written, on French politics, which usually hit the front page. Much of the material was fed to him by a remarkably knowledgeable sybarite named Jules Sauerwein. If Aristide Briand were the premier and Jimmy wanted to clarify some angle of a story, Sauerwein would pick up the telephone and one would hear:

"Bonjour, mon vieux. Comment ça va? Et Madame? Dites . . ." And the answer would come from Briand himself. Sauerwein did that often for me when I was in the bureau. I never ceased to marvel at the variety and importance of his contacts and his ability to get precise information.

Jules Sauerwein was fat, gay, witty, a lover of food, wine, and women and a piano player of considerable talent. All of which made him a natural boon companion for Jimmy James, who loved the same things, although he lacked the artistic musical touch. Jimmy was an excellent administrator with a shrewd financial sense, a flair for news, and an ability to get along with the men and women who worked with him or under him. These were gifts for a managing editor more than for a correspondent.

Jimmy James was loyal to his men and would stand up for them against the publisher and the other higher powers on *The Times*. No managing editor since his time has had those qualities or so received the affection of the staff. He talked tough and was a bit rough, but the inside was soft.

The second man in the Paris bureau at the time was Percy J. Philip, a Scot whom Jimmy had hired at the end of the war. He was to succeed James as head of the bureau and in 1931 I was to become the second man of the four-man staff but, of course, I could not dream of that in 1926.

I sailed for home, in June, on one of the long-ago-scrapped, one-class tourist ships, the Minnetonka. It proved the most memorable journey of my life, because a fellow passenger was a young Englishwoman—who was to become my wife—Edith Crosse, but always known as Nancie. It was a case of love at first sight for me. The course of true love did not run smoothly, but at length we were married on February 21, 1931.

Louis Wiley, the business manager of *The Times*, was short and squat and inevitably earned the sobriquet of "the little Napoleon." Being inordinately vain, he liked the association. He was also a petty, stingy, small-minded martinet who made a practice of turning off electric lights. Small details seemed to absorb his working hours.

I began with *The Times* at twenty-five dollars a week as a secretary to Edwin S. Friendly, assistant business manager, who, a year later, became publisher of the now-defunct New York evening paper, *The Sun.* (Friendly had courted Iphigene Ochs in vain.) His successor, Arnold Sanchez, put me on the Christmas list in 1924 to get a raise. Wiley condescended to make my salary twenty-seven dollars a week, at which I squawked loudly. With Sanchez's backing, Wiley reluctantly agreed to do better—twenty-nine dollars. This seemed ludicrous to me, but the little Napoleon was not going to accept another defeat and raise the ante to a round, magnanimous thirty dollars.

Yet Louis Wiley must have been a financial wizard, a brilliant administrator, and an extraordinarily shrewd businessman. The growth in advertising and circulation, which made *The Times* profitable and helped establish its power, was his doing. He was, of course, seconded in an equally important way by the first and, thus far, only great managing editor *The Times* has had, Carr Van Anda. Over them both was Adolph S. Ochs, whose concept of a serious, honest, fair newspaper, printing "all the news that's fit to print," made American journalistic history at the same time that it made a great newspaper. I did not work under Van Anda and knew him only by reputation and office gossip.

Ochs has been written about enough not to need any encomiums from me. His biographers tend to ignore the fact that his greatness lay in simplicity and shrewdness, not in an understanding or flair for news values, or a penetrating comprehension of what was happening in world affairs. He clung to solid virtues—honesty, fairness, thoroughness, loyalty, courage in crises. He was not intellectual.

Elmer Adler, a well-known publisher of fine books and limited editions, who founded the Pynson Printers, which then had offices on the seventh floor of *The Times*, was a typical detractor. (I helped Adler in the 1920's to creat the "Museum of the Printed Word" which is now a permanent exhibit for schoolchildren visiting the plant.) "Ochs was just lucky," Adler would say, "a mediocre mind who hit on a golden formula and found geniuses to make it work." This was the age-old habit of picking on weaknesses in great men. One can do it with Caesar, Napoleon, Churchill, and many others. *The New York Times* could not have been made into a great newspaper by a mediocre man.

What Adolph S. Ochs lacked did not handicap him. One could be amused, as my wife and I often were, by his foibles. He absorbed the snobbery of his adopted town, Chattanooga, Tennessee. He had married Effie Wise, daughter of one of the most prominent of American rabbis and through her, and his initial success with the *Chattanooga Times,* had an unrivaled place in the Jewish community—which was not enough.

Vicariously, through his brother Milton, Adolph Ochs became a figure in high society in Chattanooga. A Miss Van Dyke, of one of the oldest and most prominent Protestant families of the city, fell in love with Milton and insisted on marrying him. She was an exciting, glamorous beauty who retained her glamor and *joie de vivre* into very old age, as we saw on trips south.

The other female in the family, on whom Ochs doted, was his only child, Iphigene. Our personal recollections of Adolph Ochs were of a man made socially happy through the women who surrounded him. His wife was a home body; Iphigene a serious, though attractive, bluestocking; while his sister-in-law provided the glamor and social connections. Ochs used to take Miss Van Dyke, as she was always called, on trips abroad, where other socialites and famous actresses would flutter around him. No man, as my wife and I discovered in many countries, is so sychophantically treated as a famous and successful newspaper publisher. This applied tenfold to the publisher of *The New York Times.*

Iphigene used to read bits of letters to Nancie from her father on his trips, laughing over them. "Pa's happy. Such and such an actress was on board the ship and he had a wonderful time." Ochs, however, was not a philanderer; he simply loved adulation and the social status that his family and fame brought him. He was not only very fond and proud of Iphigene, but he also wanted her to look glamorous, too—which she could not and did not want to do. "Pa's rich," she would say with droll resignation when he showered fur coats and jewels upon her. "I wouldn't do it, but father insists."

Iphigene, to her father's satisfaction (although he never became fond of him or close to him), fell in love with and married Arthur Hays Sulzberger who, on his mother's side, was a Son of the American Revolution.

Adolph S. Ochs, *en pantoufle*—in slippers, as the French say—was a good, simple, kindly man with all-too-human foibles. He did not have two contrasting images, public and private. His life was a study in harmony.

My three years in the Business Office taught me the importance of advertising and circulation to a newspaper. Those three years were good riddance, however; the next five were to lay the basis for my career as a newspaperman, by which one always means someone who writes for, or edits, a newspaper.

I had written Arthur Sulzberger, then vice-president of *The Times* from London in 1926, expressing the hope that I could find a place on the Sunday *Book Review*. It was a natural aspiration because I had lived immersed in books. Fortunately, there was no vacancy, or I would still be there. However, the acting managing editor, Frederick T. Birchall, needed a secretary. I took the post with misgivings, but anything looked better than returning to the Business Department. I soon became an undistinguished reporter on the City staff, after proving to Birchall that I could write. Bosley Crowther, who later became movie critic, had the desk next to mine. Hanson Baldwin, the future military editor, shared a desk with him. George Horne, who was to succeed the then famous "Skipper" Williams as ship news editor, was nearby. All three "outlived" me on *The Times* and so did some others from the 1920's. One of the few who left *The Times* in my early years was Robert S. Bird, who moved over to the *Herald Tribune* and in time became its star reporter. In those years, one could say: "Join *The New York Times* and you have a job for life." One had to commit murder, or be utterly impossible, to get discharged. *The Times* has had some of the worst

correspondents in the game through unknowingly hiring in-
competents or misfits and then being too loyal to fire them. A
one-time rival of mine in the 1930's was bribed with six months
pay in order to induce him to condescend to retire. Those days
are gone, no doubt forever. Now men come and go, and sometimes are humiliated or kicked out unceremoniously—even old-
timers who have deserved an honored send-off. This happened
to assistant managing editor Robert Garst and even to Brooks
Atkinson, our noted drama critic. The paper is more businesslike now—alas! It is also a better newspaper.

One afternoon in the spring of 1928 I told Birchall that I
would like to try my hand at copyreading on one of the two night
editing desks—City and Telegraph. He let out a whoop (Birchall
was a little man with a big voice) and called to Joseph Tebeau,
who headed the bull pen—the small group of night editors who
command the news columns.

"Here's a lad who actually wants to do copyreading," Birchall
chortled. As I learned later, good copy editors were hard to find.
It is a night job on a morning newspaper and a nerve-wracking
one because of the grueling and ruthless pressure of the hands
moving round the clock toward deadlines that must be met.

Those who work in the mass communications media are the
greatest of all slaves to time. When my wife says: "It's seven
o'clock, isn't it?" I will answer, "No—it's two minutes to seven"
—which is very annoying to most people, but to a newspaperman, two minutes can make all the difference in the world.

Anyway, I became a copyreader on the City Desk, then headed
by Raymond McCaw. In those days foreign news was handled by
the Telegraph Desk, but as our small staff of foreign correspondents grew, it was decided also to create a Cable Desk as
an appendage to the Telegraph Desk. Four men were chosen,
with myself as second in charge because I knew something of
Italy, France, and Britain and knew languages. The head of the
desk was Clarence Howell. Tebeau's second man was Neil
McNeill. As I have said earlier, McCaw, Howell, and McNeill—
and a fourth named Harvey Getzloe—formed the bull pen during the whole course of the Spanish Civil War.

Since I was on the Cable Desk, I was among the first to learn, in the autumn of 1931, that the second man in the Paris bureau was quitting to join a business firm. Life was difficult for us in New York. Our first child was coming, and my night schedule created its own peculiar difficulties. Nancie never did like New York City and I was longing for Paris, not to mention for a better job with higher pay. After an initial disappointment I was chosen.

We sailed a few weeks later on the Hamburg-America liner Albert Ballin. I have only two memories of the trip, aside from the fact that it was a happy voyage. One was that, sitting at the purser's table in the dining salon and he being a gourmet, we had all the caviar we could eat. The other memory, which has remained a poignant one all my life, was of a young, upper-class German businessman and another young German, but a Jew, who was a bit loud and pushing and ostentatious. I remember the fury and hatred with which the first German talked of his Jewish compatriot one evening. "He won't have long to flaunt himself," he said.

Being second man in a foreign bureau is rarely a happy condition, and I did not find it agreeable during my four years in Paris. Philip, the bureau chief, never took to me and vice versa. "P.J.," as he was called, was a tall, saturnine-looking Scotsman (I was a tall, saturnine-looking American) who was a competent correspondent, with long experience in French affairs and a redeeming love of France and the French. I am hard to get to know and have had few intimates in my life. To Philip, I was a strange and exasperating character.

There were two other men in the bureau, both Americans: Lansing Warren, the sweetest, gentlest, nicest character I ever knew on *The Times,* and William P. Carney, who was later to be my opposite on the Franco side in the Spanish Civil War.

I could hardly claim to be more than competent myself—probably less than competent in the first few years. Life in Paris was more civilized than in New York but had its own distracting difficulties, which were chiefly financial. The great crisis that smote the United States in 1929 had reached France. The depression so affected *New York Times'* income that all salaries were cut 10 percent for many months. Our expenses were rising as first our son, Eric, was born in 1932 and then our daughter, Priscilla, in 1934.

We were always hard up during those years in Paris, but it was better than New York. A *nou-nou* for the children and a *bonne à tout faire* for the house were still easy to get at low wages. The food, the wines, the coruscating beauty of Paris; living in the world's capital of art; the penetrating sense of a glorious history; the sophisticated, fascinating, attractive people—had we been "down and out" as Orwell and Hemingway were, Paris would still have been the most wonderful place in the world to live.

For Frenchmen it was a period of distress, ferment, and discontent. Forces were shaping up for a great national, as well as world, tragedy. The Third Republic was decomposing in an atmosphere of weakness, corruption, cynicism, and divided counsels. A government that lasted six months was a marvel. Politics was a merry-go-round with the same group of men on the tread, now one flashing by, then another and another until the first one came back.

"The trick," I heard Edouard Herriot say when he saw one of his many terms as premier ending, "is how to fall off the horse gracefully." The Maginot line was the symbol of French futility in the 1930's.

The year—1931—when I joined the Paris bureau saw the rise of Pierre Laval, who became premier for the first time. Hitler was gaining power. The customs union (the Anschluss) of Germany and Austria was completed in March 1931. Gustav Stresemann had died in 1929; Aristide Briand was to die in March 1932—a story I covered for *The Times.* Dreams of a united Europe had faded away, and power politics was at its height. The names of the premiers were always familiar—Edouard Herriot, André Tardieu, Joseph Paul-Boncour, Edouard Daladier, Pierre Etienne Flandin, Pierre Laval, Camille Chautemps—professional politicians, appeasers, and right-centrists all. There were exceptional men in the 1930's—Paul Reynaud, Albert Sarraut, Georges Mandel—but they could not stop the rot. The French press and weekly reviews were mostly rightist, either because they were conservative (like *Le Matin, Le Journal, Gringoire, Candide*) or militantly political (like the *Echo de Paris, Figaro* and *Le Jour*).

It was paradoxical that World War I, still the most devastating conflict in history, hardly interrupted the course and development of the Third Republic. French institutions were not shaken. The lesson for a journalist was that dividing lines between epochs—historic watersheds—have qualitative rather than quantitative factors. War consolidates a nation. The postwar inflation and financial scandals were more corrosive and diversive than the loss of hundreds of thousands of men at Verdun.

The French are the most stable as well as the most revolutionary of peoples—which is not a paradox because France had her social revolution once and for all in 1789. Later revolts were echoes or waves lapping against the inherent stability and maturity of French society. It was apt that the French should have invented the phrase: *"Plus ça change, plus ça reste la même chose."*

The years I was in the bureau—1931 to 1935—were politically sordid, ignoble, and cynical. When it comes to politics in France, the cynicism seeps downward to the people who tend to dismiss their politicians, as they did then, with Gallic shrugs of the shoulders. French politics, anyway, are always more dramatic in expression than they are in reality and substance. The surface is exciting, but there is a stolidity underneath. French society is only now changing from the form it took after the Revolution. Now another great revolution is taking place, but it is demographic, not political. Marianne, who was a good, wise, mature bourgeoise, is now an ebullient, mini-skirted teenager. France is becoming a young country.

This was not yet the case in the 1930's. The old France went on decomposing. She might have died peacefully on her sickbed if there hadn't been an Adolf Hitler and a resurgent Germany on the borders. My memories of the period were as much of the impact of the Nazis as of French internal affairs. I could not help being impressed by the determinism and activism of the Germans, Italians, and Japanese (the future Axis) when compared to the dithering of France and Tory Britain. I had enough sense to grasp the horror and danger behind Hitler's racism and expansionism, and the ruthlessness of the Japanese. I did not underestimate the mischievousness of Fascist Italy, but I was too fond of the Italians and knew them too well to take Mussolini very seriously. My real failure—an inexcusable one in the light of what happened—was to feel so contemptuous of French and British appeasement and of American isolationism that I almost admired and rather respected the leaders who knew what they wanted and were in the process of grabbing it. I was tolerant, which was very silly considering that the end result was bound to be mortal danger to my own country and to all the things we stood for. At least I did have a proper sense of the futility of French, British, and American statesmanship in that period.

There is no need to dwell upon the petty details pertaining to France, except to touch upon the uprising of February 1934. At that time I saw Parisians rise to fight at the barricades, an almost necessary experience in understanding the French. The "mystique of the barricades" goes back to medieval Paris and has never lost its appeal. (In England, arson—for instance, burning farmers' stocks of corn or hay—was more common.)

I was thoroughly confused about the meaning of the riots in Paris at the time—and so were most other people. None of us in the bureau analyzed it properly. In the midst of a violent, stone-throwing mob, with brutal *Gardes Mobiles* on horseback swinging their clubs wildly at everyone in sight—including myself and, at one time, my pregnant wife—it was hard to see the forest for the trees.

There had been a typical French financial scandal centering around a foreigner, Serge Stavisky. News of an embezzlement appeared in a provincial newspaper on January 3, 1934. It said that the culprit had fled. Stavisky had gone to Switzerland, where he committed suicide on January 8. In the intervening days the vast proportions of his financial swindle had emerged, implicating Cabinet ministers, among others.

It was a period when war veterans, superpatriots, militant youths, and would-be Fascists were forming associations and "leagues" as channels of protest. They were nearly all right wing, having in common a strong antiparliamentarianism mixed with the typical French nationalism, which, in extreme forms, turns toward, or looks for a charismatic, Napoleonic leader. This is not Fascism or Communism. It is a refuge against disorder, violence, and illegality. Caesarism, authoritarianism, plebiscitarianism—these are all normal historic phenomena in France. Fascism has been called "a heresy of democracy." So was Gaullism in its heyday. Charles de Gaulle came naturally out of French politics and society.

But in 1934 there was no strong government leader. Premier Camille Chautemps tried, inexcusably, to hush up the Stavisky scandal. The popular clamor was too great. Daladier took over again, but also tried to avoid a full investigation and airing of the scandal.

On February 6, the new government was due to make its first appearance in the Chamber of Deputies, secure in its majority. But Parliament was in a wild turmoil as a mob of 200,000 gathered in the Place de la Concorde across the Seine. They rioted so fiercely that it seemed to be exploding into an uprising. Barricades sprang up in other parts of the city. Spikes, bottles, and stones were hurled. Razors were used to hamstring the horses of the *Gardes Mobiles.* Then came arson and looting the next day, as criminal elements swarmed out, destroying and pillaging. On February 9 there was more bloody rioting, although only in the poorer quarters. On the twelfth a general strike was called by the General Confederation of Labor in which Socialists and Communists united for the first time.

This uprising was not like 1848, 1870, or—skipping ahead—1968, in its revolutionary scope. It was simply a series of massive street demonstrations against political and financial scandals, against the distress of the economic depression, against the lies of the successive governments, against corruption. That it had no greater depth was proved by the fact that it was scotched by calling in a gentle ineffectual old ex-President—Gaston Doumergue—to take over a new government as premier. René Rémond, in a book called *The Right Wing in France, From 1815 to De Gaulle*, quotes Henri de Kerillis of the *Echo de Paris:* "It has become a sort of rite with us to appeal to an old man, to a father of the country." He was referring to Clemenceau, Poincaré, and Doumergue, and unwittingly prophesying a De Gaulle.

The Stavisky scandal was a catalyst more than a direct cause. The economic crisis had brought high unemployment and much suffering that the bumbling, corrupt Radical governments could do little to alleviate. Léon Blum thought he was witnessing an attempted Fascist *putsch* in February 1934, aimed at bringing on a dictatorship. He later claimed that the Socialists would have joined a government of national unity.

Looking back, the 1934 uprising was the major event that gave the French Socialists and Radicals the anti-Fascist mystique that was to spread over Europe and even affect the United States, reaching its grand climax in the Spanish Civil War and World War II. But this could not have been foreseen at the time; it could have been sensed only in a vague way.

It was thirty-four years before France was to have another great internal social upheaval. The *événements* of April–May 1968 were comparable to 1934 only because all mass street rioting looks superficially the same and because in both cases there was profound popular discontent. If I had been covering the 1968 riots (my wife and I were in France for the first part of them), I would have stressed their revolutionary character. The 1968 target was no less than the established social and political structure of France.

A parliamentary commission of inquiry in 1934 concluded that the rioting had been provoked, in large part, by the right-wing leagues. They had disciplined members under paramilitary leaders. However, it was not a premeditated or coordinated plot. Some Communists took part in the rioting, but as troublemakers, not as allies of the right-wing organizations. There were no equivalents of 1968 student leaders like Daniel Cohn-

Bendit and Alain Krivine. Thousands of youths rioted in 1934, but not as university students. Colonel de la Rocque of the *Croix de Feu*, Jean Renaud of the *Solidarité Française*, Taittinger of the *Jeunesses Patriotes*, Maurras of the *Camelots du Roy*, were figures in the background.

I had seen Fascism at work during nearly a year in Italy (1925–1926) and was not confounding the French fascistoid movements with Mussolini's system. The fear of all leftists and liberals in 1934—and at all times—was that right-wing, militaristic, law-and-order movements inescapably lead to some form of Fascism if permitted to follow their natural evolution. The French militant, ultranationalistic, and anti-Semitic organizations were frightening in 1934 because of their resemblance to Hitler's Nazi movement, which had triumphed the year before, but 1934 taught the lesson that France would not "go Fascist." I would add that it cannot go Communist, either.

In the 1930's Paris had ceased to be the mecca of the restless expatriate authors and artists that it was in the previous decade. The picture that Ernest Hemingway drew in *A Moveable Feast* had faded away. Perhaps it was because of the economic depression, which struck France with a delayed, but heavy, blow in the early 1930's, just as I reached Paris to take up my post in *The Times'* bureau.

Ford Madox Ford, then about sixty years old, asthmatic, poor, but still steadily producing novels, was the author we came to know best. Janice Biala, the painter, was living with him, and although he was a fine writer and she a fine painter, they earned little between them. They made just enough to go south to Toulon each winter to relieve Ford's asthma. We still possess a lovely oil by Janice of a square in Toulon.

Ford was a wonderful raconteur, for he had known many authors and artists and at the beginning of the century had collaborated with Joseph Conrad in writing *The Inheritors* and *Romance*. But he was notorious for telling stories that were much too good to be true.

One of our favorite authors, then and always, was the naturalist W. H. Hudson whose wonderful books are so seldom read nowadays. Ford told us that Hudson's wife had been a marvelous pianist when he first met her and that he married the young woman because he loved so to sit and hear her play.

"And do you know," Ford said, "from the day they were married she refused ever to play a note again."

We were at Katherine Anne Porter's wedding feast—such as it was—which took place in Ford's modest apartment. This was her first marriage, on March 11, 1933, when she was thirty-nine or forty. Her husband, who was a clerk, I believe, at the American embassy, was at least ten years younger than Miss Porter. She seemed old-maidish to us, which was ironical considering that this was the first of four marriages. By that time she had published two books of her exquisitely written short stories, but was still far from the fame she was later to achieve.

There were only about eight of us present. Ford, who looked a little like Falstaff in those days, was a gourmet and a first-rate cook. We remember his exploding when someone wanted to be helpful and *chambré* the red wine by standing it in front of the fire. He had cooked one of his favorite dishes, *veau Mistral,* a Provençale recipe—roast veal with lots of olives and tomatoes and a touch of garlic. (He gave the recipe to Nancie, who liked to make it now and then.)

There was something pathetic about the scene and the people —a famous English novelist living in semipoverty; a waspish, middle-aged spinster marrying a gentle, shy young man; no presents; and although there must have been gaiety, my recollection is of a sort of joylessness. Nancie and I can wonder today what Katherine Anne Porter thought of us—the woman who wrote the bitter *Ship of Fools.*

One of the weaknesses of *The New York Times'* coverage of France under Percy Philip—and me, while I was there—was its concentration on Paris. I can only plead that France was my first post abroad and I was not in charge, for I did not make the same mistake when I headed the Rome and London bureaus. It now seems an obvious thing to make frequent trips to all parts of the country concerned and to cover, or send a bureau member to cover, important events taking place outside the capital. *The Times* today demands such coverage and has a large enough foreign staff for it, but the rule is still hard to enforce.

My knowledge of France as a whole during my third sojourn was confined to the region of Paris and to holiday trips further afield. I did not grasp that France was—and still is, although less and less so as the years pass—a peasant country with a basically peasant mentality. It took me years and other trips to understand how different a Breton or a Normand is from a Provençale Frenchman, or what qualities give a special cachet to Auvergnats like Laval and Pompidou.

I had a sound indoctrination in French politics, which stood me in good stead during the years I was to write many editorials on France. I saw the power of the French *patronat,* the business and financial leaders who shrewdly defend their own private, family, and capitalistic interests against their workers and the state. I saw that the big banks exercised great political, as well as financial and economic, power, naturally of a conservative nature. Their directors, like the Regents of the *Banque de France,* came from the great banking and business families with interlocking directorates in railways, insurance, defense, and industrial trusts. It was a real oligarchy of the so-called 200 families. The figure came from the 200 with the largest holdings in the Bank of France who alone could vote at annual meetings. Peasants and bankers are very conservative. They make for stability; they vote for counterrevolution.

"A struggle between the revolution and counter-revolution has been in progress in France, under varying forms, ever since 1789," Hamilton Fish Armstrong wrote in 1940 in his book on the French military collapse, *Chronology of a Failure.* I agree.

On the whole, what I felt in 1931–1935 was an all-pervasive defeatism at a time when the losing power in World War I—Germany—was in a state of galloping euphoria. As I realize now, nobody wins wars in our age. After the devastating toll of World

War I, the political pressures for "peace" in France were so strong that even Premier Raymond Poincaré, wise, experienced, and patriotic in a nationalistic sense, felt compelled in 1923 to reduce the term of military service from three years to eighteen months and again, in 1928, to one year. Although it was lengthened in March 1935 by Premier Flandin ("London's man," as he was called), it was too late. Anyway, France was still defeatist.

Under Hitler, Germany had already denounced her disarmament obligations and reintroduced conscription. Far worse was to come, but by that time I was off on a war corresponding career that was to last ten almost uninterrupted years and to encompass three wars. The first—1935–1936—was the Abyssinian War in which France made a much-criticized but not unreasonable effort to find a compromise. The luckless Pierre Laval was premier again. He had already made a classic French move to contain Germany by signing a pact on May 2, 1935 with the Soviet Union. He also wanted to keep Italy and Germany apart, and so followed a pro-Italian policy. He joined with Sir Samuel Hoare, the British foreign secretary, in proposing a compromise that would have left Emperor Haile Selassie with a central nucleus of his empire but would have given Italy a large slice of Abyssinia. A great howl went up, especially in England, over this attempted appeasement, and as a result the Emperor lost the whole of Abyssinia. It took the world war that Laval was trying to avert to restore the country to its rightful owners.

I am getting ahead of my own story since by that time I was down in Eritrea with the Italian army. Going off to the wars, except for professional soldiers, is, I suppose, unfair to one's wife and children. Yet I was not a prize package as a husband and father, and in the circumstances I am still convinced that I did what was best for all of us, especially financially and professionally. We had ten years of relative affluence, during my period as a war correspondent, with happy interludes when I could get back to the family wherever they happened to be. I would certainly have been a worse husband and father, staying home, doing mediocre work in mediocre jobs.

The wars, among other things, were a genuine professional

reward. It is unfortunate, but calamities provide journalists with their best stories. This does not mean that newspapermen approve of wars any more than doctors approve of disease. Your dedicated professional, whether scientist, artist, or scholar, is a social maverick. He is, in his career, "wedded" to his work, which tends to make him an abnormal—and in some respects unsuccessful—human being.

One is what one is what one is. With which profound remark I will get back to France—always a professional concern, and always a haven of civilized living in somewhat barbaric times.

In the 1936 general election the Socialists became the strongest political party and the Communists doubled their votes. Not only the right, but the middle-ground Radicals lost heavily.

On March 27 Hitler had invaded the Rhineland, violating the Versailles and Locarno treaties. Militarily, the French and British were strong enough to stop Hitler, but politically and morally they were weak and timid. The British were already appeasers and the French were afraid to go it alone. Instead, France got the pacifist, Léon Blum, and the *Front Populaire*, which came in on a great wave of popular enthusiasm with a large majority in the Chamber of Deputies. The Senate remained rightist.

Léon Blum was a great politician whom I came to despise. He had the power, briefly, but not the courage to stand up to the Nazis or the British. I had met him in the course of work as the Socialist leader. He was a wealthy man, for he did not let his Socialism interfere with his lucrative practice as a lawyer. He had become known after World War I as a brilliant young intellectual, a drama critic, a polemical writer of great talent for the Socialist press, a first-rate debater and dialectician on platforms and in the Chamber. He was no hero in peace or war, no Mandel, no Mendès-France, no revolutionary—just a clever, supple-minded, well-meaning, patriotic, spineless politician.

The Communists, who had profited most from the 1936 election, refused to take office and so got the best of both worlds.

As they were to demonstrate many times in every continent, they were counterrevolutionary.

The Popular Front weakened swiftly because it could not inspire confidence either with the *patronat* or the workers. There was a flight of gold, inflation, and the franc had to be devalued. Britain had abandoned the gold standard in 1931, and the United States in 1933, but France's conservative governments followed deflationary policies. French prices were high and so was the cost of living.

No doubt the Popular Front faced an economic situation beyond its power to resolve. The workers' protest took the form of the famous "sit-down" strikes, and for the first time factories were occupied by the workers. This spontaneous movement began on May 26, 1936. Although self-disciplined and only quasi-revolutionary (for the workers were not organized and were not aiming at the overthrow of the regime), it demonstrated a rebelliousness that frightened the government, the employers and, incidentally, the Communists. The *patrons* made concessions, including acceptance of compulsory collective bargaining. Wage increases of 12 to 15 percent, a forty-four-hour week, and paid holidays were granted. (Note the resemblance to the Pompidou concessions made after the 1968 rioting.)

The Blum government, for its part, introduced some long-overdue social reforms. But neither the reforms, nor government expenditures, nor two devaluations could halt the decay. A whole postwar generation of political, military, and business leaders had done the wrong things. The price was the collapse of France.

I tell this sad story in some detail because it affected me profoundly as a journalist in the Spanish Civil War and World War II. It is ancient history, and no longer fresh in people's minds like the postwar Gaullist period. One needs to understand why France collapsed to appreciate how much Charles de Gaulle did for his country.

I was bitter in the immediate prewar years against France and wrote many harsh words about her. For me 1936–1939 was absorbed and consumed by the war in Spain, in which France played a shameful role—along with Great Britain who called the tune.

"The French Government would not only do nothing out of the way to help the Spanish Government," Denis Brogan wrote in his book *The Development of Modern France*, "it would deliberately not permit the Spanish Government to buy arms, although the Spanish Government had the money to pay for them, the means of importing them and, by all international precedent had every right to buy them. . . . The policy of M. Blum was to allow Britain to put the leash on the neck of France." (Brogan was referring here to the misnamed "nonintervention" which doomed the Republican government.)

One of my Spanish friends during the Civil War told me of going to see Blum about French policy. The premier wept, (it was by no means the only time) perhaps out of despair and frustration. He really wanted to help the Loyalists. He was like that other weak intellectual in the Spanish War—President Manuel Azaña. Blum's excuse was "horror of war," but his appeasement helped to bring on the great war. Moreover, as Brogan wrote, the nonintervention policy "took the life out of the *Front Populaire.*" Blum resigned in June 1937, but the Popular Front continued lamely under Chautemps. The Socialists got out of the government early in 1938 and returned later under Blum again for just one month when the Popular Front gave way to the "Government of National Defense" under Daladier.

Nazi Germany invaded Austria in March 1938. The Munich crisis came in September. France was hardly more than a spectator in the betrayal of Czechoslovakia, but a partisan one. The French Parliament had no role except to ratify the Munich agreements.

I had come out of Spain briefly for a rest and was in Talloires, France, with Nancie and the children at the time of Munich. During the few days when it looked like war, the Frenchmen around us behaved with a courage and firmness that may or may not have been typical of other Frenchmen. Premier Juan Negrín of Spain had come over from a League of Nations meeting in Geneva, and I commiserated with him, for it meant the end of any possibility that Britain and France would fight while the Spanish Loyalists still held enough territory to help reconquer Spain for the Allies. Negrín would not give up, and the Republicans went on fighting doggedly in the forlorn hope that the foreseeable European war would break out before complete defeat.

The twelve months between Munich and the world war were a period of gloom and despair for me and for everyone who could see what was happening. The triumphant Hitler, the gloating Mussolini, the ominously quiet Japanese, the smug Neville Chamberlain; fearful, complacent France; unaware, isolationist America—they made up a nightmarish picture.

Britain was to redeem herself quickly, but not France. There had been no leader, no political party, no popular movement in favor of sacrifices to sustain a military edge on Germany, which went on rearming. The Maginot line nurtured a cruelly deceptive sense of security.

Democracy shows one of its weak facets in such a situation. Nine out of ten people—inexperienced, unimaginative, engrossed in their own affairs, naturally wanting nothing so much as to be left in peace to cultivate their gardens—are against expenditures for war. In December 1939, three months after the war had begun, Premier Edouard Daladier promised that France would engage in no offensives and that any operations would be "sparing of French blood."

Denis Brogan ends his book at the beginning of the war with these words:

"In the days of Munich when, with varying degrees of candor, the escape from the ordeal was being celebrated, Georges Duhamel had bitterly noted that France, in withdrawing behind the Maginot line had lost the Descartes line, that intellectual tradition of being the European home and friend of liberty of the body and liberty of the mind. It had now been discovered that such a retreat was impossible for France; that the Descartes line and the Maginot line were one. An unknown soldier in

September 1938 had known that. Across the Rhine the Germans had hoisted a placard, *'Ein Reich, Ein Volk, Ein Führer.'* He, in reply, put up his board. On it was written *'Liberté, Egalité, Fraternité.'* The battle between these two ideals has begun."

Germany lost, and so, in most ways, did France, but the French soldier spoke for an eternal France, which can be eclipsed but can never lose her ideals of liberty, equality, and fraternity.

The French army was defeated in six weeks. It was unprepared and badly led by generals fighting the previous world war and making every conceivable mistake. The Maginot line proved useless and has left nothing except an ineradicable symbol to prove that fighting spirit, not cement walls and blockhouses, is the main ingredient for victory or for honorable defeat.

A degree of French honor was saved, thanks to a heroic resistance movement and the gallant, indomitable leadership of Charles de Gaulle. It was late, but France had found a true spokesman, one of the very great figures of French history.

I was to have my Francophile heart warmed outside and finally inside of France by the eternal flame that De Gaulle relit and kept alight in those tragic war years. As far away as the tiny French colony of Pondicherry on the east coast of India, I well recall the governor pouring his heart out to me in sorrow for France and in pride for the General and the Free French movement that he led. In Algiers, as the Allies were preparing to invade Italy, I met De Gaulle and attended several of his press conferences. One learned immediately why Churchill found the "Cross of Lorraine" (the emblem of the Free French) so hard to bear and why Roosevelt was in despair dealing with the General. The haughty, arrogant, bristling, sensitive character made an immediate impact, and a permanent one, for it was his image, and it never changed.

De Gaulle, in his early fifties, with his great height, erect bearing, and handsome face (his nose was less overwhelming than it became in old age when his cheeks were lined and sunken) was immensely impressive. He could be almost charming, and in those uncertain months he made an effort to impress foreign correspondents favorably, something he never did as President in later years. De Gaulle was not a man to seek sympathy, but I recall a sense of warmth as well as respect. He seemed to be forcing himself to be aggressive against all logic, because he knew that his position was weak and that occupied Vichy France had a weak case. It was as if he had written a drama when France was first overrun and then played the leading role in it. I never lost the sense, all through his years as President, that I was watching a consummate piece of acting. No one will ever know the extent to which he believed the things he said.

Algiers was Act II of the drama in which De Gaulle was fighting desperately to save the honor of France. Although he could not muster a wholly French force to take part in the forthcoming invasion of Italy, he managed to create a "French" division in which the officers and noncoms were French but the soldiers were Senegalese and other black Africans.

During the Italian campaign I was in contact now and then with French officers who were leading their African troops along the mountainous spine of the peninsula. Some of us war correspondents dined with the French General Guy de Montsabert just below Siena, which his division had orders to take. I was impressed and deeply touched to learn that he knew Siena like the palm of his hand and loved it—as I did, for I and my companions, Reynolds and Pibe Packard of the United Press, had been interned there after Pearl Harbor. De Montsabert said he had given orders that not a gun was to be fired at Siena and his plan was to circumvent the city unless the Germans made a stand there. Happily the Germans didn't, leaving it to me and the Packards to ride on ahead of an attached American unit to "liberate" Siena.

Later, I was in on the last great amphibious operation of the war in Europe—the landing on the French Riviera on August 15, 1944, ten weeks after the Normandy invasion. Journalistically, it was the best break of the war for me, for I was the only newspaperman to reach my division's (the American 45th) radio transmitter on the beachhead the evening of D-day, and so I was the only correspondent to get out a full, firsthand story of the landing.

The sea voyage from Naples to the landing zone gave me my first glimpse of Winston Churchill. He sailed by us on a command warship, which was supervising the operation. As she breezed by and our men cheered, he gave his V for Victory signal. He, no doubt, like the American naval and military leaders, thought that if the landing succeeded, the war would be as good as over. They were wrong by nine months.

The last of anything has a special quality, and we expected this to be an exceptionally tough fight. The whole Côte d'Azur was heavily fortified by the Germans. One doesn't want to be killed or wounded on any given day, but the final time round has a brittle, breathless tension. You think what tough luck it would be to stop a bullet right at the end of the journey. (My oldest brother, Hilliard, was dangerously gassed on the morning of Armistice Day, 1918.) I had gone through nine years of often dangerous war corresponding, and like a character in the then Sergeant Bill Mauldin's cartoons, I felt like a fugitive from the law of averages.

For the only time in all my war corresponding days I did what almost every soldier does on the eve of a D-day. I wrote my wife the kind of letter one wants to leave behind—not a farewell, no heroics, something nice and a bit sentimental. As a valedictory, it was fortunately wasted. The Germans put up only a token resistance.

The days and weeks that followed were thrilling, dangerous, and nostalgic. The French were fighting again like the great soldiers they had always been in history—the Free French and North African forces, under General de Lattre de Tassigny, and the *maquis*, who fought with renewed and desperate courage as we approached each town and the great port of Toulon and, finally, Marseilles. In a nostalgic piece, written before Cannes on August 21, I said:

"It isn't only a Frenchman whose heart jumps at the sight of Cannes lying bright in the sunlight across the Gulf of La Napoule. All of us who remember it in the great days when it was the most fashionable spot in France, if not in the world, are entitled to skip a beat or two at seeing it there and thinking that soon the world should regain some of its sanity, and we can sit again on the terrace of the Carlton Hotel and order cocktails such as only its famous bartender can make, and then eat such a meal as none but a French chef can concoct.

"These were daydreams today, because the Krauts were across the ridge in front of us, shooting in our direction, and yet the thrilling and wonderful thing about it all and about this flaming invasion that within a week has taken us this far at one end, and to Toulon and Marseilles at the other, is that they are dreams which are coming true."

Well, yes and no. Nancie and I did return to Cannes for visits and for two long stays after my retirement. It is still fashionable, still lovely, still peopled by the nicest French of all—the Provençals—but no place is what it used to be before the war, and it seems that as we grew old so did *that* France, so brilliant, so urbane, so polished, so aristocratic in its culture. *Où sont les neiges d'antan?*

After sending that despatch, I was on a grim perilous swing along the coast with the French forces until, in a few glorious days, we took Marseilles. I say "we" because I felt at home once more and because I went in with the attacking troops. To see France rise again from her shameful past was of all things in that campaign the most thrilling and heartwarming. Paris and Marseilles were liberated on the same day—August 23, 1944.

"The next day," I was to write (and I will feel so as long as I live), "was one of the great ones of my career. There was a surge and sweep to that day which caught me up and lifted me on its rushing current. It was one of those moments which held within itself the end of one era and the beginning of another. If you can catch such a moment, you have, indeed, caught history on the wing."

I look back now after more than a quarter of a century, not to retell a twice-told tale, but to brood nostalgically, and to think that some rare days such as that one make a life and a long newspaper career worthwhile. To be where history is made; to survive danger; to get off a whacking good, firsthand story for one's newspaper and get it off in time—this is what makes journalism a great and attractive profession.

Marseilles in 1944 revived in me the persistent sense that the French Revolution has never ended. I met a group of youngsters led by a pretty, helmeted girl in slacks with a pistol in each pocket. One of the lads juggled four grenades perilously in order to shake hands. They belonged to the *maquis* and had been fighting for days. The girl described to us how she had shot two German soldiers in the back the day before. On parting, I said, "Good Luck." *"Chez nous on ne dit pas 'Bonne chance,'"* she replied. *"On dit 'Merde!'"*

That parting shot was a vivid reminder of the Spanish Civil War for me, but so was the whole day with its street fighting and its aura of passionate hatred and courage. I had an atavistic feeling—and perhaps a prophetic one, too—that this was 1793 all over again. The youth of France were rising out of the ashes their parents had let grow cold. So far as the Free French were concerned, Marseilles was reconquered by the youth of the *maquis.* There was revolution in the air that day.

Marseilles was by no means my last war corresponding job, for I returned to the Italian campaign, "liberated" my beloved Florence, moved north, but then I went off to the States for an overdue vacation. I was caught there ignominiously on VE day.

For my personal "farewell to arms," I want to hold in my mind, and be remembered for, the day we took Marseilles. The ignominious years of appeasement and Vichy were never-to-be-forgotten pages of history, but Marseilles turned a new page for me. My faith in France was restored. The future held promise because the spirit of that day was one of youth and high hope.

The future has, happily, proved generally better for France despite her trials. She has been a stronger country in every way

than the despondent, cynical, defeatist France of the years between the wars.

Yet World War II was a traumatic experience for all but a
minority of Frenchmen. Nothing can hide the fact that Vichy
France was a betrayal of French history, sentiments, and ideals.
France surrendered quickly and easily to the Nazis; France collaborated with the Nazis. There was a sense of shame that
gnawed at French vitals during and after the war until a new and
untarnished generation came along. Middle-aged and older
Frenchmen hate to talk about World War II, even today, unless
they were in the Resistance or with the Free French.

France has had a glorious history, but not between 1939 and
1945. Few knew at the time or remember it now, but those who
fought in the underground or suffered torments in silence took
a terrible revenge in 1944 as the country was being liberated. I
saw a little of it as I went along the southern coast with the Free
French forces, and I heard more about it later in Paris. It was
a species of revolution, bloodier than anything of the sort since
1793 when Frenchmen guillotined Frenchmen. The Communists of the Committees of Liberation and partisans of the FFI
(*Forces Françaises de l'Intérieur*) and FTP (*Francs Tireurs et Partisans*)
had cleanups in the provinces that were carefully planned. The
extent of this "cleansing" was only realized later. At the time,
the Allies blandly let it continue as a war reaction against war
criminals. In reality it had the distinct flavor of a social purge,
which is why I called it pseudorevolutionary. It might have got
out of hand if General de Gaulle, in 1944, had not taken Communists into his provisional government and made a friendly
trip to Moscow. The country was then open to the Communists
who had the strongest movement. They alone among the political parties had a definite plan to take power.

During the German occupation and the Vichy period, a great
class of petit bourgeois middlemen grew within the economy.
This powerful element was also in a revolutionary frame of mind
in 1944–1945 until the De Gaulle government consolidated
their position in the economy, thus creating a force as stable in
industry as the peasants were in agriculture. However, the result

was a high price level, which has never come down. Tourists going to France and foreigners living there understandably bemoan the high prices, but the real burden is borne by the workers in the high cost of what they buy.

Here, too, is a perennial cause of the revolutionary potential in France. The laborers' struggle to keep the wage level equal to, or ahead of, the price level was often a losing one. This was a key factor in the workers' joining the students in the 1968 uprising. They were then placated with wage rises so high that the economy was thrown out of kilter. Yet before the increases, the French workers were among the worst paid in Europe. Moreover, the workers have never gained enough political strength and cohesion in France to force their will on Parliament, as they did in Britain. The traditional French industrial structure is low wages, few social services, low productivity, high prices for the industrialist without heavy taxation, and no high mass consumption to encourage expansion or lower prices. Lobbies and vested interests are even stronger than in the United States.

In the Anglo-Saxon countries it is customary to say the Frenchmen—and Latins generally—lack civic virtues. This is nonsense. Latins simply have different social characteristics, which are better and worse than ours. We point to the fact that there is a high degree of tax evasion in France and an unwillingness to pay extra-high taxes when required. On their part the French can point to defects of civic virtues in the United States —violence, for instance.

A newspaperman living in one country after another happily loses his native "holier-than-thou" attitude. This is one of the first steps that have to be taken in learning to understand a foreign nation. Besides, it is only a case of facing reality. It should be a truism, but only experience teaches us that no nationality, no race, no color, no religion (infinitely harder that!) is better than the others.

Foreigners—I am not thinking of tourists—get their picture of France from about 15,000 parliamentarians, lobbyists, businessmen, and journalists who speak for France but do not represent her. Once you get away from Paris, the picture is different, more solid, more commonsensical, economically better off, generally indifferent or disgusted with government politics. French politics are exceptionally strong in hatreds, jealousies, backbiting, and personalities. The stronger the premier (Mendès-France, De Gaulle), the more violent the quarrels. Popular French cynicism and indifference to politics are hard to shake. Only exceptional cases arouse people—exciting or Napoleonic figures and crucial elections.

Personalities make journalism, as they do history. In terms of creating news interest, there were only two outstanding leaders in postwar France—Mendès-France and De Gaulle.

Americans should not forget that it was Mendès-France who cut his country loose from Indochina and thus left a supposed vacuum that the United States felt it had to fill. President René Coty called my attention to the fact that this was the first time since Louis XV—Canada—that France had lost any imperial territory.

Pierre Mendès-France was premier in 1954 when I spent some weeks in Paris, and he visited Washington after I returned to the United States. He aroused great controversy on both sides of the ocean. Like De Gaulle, Mendès had a notable war record, in his case a heroic one in the Resistance. Being a Jew, he brought out the latent anti-Semitism that never disappears in France but rarely comes to the surface. It is fed by big business interests. Mendès was a friend and disciple of Léon Blum. The four leading members of Mendès-France's brain trust were Jewish. His friend and closest adviser in 1954 was Georges Boris, who was socialist-minded but not fellow-traveling. The brilliant journalist, Jean-Jacques Servan-Schreiber was another member. The whole group was radical and leftist, which contributed to the suspicions and distrust of Mendès-France in France and the United States. They tried to re-create a strong, and this time leftist, Radical party. Servan-Schreiber is still at it in 1971.

Mendès was not only a strong figure; no leader in postwar

France had such reformist, social-minded, and liberal ideas. With hindsight one could say that had he retained power and influence the explosion of 1968 and its difficult social effects might have been avoided. It was his misfortune that the loudest praise and the strongest support came from Communists and neutralists and from sympathetic publications like *Le Monde, Express,* and *L'Observateur.* In reality Mendès was one of many modern political leaders who was willing to use Communists while being personally anti-Communist.

This worried Washington and created the first and greatest crisis of any importance in Franco-American relations until De Gaulle started weakening the Atlantic alliance. Mendès had earlier gone to Brussels and wrecked the almost completed European Defense Community (EDC), which the Americans and virtually all European statesmen felt could form the best possible bulwark against the Soviet Union. I went down toWashington in mid-October 1954 to speak to a number of government leaders in order to make a confidential report for *The Times'* editors, which I quote here in part as an indication of the information I gathered.

"Dulles has not made up his mind about Mendès. He thinks it is still possible that Mendès will switch or could switch to the neutralist position if the internal political situation calls for it or if the Russians make proper moves. I said this was a very grave reservation to have in his mind about Mendès, and he said, Yes, it was. . . . The French have always claimed that Mendès is heart and soul with the Atlantic Community and the West. Dulles did not deny this, but does not consider it a fundamental and unalterable policy of Mendès, but only an expediency or calculation of what is best for France and he could, Dulles thinks, change his mind.

"Dulles feels that Mendès has the conviction of many statesmen (he mentioned Hitler, although disclaiming a belief that Mendès is a Hitlerite type) that he alone is the man who can save France and consequently what is good for Mendès' position as Premier is good for France. Dulles does not at all agree with what [Undersecretary] General Bedell Smith said to me that

Mendès is 'a lying son-of-a-bitch.' The reason Bedell called him this was that he received from Mendès at Geneva a commitment —he thought—that Mendès would back EDC. [French Ambassador] Bonnet said Mendès only promised to back EDC 'with slight modifications' and he considered that the protocols he took to Brussels were reasonable enough to come under that heading. Dulles, however, says that when he saw Mendès in Paris on July 14, Mendès also promised him he would back EDC, but as Dulles put it, statesmen often have to make promises and sometimes circumstances change and they have to break them, but it is all in the game and not enough in itself to brand Mendès as worse than any other, including himself, in that respect. Mendès, he said, is obviously a man who excites strong emotions. He has passionate friends and passionate enemies. Dulles feels he is an enigma and not a type that one could like—only respect.

"It is agreed that Mendès is the sharpest and toughest bargainer to hit the international scene in years, and that he carries his 'realism' too far. Dean Acheson pointed out that he is the first realistic Premier France has had since the war, but [Assistant Secretary] Merchant and a few others felt that he is too sharp a bargainer for his own and France's good. . . .

"The man shapes up more and more as a 'man-of-destiny' type in his own mind, and a lone wolf."

"The main field of distrust is in Mendès-France's character," I wrote in another report after Mendès-France visited Washington in November 1954. "Americans who had anything to do with the actual handling of the EDC affair (and this is doubtless even truer of the Benelux crowd) seem convinced that Mendès showed bad faith and trickery, and they argue that if he was capable of behaving in this way once, he may repeat when faced with a crisis that threatens his career or his idea of what is good for France. His personal ambitiousness, his secretiveness, his conviction that he, alone, can save France, his inexperience, his vulnerability (no one expects his present Government to last long) and his penchant for the spectacular, all add to the tendency toward caution. . . . The main source of satisfaction is that

Franco-American relations are now back on a cordial basis and Mendès has convinced them that he is anti-Communist and bound up with the ideals of the West."

So closed a typical exercise in American diplomacy—and in behind-the-scenes journalism. I put the spotlight on Pierre Mendès-France because he is, for Americans, a forgotten man. His government really was vulnerable; it fell on February 5, 1955. But he had been an important figure for the United States because he was the only French politician strong, courageous, and sensible enough to take France out of Indochina.

The American military men learned nothing from the French experience. General Bedell Smith, who told me Mendès-France was a son of a bitch, also angrily labeled the French commander and his staff at Dienbienphu—General Henri Navarre—as "cowards." "They didn't have the guts to get up out of their dugouts and fight," was the way Bedell put it. Considering that class after class of St. Cyr (France's West Point) had sacrificed their lives in Indochina along with thousands of French soldiers and untold French wealth, these were harsh words. A tragedy was in the making back in 1954 because American generals were too ignorant to appreciate the courage of the French and Vietminh or the military problems involved. The only difference was that the United States had more men, more war matériel, and more wealth—to try the impossible.

France had one more imperial problem as costly in lives and wealth as Indochina. This was Algeria, whose liquidation required another "man of destiny" also convinced that he, alone, was capable of leading France through a national crisis. General de Gaulle was waiting to be recalled by an ungrateful nation. He had been in retirement at his home in Colombey-les-Deux-Églises since he resigned his provisional presidency on January 20, 1946.

The call came in May 1958 opening a decade of power which began in greatness and ended in humiliation. There is no need to detail the well-known story here. General de Gaulle had learned the lesson taught by Indochina, and although the French were militarily dominant in Algeria, he knew they could never win politically. It took great moral courage and political skill to pull out in the face of a counterrevolutionary drive that at one time held a threat of civil war. The President was fortunate to escape several attempts to kill him. His life was so endangered that I wrote an editorial obituary to be used in case news of his assassination came through at night.

It is probable that future historians will give General de Gaulle only two really high marks for his terms as President. One will be for granting independence to Algeria and the French African colonies south of the Sahara. The other will be for supervising the remarkable postwar development of French industry. The General knew nothing about economics or finance, but he had the judgment to allow the right men to follow the right policies—notably Antoine Pinay and Jacques Rueff.

It was Charles de Gaulle's tragedy, politically speaking, that he lived to mar his great historic record. Certainly, he stayed in office too long. The defects of his virtues undermined him—the stubbornness of his courage, the xenophobia of his patriotism, the narrowness of his vision, the petty, mean, suspicious streak in an essentially noble character. He again became a heavy cross to bear for the United States and Great Britain. The United Nations, NATO, European unity, the Common Market, the dollar, the pound sterling, all suffered from De Gaulle's nationalistic and personally vindictive policies.

The fascinating and terrible thing about De Gaulle's political downfall was that he had gone blind. The clear, if narrow, vision had failed. The self-assurance that was part of his arrogance and pride prevented him from seeing that the country was no longer behind the person, Charles de Gaulle. Worst of all, he did not sense, even after the great upheaval of May–June 1968, that there was a deep and widespread popular discontent, and for valid reasons. Even when the very structure of France was almost torn apart, President de Gaulle failed to grasp what had happened. "Better is a poor and wise child than an old and foolish king, who will no more be admonished."

It was the student-worker uprising of 1968 that most interested me as a journalist and observer, for I rate it as a landmark in modern French history. Although it was an abortive revolution, it had the quality of a chain reaction with long-range effects, because the drive behind it came originally from the students—from the young who will soon be taking power. For the first time since the Revolution of 1789, France will be dominated by her young people. In the nineteenth century, as Denis Brogan points out, "the decline in numbers of one of the most talented national groups in human history was a loss for the world and a disaster for France." The dreadful toll of World War I masked a vitality that finally flourished after World War II in a sudden and unexpected increase in the French birth rate. Unforeseen, unprepared for, it has bewildered and flabbergasted the older generations. Prewar France was aging demographically, and we who lived there in the interwar years felt it like a heaviness in the atmosphere, as if the nation were slowly dying. It is so much more alive now—and what better proof could there be than the *événements* of May—June 1968?

The French student uprising was not the first such manifestation. It was unique because it came within an ace of bringing down the whole structure of French government and society. In no other country had a whole labor movement joined the rioting students, enhancing the revolutionary effect, although the workers were striking for economic gains, not to overthrow the regime. Daniel Cohn-Bendit, the Franco-German student leader of the upheaval, was credited afterward with the judgment: "We should have realized that for the workers, the automobile is a fetish." As Prime Minister Pompidou did realize, they could be bought off with higher wages and fringe benefits. Economically, the gap between workers and students was the widest in Europe. Once it was temporarily closed by concessions (inflation and a monetary crisis were soon to nullify some of the benefits) the workers ended their awkward alliance with the *fils du papa*—the pampered university youth who came from middle-class, relatively well-to-do families.

Yet the rank-and-file workers had forced their union leaders to call a general strike whose effect was to endanger the regime. Before 1968 French workers had been taking out their grievances by the sterile process of voting Communist. A general strike does not add up to "revolutionary syndicalism," as Georges Sorel called it, but it is theoretically capable of breaking down a national structure if kept up long enough. The French workers had to be appeased to stop the revolutionary momentum of a student minority. The French Communist party, characteristically, was counterrevolutionary. There is no country where the Moscow-oriented Communist parties want to make a revolution or take power. The revolutionary Communists are the Maoists and Trotskyists who are rebels in the Communist camp. In France, the orthodox Communist party is leftist and socialist, but not at all revolutionary, as the students discovered.

Revolutions—or in this case a nationwide uprising—seem to explode unexpectedly. In reality the forces always build up gradually beneath the surface, as in a volcano which finally erupts. My wife and I were in France from November 1967 to May 1968, but we were in a backwater down at Cap d'Antibes on the Côte d'Azur. None of the tradespeople, shopkeepers, restaurateurs, or workers knew what was shaping up. Afterward, it was obvious that the first violent student riots, on March 22 at Nanterre in the suburbs of Paris where the Sorbonne had a branch, should have been a clear signal of a coming national crisis. The De Gaulle government did not realize it and was caught unprepared and aghast. The people did not realize it because their press had not warned them. Radio and television were controlled by the government and forced to play down the seriousness of the situation. Not even the students at first realized what forces they had set in motion. Yet historians of the 1789 French Revolution tell us that in the preliminary riots of 1787 and 1788, students played a prominent role, as they have in all modern revolutions.

Cohn-Bendit, in a much-quoted interview with Jean-Paul Sartre, did not make exaggerated claims for the political achievements of the *événements* at any time. At the height of their effectiveness, he saw that the students by themselves could not possibly achieve any kind of revolution. At most, he felt, they could play an important role in overturning the Gaullist regime —and indeed, there was a brief period when it looked as if they were going to do it.

What the students had done, he said, was "to launch an experiment that completely breaks" with existing society, "an experiment which will not endure, but which permits a glimpse of a possibility; something which is revealed for a moment and then vanishes. However, that is enough to prove that something could exist."

This was an acute way of describing the significance of the students' role in the "happenings." There had been no clear indication that a deep and strong dissatisfaction against the Gaullist regime had permeated most of French society. The youth rebelled against an educational system and an establishment that did not answer their needs and desires; the workers came out against an unjust, antiquated economic system; the intellectuals, whose role in French history has always been crucial, were bored and critical of the old and rigid social structure; everybody resented the high taxes that had to be paid for a vainglorious President's defense and foreign aid program at the expense of badly needed social reforms and a higher growth in living standards.

The result was a seismic shock that temporarily made a shambles of the Gaullist regime, which was so sure of itself, so prosperous, and so strong politically. Everywhere in the world thoughtful people began to wonder whether the modern, Western, democratic-capitalist state is as strongly entrenched as it seems. If the leaders in the Kremlin had been able to open their minds, they, too, could have stopped to wonder whether the supposed impregnability of the totalitarian Communist states was as real as they had believed.

In France the structure of society withstood the shock of the May-June uprising and doomed the hopes of the students for political results. While the revolt was aimed against the overcentralized, heavily institutionalized society, which was basically un-changed since Napoleon's time, the rebels were not strong enough to overthrow it. The always-present counterrevolution-ary forces won when Pompidou cleverly appeased the workers and isolated the students.

Yet neither the students nor the workers had lost; the "Revo-lution of 1968" was a partial victory; it was a watershed, for France will never be the same France again, as Pompidou said. Decentralization is coming, economically and politically. Some long-overdue reforms were granted to the students, and educa-tional changes are being made to give opportunities to classes who have been barred to higher education. However, the stu-dent movement was badly split in 1970. Maoist left- and right-wing extremists are fighting each other, as well as the police and the university administrators. The great majority of moderates are only rarely combative, but the government knows that what happened in 1968 could happen again.

I am afraid that the superb civil service—the so-called man-darinate centered in the Foreign Office on the Quai d'Orsay—is doomed in its present form. There is nothing comparable to it in the world, not even in Britain. Like so much in modern France, it dates from Napoleon, and therefore from the Revolu-tion. Nothing about the running of France, her diplomacy, and her colonies impressed me so much as my decades of contact with French civil servants in Paris and around the world.

A major element of French stability during the innumerable political crises of the Third and Fourth Republics was the un-changing civil service. The economic "miracle" of the De Gaulle regime was carried out by civil-service technicians. Because of the strict requirements for entry into the higher posts—long education, rigid examinations, dedication to a very poorly paid profession—it has been hard for politicians or lobbyists to influ-ence the service officials. As in England, there is a social class that puts its sons into the civil service, generation after genera-tion, even though they can earn many times as much in other fields. The attractions of the French service are its prestige, the social status it confers, and an *esprit de corps*, which is as strong as in the armed forces. Besides, men often have a vocation for government service, as do teachers, doctors, scientists, and soldiers in their fields. The system restricts members to what the British call an "old-school-tie" class, and therefore it is doomed in its present form in both countries.

Count Nicolò Carandini, the Italian ambassador to London just after the war, once said to me: "Whenever I go into the Foreign Secretary's office I wonder which is running Britain's policy—the chair (meaning the civil service) or the man (who was then Ernest Bevin)." Such a question would not have been asked while De Gaulle was President of France, but it could have been for a century and a half before.

It has taken an upheaval like the *événements* of 1968 to shake the civil service to its depths. The men are neither conservative nor radical; they are technicians, but 1968 signaled a change in French life. The conservatives—meaning everyone who stood to lose by a revolution or who feared the idea—understandably renewed General de Gaulle's mandate with a big majority in the June election. But your conservative is a perennial loser, ever since the world began. He opposes change in the midst of an eternal dynamism. At best he can preserve what is good.

What the complacent De Gaulle did not realize, as I said, was that the French temper had already changed and that he was no longer indispensable. Although he, Charles de Gaulle, had never changed, France had. When the old sorcerer tried once more to conjure up personal mass support for himself in the plebiscite of April 27, 1969 ("Vote for my plans or I will resign"), he lost. A vindictive, embittered old man went off to Ireland to be away from it all, rather than see the man who saved him in 1968—Georges Pompidou—elected in his place.

Yet Charles de Gaulle was truly great, and so will he be regarded by all Frenchmen for all time. He had powerful detractors, especially among liberals and "Europeans," who worked for a united Europe. I remember Paul Reynaud from before the war when he was an "old man" in his fifties. I used to see him after the war on my trips to France as an editor. Few French politicians had his wealth of experience or were so shrewd and worldly-wise. De Gaulle's narrow nationalism and conservatism were anathema to Reynaud, who was liberal, practical, sensible, and international. I found a note of a talk with him in 1960 (he was eighty-one with an eleven-year-old son) during which he blamed himself angrily for having given De Gaulle his chance in World War II. "But for me, he would be a retired colonel today," he said. From what other political leaders told me, this was true.

The most embittered figure of all was Jean Monnet, always considered the "father" of the European idea in its various forms, starting with the European Coal and Steel Community. De Gaulle embodied everything that Monnet opposed. Listening to Monnet in his beautiful apartment overlooking the Champs Élysées, or at lunches in *The New York Times'* building could be uncomfortable. He spoke of De Gaulle with passion and fury. I also remember how—on a visit to Paris in 1965—he drew comfort in predicting that De Gaulle and Gaullism was "a passing phase in French history—an interruption," after which the normal history would resume.

It was true that De Gaulle could not destroy the Atlantic community or NATO, or mould the Common Market to his desires, or seriously undermine the dollar. He was obstructive rather than destructive.

Gaullism was not a philosophy, a system, or even a unique movement. It was a congeries of policies, more often negative than positive—against the United Nations, NATO, the Atlantic Alliance, the American-controlled gold standard, nuclear disarmament, the United States, Great Britain. It has a positive aspect because Algeria and the sub-Saharan French African colonies are now independent, and because the French political system has been restructured to make a very strong executive—a President elected by direct suffrage—and a weak legislature. The setup, as De Gaulle created it in the Fifth Republic, is the President plus the "legitimacy" that the people confer by means of plebiscites, referendums, and elections.

Gaullism without De Gaulle continues, but it is like the smile without the Cheshire cat. The system is weakening already under President Pompidou. *Grandeur* was not a policy; it was a magic token to provide inspiration, like the tricolor flag. "All my life," as the General wrote in the now-famous opening paragraph of his memoirs, "I have thought of France in a certain way. France cannot be France without greatness."

Charles de Gaulle was a legend, not just a man, a general, or a statesman. His name was a prophecy: Charles of Gaul. His life was constructed on a mystical conviction that he was to save France. "I am the Joan of Arc of modern France," as he told President Roosevelt during World War II. In his first broadcast to the French people from London on June 18, 1940, after the Maginot line had collapsed, he said: "I, General de Gaulle, soldier and officer of France, know that I can talk in the name of France." By this calculation, De Gaulle was great because he was French; because he was the expression of what was great in France; because he led France in her direst hours along a path toward greatness; because he was the symbol of France.

The foolishness, pettiness, and spite that accompanied his downfall in 1969 will be forgotten. History does not judge a man by his mistakes and weaknesses, but by his accomplishments. De Gaulle lived for me, personally, from my first contacts with him in Algiers in 1943. I think of him always as I saw him then—an arrogant, unapproachable, austere, tenacious, brave, inflexible man. "I was too poor to yield"—that was one of his most famous remarks. When he had little, he staked everything and won. When, in 1969, he had much, he still staked everything—and lost. The turbulent life ended peacefully on November 9, 1970. Charles de Gaule did not live by halves—nor does France for very long. She is the most exciting and fascinating country in Europe.

Chapter 4

ITALY

Early in January 1939, while I was still covering the Spanish Civil War, Arthur Sulzberger wrote me to say that *The Times* wanted me to take over the Rome bureau after the war (which was obviously nearly over) had ended. I was so bitterly against Mussolini, Italy, and the Italians at the time that I emphatically said "No!" The publisher persisted.

"Congratulations on that story of yours about the flight from Tarragona—it was a beautiful job," he wrote on January 16.

"Incidentally, while I am writing, let me advise you not to pass up this Rome opportunity. I fully appreciate your desire to stay with the present situation until the end, but frankly, it seems shortsighted to me to pass up this kind of a chance. There are, of course, other posts; none, however, which could as rapidly reestablish your position among your critics as the Italian one. Don't forget that you have a lot of enthusiastic admirers, and a lot of equally enthusiastic people who feel just the opposite. Our position here has been that you are a good reporter, not an advocate. The Rome post would give the opportunity for demonstrating that.

"We will endeavour to fill the place temporarily for as long as possible, but my own impression is that it would be wise to order you to Rome when that period expires. One advantage of 'ordering' you is that it doesn't leave you any choice!"

The letter did not reach me until February 3, when Catalonia had fallen and I was in Perpignan. My reply, among other things, summed up a personal philosophy of journalism that I still consider valid.

"Your letter of Jan. 16 reached me today. Thanks for the kind words about the Tarragona story, but I trust you also noted that the desk preferred to front page Carney's story from faraway Burgos [Franco's wartime capital], meanwhile cutting my piece up.

"As for the Rome proposition, I believe it would be a serious mistake, not only for my particular case but as a matter of policy, although I realize, as you say, that if I am ordered to go I would have no choice—if I wanted to remain on *The Times*.

"As I see it, it is essential for a newspaper to employ in any country correspondents who sympathize with the environment they work in. This is necessary for three reasons. First, there is the need for confidence of the particular regime if one is to have the influential friends, confidential contacts and trust that permit one to collect the true, inside information. Secondly, a friendly correspondent is in a better position to send unfavorable news under censorship or other restrictions than a critic. I don't suppose the paper has realized it, but it is true that nobody —not even Carney when he was in Madrid—got as much bad news out of Loyalist Spain as I did. For instance: the first accurate account of Russian aid two years ago. I could give innumerable instances of that from my copy. Thirdly, there is the question of personal satisfaction in one's work. When you consider my political opinions, the religious [i.e. Roman Catholic] difficulties, and my personal reactions to seeing Italians work in Spain, how can you think that I should welcome taking such a post? So far as being a human guinea pig is concerned and demonstrating to the world and my Catholic critics that I am a 'reporter and not an advocate,' I see no necessity to go to Rome to prove that. The proof—clear and definite—for both me and

The Times lies in the historical accuracy of my position and my stories. The world has already had proof on the Internationals and the bombing of open cities from League [of Nations] commissions, and every day brings new proofs. If *The Times* needs any demonstrations or apologies it is not from the Loyalist side of the war.

"I should add one more consideration, particularly as it is the most important: in addition to sympathy there must be absolute honesty. Get that combination plus the courage to print the truth, and you will have the solution of your troubles with the foreign staff. It isn't going to do *The Times* any good to have its correspondents kicked out of various countries, as I almost certainly would in time from Rome, despite—or rather because—I tried to make an honest job of it.

"Personally, I believe the European situation is going to blow up too soon to make this a very live issue. In any event, I must point out that I am very tired and will need a good, long vacation after Catalonia is cleaned up. There is physically no possibility of my taking right over, for the last campaign, coming on top of two years war, has done me in. As I cabled Mr. James, I shall run over to New York during my vacation, and the matter can be settled then. Meanwhile, I think it ought to have some second thoughts."

I did go to Rome, having calmed down a bit in New York when I had a chance to rest. The publisher's unfailing loyalty and fairness was evident in this matter, as in others. His praise was gratifying, but I never believed that the news editors shared his opinion.

It is one of the ironies of modern history that Italy was truly important only when she was at her worst—during the Fascist era from 1922 to 1943. No twentieth-century leader has been so drastically debunked as Benito Mussolini; no powerful seminal movement has fallen from such dizzy heights as Italian Fascism. The rise, decline, and fall were uniquely Italian. No other European people could have been so brilliantly wrong.

I watched the process from 1925 onward as student, war correspondent, foreign correspondent, and editor, going through
a cycle of tolerance, sympathy, criticism, dismay, contempt, antagonism. Not for one day did I have anything but affection for
the Italian people, nor did I ever lose my love for that cultured,
beautiful, capricious country. In this I was like everyman; Italy
is an enchantress who weaves an irresistible spell.

Institutions change, not people. Italy during my time went
through Fascism, three wars (Abyssinia, Spain, and World War
II), the transition from monarchy to republic, and economic
reconstruction. Yet the Italians I came to know as a student in
1925–1926 and the Italians I wrote editorials about in 1967 were
alike except, of course, that new generations had come along.
To say this may seem too obvious; how could a race change so
quickly? Yet Americans, at war with Mussolini's Italy, identifying
all Italians with Fascism, drew a picture in their minds of the
Italians that conformed to their animosity and contempt, and
not to realities.

In all that I wrote during those bitter years—and I wrote a
great deal—I claim never to have made that mistake. No journalist who approached Italy with understanding and an open mind
could have been misled. This is an invariable rule for any nation,
anywhere, anytime. It is a rule that does not inhibit criticism of
what a people do—and Italians, following Mussolini, did some
bad things. I am arguing that those who knew the Italian people
could confidently expect them to get over what the philosopher,
Benedetto Croce, described to me as *un morbo,* an illness, although traces of Fascism would always remain.

The characteristics that make up the Italian race are so complicated that one feels inclined, like the farmer looking at a
giraffe for the first time, to say, "There ain't no such animal."
No nation in Europe is such a mixture of races, customs, languages, and culture, with such different regional histories. Describing and interpreting the Italian character is a fascinating
game that one can never quite win. There is no such thing as
a typical Italian. Italy has been a nation only for a century. For
a millenium and a half before, she was a collection of warring

cities and states. So everybody has his or her Italy, and I have mine, a fond, happy, sympathetic one, plus a large admixture of respect and admiration. If I claim the right to speak of her with some authority—as I have done in *The New York Times,* and in books and articles—it is not simply because I have known the country and its people intimately since I went there as a graduate student in 1925. I learned in my career that nobody can be so misleading about a country as a person who has lived in it for decades. Length of knowledge is an opportunity, not a guarantee. I claim to know Italy because I love her and her people, and because some of the best friends my wife and I have had in our lives were Italian. I could furnish reasons, but they are implicit in everything I have written about Italy and will write. When it comes to the heart, as Pascal said, reasons do not enter: *"Le coeur a ses raisons que la raison ne connait point."*

The Italians are a very old, very civilized, politically astute people. No race in Europe is so resilient, so vital, so mature. Their political genius has never given them a real, grass-roots democracy, which is what they sought after World War II. Nevertheless, they are a people who cherish liberty and who have an age-old experience in the practice of politics. The "fine Italian hand" has never been lost.

They are not, like the Germans, a disciplined people who will gladly accept dictation from above; they are not, like the Spaniards, a people swinging from extreme political ferment to apathy such as Franco exploited for twenty years; and they do not possess the civic virtues of the British to build up orderly political institutions as well as freedom. They do not have the stability of the French nor their revolutionary spirit.

The most intelligent Italians are consistently inconsistent. They are "transformists," adapting themselves to changing circumstances, lacking in faith, cynical, critical, negative. They are not unprincipled, but their codes of right conduct are changeable. They adapted themselves to Fascism and, while considering it ridiculous and reprehensible, they got what they could out of it as long as they could. When it failed, they had no problem adapting themselves to the new situation. "After all," they asked, "were we not anti-Fascists?"

This was not naiveté or hypocrisy; at worst—to use a good Italian word—it was *furberia,* a mixture of slyness, artfulness, shrewdness, and cunning. Only in the case of the beguiled masses was it ignorance and simplicity. The Italian people have always been better than their political institutions—a sound, wholesome race, not nervous, not domineering, and cultured in the truest sense of the word, not only in letters but in the values of civilization, a heritage from ancient days, but an infinitely complex heritage.

Let us take two contrasting personalities—Benito Mussolini and Pietro Nenni, the strangest pair of newspapermen I ever came across. They were both from the turbulent northeast coastal province of Romagna. (In later years, Nenni was facetiously called by his opponents, *il Romagnole di turno*—the Romagnole who is taking his turn.) Both men were Socialists, both journalists in their early careers.

Nenni, in his 1932 book, written from exile in Paris, told how, in 1921, he and Mussolini walked along the Croisette in Cannes as equals for the last time. They were united by the bonds of old friendship and of battles in which they had fought side by side. They had even been in prison together. Now their ideals, opinions, and ambitions were widely divergent.

One went on to be a Fascist dictator, an enemy of Socialism, a vainglorious statesman who had his day in the sun when Abyssinia was conquered, only to end in 1944, shot in the back by Communist partisans and his body hung upside down in a square in Milan.

Pietro Nenni remained true to his Socialist beliefs, his democratic ideals, his decent humanism. For them he suffered years of exile in France. When I first knew him in the Spanish Civil War he was a company commander with the Garibaldini, the Italian battalion of the International Brigade. I used to see him often in Italy, during and after World War II when he led the orthodox Socialist party and was a Cabinet minister and deputy premier.

Mussolini will always loom larger in history, much larger, than Nenni. By historic standards—and by journalism's measure—he was incomparably the greater figure. I met with and talked to Mussolini in his long and slippery-floored room in the Palazzo Venezia (this was after the Abyssinian War), and I watched him many times at ceremonies and speeches. Although I have known Nenni for thirty-five years and I like, admire, and respect him, Mussolini would have been vastly more important and useful to me as a journalist if I could have got at him often enough.

I had studied the Italian language, literature, and history in college before first setting foot in Rome in June 1925. I was on a fellowship from Columbia University and on leave from *The New York Times*. My special study at the summer session of the University of Rome and elsewhere for eight months was Dante. Everything is grist to the mill for a journalist. A long immersion in *The Divine Comedy* is one of humanity's richest literary experiences. Great books seem to melt into one's subconscious and emerge in bits of wisdom and glimpses of beauty—two commodities that are useful in journalism. Forty years after I took the road to Rome, I had occasion to write an editorial column for *The Times* on the 700th anniversary of Dante's birth. It was reprinted in 1968 in a collection of *Times'* columns edited by Herbert Mitgang, *America at Random*.

When it came to politics and the current history of Italy in 1925–1926, I paid no attention. Yet it was a crucial period in the history of Italian Fascism. In June 1924 the Socialist Deputy Giacomo Matteotti, an opposition leader, was murdered. The deed was probably not done at Il Duce's orders or with his knowledge; he was taken aback and frightened by the consequences. Mussolini, according to Italians who knew him well and wrote and spoke about him after his death, was not as brave, resolute, tough, or authoritative in private as he seemed to be in public. In fact, there are many apparently valid stories of his weakness, fear, and hysteria at critical moments such as the Matteotti affair.

In 1924 his enemies were as weak and timid as he was. The opposition deputies foolishly withdrew from Parliament in protest, forming the so-called Aventine, and thus rendering themselves ineffectual. Dictators are not overthrown by dignified censure; they have to be kicked out. Mussolini picked up courage, and in a famous speech on January 3, 1925, struck back. While I was studying Dante, Italy developed its Fascist philosophy and regime, which I learned and wrote a book about years later.

With some brilliant support Mussolini groped his way step by step until, about the time I left Italy for France in 1926, he had constructed a monstrous new edifice which his poor old country could not support, but which showed Adolf Hitler the road to catastrophic glory. The famous phrase, *Mussolini ha sempre ragione* (Mussolini is always right) was coined at that time by the journalist, Longanesi. (As an aside, let me note that Longanesi, one of the most violent of early Fascist apologists, survived Fascism, the war, and the "purification" that followed, and was an influential journalist for another quarter of a century. He is a good example of the *trasformismo* I have mentioned.)

The definitive article for the *Treccani Enciclopedia,* which was to give the philosophical and rational formulation of Fascism as a doctrine (written by Professor Giovanni Gentile but signed by Mussolini), also came out in this period. It contained one of the might-have-beens of history: "If every century has its doctrine, it appears from a thousand indications that this is the century of Fascism."

It is often forgotten that Fascism was—and still is where it manifests itself—a revolutionary movement. Like today's student rioters, the early Fascists took to violent action without any definite objective. The Fascisti were a minority even at the time of the tragi-comedy of the "March on Rome," October 28, 1922. In the last previous general election, May 1921, the Fascist party had won only 35 seats out of 535 in the Chamber of Deputies.

Power forces a movement, a party, a group, or just one man to create a structure or perish. Lenin had discovered that before Mussolini, and Fidel Castro was to discover it long after Il Duce.

The Fascist revolution taking place around me in 1925–1926 was a more complex phenomenon than Russia's Communist revolution because of its right-wing supporters, its militarism and—in the case of Germany—its racism. Mussolini was backed financially by the big Italian industrialists and landowners, especially of central and northern Italy. The vanguard were the *Squadristi,* the activists who provided the violence. The "mass of maneuver" was made up of the discontented, fearful petit bourgeoisie, not the urban industrial workers, who were Socialist and Communist, and not the peasants, who were apolitical.

The ingredients were both universal and peculiarly Italian— the wounded patriotism of the war veterans, the fear of revolution after the occupation of factories in September 1920, the dread of disorder and anarchy, a charismatic leader, a violent vanguard of extremists, an Establishment that wanted to restore order, maintain stability, and, at most, accept some reforms. The opposition was split and without strong leadership. As in all revolutions, a fighting minority defeated a disorganized majority. The revolutionary process makes a pattern that all revolutions, left or right, have followed in modern times. As with Franco and Spain, there was a myth that the Fascisti saved Italy from a Bolshevist revolution—but it was a myth in both cases.

During my first sojourn Italy was settling down to ten years of peace during which, it must be conceded, Mussolini did a great deal, materially, for Italy aside from making the trains run on time.

Paolo Monelli, one of the privately anti-Fascist, publicly pro-Fascist journalists who carried through into the postwar years, wrote a biography of Mussolini in which he said: "There was something in him of every Italian and he did what the ordinary person would have liked him to do. . . . These were years when

Lady Chamberlain visited Italy wearing the Fascist badge and Fiorello La Guardia (Mayor of New York) declared that there was all the difference in the world between Hitler and Mussolini to whom he wished every success. Premier Pierre Laval of France described the Duce as the greatest man of the Old and New Worlds."

Mussolini was fooling some of the most intelligent people in the world in the first dozen years or so of his dictatorship. His most notable fan on *The New York Times* was Mrs. Anne O'Hare McCormick, who was a free-lance writer when Fascism began and then a staff member doing her famous columns on foreign affairs. There was nobody in American journalism who acquired a wider knowledge of European affairs or a more extensive collection of acquaintances among European statesmen than Mrs. McCormick.

Unlike her successor, Cyrus L. Sulzberger, she never went to Africa, Asia, or Latin America, but she was incomparable on European affairs. Her weakness was a tendency to project her own goodness, decency, and morality to all concerned. It was her instinct to see the best in everybody, including statesmen who did not deserve her sympathy. The result was a certain blandness in her column, an unwillingness to hit hard, a tolerance (she was a devout Roman Catholic) that was more religious than journalistic. This attitude was applied to Mussolini, so that even in 1940, after Abyssinia and Spain, I recall, she wrote a column saying that Il Duce's main interest was in the great exposition—the E42 (Exposition 1942)—which he was then preparing. He gave her that impression; then he stabbed France in the back and joined Hitler for what he thought was going to be easy pickings.

The Rome correspondent when I first went there was Salvatore Cortesi, who also worked for the Associated Press. He was deservedly the most famous correspondent in Italy and, as I discovered then and for years after his retirement, he was a man of exceptional charm and culture—"old world" in a once overused phrase. When he retired his son, Arnaldo, inherited *The Times'* Rome post as a full-time job. He held it, except for an interlude, which I filled, for more than thirty years.

Arnaldo Cortesi was an example of *New York Times* tolerance and ignorance. It was never realized in New York what a poor job he consistently did as a foreign correspondent. He was half-English and all-Italian, to paraphrase Churchill. He not only never left Rome for a story unless ordered to do so by New York, but he rarely did more than drive from his apartment to the office and back. He had little interest in Italian politics, none in the Italian economy or culture. Although he was only mildly anti-Fascist this was enough to induce the government to pass a law in 1939 that no Italian could work for a foreign newspaper, which meant that Arnaldo Cortesi could not continue working for *The Times*. The paper brought him over to New York, where he applied for American citizenship—a five-year process. In the meantime, he was made our Buenos Aires correspondent. This was the period when Spruille Braden was American ambassador. Braden was famous for his anti-Peronism. Cortesi, colleagues in Buenos Aires told me later, spent all his time between his hotel and *The Times* office, with side trips to the nearby American embassy. As one result, his despatches were anti-Peronista, and as another, a really remarkable result, *The New York Times* arranged to get him a Pulitzer Prize.

Fascism grew out of Italian history and character, and if it was an illness, as Croce said, it was hereditary, although it was borrowed from German philosophers like Hegel, Nietzsche, and Haushofer.

Mussolini took a principle as old as the hills—authoritarianism—added a one-party system such as the Russians had, built a façade called the State in which everything had to be contained, and glorified aggressive militarism.

In Germany Hitler's innovation was to add the concept of "blood and race"—the supposed Aryan race and its evil corollary of anti-Semitism. The Fuehrer got his Italian Axis partner to introduce an anti-Semitic law in Italy. Nobody appreciated the ridiculousness of being "Aryans" more than the olive-skinned, dark-haired, racially mixed Italians. Anti-Semitism had gone into history centuries before in Italy. As with some other

Fascist laws, Mussolini strutted ahead and alone while the Italian people did their best to soften the measures and to help the Jews.

The picture of Fascism is confused by the difference in stature, aggressiveness, strength of character, discipline, and traditions of the Germans and Italians and—individually—of Hitler and Mussolini. The Nazi Germans were among the most formidable people in history; the Italian Fascists were weak, futile, ludicrous, corrupt. Fascism wrote a terrible page in Italian history because of the Germans, not the Italians, but since Fascism was, intellectually, an Italian creation, it has that cachet. Mussolini lamented that his people were such poor material for his creation. "The trouble with applying Fascism to Italy," the philosopher Santayana said to me during one of our conversations in Rome in 1944, "is that the people are undisciplined. They often make good Fascists from 18 to 25, but after that they become individualists again. One can say that they are not on a high enough social level to become good Fascists."

That was a point of view which can be applied to any political system; they all require civic discipline and a "high social level" in order to work well. The puzzle about Italy is to reconcile the essential unsuitability of the Fascist system for Italians with the fact that it did work, although badly, for more than twenty years. This must mean that Fascism was not as completely unsuitable as it seemed, and also that an extremely complex conjuncture of events and emotions permitted Mussolini to conjure up a mirage of glory that lured his people on.

It was not a gigantic hoax, as it was afterward described, nor was Mussolini "the mountebank" that many historians called him. Had the Axis won the war in Europe, as they were close to doing, Fascism, as an instrument of rule, power, oppression, and territorial expansion, would have been real and rather terrible.

I agree with something I read in *The Times* of London that it is "horrifying to see what could be accepted by a civilized nation." (One can say the same, incidentally, of the Japanese in World War II and the Chinese under Mao Tse-tung.) The Italian liberals, including the Christian Democrats (then the *Partito Popolare* of Don Sturzo who initiated the Christian Democracy which became an honored, worldwide postwar movement), accepted or worked with Mussolini for two or three years after he took power. In this case it was an honest error, but a costly one for them and for Italy. Liberals and Christian Democrats joined Mussolini's first Cabinet. Even Benedetto Croce was misled at first and wrote articles that seemed to interpret Fascist ideas favorably. However, he soon changed and was Mussolini's most formidable intellectual enemy—fortunately untouchable because of his fame, although he was isolated by being deprived of academic and political posts.

The often-noted affinity of Fascism and Communism to religion sometimes traps intellectuals. Croce was anticlerical, but those Italians who were religiously inclined were easily lured at first into supporting Mussolini. The typical Catholic intellectual's attitude was expressed decades before by Lord Acton, writing about himself. "Politics come nearer religion with me," he said, "a party is more like a church, error more like heresy, prejudice more like sin, than I find it to be with better men." And much earlier, William Blake in his "Jerusalem" had asked: "Are not religion and politics the same thing?"

Mussolini was shrewd enough not only to recognize this, but to realize what enormous prestige he and his movement could gain in Italy and the world by a reconciliation with the Holy See. The Popes had remained "prisoners" in the Vatican since Pius IX foolishly decided to immure himself there after the forces of the *Risorgimento* had seized papal territories and then occupied Rome in 1870. Succeeding Popes must have realized what a crippling restriction this placed upon them, but they were in no position to say, "Pio Nono was wrong." They had to wait until an Italian government both sought a reconciliation and offered to pay handsomely for it. Unfortunately for Italy and the world, the anticlerical, cynical, unprincipled Duce was the one who made the offer, as soon as his regime was firmly installed in

1926. The result was the Lateran Pact of 1929, which enormously increased Mussolini's prestige and was to strengthen Fascist, Nazi, and anti-Communist dictatorial regimes everywhere in the world down to this day.

The simplistic, but very effective, argument was: Communism and all forms of Marxism are atheistic; therefore anti-Communist regimes and dictators who say that they are anti-Communist must be supported. One can add that the Catholic Church frowns on revolutions aimed at overthrowing established ruling classes of which the Church and clergy are a part.

Mussolini was primarily concerned with strengthening his regime and winning universal acclaim. He had no reason to antagonize the Vatican. *Qui mange du Pape en meurt.*

Cynics point to the fact that the Roman Catholic Church is authoritarian. "When I am the weaker," Montalembert said of the Catholics at a time when the Vatican ruled large regions of Italy, "I ask you for liberty because it is your principle; but when I am stronger, I take it away from you because it is not my principle."

Mussolini applied exactly the same principle, first in getting power through the democratic parliamentary system, and then in suppressing freedom in the name of his totalitarian system. In fact, he taunted the liberals in 1926 by calling their attention to the weakness of democracy which permits democracy to be destroyed. Of course, Communists use the same technique. "They demand liberty in the name of your principles, but deny it in the name of theirs," as Croce said.

Democracy, by definition, must permit dissent, opposition, protest, and agitation so long as it is nonviolent. A line is drawn against treason, and all governments try to prevent revolution sought by violent means, but the traitor is protected in democracies by laws like habeas corpus, trial by jury, the right to legal defense, and a hierarchy of courts which delay and sometimes forestall justice. The lines between revolutionary activity, mass protests, and unruly agitation are blurred in the democracies.

These are handicaps that dictators and authoritarian regimes do not face. Four American Presidents since 1954 have been unable to enforce the desegregation laws. Powerful opposition to a war the United States is fighting is permissible. Demagogues like Huey Long, Joseph McCarthy, and Spiro Agnew can weaken and divide the nation with impunity. The United States has a grass-roots democracy, and one cannot see how it can be destroyed in the foreseeable future, but it can be, and is being, weakened. There has been no great national crisis since the War between the States, unless the conflict over Vietnam is considered to be one. It is not safe to say that "it can't happen here." Huey Long had the idea that the United States could go Fascist, but it would have to be called by a different name.

Italy has never had a deeply rooted democracy, nor has Spain, Germany, Russia, or the Arab, African, and Asian nations. They are all vulnerable to takeovers by dictators and, of course, most of them already have authoritarian governments. Italy was shaken to her depths by World War I, and, nationally speaking, was off her guard. Her weak and uncertain democracy was an invitation to a mediocre demagogue who made himself Il Duce, the Leader, and even became an ally of the Holy See.

Modern history has seen some queer paladins of Christianity. Il Duce was one of a line that included such figures as Generalissimo Franco of Spain, Salazar of Portugal, and Generalissimo Trujillo of the Dominican Republic. The last named was one of the monsters of modern history, yet Cardinal Spellman, on a visit to Santo Domingo, lavished high praise on "The Benefactor," presumably because he claimed to be anti-Communist and because he protected the Catholic Church and the right to worship.

The power politics factor, which is paramount for the United States and the other Western governments, is of minor interest to the Vatican, except as the weakening of Moscow would weaken Communism everywhere. The two primary factors for the Vatican are that it will tolerate any regime that respects the Roman Catholic Church and that permits the faithful to worship. It does so on the principle that the Church is above politics. However, when it is desirable to oppose anticlerical regimes or movements, or to support proclerical or anti-Communist

parties, the Church is right there, working through its ubiquitous clergy. Sometimes even the Vatican gets indirectly involved
in its quiet way, as in the steady support its priests have given
the Christian Democrat party in Italy since the war. Sometimes
the Pontiff himself will take a public stand, as Popes Pius XI and
Pius XII did in the case of Franco in the Spanish Civil War.

None of this is unnatural or surprising, although in my career
I at times felt bitter or sorrowful about it. Years before Rolf
Hochhuth made his dramatic attack on Pius XII for favoring the
Nazi Germans, I had written in *The Education of a Correspondent*
at the end of World War II:

"This Pontiff is going to be the center of great controversy in
the years and centuries to come. I have heard him strongly
criticized by Catholics in Rome, and even by priests of the Holy
See, for having been so completely diplomatic during the war
and holding the scales even as between the Axis and the United
Nations. Fascism, in all its forms, threatened to be an even
greater anti-Christian force than Communism. The Church has
taken a strong, open stand against Communism, but it never has
done so against Fascism. I can see the practical reasons for that,
and there is no reason to doubt that the Pope was, personally
and behind the scenes, anti-Fascist, yet I, like millions of others,
could only feel discouraged that the most important religious
figure in the world felt it was not desirable or possible to condemn in public an evil which he deplored in private."

I wrote that, although I had a high respect for the Pope. In
fact, in my next paragraph I said: "The difficulty (although it
may seem paradoxical and sentimental to say so), is that Pius
XII's character has all those elements which in the course of time
will almost certainly lead to his sanctification. No one can question his piety, goodness, humility, charity, self-sacrifice and
other characteristics which go to make up a saint. However, a
saint in this wicked world is about as much at home as a man
from Mars, and when you are dealing with men like Hitler,
Mussolini, Franco, Pétain and their ilk, it is not saintliness you
need, but the whip which drove the money-changers out of the
temple."

Pius XII was the only Pontiff whom I got to know. He was elected in April 1939, shortly before I arrived to take over the Rome bureau. However, it was not until the Allies entered Rome that he began to receive me in private audiences. Myron Taylor, the one-time head of U. S. Steel, was then President Roosevelt's special representative to the Vatican. He, of course, was a Protestant, one of those American tycoons whose considerable intellectual ability was strictly limited to business; in politics he was out of his depth, and in coping with the extraordinary subtleties of the Vatican's operations, he was like a child.

My last audience with Pope Pius as a Rome correspondent was when I went to say goodbye to him in June 1945, before being transferred to London to head our bureau there. Myron Taylor accompanied me. In the anteroom, as we were waiting, a Monsignore took me aside and said that His Holiness merely wanted to see me, and perhaps Mr. Taylor would wait. I had been told before, perhaps by Harold Tittman, the United States minister to the Vatican, a career officer who stayed on with his wife throughout the war, that while the pontiff respected Taylor and was gratified by Roosevelt's gesture in sending a representative, Taylor was a bore and made requests that were sometimes embarrassing.

Unfortunately, when the door was opened to let me in, Taylor also got up and preceded me. I caught the Monsignore's eye; he grimaced at me resignedly. The Pope exchanged courtesies with Taylor in his rather halting English, after which we spoke Italian, without the ambassador understanding a word. Pius, as would be expected of someone whose career had been spent in diplomacy, was a fluent and easy conversationalist. Not being a Catholic, I was not inhibited by the tradition of not speaking except when asked a question by the Pontiff. I had learned from previous visits that he did not expect or want this. Anne O'Hare McCormick, who was a Catholic, had the same experience.

Pius was not only by his office the Bishop of Rome, but he was heart and soul a Roman, with a deep, emotional feeling for the Eternal City and its people. It was a terribly difficult time for

Rome and for Italy. When I told him that I was being transferred and had come to say goodbye, he said (I must translate, since we spoke Italian together): "Oh, Signor Matthews, could you not get your newspaper to allow you to stay in Rome for a while? There are so few foreign journalists who know and love Italy."

Pope Pius XII was a careful reader of the foreign press in general and *The New York Times* in particular. He knew that I had covered the Spanish Civil War on the Republican side, and perhaps about my having expressed my distress that he had remained so diplomatic between the Axis and the Allies and had done so little publicly to condemn the horrors of the Nazi genocide of the Jews. Yet, as I said, I had a deep admiration for Pius —his great intelligence, his sense of mission, his complete dedication to the high office to which he had been elected.

I felt deeply moved at the compliment he was paying in asking me to try to remain in Italy, although he was not asking it as a churchman, of course, but simply as an Italian. It gives me a sardonic pleasure to think that the Supreme Pontiff should have paid a small tribute to my journalism, for I have been battered about for a great many years by American Catholics. But the pleasure I feel in thinking of this incident is much deeper than such a petty reaction.

The consolidation of Fascism in its fully developed form in 1926 gave Mussolini the launching pad from which he soared into Abyssinia and Spain, and then crashed to death in World War II.

The decade between 1926 and 1936 offered Mussolini a spurious greatness—or perhaps it was, in a sense, true greatness. Judgment depends on the measuring rod. He was one of the leading statesmen of Europe. The Fascist movement, which he created, was praised inordinately and then feared with good reason; it was never ignored. Once the Axis was formed, the essential weaknesses of Italian Fascism were masked by the power and menace of Nazi might.

Historic greatness is not—or should not be—a moral dimension; otherwise some of the greatest figures in history would have to be minimized. The impact that Mussolini made on history between 1926 and 1936 was great. This is why he cannot be called a phony, a four-flusher, a mountebank, or other epithets that were later applied to him. By the same token, he was very far from the glorified figure of his own megalomania and his worshippers' praise.

I was half-bemused under his spell when I went off for *The New York Times* in the beginning of October 1935 to accompany the Italian Army for Mussolini's and Fascist Italy's one great international triumph—the Abyssinian War.

It gave me a certain malicious pleasure, in writing about Mussolini's conquest of Ethiopia in 1935–1936, to point out that while it was cynical and immoral, the issues were neither simple nor one-sided, and that the outraged democratic nations were just as cynical and immoral. The Italians had historical, social, and practical reasons to do what Britain, France, Germany, and Belgium had done in Africa before them. The League of Nations did precious little to help the Ethiopians, and the United States, particularly the American oil interests, actually worked to deprive the weak League sanctions of what little effectiveness they might have had. Moral indignation did not provide Emperor Haile Selassie with guns or material support.

It was my first war as a journalist (in World War I, I was, of course, merely a soldier in the army), but if I was on the wrong side of the fence in Abyssinia, I did realize that no altruism or morality existed among the supporting nations like Great Britain on the other side. This was a cynical attitude to take, but my coverage of the war was as straightforward and frank as censorship would allow.

As I wrote later: "If you start from the premise that a lot of rascals are having a fight, it is not unnatural to want to see the victory of the rascal you like, and I liked the Italians during that scrimmage more than I did the British or the Abyssinians." I added: "My own sentiments at the time were purely professional. All I cared about was to get to Abyssinia as quickly as possible, and I was willing to leave the moral issue to the moralists. I will never get over a profound conviction that only acts count, that only the possible is worth trying, that life is adaptation and compromise, that common sense demands we should make the best of a bad world.

"No Utopia, no myths and no bunkum! If I failed to take up cudgels for the lamb in this situation (which it was not my business to do in any case) at least I did not contribute at any time in the war to befuddling the issues by ignoring, distorting or hiding the realities."

Thus spoke Sancho Panza! I am more proud of the fact that I became quixotic afterward in the Spanish Civil War.

I still say: "Read my despatches on the Abyssinian War to *The New York Times.*" They were as honest and as accurate as I could get them. They, and the book I wrote about the war, *Eyewitness in Abyssinia,* are still consulted by historians writing about the Abyssinian conflict. The "facts" and the "truth" are there, as well as one observer could get them.

The war was my first big story, which gives it a special place in my heart. I am not proud of my sentiments at the time, nor of my inadequate knowledge of politics, nor of the fact that I enjoyed myself, but I am proud of the professional job that I did. Abyssinia taught me that I had certain capabilities as a war correspondent and that I was not any more afraid of danger and death than I should have been.

I got the biggest—and I think the best—story of the war in November 1935, when I was the only foreign correspondent attached to an Italian flying column that went across the Danakil desert, where no white men had been before. Luigi Barzini, Jr., of the *Corriere della Sera* was the only Italian correspondent present. The column was ambushed in Ende Gorge by the Ethiopians who had us at their mercy after one desperate day of fighting and then, amazingly it seemed to us, melted away.

An English Colonel, A. J. Barker, in a book called *The Civilizing Mission,** used my account for his pages on the battle. "If they

---

*New York: Dial Press, 1968.

had chosen to fight the battle of Ende Gorge to its limit," Barker wrote, "the outcome should have been the massacre of [Italian General] Mariotti's column. While it is possible that they were short of ammunition and that there was bad leadership, probably the real explanation was that the Ethiopians did not relish a prolonged battle. Their mentality was conditioned to quick shock actions and they were incapable of sustained effort."

My luck. We had a tough time scrambling up to the plateau and joining the main body of the army. There were four days without food for me and only one canteen of water because our supplies had been cut off in the ambush. But I was only thirty-five years old then—*nel mezzo del cammin di nostra vita* (in the midst of this, our mortal life). I noticed in later wars that this is the best age for sustained physical exertion and for control of one's nerves. For violent effort, one should be much younger, of course.

The adventure rated the longest single story by a correspondent published in *The New York Times* up to that period, or perhaps since. We had printed documents, like the Versailles Treaty, which were much longer, but not stories. Mine covered thirteen columns and was tossed off in eleven uninterrupted hours of writing. It took the inadequate Italian radio two days to send, and as column after column flowed into the New York office, the managing editor, Jimmy James, groaned in mock anguish. But he printed every word of it.

That was a good story—as a story—but there were much more important ones to come about the war as history.

The Battle of Endertà, fought on and around the towering mass of Amba Aradam in February 1936, made history. It was decisive in that it routed Haile Selassie's main army, and from the viewpoint of news value it was the most important story of the war. I watched it at the front, sometimes standing with Marshall Pietro Badoglio, the tough old soldier who led the Italians to victory. He had prepared his attack methodically and cautiously while the Ethiopians under Ras Mulugheta waited on the heavily fortified Amba Aradam with a force of some 50,000 men. Badoglio used five Italian divisions of about 70,000 soldiers.

Amba Aradam was an immensely strong natural position and strategically vital, for it commanded the only good passage south to the Tembien.

The plan of battle involved two masses making a pincerlike movement around the huge mountain. The Italians had the superiority in artillery and in the air that was to make a vital difference throughout the war. The roar of the guns was a sound that never stopped during the five days of the battle.

Badoglio would not allow us to get up with the troops. It being my first battle as a war correspondent, I did not realize what a handicap the Marshal was imposing. Watching the battle from command posts was almost boring. Battles, I remember thinking, were fought much better in the movies. Amba Aradam gave me my first realization that war is really like a game of chess to commanding officers and commanders-in-chief. Men have little more value than so many pawns.

Yet the Battle of Endertà, as it was officially called from the name of the region, was a great one, gallantly fought on both sides. There were hand-to-hand fighting, heavy losses, and slow, exhausting work. I stood next to Badoglio when he telephoned the order that decided the battle, sending in two battalions of Alpini—Italy's finest troops and ranked with the best mountain fighters in the world—to reinforce a Blackshirt division held at a key point high on the mountain nicknamed "the Priest's Hat."

There were two days of rest for the troops afterward, which the Ethiopians foolishly took as an end to the battle and a victory. For them Adowa in 1896, where the Italians were routed, was the classic type of battle. On the morning of Febuary 15, 1936, the Italian artillery opened up; the troops moved forward against desperate resistance; and the pincers closed around Amba Aradam. By nightfall Ras Mulugheta and his shattered forces were in wild flight southward.

By quick writing, luck, good transmission, and the intervention of Sunday, when there were no evening papers in the United States, I was able to give *The New York Times* the only personal, by-line account, as quickly as any agency correspondent could flash the news.

It was the beginning of the end for the Abyssinians. Badoglio was beaming with joy—and not at all a generous and chivalrous victor. He was a hard man, limited as only army officers can be, a monarchist but otherwise apolitical and completely professional. He did not fight for the greater glory of Fascism, but when, at the end of the war, Mussolini made him Duke of Addis Ababa, he was delighted.

I saw him several times in Rome during the Allied occupation in World War II and he argued with me that the title should remain his, even though Addis Ababa and Italy's Abyssinian Empire had been lost. "I *am* the Duke of Addis Ababa," he said emphatically to me one day. "Historical facts cannot be canceled by political events. Napier was called Baron of Magdala, although Magdala was retaken by the Abyssinians. No one thought that Marshall Ney should not be called Prince of Moscow because of Napoleon's retreat."

Abyssinia was the first assignment on which I learned what tall tales are printed by the most respected newspapers, mainly because they will print anything official. A foreign news editor in New York has no immediate way of knowing whether a story is true or not, if it comes from official quarters. Nothing is so misleading as war bulletins. This is one of the first lessons that war correspondents learn. In Addis Ababa the Emperor's headquarters denied that there had been any defeat, and this was accepted by some papers.

There are peoples—the Chinese, the Arabs, the black Africans for instance, and we should not forget the South and North Vietnamese—for whom real, objective truth is meaningless. What they want to believe and what they want to be believed are important. Lest this be considered a racist criticism, let me add that the Italian Fascists and Franco Nationalists during the Spanish Civil War were brazen in their lying and did not have the innate characteristic of fooling themselves or of having a flexible and allergic attitude toward unpleasant facts. Communist governments, of course, are equally untrustworthy.

The Abyssinian War also provided my first experience in the impossibility of convincing readers of truths that they do not want to believe. Anthony Eden, then the British foreign secretary, sadly confessed after the Abyssinian War that "there was a miscalculation by military opinion in most countries that the conflict would last very much longer that it has, in fact, done." Had there been sense enough to trust what the neutral journalists on the Italian side were writing from firsthand, eyewitness accounts, there would have been no "miscalculation."

During all my career as a foreign and war correspondent, I found that not only readers, but editors, believe that when there is a censorship the truth cannot be sent. Often, the *whole* truth cannot be sent, but no censor can force an American or Western correspondent to send unqualified falsehoods. When reputable correspondents write what they see and hear, they should be believed. The phonies and liars are found out soon enough.

The correspondent must take his knocks. I was labeled a Fascist during the Abyssinian War, a Communist in the Spanish Civil War, a tool of the British in India during World War II, and a Communist again in the Cuban Revolution. Last heard, I am down on the lists of the John Birch Society as a "radical leftist." Since the accusations are false and *The New York Times* knew them to be so, I could be tolerant. Other newspapermen, equally innocent, have been less fortunate in my time, especially during the insanity of the McCarthy period.

Contrary to popular belief—and the belief of most editors—bias, in itself, does not destroy or even weaken the validity of news coverage. The qualities that really matter are honesty, understanding, and thoroughness. A reader has a right to ask for all the facts; he has no right to demand that a journalist or historian agree with him.

Here is an example. In a long despatch of October 22, 1935, sent by courier to Asmara, Eritrea, datelined "With the Italian Forces in Ethiopia, Amba Augher," I wrote: "After a two-day trip by truck and muleback and a day spent inspecting the front-line positions, visiting native villages and talking to Tigreans through an interpreter, the writer is convinced that the Tigrean, who has a reputation of being a fine fighter and among the best in Ethiopia, completely belies that reputation and, moreover, that he wants nothing so much as Italian good-will."

I gave ample evidence to prove my point. This was not what Americans or Britons wanted to read, but it was true. If I had felt that the Italians were war criminals, if my heart and soul were with the Ethiopians, it would still have been true and there would have been no excuse to repress the information or distort it.

What does seem to me misguided and uncalled for in some of my despatches was the drawing of contrasts between the way Italians and Ethiopians acted. Here is a case in point sent from a post at the front in northern Ethiopia called, in Italian, Entisciò.

"One Italian column was defeated near here in 1896, and in a house at Entisciò a number of Italian officers were immured and burned to death. The difference between that, as well as similar atrocities in 1896, and the kindliness with which prisoners and the populace are now being treated by the Italians, is very striking. It is impossible to observe and not be deeply impressed by the civilizing influence Italy is bringing here, and the fact that there is a steady stream of submissions proves that the Tigreans appreciate this."

What is wrong in this paragraph is obvious to me in retrospect. The facts are correct; the deduction is unwarranted. It is doubtful that the Tigreans appreciated "the civilizing influence" of the Italians, or even considered the Italians to be civilized. The comparison between Tigreans in 1896 and Italians in 1935 makes no sense. And the whole paragraph is more editorial, or opinionated, than it is interpretative. It is also naive.

I did not underestimate how well and how hard the Emperor's soldiers fought, although this was by no means true of all of them. The leadership was weak because commands were given to unruly feudal chieftains and relatives regardless of their ability. The strategy was tragically ill-advised. The Ethiopians' only hope lay in guerrilla warfare which, with the exception of Ras Imru in the Tembien, they used sparingly. However, the local population was unhelpful or even, as in the case of the Gallas, hostile. The Italians won with aircraft, mustard gas (used far more than I knew at the time), and artillery, plus well-armed troops. The Italians had no picnic, but once they broke through at Amba Aradam, the end was merely a matter of time.

Neither Great Britain (Baldwin and Chamberlain) nor France (Laval) had any direct interest in saving Ethiopia if it meant fighting Italy. Hitler's star was rising, and so was German rearmament. Abyssinia, they said, was not worth a European war, nor was Spain afterward—but both inexorably led to World War II and to the decline and fall of the League of Nations.

Emperor Haile Selassie's headquarters at Dessye and in the capital of Addis Ababa, 260 miles to the south, continually gave out stories of campaigns and victories that had no relation to what was really happening. The sources being official, the information was duly sent to newspapers and printed.

Those of us on the Italian side had two advantages. Since the Italians were winning for nearly the whole course of the war, there was little need for them to embroider or falsify. Moreover, once Marshal Badoglio got going, we correspondents were able to get about and see for ourselves. Foreign correspondents on the Abyssinian side were rarely allowed to leave Addis Ababa.

Sentiment in the United States understandably favored the Abyssinians. In any circumstances, as I said, it is rightly an invariable rule of serious newspapers—certainly *The New York Times'*—to print official information, or any information coming from an authoritative source. Official statements must be sent, but they must be labeled for what they are.

I never became sufficiently philosophical to accept my newspaper's rigidly "correct" policy of printing both sides, one right, one wrong or doubtful, even when the editors knew, as in the Spanish Civil War, that *The Times'* correspondent on the Franco side could not be trusted. In the Abyssinian War I had a feeling until near the end that the Italian victory must have come as a surprise to most American and British readers.

The fighting virtually ended with a battle at Mai Ceu on March 31, 1936. Haile Selassie's troops fought with great, but unavailing bravery. It was the Emperor's last stand, although he wanted to keep on and to go down fighting. The Empress, the court retinue, and his timid princely chieftains said, "No—go to Geneva," where, as could have been expected, the League of Nations' members behaved disgracefully.

Mai Ceu led to a remarkable journalistic coincidence for me and Haile Selassie. I was on the battlefield just after the fighting ended and ran into an Italian sergeant who had picked up a sword thrown away by what must have been an Ethiopian chieftain. A nephew of Haile Selassie, Ras Mangascià Ilma, was among the officers of the Imperial Guard killed that day. Perhaps the sword was his. The Italian soldier showed his booty to me, a singularly beautiful sword, made by one of England's most famous swordmakers, with a finely engraved inscription in Amharic and a crest, or crown. The sergeant did not want to be encumbered with it, so I bought it from him. When I got back to New York months later I presented it to *The New York Times* as a souvenir. It was placed in a glass case on the publisher's floor.

On October 5, 1963, Haile Selassie came to *The New York Times* for luncheon at Arthur Hays Sulzberger's invitation. I suggested in advance that *The Times* give him back the sword, which belonged in his family. In its account of the Emperor's day in New York City, *The Times* inserted a few paragraphs:

"Before the luncheon started, Arthur Ochs (Punch) Sulzberger presented the Emperor with a century-old ceremonial sword once owned by Emperor Menelik of Ethiopia. The sword had been picked up on the battlefield of Mai Ceu in the Ethiopian campaign by an Italian sergeant who gave it to Herbert Matthews on July 14, 1936. [He sold it, and the date was April 1, 1936.] Mr. Matthews at that time was the correspondent of *The Times* with the Italian forces.

"As Mr. Sulzberger drew the sword from its brown leather scabbard, the Emperor recognized the inscription of 'The Lion of Judah,' one of his titles, on the blade and expressed appreciation for the gift."

In a profile of Punch Sulzberger for *The New Yorker* of January 18, 1969, Geoffrey Hellman has Punch saying to him, apropros of the sword, that the Emperor was "astounded." As it was told to me after the luncheon, which for obvious reasons I did not attend, Haile Selassie's face was expressionless as he received the gift, and there was no telling what he felt or what he thought.

When I thought about it myself, I realized what a sense of bitterness the Emperor must have felt. Menelik (Haile Selassie was a grandson of his cousin Ras Makonnen) was the emperor who defeated the Italians so decisively in 1896 that they had to acknowledge the independence of Abyssinia. The end of that independence pretty well coincided with the Ethiopian defeat at the Battle of Mai Ceu. Perhaps Haile Selassie thought once again, as he held the sword, that it would have been better for an Abyssinian emperor to have died fighting, as he wanted to do in 1936. It was better for his country that he lived, but his throne was regained for him by British troops, not Ethiopian. Colonel Barker, whose book *The Civilizing Mission* I have already cited, had a conclusion that I believe is undeniable.

"The Italian occupation of Ethiopia lasted just over five years," he wrote, "and during their stay the colonizers conferred many obvious and acknowledged benefits on the country they had assaulted. . . . Whatever their motives and notwithstanding the impress of Fascism, the point must be made that it was the Italians who laid the foundations for Haile Selassie's modern state."

When the Italian Army under Marshal Badoglio entered Addis Ababa on May 5, 1936, it was rightly for much of the world the completion of a crime—a piece of old-fashioned colonial imperialism at its worst. Moreover, it was perpetrated by a man —Mussolini—regarded as an ignominious and ridiculous dictator. The white man, using his superior military and technical strength, triumphed over African natives who had fought bravely to preserve their independence.

This was, indeed, a true moralistic and legalistic description of what had happened. Theoretically, I, who had chronicled the Italian adventure from its beginning to the end, when I rode into Addis Ababa a few yards behind Badoglio, should have been ashamed of myself. I was nothing of the kind. Personally, it was a thrilling experience, the climax to nine difficult, grueling, and sometimes dangerous months of war corresponding. I felt a professional pride in having stuck it out and, on the historic record, having been right in the information I sent to my newspaper. Perhaps only a newspaperman could have understood and appreciated the professional satisfaction involved.

Rereading the despatch that I sent to *The Times* within minutes of our entry into Addis Ababa, I can still feel a sense of journalistic exaltation. Rereading my last despatch on the Spanish Civil War, written four years later, I can still feel the sense of profound despondency and weariness of spirit which engulfed me in those days, although I had done a much better job, professionally speaking, than in Abyssinia.

The difference was one of personal feeling. In Spain I was caught up, committed, biased, emotional. In Abyssinia I had no deep feelings either about the Italians or the Ethiopians. Being with the Italians, knowing them, liking them, and, in many cases, admiring the courage and fortitude of the individual soldiers and officers with whom I had lived, I could not help sharing some of their satisfaction on successfully completing an arduous task. For me, as for them, it meant going home soon to one's family and to the material pleasures and comforts of Western civilization.

So I sat on the fender of the automobile in which I had come from Dessye, with my typewriter on my knee, and wrote:

"ADDIS ABABA, May 5—Ethiopia's era of independence, which had lasted since biblical times, ended at 4 o'clock this afternoon when the Italians occupied Addis Ababa. The newer empire founded by Menelik received its quietus at the same time, and a new epoch in the history of this ancient country begins. . . ."

It was not to last long, of course. Before taking world opinion too much for granted, and before condemning us journalists who were covering the war from the Italian side, I would like to cite some facts—and they were facts—from an interpretive despatch I sent from Dessye on April 24, 1936, published May 5 with the war approaching its end. History is rarely so simple as it is made out to be when historians look back, select their facts, summarize, and pass judgment.

"The Danakils, the Tigreans and the Azebu Gallas definitely favored an Italian invasion," I wrote. "The writer has had personal experiences that have convinced him of that fact. There are excellent historical reasons, too, and the fact that the Danakils joined General Oreste Mariotti's column [the one I was with] and the Azebu Gallas have carried on guerrilla warfare against Emperor Haile Selassie's forces bear out this statement.

"Gondar, in Amharic territory near Lake Tana, was occupied without the firing of a shot because the natives wanted the Italians to come on. The populace in other regions, such as Tembien, Scirè and Semien, however, showed a distinct disposition to oppose the Italians and in many cases joined the Negus's armies. . . .

"Like most peasant folk, the average Ethiopian does not care much who rules him. He wants peace and an opportunity to till his land, reap the profits it brings him and enjoy his home and family life undisturbed. He is not patriotic in the white man's sense of the term. Indeed, the writer has oftener than not found a definite hostility toward Addis Ababa. . . .

"No consideration is being given to the ethical problem behind the Italian invasion. The only point which is being made in this article is that, as far as this correspondent's personal contacts and journeys have extended, it would be unfair and bad journalism not to call attention to the fact that a vast majority of the native population now favors the Italian occupation."

There is always a problem for a newspaperman who is on the unpopular side, as I was in Abyssinia and Cuba, or who is covering a controversial situation like the Spanish Civil War: it is hard not to be on the defensive and not to be answering criticisms. The instinct is to prove that one is right by going out of the way to present favorable news, but reason impels one to lean over backward to present the unfavorable, so as to show that one is being fair.

There was a war psychology animating the Italians just after their victory in Ethiopia. I sensed it before I left the country and in a despatch of May 22, 1936, from Diredawa, between Addis Ababa and Djibouti, the French port on the Red Sea, I wrote:

"We have been out of touch with Europe here, but there is no doubt that everyone in East Africa talks as if the war just ended were merely the first of a series. Italians here say openly that they would like nothing better than to receive orders to march upon the Sudan, Kenya, British Somaliland and even Egypt.

"The hounds of war have been unleashed and it is obviously going to be a difficult task to hold them in check now that they have had this first juicy morsel."

In my book, *The Education of a Correspondent,* I expressed my feelings about Abyssinia in these words:

"The invasion was going to take place whatever I did. . . . I was a journalist and this was going to be a great story, probably the greatest since World War I, and as I spoke Italian and knew Italy, I felt entitled to cover it from the Italian side.

"I was, in the Dantesque sense, in the midst of this, our mortal life, and quite capable of a hard campaign. All the old dreams were surging up, the lure of adventure, the longing to go to strange, far-away places, to face danger, to distinguish myself, to be anything but a 'second man' in the Paris bureau living an uninterruptedly humdrum existence. I little realized then that I was embarking, not on one adventure but on years of adventure, on a whole career of danger, hardships and loneliness—the loneliness that any man must feel away from the ones he loves. But they have been great years, full and rich, and I would not exchange them for a lifetime of ease and safety."

Back in Rome, in a despatch which I cabled on June 26, 1936 I pointed out that: "There is not an Italian who is not now convinced that Italy has won her spurs and ranks as a first-class power. . . . There is the same talk that one hears in Africa about

its being Italy's 'manifest destiny' to control the Mediterranean."

Il Duce was talking of *Mare Nostrum* as if he were an ancient
Roman.

Ironically, the decline of Italian Fascism began with its greatest triumph. Had Mussolini been content to rest on his laurels
and develop Ethiopia with investments and colonization, he
would have proved himself a sensible, far-sighted, prudent
statesman. Being none of these things, he turned to where, as
he thought, more glory beckoned. Although Germany and Italy
won the war in Spain for Generalissimo Franco, the Italian army
and economy paid so high a price that Italy could not join
Germany when World War II started. Mussolini waited until he
thought it was safe and then made the greatest of all his mistakes.

By that time I was in Rome as head of *The Times* bureau, and
I knew what great concessions Britain and France had offered
the Duce to stay out of the war. French Ambassador François
Poncet said to me in despair: "I cannot understand this man.
We have offered him everything he could gain by war if he
would only remain neutral." Poncet was using French logic.
Mussolini was a megalomaniac Italian; he wanted Italian blood
to be shed. It was part of the Fascist psychology of "glory" and
"heroism."

I had some bitter moments in the early months at the Rome
bureau, especially having to witness and report on the triumphant return of the Italian expeditionary force from Spain.
However, my love of Italy, which my wife and children shared,
and the fact that all our friends were anti-Fascist and (I guessed)
so were at least nine out of ten Italians, made it bearable.

We had no illusions. If Mussolini had guessed right and the
Axis had won the war, nine out of ten Italians would have
cheered him. There was no moral issue involved for them. We
were disgusted at the complacent way even our friends contem-
plated the German bombing of England, and at their conviction

that the British would give up the fight any day. The gloating of the Italian press was especially hard to take.

We lived in a sort of limbo, because although the war began for Europe on September 3, 1939, it did not begin for the United States until Pearl Harbor, more than two years later. As American citizens we were left alone. I was having my final lesson in Italian Fascism, Mussolini's style, but I was still naive enough to be shocked when Hitler and Stalin made their pact on August 23, 1939. I had retained from Spain a belief in the determination of Moscow's anti-Fascism. I still thought that Communist ideology had a consistency divorced from purely nationalistic considerations. To me the pact was a betrayal of those genuine Communist idealists who had come from all over the world to fight in the International Brigade in Spain. The Russo-German agreement at least started me on an intensive effort to understand Soviet foreign policy and how international Communism works. I realized, belatedly, the affinity of all totalitarian systems—Fascist, Nazi, Communist, and military dictatorship. They all use the same methods and have a common enemy in liberal democracy. As Hitler said in *Mein Kampf*, they all "come together."

Rome was a grandstand from which to watch, in bitterness and despair, the "phony war" of 1939–1940, the collapse of France, and the initial defeats of the British. President Roosevelt was a hopeful beacon in the distance, for one could see where he was trying to lead the United States. So could Italy and Germany. During Roosevelt's presidential campaign of 1940 against Wendell Willkie, I sent a despatch from Rome saying that Hitler and Mussolini wanted to see Roosevelt lose. The Germans were so furious that they had the Italians expel me, but my friends in the Ministry of Information were reluctant to do this, and let me understand that if I stayed in Switzerland for a month or so, a return could be arranged. My wife and I went to Berne for a pleasant holiday and word was duly sent to me that I could come back to Rome. A few years later, when I was in New York on leave, I was introduced to Wendell Willkie at a dinner party. "Ah!" he said. "Here's the man who lost the election for me"

—an exaggeration, of course, but it must have been true that F.D.R. gained votes by being depicted as the man the Fuehrer and Duce feared.

As 1941 drew on it was obvious that the United States would be drawn into the conflict. The food situation in Rome was steadily getting worse and our chidren were showing the effects. Nancie took them to New York on a ship bearing the families of American diplomats in Europe. I stayed on, in an invariably friendly atmosphere. Italy was so weak and Fascism so unpopular that we all had the impression, when disaster struck Pearl Harbor, that the Duce would have liked to avoid war between Italy and the United States. He had no choice, although he hesitated for several days before declaring war.

On the morning of December 11, 1941, U.S. Ambassador William Phillips told me the blow was coming that day. I went down to the Piazza Venezia and stood directly under the famous balcony of the Palazzo and for the last time heard Il Duce make one of his declamatory harangues. It was monstrous to think of our countries being at war, and incredible to think of myself as an enemy alien in Italy, but at least I knew that most of our Italian friends felt as I did.

I did not know what would happen next, but took no chances and went to one of our favorite restaurants—the Ristorante Umberto, now gone—and had a bang-up lunch. Back at the office two detectives were waiting, and I was soon a prisoner in Rome's grim medieval prison with the incongruous name of *Regina Coeli*—Queen of Heaven. Others in the small group of American newspapermen had also been arrested. We learned later that Rome had received a false report that Italian journalists in the United States had been jailed so they, as they thought, retaliated. In fact, the Italians in America were simply interned with their diplomats, so we were taken out of jail in three days and ended up *in confino* in Siena, the loveliest spot that could have been chosen. My brief sojourn in a small, dark, very dirty, and very cold cell with two of my colleagues—Reynolds Packard of the United Press and Richard Massock of the Associated Press —was a salutary experience.

It was a bad one, too, especially as I have a tendency to claustrophobia. No concessions were made to us as political prisoners, although I remember once giving back the bowl of minestrone that constituted one of our meals and telling the guard it was cold and I wanted hot soup. The young man looked at me in astonishment, but took it away and came back with hot minestrone. Italians are like that.

My most ticklish moment in jail was immediately after the iron entrance doors clanged shut—a dreadful sound—when I realized that a book of the names, addresses, and phone numbers of all our Italian friends was still in my pocket. I told a guard that I had to go to the toilet, where I tore the book into shreds and threw them down the hole.

Ever since *Regina Coeli* I have known what it feels like to be in prison. It is a terrible thing to be deprived of one's physical liberty. I recommend just such a brief sojourn to those who want to know how the world is going—even in our United States where so many thousands are jailed for political protest.

The five-month internment in Siena was no hardship. We newspapermen lived in a hotel and had the run of the city. I even went for daily bicycle rides in the lovely Tuscan hills while Fascist officials looked the other way. All the Sienese, of course, were friendly. Then we were exchanged for the Italian newspapermen, and after a year in India I was called over to North Africa to take part in the invasion of Sicily and the Italian peninsula.

The Italian campaign probably was, as the military experts said, badly conceived and unnecessarily long and costly, but it made a contribution to the final victory. Personally and professionally, it gave me a great assignment and, often, a heartbreaking one, as I saw so much of Italy's wonderful art treasures destroyed and so many familiar towns and villages irreparably damaged. No doubt "art is long and life is short," but bombs and shells put an end to art as well as lives. The war corresponding was an adventure. It was more rewarding for my future career as foreign correspondent and editorial writer to be able to follow postwar Italian politics from its inception.

Mussolini, as I said before, had been shot in the back by Communist partisans and his body hung upside down in a Milanese square where Italians, who had toadied to him and cheered for him in life, took their cheap and shameful revenge. Dino Grandi, who had presented the letter at the Fascist Grand Council meeting in Rome on July 24, 1943, demanding Mussolini's retirement, had written, only a few years before: "My life, my faith, my soul are yours." This was why Italian Fascism proved such a hollow shell under hostile blows, while German Nazism fought to the end and has refused to disappear to this day.

What price charisma? Benito Mussolini seemed so easy to characterize—well or badly—in his years of power, but hardly anybody really could have known him. Such men do not have intimate friends. He never inspired personal loyalty or affection. His mistress, Claretta Petacci, was one of the very few who stood by him to the end. He wore the trappings of power and these, not his will, courage, brains, or character, permitted him to rule for twenty-two years. He fooled the world—those who worshipped and those who despised. The leading figures of history, I discovered in my career, are all enigmas.

"Liberated" Rome, during 1944, was an unhappy city. I made the following note after dinner one evening with three of Italy's outstanding intellectuals, the Contessina Irene di Robilant, the journalist Mario Vinciguerra, and the philosopher Professor Guido di Ruggiero:

"How well these Italians solve the problems of the universe and what a mess they make of Italy! The realization that Italy no longer counts, even journalistically, made Di Ruggiero say that Italy is now object, not subject. 'People who write history a century from now will see this era perhaps as one of great travail from which a better world came, but for us who have to live in it there is only suffering!' "

Italians, like the French but for different reasons, felt ashamed of their country. Yet—as in France—there was a superb resistance force in northern Italy. After the capture of Rome there was also an Italian unit that fought well by the side of Allied troops.

No people are more willing to live and let live than the Italians. It was amusing to see the Allies at first try, and then give up, their determination to punish ex-Fascist leaders. Had all Fascist officials been "purified" in what was called "defascistization," there would have been no one left to perform the myriad tasks of running the state, the army, police force, post office, no teachers, musicians, or journalists. They all had to have their Fascist uniforms and swear an oath of allegiance to Mussolini to get and hold jobs. Everybody was a Fascist before liberation and nobody was a Fascist after the liberation. It was amazing how many spurious "partisans" appeared all over Italy.

Count Carlo Sforza was High Commissioner for the Punishment of Fascist Crimes in the Rome government. He was a perfect choice because of his pre-Fascist distinction as minister of foreign affairs and, especially, his exemplary record as an anti-Fascist exile in the United States for almost twenty years. Nancie and I came to know him and his gentle wife well in the United States, and I saw him often when he came to Naples, as soon as it was liberated, to join the government. He had lived abroad with great dignity, earning a living by lectures and books.

His anti-Fascism was urbane, cosmopolitan, philosophical, aristocratic, and understanding—but very firm. Whether he was a descendent of the Renaissance family of Ludovico Sforza, and whether his title of Count was legitimate, was uncertain and unimportant. As Benedetto Croce said to me about him, "I knew his father, who did not call himself a Count, but what is the difference?" If Sforza had enemies and detractors, it was because of a certain haughtiness and an overweening vanity—peccadilloes that did not nullify a noble character.

Such a man was not going to be vindictive or dogmatic in "purifying" Italian society of Fascists. This was true of all the men who took power as Italy was freed. Even so right-wing a politician as the tough Minister of the Interior Mario Scelba, a Christian Democrat, argued with me that there was no need to be afraid of the ex-Fascists or to be too dogmatic about them.

The easing up of the *epurazione,* he said to me on a trip to Rome in 1949, was effective because it avoided creating a class whose primary interest would have been to overthrow the existing order and make a comeback. Instead, it gave the ex-Fascist officials a vested interest in democracy. Now these elements, many of them prefects, police commissioners, and military officers, would have feared a return of Fascism.

The neo-Fascists (who have been gaining strength in the last few years) lacked strong leaders. Their following, curiously enough, came largely from the very young, who did not know Fascism but were moved by nationalism and the legends that quickly began to gather about the figure of Mussolini.

I argued at that time—and even wrote a much-quoted article for Alba de Cespedes's magazine *Mercurio*—that Fascism was not dead and would not die; that it was a permanent feature of Italian life. In so doing I went against the opinion of Benedetto Croce, who assured me more than once that Fascism was an illness (*un morbo*) from which Italy had fully recovered and which would not recur. In an article he wrote for *The New York Times* at my request Croce said: "And now Italy is free of the Fascist infection, and although still in grave danger, she can die any kind of death but no longer that death."

He was closer to the truth than I was, I am happy to say, but it is obvious that the Fascist germ has by no means been eradicated from the Italian body politic. I do not think it ever will be, because Fascism—or something similar—was a natural development from Italian history—a dream of "glory," an atavistic survival of "the grandeur that was Rome" in ancient days.

All the same, should there be a Judgment Day, I would still say that Italians will be punished for creating Fascism. When Mussolini wrote of "the universality" of Fascist doctrines, he was right. Even Croce conceded that "the ideological danger of Fascism persists" and that men are still "prepared to adopt Fascist methods." Often in my work thereafter, in many countries, I would see these Fascist "methods" at work. Juan Perón in Argentina modeled his regime on Mussolini's. George Wallace and his running mate in the 1968 presidential campaign,

General Curtis Le May, were crypto-Fascists without realizing it. Wherever the State is made all-powerful, one has a form of Fascism, as distinct from Communism where the party is all-powerful.

"It is not for an outsider like myself to deliver a lecture on the deep roots of Fascism in Italy," I wrote in my *Mercurio* article, "but nobody who studies your history from—let us say—Cola di Rienzi to Crispi, or reads your philosophers from Machiavelli to Gentile, can escape the conclusion that Fascism was to a certain extent a natural phenomenon in Italy. Moreover, I must repeat, Fascism is a world force. As has happened before in history it was for Italian genius (in this case an evil genius) to give expression to a powerful and previously unformed urge of the contemporary spirit."

I can no longer feel about Fascism and Communism as I did in the 1930's and 1940's. The movements have changed; the world has changed; and we must all either change our ideas or be ossified reactionaries. I find it impossible to label any political movement as "evil." Fascists, Nazis, and Communists have done evil things, but this was because they used their movements for militaristic, racist, and oppressive policies.

A movement of such broad scope as Fascism has its good and bad sides. The temptation is to contemplate Fascism's worst features and judge it solely by them. Lack of civic freedoms, military aggressiveness, extreme nationalism, a police state— these are enough to lead a liberal democrat to say that Fascism is unbearable. Yet in Italy the Mussolini regime did a great deal for ordinary people. It maintained order and unity; it improved the educational system and public health; it did much in the fields of public works, women's rights, and child welfare. It sustained a high level of employment and did more to redistribute national wealth than the postwar democratic governments. It took a nation that was in disorder and despair after World War I and, for some years, gave it a sense of national dignity, which turned out to be hollow and spurious because of Mussolini's folly, not because his Fascist system drove him into mad adventures.

Fascism is one form of authoritarianism. As such we reject it, but it does not follow that it need be unsuitable to a backward and underdeveloped African country, or an Asiatic nation that has always known autocracy and never known democracy. Nor does it follow that many millions of Italians who considered themselves Fascists were evil men and women. If Nazism retains an evil connotation, it is because it added racism to the Fascist system. Racism is evil, but it is not a political system.

It has always been recognized that if the Communist ideology could be carried out to the full in its theoretical form, one would have a society as admirable as an ideal state run on the highest Christian principles. Anyone who says that Communism has no good in it and that all Communists are evil is an ignorant fool.

Our fear and hatred of Fascism and Communism were based in part on a mistaken belief that they could make the State invulnerable. Everywhere, even in the Communist bloc, the State is being weakened by pressures and demands from below. Orwell's *1984*, which seemed so chillingly possible when he wrote it, is now recognized as a *reductio ad absurdum* of some aspects of authoritarianism. Totalitarianism, like the violent stage of a social revolution, is a passing phenomenon; nations recover from it as men do from devastating illnesses.

It is no accident of nature or politics that in the Italian transition from Fascism to democracy, from monarchy to republic, a huge Communist party and movement grew up. Fascists easily become Communists, or vice versa. They are like the hands of a clock: follow the two movements around far enough and they come together. Each, paradoxically, leaves fertile ground for the other. I had seen in Spain how easily Communists and Anarcho-Syndicalists went over to the Falangist party after Franco's victory.

Throughout the whole course of postwar Italian politics, two parties have been dominant—the Christian Democrat and the Communist. The former is considered a natural development; the latter an aberration. In truth, both are "naturals." Christian

Democracy is easy for Americans to understand, but they are bewildered and resentful over Italian Communism and have helped to fight it. The Communist movement needs an explanation.

I do not mean to give the impression that Italian politics can be simplified into two parts. On the contrary. Every Italian party has its shifting factions and personalities, so that the analysis of today will not be valid in a few months. Each region needs to be weighed before judgment. So far as my knowledge goes, there is no country where the political situation is so complex or so dependent on a day-to-day assessment.

Wherever one goes in Italy, history and its centuries-old quarrels intrude in new-old forms—Guelf-Ghibelline, clerical-anticlerical, north-south, rural-urban, all the rest against Rome. Within the boundaries of the old Venetian Republic, north of the River Po and east of the Adda, the political coloration is "white," which is to say, anti-Communist. Cross either river and it is Red. In the old Papal States—especially in Emilia and Romagna—the complexion is now Red; wherever there was freedom, as in Florence and Siena, it is white. In the regions where the foreigner—Austrian and French—ruled, there is a persistence of being against the government, any government. Communism in Italy is in part a historic movement of protest against government.

Factionalism is ages old; it is an ingrained quality of the Italian character. Surface manifestations are never to be trusted, for there are always currents and cross-currents of extreme complexity. Italians do not vote for programs; they vote for personalities and for something that arouses their passions. There were only two voting traditions—monarchism in the agrarian south, and socialism in the industrial north. The monarchy is gone and the Communists inherited the bulk of the Socialist vote. "They keep reproaching me with being always in alliance with the Communists," Pietro Nenni, the Socialist leader said to me in 1954 (and not for the first or last time), "but how could I do otherwise when I am always forced into a defense of exactly the same positions that the Communists also have to defend?"

(136)

When, eight years later, he broke with the Communists, and the Socialists entered the government, the strains were so great that the Socialist party split wide open.

United States policies, ironically, consistently played into the hands of the Communists. The Communist movement got its powerful, and thus far unbreakable, grip in Italy when the country was being "liberated." The Russians were so much more astute than the Americans and British that it was pitiful. The Allied Control Commission in Algiers, among whose leaders were Robert Murphy and Samuel Reber for the Americans, Harold Macmillan and Harold Caccia for the British, invited a Russian advisory group. Moscow sent a big delegation, all authorities on Italy, all speaking Italian fluently. We had nothing comparable. Alberto Pirelli, then an old man, head of the famous international concern of that name making tires, tubes, and other rubber products, claimed to me that Murphy had answered his warning about the Reds by saying: "Well, if Italy goes Communist, it will be all right. The Communists are now a part of the democratic community."

The Russians, with Allied consent, arranged in March 1944 to bring in an Italian Communist named Palmiro Togliatti, who had been a leading figure for years in the Comintern. Togliatti had played an important role with the International Brigade in Spain. Thanks to Allied insistence on trade union unity, Italian Communists quickly got control of the main labor organization, the General Confederation of Italian Labor (CGIL)—a control they still hold in 1971.

Togliatti, as anyone who knew his record could have expected, became an outstanding figure in Italian politics. He built the Italian Communist party into the largest Communist party outside the Soviet Union—which it still is. No Italian politician, except De Gasperi in his day, could match his remarkable qualities of intelligence, shrewdness, and administrative ability. He was so astute that he weathered the transition from Stalin to Khrushchev without a hitch. Even more than Tito of Yugoslavia, and earlier than he, Togliatti was a pioneer in creating the type of national Communism that has so weakened the Kremlin's hold on the non-Russian parties. It was Togliatti who coined the word and implemented the concept of "polycentrism"—the right of each individual Communist party to find its own road to "socialism" without taking orders from Moscow. This policy made it easy for Luigi Longo, Togliatti's successor, to side with mavericks like Rumania and to condemn the Soviet intervention in Czechoslovakia in 1969. Guiseppe di Vittorio (like Togliatti and Longo a "graduate" from the International Brigade) organized and headed the CGIL with remarkable ability until his death in 1958. Another ex-Brigader was Vittorio Vidali (Carlos Contreras) who became—and still is—the Red leader in Trieste.

I knew and admired all these men, but liked none of them. The two I both admired and liked were Pietro Nenni, the Socialist, and Randolfo Pacciardi, the Republican. Pacciardi, a tall, handsome young lawyer in 1936, had been in exile from Fascism in Paris. He was not a Communist and, in fact, had to be secretly rushed out of Spain in 1937 when he learned that Communists from the Brigade were going to kill him. He later became De Gasperi's minister of war and a formidable enemy of the Italian Reds.

Togliatti rarely talked in Marxist terms. He made speeches that could have been accepted by the staunchest democrats. The last thing he or Moscow wanted was a revolution or a Communist government.

The other political parties and movements could not be formed so quickly; they lacked the cadres, the trained leaders, the money, and the already formed policies. When the non-Communist parties developed policies that were naturally democratic, they found that the Communists had got in ahead of them, and that the worker could see no reason to change. The fact that the Italian Communists were strongly anti-Fascist, and always had been, helped the Reds. Another factor was the superb fight that the Russians had put up against the Germans. Italians had seen their own tricolor disgraced and hauled down; the Red flag had a proud history. The big businessmen and landowners had been linked to the Fascisti and were in bad odor. The Reds made their major efforts in the rural areas. This was dangerous in Italy because the sharecropper and farm laborer had not, as in France, had a revolution that created a vast class of small, conservative proprietors. There has been no social democratic movement, as there was in Sweden, Norway, Denmark, Holland, and Britain, to introduce a welfare state. In those countries labor, organized in powerful free trade unions, could win their battles against enlightened industrialists who saw the value of yielding with grace. On the other hand, the Italian industrialists, except for the biggest companies, were trying to pay low wages and gain high profits. Redistribution of wealth through graduated income taxes is not effective in Italy. There are still extremely wealthy men who pay relatively small taxes. The countries mentioned have abolished dire poverty, but there is terrible poverty in Italy.

Where are the Italian workers, sharecroppers (*mezzadri*), or agricultural laborers (*braccianti*) to turn? Except in the backward south, they are anticlerical by history, tradition, family, and upbringing. They will not turn to the Church. The Christian Democrat party is politically Catholic, and so is the trade union federation linked to the DemoChristians—the CISL. The Social Democrat federation—the UIL—is small and weak. Neither have the men, money, or organization to compete with the Communists and the CGIL.

One of the top executives of the huge Montecatini chemical works in Milan listed for me the elements that pushed Italian workers into the Communist movement: fear, comradeship, traditions, history, anticlericalism, lack of political experience, illiteracy, tolerance, the feeling of the miserable that there is nothing to lose; the unemployed, the poorly paid, the landless peasants. To these can be added Communist organization, unlimited funds, first-class leadership, dedicated agents at the grass roots, intelligent propaganda, and caring for the workers as individuals.

All these factors, incidentally, help to explain the strength of Communism in France, too, and they will operate in Spain after Franco dies. When it comes to voting in elections, the Communist parties attract support far beyond their membership. In

Italy, with less than two million members, the Communist candidates get about eight million votes in general elections.

The second period of United States bungling on the anti-Communist policy in Italy coincided with the ambassadorship of Claire Boothe Luce, from 1953 to 1956. In fact, the policy seems to have stemmed more from her ideas than the career officers of the State Department. There was an amateurishness about the process, although in 1943 and 1944 the guilty parties had been professional. The madness of McCarthyism was still operating in the United States, and it is possible that Mrs. Luce was emotionally driven by her religious feelings, for she had come to Rome as a crusader against the heretics.

The basic idea was to use the power that Washington possessed through aid and trade with Italy to force the big businesses to threaten workers with loss of employment if they did not quit the Communist-led CGIL for the Christian Democrat CISL or, as a second choice, the Social Democrat UIL. The American Embassy gave funds to the CISL. The Christian Democrats were also helped politically.

The results, as could have been foreseen by anyone familiar with Italians and the labor situation, were counterproductive. The program did not tackle the roots of the problem, which were demands for steady jobs, security, and social reforms.

I had a long talk with Dr. Angelo Costa, president of Confindustria, the great employers' federation, in 1954. He argued that a direct attack on the Communists, such as Claire Luce was then carrying out, did not take account of the basic, complex factors behind Italian Communism and the psychology of the workers. The Italian, he asserted, has a strong sense of right and justice, and Communism was not illegal. Dr. Costa asked why a man should be punished for taking a position that was within his rights. Fellow workers, even if they were not Communists, would sympathize with those penalized.

Italians are not Communist for ideological reasons, Costa pointed out, but this does not mean that the answers to Communism lie wholly in the field of material betterment or short-term, opportunistic tactics.

"I am sure," he continued, "that a worker, seeing that he will lose his job if he remains in the CGIL and thus switches to the CISL or UIL will still, when it comes to voting by secret ballot, vote Communist. This is in the Italian character, and it is not taken sufficiently into account by Mrs. Luce and the Americans. The fact that the [Christian Democrat] Scelba Government is taking anti-Communist measures at the behest of the Americans is enough to make the measures ineffective."

Actually, Mario Scelba complained to me (as an editor I always conversed off the record) during that same visit to Rome that the open American fears and pessimism disheartened Italian anti-Communists by depicting the Reds as stronger than they were. This, he said, is exactly the impression that the Communists wanted to give.

The Luce process reminded me of the Fascist era. When Italians were ordered to join the Fascist party or lose jobs, they joined—but it meant nothing. Americans were happy when an Italian worker *said* he had ceased to become a Communist, which overlooked the fact that seasoned Reds would be the first to say so. The Communist party was more sophisticated than Mussolini; they wanted the substance of support; the form was unimportant.

Ambassador Luce was out of her depth and making a common American mistake of applying American psychology to foreigners who have other ideas and ways. To be sure, she was up against a universal postwar puzzle—how to define and make the tenets of liberal democracy understandable and attractive. As abstractions they could have little appeal to Italian industrial workers and agricultural laborers who had no experience of democracy.

For instance—Giulio Pastore, who for years headed the CISL, the Catholic labor confederation, told me that he had asked the Americans not to back him so ostentatiously. It was an open secret that he was getting money from our embassy. He said that he had warned Washington that such tactics ran the risk of merely affecting the façade. Many Italians, I know, gave the Americans this advice, but it was not heeded. My Italian friends even claimed that Claire Luce was responsible for Giovanni Gronchi getting elected President in 1955, by opposing him openly.

Giovanni Malagodi, the Liberal Party leader and one of Italy's most brilliant, cultured, and practical conservatives, told me in 1960 that when Mrs. Luce arrived full of energy and enthusiasm to defeat Communism in Italy, he said to her that it would take a generation or two. She scoffed, but when she left she ruefully argued that Italy would never get rid of Communism. Malagodi said that he told her she was wrong in the beginning and wrong again. Italy will get rid of the Communists, he asserted, but very slowly. If so, it is indeed a very slow process. Fifteen years have passed since Mrs. Luce left and the Italian Communists are as strong as, or stronger than ever, although split into factions.

Italians like to be on the winning side, and the Reds always managed to give the impression that they might gain power. Workers and peasants knew that the democratic regime would not persecute them for being pro-Communist, but they feared that a Red regime would punish them for being anti-Communist.

It is a worldwide experience that Communism profits from the phenomenon of rising expectations. I have seen this on four continents, but nowhere more remarkably than in southern Italy, a region oppressed and impoverished for 2,000 years. Even the Fascist regime neglected the south, which was overwhelmingly rural, feudalistic because of the landowning aristocracy, and monarchist because the wretched, illiterate peasants voted as they were told. The south was Italy's "colony."

At long last, in 1950, the Christian Democrat regime under Alcide de Gasperi started to do something. A large fund (the *Cassa per il Mezzogiorno*) was allotted and an ambitious plan drawn up, which has done as much as humanly possible. But a democratic regime has limited resources; it can only do so much. When a peasant received a farm, a house, and some livestock for small payments over thirty years, a Communist agent would come along and say: "Vote for us and we will give you all that and more free." Rome was far away and alien; it always had been. Democracy was strange, demanding, and incomprehensible. Communism was the only modern manifestation of political life that adapted itself to backward conditions in the south.

A subproletariat became a proletariat; there was time to think about politics, and freedom to vote as one pleased; a national consciousness was awakened. But rising expectations could not be satisfied in a region with the highest population density in Europe. So southerners became emigrants again, this time to the industrial north where, being unskilled, they lived in poverty and, in many cases, were lured into the Communist fold.

Becoming attuned to southern Italy is a sad experience. Surface appearances are unattractive. Most peasants live in "monster villages," which are residential and market centers. No southern town except Naples was touched by the Renaissance. None has the artistic and cultural fame or beauty (again excepting Naples) of the hill towns of Tuscany, or the great cities of the north. Those accustomed to the supreme beauty of the northern cities will be dismayed by the ugliness and drabness of southern towns like Foggia, Bari, Taranto, Crotone, Cosenza, Canossa. Yet these are very ancient places; some were famous in Roman times.

There is an ingrained civilization and culture, which is felt, rather than seen. Phoenicians, Greeks, Romans, Saracens, Normans, and Spanish Bourbons came and went but left subtle imprints. These people are ignorant in letters and the fine arts, but not in the wisdom of the ages or the refined sensitivity which comes from civilizations that have gone into history, but left their natural inheritance.

The hospitality is heartwarming, perhaps especially so for Americans. Few of the families cannot boast of relatives in the United States. Many went to America before the immigration bars were put down in 1921 and returned with a "fortune," enough to build a house or start up in trade. The southerner will feel badly if the stranger does not accept something—cherries, eggs, a cup of coffee, a glass of wine. Gracious hospitality, I have discovered, is a mark of the poorest classes in ancient civilizations—Mediterranean, East Indian, Chinese.

Naples is an exception, because the foreigner is *ipso facto* taken in—literally—as a tourist. It is an unpleasant city to visit, despite the beauty of its setting. Northern Italians feel as uncomfortable and as critical in Naples as I feel. The city is best enjoyed in paintings, songs, and movies.

Until the unification of Italy in 1870, Naples was ruled by foreigners. The last ones—the Spanish Bourbons—were famous for providing *pane, farina e feste* (bread, flour, and circuses). For years after World War II, a self-made Neapolitan millionaire and demagogue, Achille Lauro, provided the spaghetti and entertainment. He had what Neapolitans call a *carattera spagnolesca*— a Spanish character. He did much for Naples in the way of education and public works, largely at the expense of Rome and the budgetary balance. "Tomorrow is in the hands of God," as the Neapolitans say. He did transform the city; Naples has not looked so good in all its history. Nevertheless, he left behind great and heartrending poverty in much, if not most, of Naples when he retired.

The poorest Neapolitans always voted for Lauro to a man and woman. Had he emigrated to the States, he would have been mayor of New York instead of Naples.

The most extraordinary figure in southern Italy during my time was Padre Pio, who had the five wounds—the stigmata— of Christ's crucifixion on his hands, feet, and side. At least he certainly had them on his hands, as my wife and I saw when we spent a few days at San Giovanni Rotondo outside of Foggia in June 1956. He gave me a private audience and came out of his cell in the Capuchin monastery to bless my wife.

Padre Pio remains one of life's mysteries to me, for he did have the stigmata, and we were assured by those living closest to him that he ate almost nothing. Yet we found him cheerful and well, and he was eighty-one when he died on September 23,

1968. We were told of various simple divinations that his followers considered miraculous, and they sincerely believed in his
supposed powers of bilocation (being in two places at once) and
levitation (rising spontaneously into the air).

I had a brief, private talk with Pope Pius XII on June 26, after
returning to Rome. The Pope came out into the antechamber
from his office to see me and stood talking for six or seven
minutes, standing straight and looking vigorous despite a recent
illness. I told him that I and my wife had seen Padre Pio in San
Giovanni Rotondo and, while I was not a Catholic, it seemed to
me the Padre could be called a saint. I did not mean it literally,
since the process of sanctification is long and rigorous, but His
Holiness, after a brief and thoughtful pause, picked me up on
it.

"*Si,*" he said, "*è un uomo santo.*" (Yes, he is a saintly man.) He
was surprised to hear that his sister and niece (who seemed to
us to be autistic) had been there at the same time as we were,
but obviously he did not have any objection. The Pope spoke
highly of the hospital Padre Pio had founded at San Giovanni
Rotondo, which, he repeated a few times, should become an
international center.

As I have said, Pope Pius was a faithful reader of our newspaper, which he referred to as "*un gran giornale*"—a great newspaper. He spoke sadly of Anne O'Hare McCormick, our columnist
who had died two years before. "*Una brava persona*"—a fine
person—he said. He asked who was going to be elected President in November, but when I said, Eisenhower will be re-
elected, he was careful to show no feeling, merely saying in
English, with a smile, "to a second term." However, he had no
hesitation in calling the Italian elections of the month before, in
which the Christian Democrats had done fairly well: "*abbastanza
buona*"—good enough.

As always, he gave his blessing to me and to everybody dear
to me, and presented me with a papal medallion, asking first if
I would like one. I told him I had a Catholic sister-in-law and that
their children had been brought up as Catholics, so he gave me
three more and blessed them. This was the last time I saw Pope

Pius as I did not return to Rome until 1960. He died on October 9, 1958.

John XXIII evidently did not have a good opinion of Padre Pio or his hospital. He ordered an inquiry into the running of the hospital, and although the report was never published, Padre Pio was forbidden to say mass in public or conduct marriages. There was no slackening in the thousands who went to San Giovanni as a pilgrimage or for a hopeful miraculous healing, and it was said that Padre Pio received an average of 500 to 600 letters and many telegrams every day from people stricken by illness. I will never know what to believe about Padre Pio nor, obviously, did his superiors.

Pope Pius was, of course, deeply concerned over the strength of Communism in Italy. The Holy See tries to avoid antagonizing Moscow since so many millions of Catholics—Roman and Greek Orthodox—live under Communist regimes. In Italy, however, since the Pope is Bishop of Rome, there has never been any vacillation about the Communists. Togliatti, cleverly, was careful never to antagonize the Church and, in fact, came out openly in favor of including the Lateran Pact in the new Italian constitution.

The relationship between the Catholic clergy and the Reds in Italy was mutually tolerant enough to bring out the now-classic series of books and films by Giovanni Guareschi on Don Camillo, the priest who cooperated with the friendly Communist mayor of his village. It was not too far-fetched.

Bologna, politically, has been a Communist city since the war. The Saragozza Gate, now in the town center, built originally in the twelfth century and rebuilt in the sixteenth, is a famous landmark. On one side it has a shrine to the Madonna and on the other the district Communist headquarters. The shrine is visited constantly by hundreds and thousands of Bolognese, many of whom leave candles or tokens—then they vote for a Communist mayor, or go to dances organized by the Reds. I remember a talk with Cardinal Lercaro, Archbishop of Bologna, in 1956. He was rightly considered a liberal, and he talked with wry humor of his townspeople's anticlericalism and Communism. The Cardinal was very popular, and there is no doubt that many Reds paid their respects when he died.

"Don Camillo is not real," Mgr. Giovanni Battista Montini, then secretary of state and later Pope Paul VI, said to me in 1954. "There is some basis in the concept, but when it comes to the reality, as in the recent strike of the cattlemen in Ferrara, you saw that they let the cattle suffer." (The *boari* in that province are still Red.)

The Communists, Monsignor Montini argued, were profoundly anticlerical even when Togliatti wooed the Church, and the Holy See knew it. "The Vatican cannot be accused of not being anti-Communist," he continued. "The major trouble goes back to the weakness of the government setup in the crucial years of 1945–1946. Communists penetrated all the ministries at that time, and many remain. The Allies were to blame for that. Democracy in Italy means a weak government, not a government of the people. The Vatican could not intervene. We do not even try hard enough now to influence the Christian Democrats. The answer to Communism is a socially advanced program."

I would still apply to the fictitious Don Camillo a classic Italian adage: *Se non è vero è ben trovato* (Even if it isn't true it is apt.)

Luigi Barzini once told me a typical anecdote of a big landowner in the Po Valley whose land was worked by sharecroppers with a *fattore* (steward) handling the administration. All were prosperous and Communist. The owner said to the *fattore:* "Don't you know that if there were a Communist revolution I would be the first one to be shot, but you would be the second?" "O, *Signor Conte,*" the *fattore* answered, "but surely a gentleman like you wouldn't let that happen!"

The last time I saw Don Luigi Sturzo, the wise, gentle, and charming Sicilian founder of Italian and worldwide Christian Democracy (this was in 1954 when he was eighty-two and living in the Convent of the *Figlie di Carità Canossiane*), he made exactly that point. "Voting is very often an external manifestation," he said, "and that goes for Communism. It does not mean at all that the voters are Communists."

Italian Communism, like Cuban Marxism-Leninism, is *sui generis*. Italians do not worry too much about their Communism even when 25 percent and more of the electorate vote Communist. They ought to worry, and I do not believe that a Popular Front government someday, dominated by the Communists, is an impossibility. The roadblock since the war has been the Christian Democrat party, which has dominated the political sphere at all times. It started to weaken even before Alcide de Gasperi died in 1954. As the 1960's ended it was split into as many as eight factions.

American economic, financial, and political power had been mobilized to win the crucial general election of April 18, 1948, for De Gasperi and the Christian Democrats. This was the first election of an Italian Parliament under the new constitution. The Socialist party had split the year before, and the great bulk of it agreed to a common electoral list with the Communists. Fears and tensions mounted. In February 1948, the Russians had engineered the Communist coup in Czechoslovakia. The April election seemed like a climactic struggle of Rome against Moscow.

Later, it was realized that the danger had been exaggerated. The Marxist vote was about the same as in the previous election in 1946. The Christian Democrats gained because of a conservative swing to their side. With 305 seats in the Chamber of Deputies out of 574, De Gasperi's party had a majority, and the Vatican is believed to have tried hard to induce him to form a one-party Catholic government. He wisely refused, fearing a countrywide split of clericals and anticlericals. He likewise refused American pressure to outlaw the Communist and Socialist parties.

Alcide de Gasperi's career ended with a later, and this time unsuccessful, election, on June 7, 1953. Once again, the United States tried to interfere through Ambassador Clare Boothe Luce, who publicly warned Italians of the unfavorable economic consequences to them if the center coalition did not win. The

Christian Democrats received only 40 percent of the votes and 261 seats. Many Italians believed that Mrs. Luce had done De Gasperi more harm than good, which was likely. The 1953 election marked the end of De Gasperi's career. He retired and died the following year.

It is one of the many subtleties of Italian politics and the workings of the Holy See that one has to make a distinction between the Vatican and the priesthood throughout Italy. There has never been any question that parish priests have influenced voters in favor of the Christian Democrats. All Italians will tell you that the Vatican also intervenes directly, and that De Gasperi and Don Sturzo received vital support from the Holy See.

I do not believe it in their cases. I knew De Gasperi and Don Sturzo well and discussed this matter with them. Back in the early Fascist era, Don Sturzo and his *Partito Popolare* were actually sabotaged by the Vatican, which went ahead and made the Lateran agreement with Mussolini. De Gasperi would not brook interference from the Holy See, as he proved in the 1948 election. He was a devout Catholic, but felt that politics and religion, the State and the Church, should be separate. I remember him once telling me that he made his political alliance with the splinter parties (which were anticlerical) in order to *"far fronte alla chiesa"*—to be in a position to stand up against the Church.

I have already cited the then Monsignor Montini. Behind his complaint of government weakness was the fact that De Gasperi, although scrupulously honest himself, permitted great corruption around him.

A Vatican source as important as Monsignor Montini in the Papal Secretariat of State in the 1950's was the gruff, outspoken Monsignor Domenico Tardini, pro-secretary of state. He was highly critical, in a conversation I had with him, of the various governments that had come along for not taking a stronger stand against Communism. When I remarked that I could see that the Vatican did not have much influence over the Christian Democrats, he exploded, and since he had a powerful voice and spoke with great animation, it was impressive.

"Such reports [that the Vatican influences the DemoChristians] are foolishness. They never were true. Parties are formed in Europe calling themselves Christian. Perhaps it is a disservice to the Church. The Vatican does not ally itself to any political party." However, in 1970 Pope Paul did intervene politically against the pending divorce law.

It is too soon for history to pass judgment on Alcide de Gasperi. In my opinion he was one of the three or four outstanding statesmen of unified Italy. Curiously, he was half a foreigner, having been born and brought up in the then Austrian Trento. He was weak in allowing corruption, but I do not agree that he was weak in dealing with the Communists. I discussed this matter with him on several occasions, and I believe he was right in feeling that he could not have taken stronger positions and kept Italy's democratic structure together. Incidentally, he, too, blamed the Allies for permitting the Communists to get such a strong foothold in 1943–1944.

De Gasperi, as he put it to me once, started from the premise that the Italians are an undisciplined race. Nevertheless, he managed to build up a strong mass party of Christian Democrats, which, despite splits, tensions, quarrels, defections, and personalities, is still the dominant political party in Italy. It holds the bourgeoisie, the middle classes, the professionals, the tradesmen—classes that fear Communism and left-wing socialism. The women, who got the vote after World War II, are overwhelmingly Christian Democrat. The party—united or split —is a true expression of a great, central sector of political Italy.

This large, solid, relatively stable central mass has been a bulwark against Communism. It was not against Fascism. It may not be with the youth of Italy as the 1970's begin. Yet Italy is one of the cradles of Western civilization. The conflict between East and West, which in our time took the form of Soviet Communism versus democracy, with a battle line at what we now call the Iron Curtain, is one of the oldest in European history. Never in that history of more than two millennia has Italy been on the side of the East. But one cannot rely too much on history.

Italy must find a new ideology. There is a growing realization that the present political system, copied from France in 1870, does not suit modern, urban Italy. Neither the Marxism of the Communists and Socialists, nor the diluted Catholicism of the Christian Democrats, provides the answers. Debate over what to do and where to go explains why every political party is divided and quarreling.

I watched and lived with Italy's efforts to find herself, politically, through Fascism and postwar democracy. One must still watch and wait. Anglo-Saxon democracy fits awkwardly, even in highly developed countries like Italy and France. This ferment and uncertainty induces pessimism and cynicism in the older generations, but in the younger a desire to search for new answers.

One trouble, as I said, is that Italy never had a social revolution like France's, nor a revolution that evolved, as in Great Britain and the United States. President Giovanni Gronchi was one of several Italian leaders who agreed with me when I argued along those lines. He conceded that Italy still has its oligarchy and its poor masses. Wealth has not been fairly distributed. At best it is difficult for the people to make contact and to understand what the ruling elite is doing, and what the complications of party politics and ideas mean. There is a vast gap between politicians and public opinion. Twelve years of an "economic miracle" has transformed the nation but not politics or administration.

Italy in 1971 is socially the most volatile country in Western Europe. Conditions for a social crisis exist—as they do in France. When? How? The youth of Italy will answer the questions.

Chapter 5

INDIA

One of the best of the superb corps of British civil servants I met in India during World War II said to me: "Once a great power takes over a lesser country, it is almost impossible to get out or give up. You become involved, and you set standards, make connections, arouse hopes and promises, and in a sense become dependent on your dependency." So it has been with Vietnam and the Americans; so it was with India and the British.

Nations, like men, must learn by experience. India was the beginning of the end for the colonial part of the British Empire. The dominions had already gone their way in the 1920's. I watched the decline and fall of the Empire during my career and covered much of it personally as a correspondent.

As an imperial power, Britain became an anachronism. So long as the British bravely and honorably—by Western standards—bore "the white man's burden," ruled the waves, and acted as banker to the world, they seemed supremely right. When I was covering the Abyssinian War in 1935–1936, it was possible to start in Alexandria on the Mediterranean Sea and go down to the Cape of Good Hope in South Africa without leaving territory marked on the map with the famous red color of the Empire "over which the sun never set."

"The brightest jewel" in His Majesty's crown was India, which the British ruled for only 300 years—a few hours of time in India's fathomless history. The end was in sight when I was a war correspondent in India from July 1942 to July 1943. It came in 1947 when Prime Minister Clement Attlee announced in the House of Commons that Britain was granting India the independence that could no longer be postponed. I covered that story for *The Times* as chief of our London bureau.

It was in India that I realized how little our Western philosophy applies to the East, and how hopeless it is to try to foist upon Asians a way of life and government that do not conform to their profound beliefs and customs. Asia's future is for Asians to determine. Mohammed Ali Jinnah, head of the Moslem League and "founding father" of Pakistan, whom I got to know well in India, once said to me: "Let us stew in our own juice if we are willing." But Britons were not willing. At the time Winston Churchill in 10 Downing Street was saying that he was not going "to preside over the liquidation of the British Empire."

No experience in my career was so chastening or so fascinating as my year in old India. The American press had rarely mentioned her during my then twenty years on *The Times.* She was *terra incognita* for Americans. India was fresh and strange and wonderful. My assignment was, for American readers, a voyage of discovery.

"If you want to be thoroughly misinformed about a country, ask the man who has lived there all his life," wrote George Bernard Shaw. One of the extraordinary things about the then undivided India was how little the average Indian knew of his country. I have met hundreds of Indians and Pakistanis since the war, and so far as I can tell, this has not changed. We foreigners, writing about India, were often sneered at and doubted by Indians with whose ideas we disagreed. The truth was that even highly educated and cosmopolitan Indians often knew next to nothing of the people in other parts of the subcontinent where they had not lived.

Now they are divided into two countries, and one of those countries—Pakistan—is, herself, divided into two widely separated and racially and linguistically different parts at war with each other in mid-1971. In present-day India—as during the time I was there—the barriers of caste, race, religion, and language are insuperable for most Indians trying to grasp the unity of a nation.

With the Indian subcontinent, as with other vast subjects like Latin America, Africa, or Asia, there are merely degrees of knowledge—and ignorance. A foreigner is at least able to have some objectivity and to embrace a wider view. We, who were there in World War II, saw an immemorial India whose roots went back to the dawn of history. That India has gone only in a political sense. People do not change because boundaries are changed.

I flew over on an Air Force bucket-seat DC3 from Fisherman's Lake in Liberia—the first American correspondent to take the southern air route to India. Some of our stops, like Accra in Ghana, Kano in Nigeria and the Sheikhdom of Oman in South Arabia, have loomed large in the news in recent years. Another —Asmara in Eritrea—brought back memories of the Abyssinian War. We landed in Karachi from where, three days later, I cabled *The Times:*

"An American entering this gate of India finds himself caught between two fires—British and Indian. Both sides have their case and they present it with such complete conviction and intransigence that a neutral observer is left bewildered. He is given a choice between black or white; take it or leave it."

After ten days in Delhi, my predicament was no easier.

"It does not take a newcomer long to discover," I wrote, "that India is about the hardest nut to crack that any foreign correspondent, however seasoned, can have wished upon him. It would seem as well to put this on record at the beginning of what threatens to be a long and intricate quest for truth on an encyclopedic subject. The trouble with expert opinion on India, your correspondent quickly discovered, is that everybody you meet is quite certain he knows what it is all about and that the other fellow is all wrong. I have never, in twenty years' career, encountered such complete assurance on the part of all individuals, and such equally complete differences of opinion. I have never found a situation where argument gets down so quickly *ad hominem*. . . . But, then, who does know? What is the situation? What, indeed, is India?

"Time, perhaps, will tell, but it is going to take a long time and a lot of travelling and a lot of listening and seeing. At the end, your correspondent may be sure he knows all about India, but the question will be whether anybody else will agree with him."

A particular knowledge and a generalized ignorance was true of Moslems, Hindus, Parsees, Christians—and the British. I stayed almost a year, went all over India on innumerable trips, and learned a great deal, but I am glad to say that I ended with more humility than assurance. There are innumerable foreigners who know more about the United States than I do, for they have traveled all over the country, which I never did. I traveled all over India, which few Indians ever do.

Neither I, nor any Westerner, could hope to feel or think like an Indian. C. R. Rajagopalachari, one of the wisest of all the men I have met in my life, even then an old man and still active in politics in 1971, agreed with me that no individual Indian could embrace in his mind and understanding a knowledge of "All India," as the Congress party and Moslem League people called it. He claimed no special knowledge for himself—although no Hindu (Rajaji was a Brahmin) knew more of his nation than he. "But," he added during one of our many talks, "an Indian has an intuitive understanding, just as the mango tree knows the earth in which it has its roots." (I would argue that only a Hindu could have such a subtle and profound thought—and make real meaning out of it. An American, like myself, grasps the idea intellectually; a Hindu feels it.)

I remember another equally profound remark that the old Brahmin made to me during the long hours when we discussed religion. The Hindu religion—not the Moslem, which derives from the same Judeo-Christian roots as our religions—was what made India seem to me to be so basically different from any Western country. In the villages—India is above all a country of villages—Rajaji said, "Religion is like finding the carbon in the diamond; it is there, but so compressed after thousands of years!"

He conceded that the ignorance of villagers, wherever I went, of the vast country outside of them was real. In Madras Province (Rajagopalachari lived in the capital, Madras) when I went outside the city and questioned peasants, I could find none who knew where Bengal was, or the Punjab, or who remotely grasped the concept of India as a nation.

I visited many villages all around India, only to find that the peasants were not interested in the war being waged—if they had heard about it—nor in Gandhi. The Mahatma was under arrest all the time I was in India. So were Nehru and the other Congress leaders, for they had called for a civil disobedience campaign against the British. It was the height of Gandhi's fame after decades of political and social agitation. One could not find an American, I imagine, who had not heard of Gandhi in the 1940's—but I found any number of Indian villagers who never heard of him in 1942–1943. Yet from what I had read and been told, his appeal was supposed to be to the masses, and especially to the nine out of ten Indians in the rural areas. Congress was fighting the British for independence on behalf of these peasants. Congress was the greatest single force and most important political party in India. My experience, at firsthand, was that only a small percentage of the peasants was educated to the point where they understood or cared for Congress and its aims. The same went for the Moslem League. It annoyed Jinnah very much when I tried to tell him so, yet I doubt if that wily Bombay lawyer ever went to a village in the latter part of his life.

Here is a passage from a despatch I sent to my newspaper on Christmas day, 1942, from the princely state of Cooch Behar in Assam, where I and Preston Grover of the Associated Press spent a week, and where there was an American military air field.

"Here Gandhi and Jinnah are mere names," I wrote. "Pakistan, among those few Moslems who have heard of it, is something vaguely desirable that does not remotely approximate the Moslem League program. I found no one who knew that Gandhi was in jail; none could explain *ahimsa* and *swaraj* (non-violence and independence); none who wanted the British to leave India. . . . They did not know what India was. Not a single inhabitant I questioned knew where Madras was or whether Afghanistan was part of India. Hardly more than one or two men in any village knew that the central government was in Delhi. The war had come vaguely to their ears as a fight between the British and Japanese, but they could not connect it with their own lives."

The Maharani of Cooch Behar, the mother of the young maharajah who became a well-known figure after the war in what is now called the jet set of England and America, was a famous beauty in her youth. Although educated in England and very cosmopolitan, she still believed in astrology and other Hindu teachings. She persuaded me to let her court astrologer work out my horoscope, which he did—but unfortunately in Sanskrit, beautifully written on a roll of paper six feet long. Someone there gave me a very brief summary in English whose accuracy, I suspect, is dubious. It begins charmingly:

"May all the planets, the stars in their positions, give longevity to the person whose horoscope is written below.

"All other sciences are devoid of value and it is useless to have a difference of opinion on this point. The science of astrology is true, with sun and moon as witness thereof.

"The life of the man who has no horoscope, which illumines his good and bad times like a lamp in the inky darkness of night enveloping a big mansion, is practically shrouded in gloom."

There follows a series of "effects" due, I suppose, to stars or planets. They are confusing because they seem to cancel each other out. The first two, for instance, read as follows:

"*Pansha month:* The person born in Pansha month is lean, confidential, doing good to others, devoid of patrimony and would spend his hard-earned cash and will be very courageous and resourceful.

"*Effect of Masha-rasi:* A person born in Masha-rasi will be not too hairy, philanthropic, interested in neat and sweet things, talkative, not much attached to his household, cruel in looks and weak in brain."

The astrologer was an official, paid by the state. He had been trained at the Sanskrit college in Calcutta. There were a number of colleges teaching astrology, I was told. The holy city of Benares was the chief center. There they used a system that was said to be 2,000 years old, but a new version was drawn up in Indore State 175 years ago. I ended my year in India with a smattering of astrological knowledge, but completely skeptical.

It is one thing to absorb, with wonder and enchantment, the different ways of old India; it is another to try to believe them or accept them. I immersed myself in their world, and have no difficulty in recalling and reliving those times—but it was always a strange world. I am an intellectual snob, but I could never be so foolish as to place my Western "civilization" over their Eastern brand. By the same token, I resented it when Indians looked down on me.

At the turn of the century—and since—Indians were taught by scholars and gurus like Swami Vivekananda that their cultural heritage was superior to the West's, and it was for the "materialistic" West to learn from the "spiritual" East. When Jawaharlal Nehru (then prime minister) was on a visit to the United States and his sister, Mrs. Pandit, was ambassador, they both came to *The New York Times* for lunch. She put forward that superiority thesis, while he nodded agreement. In reality, as I wrote my newspaper when I was in India, "It would be hard to find a more seductive or more misleading generalization." Gandhi, himself —and Nehru even more—owed much to Western education and thought. Their Congress movement always stood for a form of Western democratization and nationalism that was foreign to Indian culture, traditions, and desires. Indians had no political system of their own to put in the place of the West's because their only traditions were the autocratic rule of princes and emperors and the isolated village *panchayats,* or councils. Their caste system, which goes back thousands of years, has rightly been characterized as "the greatest fissiparous force known to politics," and they are now trying to soften the injustices caused by caste. In the cases of the lowest castes, such as the untouchables, the system is inhuman by any standard except the Hindus' who believe in karma and the transmigration of souls. This takes in nearly all Hindus. The American task of accepting the fact that a Negro is as good as a white man and entitled to complete social equality is child's play compared to the vast gulf Indians must cross in obliterating the lines between the "twice-born" higher castes and the "once-born" low castes.

Karma has been called "the most characteristic of all Hindu doctrines." The Oxford dictionary defines it as the "sum of a person's actions in one of his successive states of existence, viewed as deciding his fate in the next." It is more than that. It is the sum and essence of *all* past deeds of a soul in his previous existences that determined his present incarnation and that, by his deeds in this life, will determine his soul's next incarnation. Such a belief, held within a caste system, destroys the concept of human equality. It induces an enervating fatalism, because an individual believes that he has earned his high estate or is being punished for his low estate because of what his soul had done in thousands of previous incarnations.

This fatalism is in process of changing, but it will take generations, if not centuries. The change is taking place among the urban elite with the painfully slow growth of the economy and education and, above all, with the impact of modern ideas from the world outside, especially from the despised West.

Time is pressing, but it is hard for the average Indian to hurry. Scholars say that before Westerners came with their sense of time, the Indian simply could not understand chronology. He was indifferent to the concept of order in the sequence of events. I was often struck by the fact that what seemed like a logical sequence to me was nothing of the sort to my Indian friends.

I got to know two very interesting Presbyterian missionaries who ran an experimental farm in the United Provinces—Dr. Sam

Higginbottom and his wife (she also ran a leper colony), who was a first cousin of Buffalo Bill. The farm was one of the most productive in India, but this was because Dr. Higginbottom eliminated religious (i.e., caste) inhibitions. The couple had been in India for forty years.

"The most consistent characteristic of the Hindu," Dr. Higginbottom said to me, "is his inconsistency. The ability of educated Indians to accept contradictions is extraordinary." For example, his experiences in his rural work, Dr. Higginbottom told me, convinced him that Indians are the most cruel people in the world to animals. If anyone could explain the logical process that leads the Hindu to believe that animals have souls and that the cow, among other animals, is sacred, and at the same time leads him to maltreat those animals, he would have the key to the Indian mind.

On the other hand, I made some true friends in India and met many men and women of the highest human qualities. When an American and a Hindu become friends, I suppose you do have a meeting of East and West. Such a friend was the Maharaj Rana of Dholpur, a relatively small princely state in the Rajputana, south of Delhi. I met him first at Dholpur House in New Delhi through the courtesy of Sir Evelyn and Lady Wrench. The former, who before and after the war was a leading figure in Anglo-American relations, was attached to the viceroy's staff. However, it was during three longish visits to Dholpur State and in other meetings in Delhi, that I came to know and appreciate His Highness (a title extended to all princely rulers).

The Maharaj Rana was the ideal type of monarchical ruler. If the subjects are poor, illiterate, and incapable of understanding or carrying out a democratic system, a benevolent despot is the best solution. Of course, it is wrong by our Western standards and the standards of independent India that the masses should be poor, illiterate, and apolitical. Moreover—a point I often made to Dholpur—while a good king or prince may bring justice and happiness to his people, there is no guarantee that his son and successor will not be cruel and incompetent. If so, he argued, it would mean that the subjects are being punished for sins in previous incarnations—but the monarch is divinely chosen and is therefore the best person for his people.

We were very quickly attracted to each other, which may have been why the Maharaj Rana felt sure that we must have met in a previous incarnation. It was a charming idea, even if I could not believe it. My sojourns in Dholpur State were not only pleasant—they were invaluable in teaching me how an orthodox Hindu believed and felt. He was a representative of old India, but he was exceptional in the extremes to which he carried his beliefs. The present sophisticated, educated rulers of India have, rightly, abolished princely rule and no longer accept the orthodox tenets of the Hindu socio-religious system. Dholpur, although of a very high caste and a maharajah, was more in tune with the immense mass of Indian peasants and artisans than, for instance, Cambridge-trained Jawaharlal Nehru.

All the ancient beliefs—caste, transmigration, astrology, the influence of gems on individuals, the sacredness of the cow (Dholpur, incidentally, was so kind to animals that I saw hyenas come up to him to be fed)—were accepted by him unquestionably, as a matter of course. He believed in the virtue of suttee—the immolation of a widow when her husband dies—although he naturally did not encourage it. Suttee had been illegal in India for a century, but the Maharaj Rana's mother committed suttee when his father died, not on his funeral pyre, but by poison after a touching farewell to her children. He was six and a half years old at the time, but it clearly left a burning impression on his mind. The account he gave me, after we became friends, was very moving. We Americans would say that the poor woman committed suicide, which was a tragedy and even a crime for one in good health with young children. For an old-fashioned, orthodox Hindu like the Maharaj Rana, it was a deed of the highest virtue. He used to send me Christmas cards after the war, always with some motto that he coined. I have one in which the saying is: "Faith defeats reason." This, I would say, is what happened over his mother's death, but he would have said that it was faith *and* reason.

We corresponded with each other for years until he died. His name, incidentally, was Sir Udaibhan Singh Lokindra Bahadur. He signed his letters "Udaibhan" followed by a little indecipherable squiggle. I believe that one of the letters he wrote me will give a better idea of the kind of man he was than anything I can say about him. It will also give an idea of Hindu thought. This one was written from Kesarbagh Palace, one of his five palaces in Dholpur, on October 9, 1945. I leave his sometimes quaint English as he wrote it. The Maharaj Rana was not, like so many Indian princes, educated in England.

"Many thanks for your letter. It was a most pleasant surprise for me. Of course, I did not for a moment think that you forget friends or that this terrible war, which has so callously robbed the world of so many precious young lives, had harmed you, but what I did think was that you were so busily occupied with your work that you were literally tied to your duties. . . .

"I, sometimes, feel quite depressed when I look at the picture of my species of today and tomorrow, because I feel we are falsely attempting to focus and aim the entire outlook of mankind, unaided and uninfluenced by religious humanity, which will alone spiritualise our future existence for a happier and more peaceful world.

"The Almighty's designs are always mysterious and it may be that the chapter of suffering is not yet finished for man and, therefore, He will direct evolution according to His own scheme to further tutor us in His own way. . . .

"Many thanks for the good wishes on the marriage of my daughter to His Highness of Nabha. He is such a nice lad and carries with him the rare combination of the real goodness of head and heart. I am glad to say they are both happy and he has been an angel to my child. When you visit us again, I shall have the great pleasure of introducing him to you. I am sure you will like him. Yes, the actual event was the successful termination of a great responsibility of a father, but the mental effect on me was extremely trying.

"We get very attached to our pet animals and birds and keenly feel separation from them but, in this case, the prospect of separation was not from a pet animal but, from the live spark of the father's own soul, the beloved daughter-child, who had been literally nursed in my arms almost from her birth. This trying thought of separation haunted me morning, mid-day and evening and I just could not shake it off. It is true, I had my State work to occupy my mind for certain periods of the day coupled with the whole marriage programme, the details of which had to be as best as could be managed under war circumstances. It also included so many religious ceremonies, their most auspicious planetary timings and so on.

"While we laboriously worked for the complete success of this great event, I could not get rid of a gnawing feeling in my heart that all this sweating effort, glamour, splendour and show was going to mean dazzling celebrations for the populace but to me a grim reality of the separation of father and daughter-child and that one day, soon, the important final ceremony will be performed, when I shall beckon to her future husband that, until now, I have been this virgin child's friend, companion, tutor, guardian and all else as a father and, from now onwards during the whole of the life-span, you carry this great responsibility as a husband and, then, I would hold her little hand in mine for the last time and put it in his hand and, then, demand a promise over the eternal fires of the world that he will vouchsafe to be an ideal husband. . . .

"As the days passed on, one after another, I was frantically trying to build up my courage to face the event boldly, aided by profound philosophies that all connections and relations in this world are really meant by Him to be of transitory natures and, even, the much cared for body of a being is designed to companion the undying Soul for the short span of human life only, so why worry?

"With this philosophy, I gradually started hardening the soft regions of the human heart and, thus, gathered courage up to a point when news came that the marriage of Her Highness's [his wife's] nephew, cousin of my daughter, was to come off that week, and all my family had to go to my father-in-law's to attend. I was left quite alone with my anxiety, State work and the same marriage programme as my only companions. The same defeated pessimism wrecked my mind's courage once again and even the philosophy aided me but little. I tried to divert my mind amid my pet birds and animals in my house and in the jungle but that scheme, too, did not help me as I had expected, as it was my daughter who completed the picture as she had been my constant comrade in the humane ministrations of, and in the affectionate treatment and feelings for those tongueless friends of ours, and as I tended on them, her innocent sincere figure imperceptibly crept into the mental picture of mine and it really seemed I could hear her soundless speech to say, 'Daddy, you will be kind and look after our little pets when I am gone.'

"As days rolled on, I got more and more miserable mentally and, then, another idea struck me and that was to attempt to write an exhaustive essay on the fundamentals of Sanatan Hindu philosophy and culture in response to a very long-standing request of so many friends of mine within and without India. So, I started and, now, you will be surprised to hear as much as I am, that those essays have developed into a book which may be published soon. . . .

"I am sending you a portion that I tried to explain to you the age-long faith in Transmigration of Souls. This belief has lived virtually in Hindu India for an unknown period and has provided most logical, understandable, and above all, satisfying answer to *life* in His vast Creation."

The last letter of Dholpur that I kept was written five years later, on October 23, 1950. He was discouraged and pessimistic.

"But such a feeling," he wrote, "I think is greatly influenced by my not being able to catch up with so many new changes of the modern progressing world marching so rapidly with long steps on the material plane on the one hand, and as rapidly forgetting the valuable spiritual side of humanity, with a sneaking fear that such a spiritual loss may mean definite lowering of the elevated position of mankind and who knows, even a tragic suicide of the prized soul. Because in spite of wonderful hourly discoveries of science I cannot gather courage to believe that man will profitably thrive aided only by wonderful but lifeless machines and then be able to possess the elevated human conscience, rich in morals and ethics—the real mother of a happy world. . . .''

Before I left India in 1943, the Maharaj Rana had written me a farewell letter in which he said:

"I hope, wherever you may be, you will carry with you the memory of her children here, who are different, with their own peculiarities of deep religious faith and various customs and ways, but entirely friendly, fruitful and humane in every sense of the word.

"Of this I am sure, that when you do return to my beloved country again, you will find India keeping up her never-forgotten traditions of kindness and hospitality to all her friends."

Now, in the 1950 letter, he was sadly writing: "I am certain if you came out you would not recognise the India you saw and knew. . . . I hope destiny will again work out a mysterious scheme for us to meet again and talk about so many things as of old."

We were not destined to meet again. He died of heart failure on October 28, 1954.

For his sake I hope he was right about the transmigration of souls. I never let on to him that I was an agnostic and did not believe in an afterlife, as it would have grieved him. I said to him once, "But, your Highness, you have such an exalted state now, what more can you achieve in another incarnation?" "Perhaps," he said wistfully, "the Creator will say: 'This prince has been a good ruler,' and he will give me a larger state in my next sojourn on earth."

I was under no illusions about the Maharaj Rana of Dholpur being a characteristic Indian prince. I met many of them, good, bad, and indifferent. To counterbalance the picture I have given of Dholpur, I should tell about another prince who was an extreme, but not atypical example, historically speaking, of the bad prince. I heard a great deal about him in India from unimpeachable sources, including some who had known him. He was the Maharajah of Alwar.

The first man to tell me about Alwar was Colonel W. F. Campbell, the resident for Central India, in the princely state of Indore. One of Alwar's wives was having a baby, which he wanted very much to be a boy. When it turned out to be a girl he beat his wife to death. On another occasion, a wife of his was reported to have fallen out of her palace window and been killed. Upon investigation it was found that she had been shot in the back of her head—undoubtedly under his orders. However, he made a great show of grief and had the palace pulled down to the ground. Once he beat to death a polo pony who displeased him.

Alwar always wore gloves, so as not to contaminate his hands in shaking hands with white people or lower castes. Once, in England, Lord Birkenhead was giving a dinner party, and when he invited Alwar he said: "Now, these are going to be all nice English people. Do be a good fellow, and leave off your gloves for once." To his surprise, Alwar agreed, and when he arrived —late, as always, to show how mighty he was—he came in without gloves and graciously shook hands with everybody. However, when the time came for dinner he had disappeared and Birkenhead looked around for him. Finally, in came Alwar, rubbing his hands. "All right, Lord Birkenhead, we can eat now," he said. "I have washed my hands."

He was repaid very well once by a brother-in-law of Colonel Campbell's who was resident or political agent in Kashmir. There was a garden party at which Alwar was expected, and the Englishman knew just what would happen. Alwar, as always, showed up three-quarters of an hour late and with his gloves on. He walked up cordially to the brother-in-law, with his hand outstretched. "Good afternoon, Mr. Blank." The Englishman stepped back a few paces, and called out: "Chaprassi!" An attendant who had been instructed in advance solemnly walked up with a pair of gloves on a platter. The Englishman put them on, quite deliberately. Then he put out his hand. "Good afternoon, Your Highness." Alwar never spoke to him again.

Once, when Alwar was traveling in Europe, a distracted cable was received at the Colonial Office, telling about Alwar in Austria. The Maharajah was to travel from one city to another, and hired an entire private railway car. However, before he would enter it, he sent his servants inside and ordered them to tear off every bit of leather—and it was covered with leather. As a devout Hindu, he felt that he could not touch cow leather.

Among his other sins, Alwar was outrageous in the amount of the state's revenue that he appropriated for his personal use— forty out of forty-five lakhs of rupees, I was told. (A lakh is 100,000; the rupee was then worth about three to the dollar.) Everyone who spoke to me about him agreed that he had a brilliant mind and was a superb athlete. The Maharaja of Kapurthala told me that Alwar's sharp tongue kept his fellow princes in "deadly fear," and that he used to make them writhe in their seats at meetings of the Chamber of Princes.

Alwar died in London shortly before World War II by falling downstairs. *Sic transit!*

When Dholpur wrote me about his daughter marrying the young Maharajah of Nabha, the name struck a bell.

"The late Maharaja of Nabha," I wrote in my notes on a visit to Lahore in the Punjab, "was another of the wicked princes, finally deposed and banished to the south, where he died. The Maharajah of Kapurthala told me of one case where Nabha coveted the wife of a prominent Sikh official. When the Sikh objected, Nabha had entirely false charges trumped up against him and had him sentenced to seven years solitary confinement. Another man, also falsely imprisoned by Nabha, told His Excellency that what he disliked most was being hung by the heels from the ceiling, and snakes and scorpions being thrown on the floor. H.E., just wanting to make conversation, said to him: 'Well, perhaps they just wandered in.' 'But did you ever see a snake come into a room backwards?' the man asked."

It was unusual for the British raj to take action against princes, no matter how badly they behaved. Alwar was never touched, although he was a monster. The British wanted no trouble, and they tried to disturb Indian life as little as possible so as to be undisturbed themselves. Throughout pre-British Indian history, the law of the jungle and of survival led to wicked rulers being killed in palace revolutions or driven out of power by their subjects or neighbors. After the British gained complete control of the subcontinent, they froze the map, leaving princely states scattered all over as in a patchwork quilt. They gave legal territorial rights to the princes that guaranteed their tenure and legitimacy for their descendants. Tyranny, cruelty, mismanagement, corruption were accepted unless they got too monstrous and, especially, too notorious. Then the prince would be deposed and the next in the legitimate family line installed on the throne.

The Congress party and—when it split on the Hindu-Mohammedan issue—the Moslem League rightly fought against this anachronism. Independence would mean an end of princely rule. However, there was not going to be any independence while World War II was in progress. This was the most obvious sort of logic to the British, who were literally fighting for their existence. Even the Americans, although carrying out President Roosevelt's anticolonial policies, much to the irritation of the British, conceded this necessity.

The Indians could not see this. The war was not their war. They had not been consulted when India was declared a belligerent. Gandhi said that he would have let the Japanese into India and then opposed them with "passive disobedience." The princes supported the British for obvious reasons. So did Mohammed Ali Jinnah, who told me once that he had no intention of substituting the British raj for a Hindu raj.

My despatches to *The New York Times* were full of the communal strife, which pro-Congress sympathizers in the United States denounced as exaggerated. The Jinnah concept of Pakistan, later carried into a reality, was obviously a monstrosity—two territories separated by 1,000 miles of India, similar only in being Mohammedan in religion. Not wholly separated, of course, for there are today many Hindus in Pakistan and many Moslems in India, which likes to consider itself as a multireligious nation. It is so, up to a point, but for practical purposes India is a Hindu nation. And within each of the countries, the two communities are forever segregated by the inescapable dogmas of their religious practices and beliefs. No Moslem, for instance, can be related by blood ties to a Hindu. If a malevolent deity had set out to make two communities of men as different as human beings could be, he would have made them Hindus and Moslems. Some day, we in the United States will achieve desegregation; this is inconceivable, ever, in India and Pakistan.

The wheel of Indian life, as I said before, turns on the hub of religion. However sophisticated politics and politicians get to be in India and Pakistan, this cannot change. Religion and politics are one; so are religion and business, religion and society, not just in the Western sense of a politician or businessman being religious.

I heard a great many stories in India about religious differences, and told a number of them in my *Education of a Correspondent.* Here is another and characteristic one, related to me by the Anglican bishop of Lahore.

He told me of an Englishman who came to see him a few days before I saw the prelate with a troubled conscience and a remarkable story. There was a Hindu doctor in a Punjab village who was continually insulting the Moslem religion and even named his donkey "*Allah.*" It was decided in the neighborhood that he must be killed.

The Englishman lived in a neighboring village, and had a young Moslem for a friend, a gentle lad, who had just graduated from college and was studying for some profession. The Englishman was going to Kashmir for a month's vacation, and the Moslem approached him, begging earnestly that he take him along, but it was not possible, so he went off.

Two days later the young Moslem went to the neighboring village, killed the Hindu doctor and gave himself up, explaining that, of course, this man was not fit to live. The instigation had come from relatives of the young man who lived in Delhi and agreed with the neighbors that the Hindu must die, so they called the youth down and told him to do it. After a protracted trial of a year (murder trials last long, and the man is usually let off, which is a great incentive to murder, said the bishop) the youth was hanged.

Gandhi, in a well-known phrase, referred to "the religious use of politics," which was an interesting way of twisting what we would call "the political use of religion." A foreigner, trying to understand Gandhi—and this was a very important journalistic task for me—really had to go "through the looking-glass" into a different world. Where, for instance, Machiavellian Westerners would say, "the end justifies the means," Gandhi said: "Means and ends are convertible terms in my philosophy of life."

In February 1943 Gandhi, who was then a political prisoner of the British, announced that he was going on "a fast to capacity" unless the British gave him his unconditional release. Lord Linlithgow, the viceroy—and any Westerner—had to say that Gandhi had no legal right to make such a demand. Emotional Hindus could see only his greatness and holiness, and that to allow him to die would be the greatest of sins—and hence, utterly unjust. The British were saying that the Indians were wrong because they did not see the plain logic of the situation, but the Indians said that the logic was wrong. Had Gandhi died, India would have suffered a profound—and doubtless violent— upheaval. "Two men with iron wills [Gandhi and Linlithgow] have been facing each other across the unbridgeable gap between East and West," I cabled *The Times.* There was no meeting place. One of them had to give in—and it was Gandhi who humiliatingly ended his fast, having kept himself for weeks, by an extraordinary control of his body, on the precipice of death. He wanted to live, and at the most critical moment switched from sour to sweet lime juice.

Sad to relate—as the United States and Europe had to learn in recent years—the only effective Indian reaction against the

British was violence, not civil disobedience. Gandhi deplored violence, but called for policies that experience had shown would lead to violence. V. D. Savarkar, head of the right-wing Hindu Mahasabha, reduced Gandhi's fast to absurdity by asking: "What would happen if Churchill fasted against Hitler?" Churchill had a characteristic description of *ahimsa*—civil disobedience: "It's plural and it bounces."

Gandhi unhappily realized that he, alone, could not gain India her freedom. "A teaspoonful of water given to a thirsty man cannot quench his thirst," he said to a friend during his fast. "It would be a different matter if a lakh [100,000] of people fasted." But there was only one Gandhi.

When I was in India during the war, there were a little under 400,000,000 inhabitants in the whole subcontinent. No more than 600 Britons were left in 1942–1943 in the wonderful Indian civil service. These were respected, liked, marvelously trained, dedicated; a great many felt a deep affection for India. But they kept apart, had their own clubs, made their own social contacts. Most Indians resented this genuine segregation. Yet I dined in the homes of Brahmins and other high-caste Hindus where the host (a few times it would be his old-fashioned parents) would eat in another room, or at least, at another table, because my presence and my using their plates and utensils were contaminating to them. More often, I was irritated by Indian servility and obsequiousness when I felt no superiority whatever and wanted to be treated as an equal.

The British were always aliens in India. The Nawab of the Moslem state of Bhopal in northwestern India, Haji Muhammad Hamidulla Khan, was like a Westerner in many ways—English-educated and one of the world's greatest polo players when I met him. "The British have never become one with us," he said to me. "If I went to your house in the United States, I would try to live with you as you live, but if a Britisher comes here, he must live as a Britisher, never as an Indian sleeping in our type of bed and eating our food at hours we eat it."

The Nawab was asking too much, but he touched a sore point. Even after three centuries of occupation, India was, in Kipling's phrase, "an alien land" to the British. I did not see how it could have been otherwise, although I condemned the calculated British policy of segregation, their exclusiveness, their feeling of superiority. Exclusivity had long ago become snobbishness, not an instrument of law and order.

Ralph Waldo Emerson wrote that the Englishman "sticks to his traditions and usages, and so help him God! he will force his island by-laws down the throat of great countries like India, China, Canada, Australia." I was hearing the swan song of that historic Englishman when I was in India.

When Edward, the Prince of Wales, visited Delhi in 1921 and stayed with the viceroy, he said, "At last I have seen how royalty lives!"

I learned for myself at my first luncheon at the Viceroy's House in New Delhi. It can be taken as typical. I was there on September 22, 1942, with four other guests, Sir Mohammad Usman, Sir Jwala Prasad Srivastava, and the Commissioner of Delhi, A. V. Askwith, and his wife. The formality was complete from beginning to end. An Indian officer checked his list as our car arrived at the inside gate, and then we drove to the main entrance, where many flunkies stood waiting. From there we were ushered into the air-cooled drawing room, which seemed like an icebox, but when someone looked at the temperature it was seventy-six.

Cocktails and talk as the various guests arrived, with three A.D.C.'s doing the honors. The two daughters came in, Lady Joan Hope and Lady Doreen Hope. At 1:04 the guests were lined up at right angles to the main door, and at 1:05 His Excellency came in, followed by Her Excellency. They passed down the line shaking hands, and Mrs. Askwith curtseying, and then they went straight on to the dining room where they sat down opposite each other in the middle of the long table. We walked in later, having been carefully shown in advance by an A.D.C. where our seats were. There were printed cards, with the Linlithgow crest, for that matter.

Luncheon was studiedly simple as to contents, but overwhelming as to service—nine footmen for eleven people. The service, however, was human enough to have forgotten to give me a plate for my food, which almost resulted in a catastrophe when I started to serve myself with a piece of chicken dripping with gravy. We had chicken, potatoes, green vegetables, salad, tipsy pudding, cheese, melon, coffee. Then cigarettes and Indian cigars with bands bearing the Linlithgow crest, which did not make them taste any better.

Their Excellencies then rose and went back to the drawing room. His Excellency went off to the opposite corner and sat down on a sofa. Her Excellency took a sofa in the middle of the room, facing the garden. Lady Joan sat on one with its back to her mother's, and Lady Doreen had the corner by the dining room. We stood around awkwardly for a few minutes while the A.D.C.'s whispered to Their Excellencies. Finally, one went up to Srivastava and said that H.E. would like to speak to him. Another went to Usman and said Her E. would speak with him. He, incidentally, was a perfect slug, a tub of guts, billowing like sails in his long garments, and most sycophantic. He was quite deprecatory about his pro-government motion in the Council that morning, and made fun of his opponents. I was told that Lady Joan would speak with me, so I joined her and was just about getting acquainted, when an A.D.C. walked up and we went through the formula again. It was the viceroy who wanted to speak with me. In my five minutes with him he said that I had not been there long enough for him to have a really good conversation with me about the Indian situation. He said he felt he had come to know India better in these last two years than in the previous five of his term. Again he said I must see village life and see how completely indifferent the people are to politics. "Don't get taken in by Indians who take you to a village they have worked over," he said. "Pick your own."

As my five minutes ended, Usman came up and H.E. said to him: "Isn't it true that the village people pay no attention to politics?" Usman goggled and said eagerly, "Yes, yes. We can't solve our problems until we get a communal settlement." I was then handed over to Her Excellency, who was as tall and big as her husband, with a charming face and grey hair, quite distinguished. She said that she always warned Americans against Gandhi who, in her opinion, was an insincere politician. She saw

Louis Fischer after his week with Gandhi and found him sold, but said that if people were warned in advance and were on their guards, they weren't taken in. That ended our five minutes but she asked whether I would come up to her bureau for a talk.

They marched out, he first, after receiving thanks and curtseys, and in a minute an A.D.C. came to usher me up to Her Excellency's study, which was a marvelous, big room, overlooking immense grounds with the Friday Mosque off in the distance. I was there an hour. More talk about politics, Gandhi, Washington. She said that she asked her husband a few days before what the British had done to merit Indian distrust. He answered: "I know India better than any living man, and I have searched my mind for the slightest case in which we have betrayed our word, but I cannot find a single case." The conclusion was that Gandhi and other political leaders fostered the distrust.

More politics and some gossip, including a current scandal about the Maharajah of Indore running off with the American wife of a British officer. Her Excellency said that at the beginning of the war H.E. saw Gandhi and wrote to her: "You will appreciate my feelings when I tell you that he said he saw eye to eye with the British and would do what he could to help win the war. Then Gandhi went off to a meeting of the Congress Working Committee where it was decided that India had not been consulted. Gandhi said he could not control the Working Committee!"

I am sure that luncheons at Buckingham Palace would have been far less ceremonious than they were at the Viceroy's House. Naturally, it was a deliberate show to impress Indians. When my wife and I dined with the Linlithgows at their home in London after the war, during the austerity period, nothing could have been simpler or more easy-going. A cook prepared a modest meal and we served ourselves.

One reason for viceregal ceremony and splendor was that the British Crown's representative had to compete with the magnificence of a great many Indian princes. The stories of princely

extravagances were legion and I heard many. Here is a typical
—and true—one told to me in Hyderabad.

The Nizam's father was a lordly spendthrift. His son, whom
I met, was a pathological miser. The Parsi businessman, Canar
Tyabjee, told me at lunch one day about a visit the late Nizam
paid to the Army and Navy Store in Bombay. The whole
managerial staff turned out. He walked through the aisles, now
and then waving his cane in some direction. Finally, he returned
to his car, and the unhappy managers saw him drive away, thinking that the biggest order of the year had failed them. Then they
learned that every time he waved his cane, he meant, "get me
those things"—and that meant hundreds of hats, a whole department, or an entire section full of cigars, cigarettes, and
tobacco.

When the automobile came into use, a salesman was sent over
to Hyderabad to try to interest the Nizam. For two months he
was a state guest in the Rest House, living on the fat of the land.
Finally, he was allowed to see the Nizam. "What is this new
contraption you are talking about?" His Exalted Highness
asked. The salesman explained that it was a coach which ran
without horses. The Nizam was intrigued. "I will take a dozen,"
he said.

The British raj was a huge mechanism, which was creaking
toward a breakdown but kept functioning during my year in
India. It was a grave period for the British and a ticklish one for
the Americans who had a large air force in India but whose
policies were anticolonial and pro-Indian. The British had been
losing the war in Southeast Asia and had been driven out of
Burma just before I arrived in 1942. "We got run out of Burma
and it is as humiliating as hell," Vinegar Joe Stilwell, the American commander, said angrily.

It was at that moment that Gandhi, Nehru, and Co. called for
a civil disobedience campaign. The government naturally
clamped down and jailed almost all Congress leaders on August
10, 1942. It was a grim, bitter business.

The many thousands of American soldiers, stationed in India,
remained outside the struggle and were unmolested. The moment an Indian learned that I was an American and not a Brit-

isher, suspicion and resentment would fall away. There was a decided coolness between Americans and Britons there, which was a reflection of conflicting policies. "Resentment is growing," Linlithgow said bitterly to me one day. "The United States' policy of Asia to the Asiatics is going to reap a whirlwind some day." (How ironical that remark seems today when we forgot the sound policy of Asia for the Asians and went into Indo-China!)

General Wavell (who later, as Lord Wavell, became viceroy) was especially angry. Americans, he said, are "letting their hearts get the better of their brains. They should realize that the British have had long experience in India and are honorable men trying to do the best thing. It is easy to sit in chairs 12,000 miles away and tell the British how to run India. Give us credit for knowing what we are doing. How could we turn this country over to Gandhi and Nehru, who have shown that the question of defense is at best secondary?"

I was unsympathetic and critical of the British at the time—more so, of course, in my notes, which were personal and opinionated, than in my despatches, which had to be as objective as possible. I stress the words, "as possible." Naturally, I could not be completely objective; no human being could have been in such a situation, but I ended up with the Indians accusing me of being pro-British, and the British accusing me of being pro-Indian, which was as it should have been. I was always treated with the greatest courtesy and friendliness by Britons, Hindus, and Moslems.

A correspondent in India at any time struggles with the handicap of trying to understand a totally foreign Hindu viewpoint and expressing that viewpoint in a foreign language so that readers will comprehend who do not have even his modicum of understanding. Nothing and no place was typical of India as a whole. When Gandhi wanted to pick a spot to settle down, he chose the geographical center of India—Sevagram, just outside of Wardha. In no other way could he get a symbolical place for his ashram (his religious community) that would be representative of India as a whole.

I once quoted a Sikh villager in the Punjab who, when I asked what he thought about freedom, said: "A belly filled with good food and a safe job. We don't care who runs the Government." This is what the British used to say in arguments with me. If the Indian peasants, nine-tenths of the population, were satisfied with their lot in life, why stir them up with incomprehensible ideas about independence? It is true that I generally encountered what has been called "pathetic contentment," but human beings should not be asked to live in the dire poverty, squalor, and ignorance that was the lot of most Indians. (Unhappily, the situation has improved very little after twenty-four years of independence.)

Another simplification is to turn to the religious tenets of Hinduism, especially metempsychosis and the caste system, and say that since this is what Indians believe, they should be allowed to live the life that they accept. It is true that the Hindu ideal has never been our passionate search for release from the cares of existence on earth. Its philosophy is a fatalistic acceptance; its goal is Nirvana where there is perfect peace, complete stillness and inactivity, where the weary round of countless incarnations ends at last—in nothingness.

"In those villages where nine out of ten Indians live and cultivate land, you find a stolid, stubborn conservativeness which still resists the impact of the West," I wrote in one of my last despatches. "It is breaking down slowly but surely, but generations of education lie ahead before the villager can play his part in an enlightened, representative government. The Hindu religion, so tolerant, so beautiful in many of its aspects, is not designed for the modern rough-and-tumble world."

One generation has passed since I wrote that Hindu India has made a little progress, but it is still true that generations must pass before a majority of Indians are educated; before the standard of living for most is raised above the poverty level; before the cruel injustices of the caste system are worn down; before a national conscience is developed among all Indians.

One can say the same for Pakistan, except that Moslems do not have the burden of the caste system. Yet, one must now add that the Moslems have something more murderous—the racial hatred of the Moslem West Pakistanis and Bengalis for each other, in addition to the abiding hatred of Moslem Bengali for Hindu Bengali. East Pakistan, at best, was one of the most hopeless and poverty-stricken regions of the world. Its concededly violent movement for independence led to an appalling reaction by an avenging West Pakistani army sent in by General Yahya Khan in May 1971. The exodus of millions of Bengalis into India and the slaughter of uncounted thousands of Bengalis led to a human tragedy whose awful scale has had few parallels in our tortured century.

The dream of those who had hoped to found a viable Moslem nation of two equal regions has gone beyond repair. The West Pakistanis have killed and devastated to such an extent that much of East Bengal will be a colonial wasteland for decades. A new area of instability and danger, comparable to the Middle East, has been created in Asia.

Although intractable problems were foreseeable during the world war, they were not a justification for withholding independence after the peace. The British saw the inescapable realities quickly enough, granting independence two years after the war ended. President Roosevelt's anticolonialism was right, but it was premature. The first task was to win the war. The assurances to me of Hindus and Moslems by the dozens, that if the British would only grant independence all of India's problems would quickly be solved, were even more premature. Freedom simply transferred the problems from the British raj to the Indians and Pakistanis. The generation of Hindus that won independence is now old and reactionary; a young generation is waiting to take over and build on the ancient structure of traditional India—but they will only be able to make a start.

I wrote a last note before leaving: "India, for the Westerner, is either to be shut out, as the British do, living their lives as nearly as possible to life in England, or it must be fought, almost physically. You must fight through its horrors of climate and disease, of ignorance and filth; its swarming people whom you can never understand and who can never understand you. Your intelligence tells you that at the core of things is much that is fine and patient and wise—only you must search for it, and to a Westerner that search is only too often a weary, bewildering task. The Indian finds it so easily because to him the impediments either do not exist, or he cares nothing about them, or ascribes them to fate and not neglect."

I have not been back to India since that day—July 5, 1943—but I have read much; talked to many Indian and Pakistani visitors to London and New York; covered for my newspaper the British side of granting independence to India in 1947; and followed with horror the Hindu-Moslem slaughter that accompanied the birth pangs of Pakistan and the devastation of East Bengal in 1971. Much of it had been foreshadowed in my despatches to *The New York Times* and in my notes.

More than a quarter of a century later, I feel sure that if I went back for another year, I would sum up my impressions of India, at least, in much the same words as I did in 1943. The surface of old India has changed; the princely states have gone and their rulers are deprived of power; and "India" is independent. Yet India—without the quotation marks—I am certain, cannot have changed in any fundamental way. Gandhi, Nehru, Jinnah, Linlithgow, Churchill are dead, along with so many of the Indian and British leaders whom I got to know. The British, under Prime Minister Attlee and the Labor party, cut the Gordian knot and so found their answer, but the Indians—Hindu and Moslem —cannot run away from themselves.

Their numbers, already enormous in 1942–1943, continue to grow. Now there are more than 530 million people in India, alone, plus about 110 million in Pakistan.

I went away, as the British did later. In my case, it was a transfer to the North African and Italian war fronts which, in its journalistic way, cut a Gordian knot for me. Professionally, India was one of the most fascinating and difficult assignments of my career, but it aroused no partisan feelings. I was mildly pro-Indian, since they were the underdogs and were striving for freedom, but I was also mildly pro-British for I could see their point of view.

Yet India did touch my emotions, and deeply. It was many bad and ugly things, but there was so much more that was sad and fine and beautiful. I do not want to end on a carping note. Come with me, so to speak, to one of innumerable lovely spots I visited

—an out-of-the-way place, not a storied wonder like the breath-taking Taj Mahal, or the three lovely pleasure gardens in Kashmir, which the same Jehangir built for his Empress Nur Jehan, "Light of the World." The loveliest of these is Shalimar, whose fame has spread, in poetry and song, over the world.

October 9, 1942, JAIPUR.

"Visited Amber at sundown with Da Costa, the Premier's secretary, and another official named Achariar. It is a dead and lovely city, up on a hill outside the first pass where tigers roam at night and the still waters reflect the marble palace hundreds of feet above. The path goes by a rose bush and by the now barren gardens where once the water cascaded, and then up the steep side of the hill through Mogul gates into the lower square.

"The palace, on its northern side, hangs over the square and is reached by a massive flight of steps. And then all is marble and red stone, intricate arches and halls with thousands of mirrors. The workmanship is exquisite, particularly on the cream-white marble—complicated railings cut from one block, and delicate flowers that are as fine as gems.

"The best thing was the peace and quiet and deadness, amidst so much beauty and in a world where there is no peace. It was sunset, and a man sitting lazily in the minaret of the temple over the square clashed his cymbals together as if to call the ghosts of Amber to evening devotion. The sound followed us down the hill where the gate-keeper, as we walked out, gave each of us a rose. For nine hundred years visitors leaving Amber have been given a rose.

"As we drove away, Da Costa pointed out Jaigarh—the big fort which surmounted the city, and where we had not time to go. Hundreds of years ago, the Maharajah had placed a great treasure in the fort, to be used only when the State was in grave danger. For two hundred years it has not been touched. No one may go in it except the Maharajah, and then only once on ascending the throne, and he must go alone.

"That is India."

Chapter 6

GREAT BRITAIN

It was "farewell to arms" when I went to London in June 1945, to head *The New York Times'* bureau. My war corresponding days were over, not by choice but—as I was told when the Korean War started in 1950—because I was too old. I had been told that before, in 1944 during the Italian campaign, when I was forty-four and had volunteered for a parachute drop into northern Italy behind the German lines. It was Tex McCrary, public relations officer for the Fifth Army, who dismissed me as decrepit. It would have been a good story, and I wasn't really too old.

War corresponding is a vicarious pleasure, I suppose. It is something like having your cake and eating it. Enjoying the rank of captain in the American army, you escape the training, the discipline, much of the hardships, and some of the danger. You share the comradeship, the thrills, the fulfillment, and, as a journalist, the satisfaction of always getting good stories and sometimes wonderful ones. There is a primitive pleasure involved, too. As I wrote during the Spanish Civil War, "Let him who loves life risk it."

A newspaperman can make no prouder boast than that he has been where danger lay, and seen with his own eyes, and written honestly. This, come to think of it, would make a good epitaph for a journalist.

When I was crossing back to Africa on a troopship in May 1944, to rejoin the Allied army in Italy, I was asked by the editors of the daily news bulletin to write something. The radio room had been unable to capture the usual news broadcast on one day due to atmospheric conditions.

"Old timers like to think that things were tougher in their day," I wrote, "and maybe they were in some respects. We certainly did not have any ships like this to go over on in the First World War, but all these things are relative, and nobody is going to insult your intelligence by trying to tell you how lucky you are. War is a pretty lousy business and the more you see of it the lousier it gets. I feel qualified to speak because this happens to be my fourth war, as I covered the Abyssinian and Spanish Civil Wars, as well as this one, for my newspaper. So I don't like it, either, when people fill me full of too much bunk about glory, democracy and a lot of things that I do not doubt are well worth fighting for, but which I would rather not hear about.

"But just because I have seen men fight on many a battlefield in many parts of the world, I also feel qualified to tell you that you are not going to regret it. There is an awful lot about it that may sound corny to say, but that is real and deep, and believe it or not, you are going to look back on it in later years with regret that these days are gone. Comradeship and danger shared and service done are phrases that may sound sentimental now, but I wouldn't sneer at them too much if I were you, because whether you know it or not, you are appreciating them somewhere inside and they will all come out in the wash some day. . . ."

True enough, but I had had ten straight years of war corresponding and it wears a man's sensibilities down. I will never forget the shock with which I first discovered, in the Sicilian campaign in 1943, that I was bored with war corresponding. There was little zest or romance in the day-to-day coverage. It took a really big story—the landing at Salerno, the taking of Naples, Rome, Siena, Florence, Marseilles—to arouse my enthusiasm.

One gets a little more cautious, a little more careful as the weeks and months and years pass. Only the biggest stories get to be worth big risks. One feels more and more that his luck cannot hold out forever. In earlier days it was only the other fellow who was going to be hit. By 1945 many of the old colleagues were gone—Eddy Neil, Byron Darnton, Robert Post, Tom Treanor, Ben Robertson, Ray Clapper, Ernie Pyle—and others.

Some war correspondents are killed, and if they aren't they grow old and descend to writing about politics, economics, foreign affairs, coal strikes, herring fishing, and Princess Elizabeth marrying Lieut. Philip Mountbatten in Westminster Abbey in November 1947.

London was *The New York Times'* biggest and most important foreign post, and this time I needed no coaxing from Arthur Sulzberger to go there.

During my childhood in New York City, as the century was beginning, the British had been in disfavor. We not only learned from our schoolbooks how the American colonies won their independence from the wicked tyrants who tried to tax them without representation, but there was a pervading atmosphere of hostility in New York created by the recent wave of Irish immigration.

I was not to see England until World War I, and then very briefly. I have only vague memories of the transit camp on Salisbury Plain in 1918 when I went through with my Tank Corps unit. I remember hearing about the Anzacs (Australian and New Zealand troops) and how rough and tough and unruly they were. The memory came back to me in Canberra, Australia, on Anzac Day in 1970 when some poor old crocks marched up to the war memorial. They reminded me of the Civil War veterans I used to watch parading down Fifth Avenue in New York on Memorial Day, fewer and feebler each year. Not for me!

I remember something else at that camp on Salisbury Plain because of the shock it gave to the boy of eighteen that I was. A few of us Americans were in the canteen drinking with some limeys. They were veterans who had been back on leave. Their language was such as I had not heard before, and they were boasting about having shot in the back and killed the son of Harry Lauder, the famous Scottish comedian whose name was a byword in those times. I had heard Harry Lauder often in my teens in New York when he appeared in vaudeville. His song, "A-roamin' in the gloamin'" still sounds in my ears. Not the Germans, but his own men had shot Captain Lauder during battle because, they said, he was mean and they hated him. Later, in other wars, I learned that such things do happen. There is no easier way to get rid of the sergeant or captain who is insufferable. But one does not boast about it in public. I believed the Lauder story, although it may not have been true. I think I was so shocked because I learned that life can be cheap.

My next sojourn in Britain was in 1926 when I went to London to finish a year abroad on a Columbia University Bayard Cutting Taylor fellowship.

I had to read later about the general strike of May 4–12, 1926, although I went to London for a few months soon after it. While I was there, I showed no curiosity about what happened, or why. I suppose it is a commonplace in anybody's life that one gets interested in subjects if there is a reason to be interested, or if the subject is already familiar. The general strike was a great and dramatic event, although, surprisingly, it had little long-range effect on industry, wages, prices, or social welfare. It did leave a long-smouldering bitterness among workers. In a curious way the strike seemed to act as a release from years of tension, unrest, and even possible revolution. It was an end, not a beginning—an end of extremism.

The hopes of a better world—"an age which is brightening," as Woodrow Wilson put it in a speech he made in Manchester in December 1918—were to prove illusory. The war had, however, brought new strength to the Labor movement, a new program, new leaders, and great new labor federations like the Transport and General Workers' Union which Ernest Bevin created in 1921.

An unhealthy postwar speculative boom began to collapse in the spring of 1920. Workers were discouraged by inflation, bankruptcies, unemployment, and unsuccessful strikes. The high, chronic rate of idleness at first brought the apathy of misery, but in time built discontent and unrest up to potentially explosive levels. At all times from 1919 onward, the threat of a general strike was in the air.

The first Labor party government in British history came in with the general election of January 21, 1924, but it was a poor and weak government under the tragically inept Ramsay Mac-Donald. Within nine months the Tories were back in office with a large majority under Stanley Baldwin. Winston Churchill was his unfortunate choice as Chancellor of the Exchequer. In April 1925 Churchill put the pound sterling back on the gold standard at the prewar parity of nearly five dollars to the pound. The results were deflation, crippled exports, unemployment—and more strikes.

The coal miners were the hardest hit. The industry had only been kept going with government subsidies. In March 1926 a Royal Commission recommended a reduction in miners' wages and a longer working day. The infuriated miners struck on May 1, and three days later the Trade Union Congress (TUC) called for a general strike. The government was prepared for a show-down, and the strike was soon broken with the help of thousands of voluntary workers.

The moderates in the Labor movement took over in 1926 after the strike and were still running the Labor party when I became London correspondent in 1945. Ernest Bevin, whom I got to know as foreign secretary in the 1940's, was the leading trade union figure of the 1920's. The British Communist party leader during the years of the Spanish Civil War, Harry Pollitt —with the Boilermakers Union in 1926—was naturally among the extremists. Churchill, with his demand for the "unconditional surrender" of the workers, was an extremist, or what was then called a "wild man," on the Conservative side, and he called the tune. He was instrumental in getting the Trade Disputes and Trade Union Act of 1927 through Parliament, severely restricting workers' rights and reducing the income of trade unions. In 1946 while I was head of the London bureau, the newly elected Labor party triumphantly repealed the act.

It is interesting to me that the general strike was precipitated by a trivial newspaper incident. The National Society of Operative Printers and Assistants at the *Daily Mail* refused, on their own initiative, to print the May 3rd issue unless an offending editorial was changed. The Baldwin government hastily used this as an excuse to deliver an ultimatum calling for "an immediate and unconditional withdrawal of the instructions for a general strike." Churchill rightly—but tragically—saw that the government could win what he called a "total victory" over the trade unionists.

Because the printers were on strike, there were no newspapers to defend the workers or present their case. Churchill created a *British Gazette* in which the government side alone was presented. The radio broadcasting was also under government control. The workers were isolated; the general strike did not bring the nation's life to a standstill. On May 12 the TUC Council called the strike off, leaving intense bitterness among the workers, especially the coal miners who stayed on strike until December, suffering, with their families, terrible privations.

"Surrender of the Revolutionaries," the *Daily Mail*'s headlines of May 14 triumphantly proclaimed. . . . "Revolution Routed." The strike was not a revolution, but had it not ended when it did—a tough, brutal ending for the workers—there would certainly have been violence. The consequences of forcing a sense of class consciousness approaching class warfare were lasting. It left a resentment among working people which had not ended twenty years later when I took over our London bureau. It also left a sense of pride, because the rank and file of the unions in the general strike had held firm and stood together unselfishly. It was their leaders in the Trades Union Congress' General Council who, as they felt, betrayed them by surrendering unconditionally.

In the latter half of May and throughout June 1926, when I was in London, the atmosphere was still heated. The general strike was an indirect result of the dreadful cost in lives and industry of World War I.

An outsider can be insulated from surrounding misery. Holidays in Britain during the Spanish Civil War were happy and luxurious times. After every war or revolution there is an inevitable sigh: "How much better things were before!" In modern times I believe it was Talleyrand who started the process with his lament that those who had not known what life was before 1789 could not conceive what *douceur de vivre* meant. But, of course, for millions of Britons there was no *douceur* in the interwar years.

When we returned to New York from London in 1949 and I joined the Editorial Board, my wife and I collaborated on a book called *Assignment to Austerity.* For three years Britain had more austerity than she had had at any time during the war.

I found three of *The Times'* war correspondents waiting for me in London. Clifton Daniel, who was to marry Margaret Truman and become managing editor; Sydney Gruson, a later foreign editor and vice-president; and Drew Middleton, who became head of the paper's United Nations bureau after years in Europe. Middleton succeeded me as head of the London bureau. Clif Daniel surprised me by calling me "Chief"—the one and only time I was so addressed in my career. London was such an important transmission center that I was soon given a news editor—Emanuel R. Freedman, later foreign editor and assistant managing editor until his death in February 1971.

What with correspondents, editors, secretaries, and a large business staff, there must have been thirty to forty people on the staff. It was an administrative, as well as corresponding, job and I was never a good administrator. My ideal was working alone or, at most, in a two-man bureau like Rome. My happiest times in the United Kingdom were going off, with my wife, on many trips to write stories about other parts of the United Kingdom and Eire, to mines, factories, conferences. I always had a good staff of correspondents and an outstanding news editor in Manny Freedman. So the office sort of ran itself, and I was not kicked up to the Editorial Board after five years; I asked to be transferred.

Journalistically, it was an intensely interesting period to be in London. I started between V-E Day (May 8) and V-J Day (August 15). July 26, 1945 was the great and glorious historic moment for the British Labor movement. The Socialists had won a stunning victory in the general election. The dismissal of Britain's wartime leader, Winston Churchill, was astonishing and revealing. Having so recently taken over *The Times'* bureau, I could only rely on the predictions of the experts, none of whom foretold a sweeping Labor victory. As King George VI said, "It was a great surprise to one and all."

To me—as to all Americans—Churchill was sacrosanct, the architect of victory, John Bull in person. I cannot believe that such a figure could be defeated in an American election. Yet the Britons, with their political maturity, realism, and common sense, did the right thing. It was time for a change; time for fresh men and fresh ideas; time for leaders in peace, not in war. To Churchill, it was ingratitude. I thought so, myself, but his people were not ungrateful, as they showed in later years; they were hard-headed. And they remembered the general strike of 1926 and the unemployment and social injustice of Tory rule in the 1930's.

No election since Lloyd George's Liberal party victory in 1906 was to have such a great, if temporary, impact on British politics and life. Looking back now, I feel that it should have been more fruitful, although much was accomplished. Austerity and crushing taxation made it a hard period internally. The loss of India and Palestine foreshadowed the end of the British Empire. But after the first few harsh years, there were full employment, the National Health Service, educational reforms, and the breaking down, or at least erosion, of some traditional social barriers.

Labor began with overwhelming popular support. The boldest measures could have been pushed through. It was a time for consolidation; it was a time for innovation, for "facing the future," as the Socialists promised. Instead, they concentrated more on avenging and correcting the past. The country was left of the government during the regime's first year or two in office, but Prime Minister Clement Attlee had appointed a Cabinet of sixty-year-old Labor movement veterans who were as moderate as most Conservatives. (The cabinet was completed, incidentally, on the day the atom bomb was dropped on Hiroshima.)

One year after the electoral triumph, Herbert Morrison, the brains behind the political victory and Labor's shrewdest politician, told the annual Labor party conference: "The Government has gone as far Left as is consistent with sound reason and the national interest." There was to be no revolution.

The British, unlike the French, are not a revolutionary people. They had their abortive peasant and religious revolutions in the Middle Ages, the most important being Wat Tyler and the Lollards in 1381. The Great Rebellion of 1640, in which the English bourgeoisie once and for all abolished the absolute monarchy—after a bloody civil war—was a sort of revolution. The one real upheaval was the Glorious Revolution of 1688–1689, but it was as much religious as political—William of Orange's Protestant crusade against King James II's Roman Catholicism—and it was bloodless. It led to wider liberties and the supremacy of Parliament, but it was not a social revolution in the modern sense.

Since Magna Carta the British genius has been for evolution, the peaceful transformation of society. This is a marvelous national trait. Nothing could be more civilized, but a country cannot "muddle through" forever.

Rudyard Kipling sensed the end of the British Empire and of England's greatness when he wrote his poem, "Recessional," for Queen Victoria's jubilee, which occurred on June 22, 1897, three years before I was born.

> Far-call'd our navies melt away—
> On dune and headland sinks the fire—
> Lo, all our pomp of yesterday
> Is one with Nineveh and Tyre!

Great Britain had come out of the war as one of the "Big Three" with the United States and the Soviet Union. However, it had neither the strength nor the wealth to sustain the position of superpower. The British had sold more than $4 billion of overseas assets and had incurred a mountain of debts. United

States terms for a postwar loan were harsh. In 1947 (the "*annus horrendus*," as Hugh Dalton, Chancellor of the Exchequer, called it) Britain became a second-rate power. That one year saw a coal, fuel and power crisis, the abandonment of Greece, the loss of India, a dollar crisis, and devaluation. It took the Marshall Plan to save something out of the wreck.

The word "austerity" was aptly coined for the period by Sir Stafford Cripps, then president of the Board of Trade. At times there was less to eat than during the war—1.6 eggs per person per week, to give a characteristic example. Even bread had to be rationed in 1947, something that never happened in the war years. The small bacon and poultry rations were reduced; rice vanished; beer was weakened; whiskey was almost impossible to get. Queues were as long as they ever had been. Foreign travel was suspended. Automobiles had to be put away for lack of gasoline.

Whalemeat, of all things, brought a little relief for a few years. It took strong stomachs to eat something looking like meat and tasting like oil-soaked fish. Our family could not eat it. Nobody liked it, but it filled a gap in the food supplies and in empty stomachs. The year 1947 also saw the arrival of a piscatory horror from South Africa called "snoek," something like a barracuda. Among other reasons, the British have survived because of their wonderful sense of humor. Snoek tickled their risibilities, not their palates, and it soon disappeared. (Australians, with their stronger palates, still eat it.)

All through, it was a remarkable exhibition of civic virtue. I was in a great many countries in my career, and I feel sure that only the British people would have accepted such hardships with such discipline and cheerfulness. British morale, curiously, goes up in the worst of times—a trait on which Winston Churchill capitalized with his "I have nothing to offer you but blood, toil, tears and sweat."

H. G. Wells, seventy-eight years old when the war ended, succumbed to despair. He wrote a last essay, published in November 1945, the year before he died, called "Mind at the End of Its Tether." It began:

"The writer finds very considerable reason for believing that, within a period to be estimated by weeks and months rather than by aeons, there has been a fundamental change in the conditions under which life, not simply human life but all self-conscious existence, has been going on since its beginning. . . .

"If his thinking has been sound, then this world is at the end of its tether. The end of everything we call life is close at hand and cannot be evaded."

As Mark Twain said of the premature reports of his death, this was exaggerated.

Britons do not ask much of life by American standards. They want a lot of food, but it can be—and is—simple and culinarily bad. They do with drab clothes (except for the mini-skirted girls, who are chic and charming, and the long-haired boys, who are not chic but are, I am told, also charming). The depth of the fuel and food crisis in February 1947 saw a revolution in fashion.

It is hard today to realize the startling impact of the "New Look," which Christian Dior launched in Paris. I am not fashion conscious, but the explosion was as inescapable as the first atom bomb. The fashion, like the later mini-skirts and hippies, exemplified a way of life as well as a way to dress. The idea, as I understand it, was that Dior made women look like women again after years of unfeminine angles, squares, and straight lines.

Poor England! Poor women! They could only sigh and goggle, for February 1947 was the worst period of austerity and shortages, plus abominable winter weather. The New Look was a promise, not a fulfillment. Sir Stafford Cripps, still president of the Board of Trade, was upset; the New Look called for long dresses (i.e., more cloth) as well as curves. He even persuaded the British Guild of Creative Designers to boycott the Paris fashion "to save material." Cripps could easier have stopped the tide from coming in than the hemline from dropping. Besides, it was not the length that made the New Look, but its femininity. The new mode came across the Channel like a tidal wave in 1948. Sir Stafford's successor, Harold Wilson, in his first big post, accepted the inevitable, perhaps not too reluctantly for there were women's votes to be considered.

For older people in Britain, clothes must be warm. They want houses—not flats if they can help it—and they must have a few fireplaces to keep some parts of the house warm. Their pleasures are simple—gambling on the football and racing pools, movies, watching sports and comedies on the "telly," a few weeks in a popular seaside resort for holidays.

Of course, tastes are changing. The middle classes have swelled in numbers and are better educated and hence demand more. The so-called working classes want their televisions and, often, their cars. Life is becoming more sophisticated, but by Western European standards the British public is not asking a great deal of life.

Or is it? I was struck during my term as bureau chief, and in later years on visits, by the inability of the government—Labor or Conservative—to make the man in the street and his wife realize that the nation was in crisis. Once the worst postwar period was over, a Britisher had a job, a home, plenty to eat, plenty to wear, and the family's health taken care of from birth to burial for a pittance paid to the National Health Service. So, when the government asked for sacrifices and harder work, pleading the very real state of crisis, workers would ask "What crisis? We don't see any crisis." In the war they saw the threat to the nation and responded to it; in peace the crisis seemed an abstraction of government economists, not a reality.

This very human and happy psychology for the individual has been a great handicap for successive governments. The need to work harder; to reduce consumption; to help increase exports; to save more—these harsh facts of life are simply not grasped. If they are, the attitude is "I'm all right, Jack," and let the other fellow make the sacrifices. Being law-abiding, they pay their monstrous taxes, but being simple in their tastes, they have enough left not to have to work harder.

This was the picture that I was drawing for my newspaper during the first Labor government of 1945–1950. It changed only in the further weakening of the economy, the currency, and the fiscal situation.

People do not change. This is a truism that we journalists can never forget. The important thing is to understand a people, to know how they feel, what makes them tick, what there is about their history, traditions, customs, and character that has moulded them into what they are today. Get the basic factors right, and everything a people or a nation does will make sense —in their terms, not yours. Americans—or anybody else—are hardly in a position to tell the British how to live. There are no people more civilized—in a true sense of the word—more civic-minded, more law-abiding, more politically mature, more tolerant than the British. Let them stew in their own juice; it is a good brew.

Nothing impressed me more, when I was running the London bureau, than the compelling demand of the British people for job security. The bitter, heartbreaking years of high unemployment in the 1920's and 1930's were fresh in all minds and all families. The whole nation and both political parties said: "This must never be allowed to happen again." An unemployment rate of 1 percent came to seem normal. However, it has gone up in the economic crises of recent years, and in 1971 is reaching distressing proportions.

The welfare state arrived in full form with the start of the National Health Service in July 1948. Four centuries of degrading Poor Law legislation went into history. Great Britain led the way that the United States took a score of years to begin to follow. The British Medical Association (BMA) was not allowed to be as obstructive and reactionary as the American Medical Association (AMA), although it certainly tried hard.

The health bill was a truly splendid social reform, which the United States will get around to one of these days. No Briton will lose his life savings through a serious illness. The Health Service was a nonparty measure (Churchill called it an "important reform"), but it was given life by the Attlee government and it ranked as Labor's greatest piece of legislation in their six postwar years in power. It is doubtful that a Conservative government would have put as thoroughgoing a reform into practice so quickly. Aneurin Bevan's measure was more socialistic than either Tories or Liberals had planned. It was considered, with justice, as the most advanced and far-reaching measure of social legislation in British history.

The nationalizations—Bank of England, coal, fuel and power, railways and aviation, wireless and cable services, iron and steel —made little difference to the life of the people, or even to industry. The succeeding Conservative governments were to repeal some of the measures—without any appreciable dislocation. The National Health Service, on the other hand, made a world of difference to every man, woman, and child in the United Kingdom. So did "full employment", while it lasted. Both were nonpartisan responses to a stage that British history had reached. There were shortages and crises, but from 1948 onward every Briton lived in a nation in which dire poverty had been abolished and medical care was available almost free to all.

During that period of 1945–1950, I was generally enthusiastic about the way of life that had burgeoned under the Socialists. We were amused—and shocked—on trips to the States, or when I lectured later about the Labor government, to find so many Americans believing that a Marxist, almost Communistic, regime had been set up in Britain. I had fun pointing to the many "socialistic" measures in force in the United States, which few Americans noticed. Fabian socialism (from which the British Labor movement grew) owed little or nothing to Marx; it was in the social democratic tradition of most of the Continental socialist movements. Whether the British had a socialist government or not, Britain was a more democratic country than the United States, except for class distinctions.

All the same, it was a hard life. I read in a recent English book that *The New York Times* correspondent in London in 1947—who must have been me—described postwar Britain as "an impoverished, second-rate power, morally magnificent but economically bankrupt." Moral magnificence, alas, does not feed or clothe or house a family. A nation can be proud, as well as poor, for just so long. There were three grave economic crises in those five postwar years. The country could not even produce the coal it needed, partly because the coal miners could not be persuaded that the nation was in crisis. Ernest Bevin had said that if the industry would give him enough coal, he would give the country a new foreign policy. But the Yorkshire miners went on a wildcat strike in August 1947, and I had the wry duty of cabling *The Times* that coal was being imported to Newcastle. "Left" after all did not "understand Left," as Ernest Bevin had boasted. What was lacking, in Prime Minister Attlee's words, were "increased effort and efficiency."

It was paradoxical that the abandonment of the Palestine Mandate in 1948 was a greater shock to the Labor government and to Britain than the much more momentous act of freeing India. An endlessly fascinating aspect of journalism is that news values very often do not match historical values. Palestine was an emotional issue, and it was also a problem that deeply and disastrously affected Anglo-American relations. Moreover, it was the one great failure in foreign relations of the postwar Labor government.

The man who felt it most—whose personal failure it was—was Ernest Bevin, the foreign secretary. It was his misfortune that a generally successful term in this—for him—truly "foreign" post will be remembered because of the way he mishandled the Jewish-Arab conflict.

"Ernie" Bevin, as he was always called, was Britain's most important and successful trade union leader of the century. He was a dynamic, as well as social, opposite of Anthony Eden, who both preceded and followed him as foreign secretary and who, incidentally, made an even more catastrophic failure in Middle East policy in 1956, when he joined with Israel and France in the Suez Canal crisis. Bevin had little schooling. He was working class, tough, bluff, undiplomatic by old-school standards, but shrewd, clever, intelligent, and at all times very impressive. In my memories of that period his figure stands up above all the

Laborites. As much as Winston Churchill, he seemed a personification of John Bull.

Britain had controlled Palestine since 1917 and was proud of her record there. Tragedy came because of a theoretically laudable principle—to hold a fair balance between Jews and Arabs. This meant that there could not be a Jewish state. At best, there might be a partition, but the Zionists had not been agitating for anything but a Jewish state. They got it through the terrorism of the Stern and Irgun gangs.

The turning point between compromise and all-out war came when the Irgun blew up the King David Hotel in Jerusalem, causing many deaths, on July 22, 1946. This, and another vicious incident a week later when two kidnapped British sergeants were hanged by the Irgun and their bodies booby-trapped to blast those who came to cut them down, destroyed British sympathy for a Jewish home and even for the plight of 600,000 European Jews who had survived Hitler.

Israel was a legitimate historic and religious ideal, created by violence and upheld by war. Less than two years after the King David Hotel incident—on May 14-15, 1948—the British gave up their Palestine Mandate.

Bevin, rashly, had earlier said in the House of Commons that he would stake his reputation on solving the Palestine question. When he failed so resoundingly, he blamed the United States, and especially President Harry Truman. What had been a tolerant British policy became, under Bevin, stupid and insensitive. The Jews, Bevin said in 1947, had waited 1,900 years for a "home" and they could wait one more year until Britain gave up her mandate.

The Irgun atrocities had caused a rare wave of anti-Semitism in Britain. Palestine was like an obsession, and nobody suffered more pain than Bevin. Later, many historians interpreted the affair in terms of the foreign secretary's irrational and emotional anti-Semitism. I saw him a number of times while bureau chief in London, and I did not consider him anti-Semitic. There was a coarseness or roughness and insensitiveness about him—a distinct element of the bully in an essentially fine character. He felt goaded by Palestine and roared with the pain.

So far as Britain and the Labor government as a whole were concerned, the failure was due to an inability to see or believe that Jews, as Jews, could form a nation. Bevin had been assured by his Foreign Office associates and the British officials in the Colonial Office and in Palestine who were almost romantically pro-Arab, that a Jewish state was impractical. He attempted arbitration, clamped down on the illegal immigration, and tried to crush the Zionists in Jerusalem.

Palestine was a neurosis—and Bevin had it badly. He decided as early as February 1947 to dump the problem in the lap of the United Nations and withdraw on May 15, 1948. Meanwhile, Britain furnished arms to the Arabs, who exultantly began to fight the Jews on May 14, 1948. They were defeated then, as they were to be again.

Arthur Hays Sulzberger, *The New York Times'* president and publisher, came over to London about that time and I arranged for him to have an off-the-record talk with Bevin. Sulzberger and the whole Ochs family had always been anti-Zionist, but in a cautious way. The Jewish readership of *The Times* was emotional and not at all cautious. *Times'* editorials condemned the Irgun terrorism but did not oppose the idea of a Jewish state, and certainly the paper was not pro-Arab.

We saw the foreign secretary in his private office at 11 Downing Street on May 24, 1948, nine days after the birth of Israel. Fighting had already begun. Afterward, I made full notes on our talk which I feel free to publish now that so much time has passed and both Bevin and Sulzberger are dead. The publisher went over these notes carefully and confirmed their accuracy.

"Bevin," my notes begin, "opened up by recalling his meeting with the Publisher in New York and he emphasized then and later that he appreciated the Publisher's attitude on Palestine and for that reason was going to say things that he has never said outside of official circles, all of which was to be very strictly off the record. He then asked what the Publisher had on his mind.

"Mr. Sulzberger replied that he was very disturbed by the effect on Anglo-American relations of the Palestine issue, which was creating a schism between our two countries.

"Bevin from then on kept up an almost uninterrupted flow of language for forty-five minutes. He began, half in earnest, half jokingly to ask why we have so many elections? We ought to have one every five years, as they do here, and not every two years. [The presidential campaign of Truman versus Dewey had begun.]

"Bevin has been seeing [Ambassador Lewis] Douglas every day for the last fifteen days. Douglas understands the situation, and so do Tuck, Wadsworth, Allen, Marshall and the State Department. 'I can get along with the State Department, but what can I do when that blessed President of yours and the State Department have different policies? If only they would let the State Department run things!' Later, he praised Douglas very highly as 'a real gift.'

"He described a critical night in his office with the Jewish Agency group headed by [Chaim] Weizmann—a friend of 35 years standing. He stressed several times that Weizmann called him 'Ernest' and he showed a high regard for Weizmann.

"(The meeting would have been in 1946. At that time the so-called Morrison Plan had been agreed to by Anglo-American experts, and Bevin was pushing it hard. He told me [Matthews] that the Arabs had privately agreed at one time to accept it. On that occasion he was trying to influence the Jewish Agency. The Morrison plan called for four cantons, two Jewish, two Arab, with a central administration in Jerusalem taking care of things like post, telegraph, railways, some economic matters, etc. Bevin's idea was that this should be tried for five years without definite commitment by either side and with the right of secession. The British, of course, were to clear out at the beginning.)

"At the end of the evening in his office, after propounding this plan, Weizmann said: 'Ernest, you've got it!' The next day Bevin —and Weizmann—went to Paris for the Peace Conference. (This would have been the Jewish Day of Atonement, for Bevin remarked that his talk had been the day before 'Atonement.') At midnight Attlee called Bevin (who was at the Hotel George V) to tell him that Truman was going to issue a statement about

Palestine. Bevin said something like: 'Oh my God, that would be awful!' and he decided that it must be stopped at all costs. So he got up and dressed and went to the Hotel Meurice where he got [Secretary of State] 'Jim' Byrnes out of bed. Byrnes agreed with him and tried to stop Truman, but the President said that Dewey [then governor of New York State] was going to issue a statement and he had to forestall him. (The Truman statement was the one asking Britain to grant 100,000 extra immigration certificates to Jewish D.P.'s in Europe.)

"Bevin then skipped to the Partition Plan (finally passed by the U.N. on November 29, 1947). 'You know how it was won,' he said. 'China was told that she wouldn't get a loan if she didn't vote for it, and so forth.' This was 'thoroughly wrong.' The British had said that they would do their best to prepare Palestine for Partition.

"The next thing that happened was the switch-over to the Trusteeship Plan—'without consulting us—that was the rub.' Previously, there had been the truce proposal, and Abdullah, 'to give him credit,' said that he would agree to a truce for Jerusalem, but the Jews (it was the Irgun, although Bevin kept saying 'Jews') broke it, and 'what could you expect the poor Arabs to do?'

"In the last days before the Mandate, Bevin pointed out, he had sent in combat troops so as to clear the way for settlement along Partition lines—that is to say he stopped the Jews in Jaffa and drove them out of Acre, and restored order in Jerusalem. Thus the stage was all set.

"On Thursday, 'before Scarborough' (that would have been May 13th, on the week before the Labor Party Annual Conference, and before the formal relinquishment of the Mandate at midnight, May 14–15) Bevin received a message from Azzam saying that all the Arab States would agree to a truce. Then, without notifying the British, Truman recognized the State of Israel, and it was all off. The Arabs blew up. He indicated later that he expected the Arabs to occupy their part of Palestine and felt that they were not invading foreign territory when they did so, whereas the Jews went over the boundaries of the Partition lines to take Jaffa and Acre after May 15th. Israel, he insisted, is not a state, not a 'third party,' and has no legal existence.

"The Publisher called his attention to the articles in the treaty of alliance between Britain and Transjordan that seemed pertinent to the matter. (These read: Third paragraph of Article 1: 'Each of the High Contracting Parties undertakes not to adopt in regard to foreign countries an attitude which is inconsistent with the Alliance or might create difficulties for the other party thereto.' Article 2: 'Should any dispute between either High Contracting Party and a third State produce a situation which would involve the risk of a rupture with that State, the High Contracting Parties will concert together with a view to the settlement of the said dispute by peaceful means in accordance with the provisions of the Charter of the United Nations and of any other international obligations which may be applicable to the case.')

"Bevin took what we called a 'legalistic' line, but he retorted, 'Of course, what else can you do?' According to him, there is no 'third State,' and hence the articles of the treaty do not apply. The Arabs, he asserted, had to enter Palestine, otherwise the Jews would have killed the Palestinian Arabs. On the Partition Line, he pointed out that it was not to take effect for two months, whereas Truman's recognition came immediately.

"The Arab Legion, he said, didn't fire a shot until they got to Jerusalem (where the Jews had violated the truce). The reports from there are very exaggerated. There has been little shelling. All the information they have points to there being no British officers with the Legion in Jerusalem. The British officers have not taken part in any fighting.

" *Sub rosa*, he said—something that he cannot say publicly—he put it up to the Jewish Agency some time ago as to whether they wanted him to withdraw the British officers, or leave them to try to maintain discipline. He couldn't say exactly that the Jews said 'Yes,' but it was recognized that the British officers might have influence in holding the Arabs in line and preserving discipline. Only last night, said Bevin, talking to important Jews among the British M.P.s, he asked them whether he should withdraw the

British officers, and they said for God's sake, keep them in.

"On the question of arms, he made the point that only those arms were being furnished which had been guaranteed under the treaty, and no new arms were being sent. He complained that 'American newspapers' never printed the true facts about this and other aspects of the Palestine situation, but the Publisher intervened to say that Bevin shouldn't use the phrase 'American' or 'New York' newspapers, because *The Times* was not attacking him and, as we pointed out, had given the true facts about the arms agreement. The Publisher also remarked that Bevin was 'generalizing' about the American press, and the Foreign Secretary did concede that there were exceptions—or that *The Times* was an exception.

"Both earlier and later, Bevin made a big point of the Moslems in the Middle East. A new situation has arisen, he said. There are 70,000,000 Moslems in Pakistan. Both for British and American interests, they must not be antagonized. If they find a leader, and if the conflict takes the form of a holy war, there is no telling what might happen. He greatly fears the possibility of the Moslems being aroused.

"In mentioning Truman's sudden announcement recognizing Israel, Bevin pointed out that it even surprised [U.S. Ambassador] Austin at Lake Success. He told us how, in connection with the truce, he had sent instructions to every British envoy in the Middle East, telling them to urge strongly upon the Arabs the desirability of accepting a truce. The sudden recognition of Israel, he said, made the Arabs give up the idea. 'How can I do business', he asked, 'when policy is so inconsistent?'

"Before the Labor Party conference at Scarborough he discussed with the pro-Zionist Laborites whether to bring up Palestine or not, and he told them he would rather not talk about it, because if he did he would only have to say harsh truths against the United States, and he did not want to harm Anglo-American relations. If he was attacked, he was ready to reply, but it would be unfortunate. It was agreed that he could maintain silence. In the same way, he wants to remain silent now. 'Poor old Winnie' wants to bring the question up in Commons, but Bevin was on to him today to see if the discussion could be postponed at least until the Arabs have had forty-eight hours to discuss the cease-fire proposal. In any event, he intends to maintain silence, because if he talks he could only make relations worse. He could demolish Truman's case completely. (The question was put by Churchill on May 25th, and Bevin refused to talk.)

"On the cease-fire proposition, he had been working all weekend trying to persuade the Arabs to accept it. At the Security Council last week, he took the line that to invoke Article 39 would not make sense, since it would mean armed intervention and sanctions. The only troops there are 20,000 British. Truman is trying to create a situation where Britain would have to use her troops to attack the Arabs. 'I am not going to have anything like that,' he said. 'The United States isn't willing to send a single soldier.' More than the thirty-six hours proposed is needed by the Arabs to study the cease-fire proposal, because of communication difficulties throughout the Middle East. Bevin's hope is that it will be accepted, with British advice. He was against a 'stand-still.' What he wants is a cease-fire, after which the Arabs and Jews would be unscrambled, each going back into the regions due to them under Partition. In general, he said he would go about a settlement the opposite way from the Jews. First have a very loose, central authority for post office, etc. (as in the Morrison Plan), then through living together, economic necessity and development, it would all be brought into a harmonious whole. He agreed that the Palestine situation is 'soluble.'

"Zionists want to rule and crush the Arabs, he said. Jews and Arabs can live together, but not Zionists and Arabs. He is convinced that the Arabs would not have a chance in hell under the Zionists. He sees the Zionists as Fascists or Communists, ruling the Jews and the Arabs. It would be like Czechoslovakia. In discussing the 'Fascist' aspect of Zionism he made the point (I remember specifically the mention of Ben Gurion) that 'they have been brought up on the Old Testament—a cruel book.' Also (I believe it was in speaking of Count Folke Bernadotte of Sweden, the U.N. representative), he said that he hoped he would be the Daniel of the present situation—but I remember being unable to fit the allusion to the circumstance, perhaps 'a Daniel come to judgment.'

"The Russians do not want a cease-fire, Bevin thought. They would enjoy seeing the shooting go on indefinitely. He said he asked the Security Council today whether the cease-fire order will go for the Irgun and Stern gangs. 'What is the use of only getting the agreement of the Haganah?' There are 12,000 in the Irgun, he pointed out.

"In discussing the force needed for imposing Partition, he said they estimated that two divisions could do it against one side or the other, but that five divisions would be needed to impose it on both sides. 'Very confidentially,' he said that he understood that Eisenhower's estimate was also five divisions for the latter.

"Britain worked very hard and puts much faith in the mediator, Count Folke Bernadotte. The British have sent a very experienced representative as Consul General, Sir Hugh Dow, who was Governor of several provinces in India and knows how to handle communal difficulties. Dow has been ordered to help as much as he can.

"At one point Bevin said that if there is going to be war (meaning world war) it would be because of the White House, never because of the State Department.

"When he was saying goodbye, Bevin again stressed that he had never spoken so openly about this to anybody, but he was doing so because he had been impressed by the Publisher's good faith, and trusted him."

The Palestine issue brought out a latent anti-Americanism that was only partly assuaged by the Marshall Plan, which came into force later in 1948. Bevin had given a press conference at the time the Mandate was abandoned. He could not forbear one brief and bitter passage which was off the record at the time, but I made a note of it for my files.

"We fought six years," Bevin said, "two of them before America came in. We are lectured on every hand. You journalists would not be in England today if we had not fought like grim death. There is not one word of thanks for anybody. Our cemeteries are evidence of it. Old England is not down yet. But we made no bargains, and we have not charged 5 percent for it, either." This was a reference to the interest the United States charged on its postwar loan, which the British considered shocking.

The day after Arthur Hays Sulzberger and I saw Bevin, I spent an evening with Hector McNeil, then minister of state of the Foreign Office. McNeil, a Scotsman from Glasgow, was about the most brilliant of the young Laborites in the field of foreign affairs. It was a great loss to Britain, as well as the Labor party, when he died of a brainstroke in his forties. He was a good friend.

McNeil told me that Nahum Goldman of the Jewish Agency had made a special trip to London two weeks before to see him and discuss the ending of the Mandate. Diplomatic recognition of Israel was out of the question, McNeil said, but the British planned to send a high consular officer and some assistants to maintain contacts with the new state in Tel Aviv. Goldman did not seem upset, according to McNeil, who told the Jewish leader that he would be *persona grata* if Israel appointed him to their London post.

From what Goldman said, the Israelis were not concerned about Egypt, Syria, Lebanon, or Iraq, but only about Transjordan and the Arab Legion. He said that they knew the Negev would be overrun, but that did not worry Tel Aviv much. What did frighten them a great deal, it seemed, was to get a heavy flow of immigration before Israel was in a position to absorb the newcomers into her economy. Weizmann had said that he loathed the idea of having to set up concentration camps in Palestine when the immigrants would come just to escape from them, and yet that was what might have to happen.

Hector McNeil was less emotional than Bevin about President Truman, but he was just as critical. As between the two evils—

bad relations with the United States or bad relations with the Arabs—the British, he said, were opting for the Arabs and Middle Eastern peace. They were "profoundly convinced" that the president's policy was not only bad, but that it was his personal policy, not the State Department's.

The British, as I knew, were genuinely afraid that the Arabs would start a holy war—a *jihad*—and, like most officials, McNeil then believed that the Arabs would win.

"The only gainer by the present quarrel between Washington and London," he said shrewdly, "will be Russia. If Truman keeps on pursuing his present policies, there will be a long and grave period of conflict."

The British correctly foresaw the consequences of an Arab-Jewish conflict, and they were right to aim for an accommodation whereby Jews and Arabs could live and work out their problems in peace. This was the statesmanlike thing to do—but it was trying the impossible. Truman was responding to political pressures from the Jewish community, especially in New York, and he was going against the advice of the State Department, but he was right in seeing that a Jewish state was logical and inevitable. However, he did not have to handle the affair in such a crude and blatantly political fashion. The Arabs will never forgive the United States. As in all such issues, there is no way of proving what did not happen. An endless conflict may have been unavoidable, whatever Truman did. The fact remains that his policies made warfare inevitable.

The decision to give up India, made in February 1947, was right but, as with Palestine, there was a costly miscalculation. It reflected an equally great miscalculation by Nehru and the Congress Hindus, who had consistently underrated Jinnah and the depth of Hindu-Moslem antagonism. The British had had ample warning of bloodshed when communal rioting in Calcutta on August 16, 1946 led to 5,000 deaths, mostly Hindu.

Lord Wavell, then viceroy, went on hopelessly pushing for a united India. Prime Minister Attlee was getting bad advice from the experts, but he knew that Britain could no longer bear the "white man's burden" in India. Admiral Viscount Mountbatten (Prince Philip's uncle) was sent to replace Wavell with a mandate to arrange for the partition of India as soon as feasible.

Few Britons, even then, appreciated how fiercely Hindus and Moslems hated each other—which was incredible to me, for I had been overwhelmed by this antagonism during my year in India. However, no one in India or Great Britain could have foreseen the appalling scale of the mass slaughter by both sides. Nehru must have been out of touch with the people; he was too much the aristocratic Kashmiri Brahmin to commune with the masses, although he always had a charismatic appeal to them. Jinnah, from what I knew of him, would have been too reckless to care what price had to be paid for his brainchild, Pakistan.

No one will ever know how many people were killed when Moslem and Hindu turned on each other and there was a desperate exodus of Moslems from Hindu India and of Hindus from the future Pakistan. About 6 million Moslems and 4.5 million Hindus were in the agonizing cross-exodus. Estimates of the dead ranged from 200,000 to 600,000.

It was terrible enough to sit in London and read about it. I saw Lord Linlithgow, the former viceroy, soon afterward and asked him whether, if he had still been in New Delhi, he could have held India for the British raj. "If they gave me enough troops," he said, "I could have held it for fifteen years, but sooner or later we would have had to get out."

Mahatma Gandhi had opposed partition from the beginning. There are few things more ironical in modern history—or more tragic and sorrowful—than for Gandhi to have had to sit back, heartbroken, and see the wreck of his "civic disobedience" policy, as Hindus slaughtered Moslems. The crowning irony came soon after. On January 30, 1948, a young, right-wing Hindu extremist from the Mahasabha party pumped three bullets into Gandhi's body as he sat in his prayer meeting. In a practical sense, no historic figure of our times had failed so completely. Mahatma Gandhi's greatness lay in the spiritual realm. He was a good man with an exalted vision. He asked more of human nature than the race could bear.

One keeps returning to that fateful month of February 1947. A historian can use it as a time reference to signal the end of Britain as a first-rate world power.

Chronologically, the Greek crisis in mid-February 1947 was the beginning of the end. Bevin had said, "Left understands Left," but when it came to the pinch, and the Attlee government realized that it could not continue pouring economic aid into Greece and Turkey and paying high military costs to defend them, Bevin turned to Washington, not Moscow, for help. Some of his Socialist colleagues in Parliament berated him for calling in the capitalistic United States to redress the balance in Europe, but he really had no choice. Britain is an Atlantic and politically Western power.

The Truman Doctrine, whereby the United States took Britain's place in Greece and Turkey, was also historic in ending the centuries-old British policy of holding the balance of power on the European Continent. From then on, Britain was simply an ally of the much more powerful United States. The Common Market will change that relationship.

Bevin was first off the mark when General Marshall, then secretary of state, made his speech outlining the economic program that became known as the Marshall Plan. The following day, the foreign secretary enthusiastically endorsed the idea, and began mobilizing the Continental powers to join in. That was one American move whose wisdom, generosity, and unselfishness was fully recognized in Great Britain. Without Marshall aid, it was estimated that the slim rations of butter, sugar, cheese, and bacon would have been cut one-third; cotton goods would have disappeared; timber would have been in short supply, heavily cutting the housing program; and the shortage of raw materials would have made 1.5 million unemployed.

The Marshall Plan aside, Britons, like the Gaullists in France, were unhappy at being told that they had to follow the leadership of the United States, and that the world was then dominated by the American and Russian governments. The British never have conceded a moral superiority to the Americans—far from it. They recognize the power and wealth of the United States, but do not consider these to have been gained by any special American virtues. I believe that if you asked John Bull to explain American predominance today, he would say: Providence, geography, natural resources, British capital and the British Navy in the nineteenth century.

The greatest shock of all to Anglo-American relations came in October 1962 when President Kennedy was prepared to fight a nuclear war with Russia over Cuba in which Great Britain would have been destroyed—without being consulted.

Despite her decline, the British did face up to the possibility of a World War III during the Berlin crisis of 1948. It takes an effort to recall how tense the atmosphere was in those days. Berlin, said Bevin, was "a symbol," meaning that it was a symbol of the liberties and ideals of Western civilization. There was talk of the Russians driving to the English Channel. Britain played a strong role in that crisis.

"We have never known what a modern war was like in the physical impact on our cities and homes," I wrote to my brother from London on October 1, 1948, "but the British do know, and yet they are facing the prospect of another war without any nerves or jitters and with typical determination. I have never felt more admiration for them as a people than in these days.

"To be sure, we all feel that war is extremely unlikely so far as one can see ahead—which these days would not be further than next spring. The fear is that the Russians might think this is their best time to strike, or that they will underestimate our determination to stay in Berlin, and precipitate a war without meaning to. . . . There was a period when I thought I smelt appeasement in the air, but now that the documents have been published, it is clear that we took a strong line all along."

During the cold war period I was as orthodox an anti-Communist as any American, so far as international affairs were concerned. I believed in the prevailing nightmare of the Kremlin seeking to conquer the world for Communism. China was simply a dark cloud on the horizon. We all exaggerated the danger greatly, just as the United States exaggerated the danger from Communist China in the 1960's when it intervened in Vietnam. The Russian moves into the Mediterranean Sea and the Indian Ocean in the 1970's are examples of old-fashioned imperialism and power politics not ideological Communism.

I think 1948 was my personal anti-Communist high-water mark. My intellectual process was probably typical of the American liberal. I preserved some scraps of writing which show the progression.

"Granting the mentality of the Hitlerites," I wrote to my brother from Rome on July 17, 1944, "it seems fairly obvious that if they have to go down, they will take Europe with them if they can. One can imagine Hitler saying: 'So you don't want a Nazi Europe! Let us see how much better you like a Communist Europe.' "

"Our twentieth century enemy," I wrote again from Rome three months later, "isn't just Fascism in its various phases, but totalitarianism. The Communist way of life is completely totalitarian and in the most devastating and sinister way, despite its many attractive sides. It seems to suit the Russians the way Nazism suits the Germans, and if they want it, okay, but if it becomes an article for export and conquest, then I don't see any choice but to fight it in the end, as Nazism and Fascism had to be fought. . . ."

A year later, in my book, *The Education of a Correspondent,* I was writing: "When the German Army went down, its last gasp was that it was fighting to stem the westward rush of the barbarian hordes of Communism. That myth will rise to plague us, and it will be the task of the liberal to avoid both the Scylla of Communism and the Charybdis of Fascism—although, as I said before, if the choice were ever forced upon me I would take Communism."

"If everyone can't see the startling parallels between Stalin's policies and methods and Hitler's, they are crazy," I wrote my brother from London on March 29, 1946. "And nothing could be more natural. It leads one to a terribly pessimistic conclusion, but in the first place, one has to face the facts and the truth, and in the second place there is no use kicking against a world force brought on by centuries of history. It is like saying you wish you were born in the eighteenth century, or whenever you please. We were born in this one, and have to make the best of it."

The shock of the 1948 Berlin crisis brought back the spectre I had mentioned four years before—of Communism setting out to conquer the world. My reaction seems to me today to have been emotional and irrational—but it was typical.

"People are moaning and groaning about what will happen to civilization if there is another war," I wrote in my letter of October 1, 1948, "and how can we all be so stupid as to let it happen, and don't the statesmen know what it means, etc. etc. —all of which is quite beside the point. Of course, everybody knows what it would mean. And, naturally, we could avoid it very easily and neatly. All we have to do is to become Communists, and let the world become Communist and totalitarian. Then there would be peace and we could all die in bed, perhaps with some slight qualms of conscience."

George F. Kennan's policy of the containment of the Soviet Union seemed logical and morally right in those cold war days. It was right only in a military and strategic sense. When the Russians tried to put missiles as close to the United States as the American missiles were close to the Soviet Union, Kennedy risked a nuclear war over Cuba to stop them. When our submarines with Polaris missiles cruised within close range of Russia, this was natural and right. When Russian submarines with missiles cruised along our Atlantic coast, it was an outrage.

The premise for this illogicality is, of course, that Americans consider themselves to be a peace-loving nation, defending themselves and Western civilization against a potential aggressor with an evil way of life. Vietnam and the Dominican Republic were paradoxical examples of this mentality at work.

The Allied reaction to the Berlin crisis was sound and sensible. Stalin had to be stopped. But I see it now simply as Moscow's effort to grab something that seemed grabable, and not as a step in the conquest of the world for a Russian-dominated Communist system. Naturally, the Kremlin would like to see every nation in the world turn Communist; naturally, Washington would like to see every nation in the world adopt a liberal democratic system. They want socialism; we want capitalism.

These are two different political, economic, and social systems. To say that one is intrinsically good and virtuous, and the other bad and evil, is a piece of nonsense that has done our postwar world as much harm as the religious wars of the past.

American policies have reacted to Communism as if it had not changed since Marx, Lenin, and Stalin. The worldwide dictatorship of the proletariat, which was basic to Leninism, is no longer to be feared. It is doubtful that the younger generations of Communists in Russia or elsewhere think of this any longer in practical terms. Even for Lenin, Marxism was a living force and hence a developing, changing, adaptable system or theory.

Professor Robert L. Heilbroner aptly called Communism "the great modernizer." It has brought about change; reached and organized the great, inchoate mass of the people in many countries; destroyed traditional and anachronistic social structures; and in so doing may have paved the way for a new and better life in the underdeveloped countries. In developed countries, clearly, the system does not work as well as capitalism.

I was far from thinking such thoughts while I was running the London bureau. However, I did respond to the mature, sophisticated, and tolerant attitude toward Communism that was common to British statesmen and politicians. The British are a wordly-wise people. The one deep, mad, stain on their escutcheon is Ireland, and that is now past history—for the British, not the Irish, although my wife and I found on postwar trips to Eire that the Irish have, on the whole, put aside animosities. The old rancor still burns in the Catholic communities of Ulster—who have good reasons for complaint—and in the eastern seaboard of the United States, where it makes no sense. I do not believe that the contemporary troubles in Northern Ireland will lead the British to harsh repression.

I like Lord Robert Cecil's characterization about the English: "It is better to have second class brains than second class characters." That is about the way it has been since the war, allowing for many notable exceptions, such as Attlee and Churchill, who could claim both brains and character. (It is tempting, but too soon, to add Edward Heath.) Lord Robert, anyway, was thinking of a general gamut from Cockneys selling fruit off street barrows to the Eton and Oxford, Harrow and Cambridge old-school-tie boys. Now and then one wonders whether the old, strong fiber has not weakened, but a race does not change.

As I said, it was wonderful the way they took shortages and monstrous taxation in the first years after the war. All things end, and so did austerity, but not swiftly. Clothes came off rationing in March 1949, milk in January 1950, and many other things before the end of that year. In 1951 the ordeal was over.

So was a hopeful idealism that had greeted the Laborites when they won the 1945 elections. I suppose that no political party could have kept its popularity after a year like 1947 and its drab and difficult aftermath. British politics, with what amounts to a two-party system, swings like a pendulum. With moderate Socialists in the leadership, there did not have to be much of a swing, in policies or ideology. There had been more danger of class warfare in 1926 than in this postwar period.

Aneurin (Nye) Bevan, the exuberant former Welsh coal miner who was minister of health when the National Health Service went into effect in 1948, was an exception. He expressed the opinion, in a Manchester speech, that the Tories were "lower than vermin."

Attlee, who was middle class and old school tie, was more in tune with traditional British political ways. I remember listening to him and Churchill (then Leader of the Opposition) having a very sharp slanging match in the House of Commons. Shortly afterward, I saw them walking through the door, Churchill with his arm around Attlee's shoulders.

Churchill was writing his war memoirs at the time, which *Life* magazine and *The New York Times* were printing in installments. I would sometimes get inquiries from Managing Editor James' office about details and I would, at other times, pass along corrections that one of Churchill's secretaries would send to me.

One evening, when Nancie, our two children, and I were playing bridge in our house on Victoria Square, the telephone rang. I grunted in annoyance, but got up to answer. "You never know," said Nancie jokingly, "it might be Churchill." I picked up the phone and said: "Hullo, Matthews speaking." A familiar voice replied: "This is Winston Churchill." When the family heard me say: "Oh, good evening, Mr. Churchill," they thought it a great joke.

The "Old Man," as everyone called him, was in no joking mood. He had just received another message, through my office, from Jimmy James complaining about Churchill sending corrections so late that copy had to be reset and editions were missed. Churchill plaintively urged me to point out to James that he was spending a great deal of time and money checking every fact in his text to get them right, and *The New York Times* should appreciate his efforts and not complain. I mildly pointed out that newspaper deadlines were rigid, almost to a matter of seconds, but that, of course, I would tell New York how he felt.

There was a charming sequel for me to the many exchanges on the memoirs in a letter that Churchill wrote me on August 27, 1949. I had written to his house at 28, Hyde Park Gate, to say that I was being transferred to New York and would like to drop in for a farewell visit. As it happened, he was on vacation, so his reply came from Cap d'Ail, France.

Dear Mr. Matthews:

Thank you for your letter of August 12, in which I learn with regret of your departure from London. I am indeed sorry not to be able to see you before you leave, but I do not yet know when I shall be returning.

I am so much obliged to you for your co-operation and help in the publication of my Memoirs. I hope we may meet again sometime if you are able to visit England in the future.

Sincerely,
Winston S. Churchill

Early in 1954, after one of my visits to Havana, Cuba, I was able to settle for posterity a point of very minor importance to historians, but meaningful to cigar smokers like myself. Churchill's monstrously long cigars were, of course, as much a part of his image as the V for Victory sign. It was widely reported and believed that during World War II the prime minister was forced by his security officers to switch from his favorite Upmann Havanas to similar-looking Jamaican cigars, every one supposedly examined by a security agent to be sure that no explosive or poison gas was wrapped in the tobacco.

It was a good story, and plausible, but a connoisseur of cigars and a confirmed smoker of them, which Churchill was, would never dream of smoking anything but first-rate *vuelta abajo* cigars if he could get them. I had to write his office about another matter and took the opportunity to ask if the story about the cigars was true. His personal private secretary, Jane Portal, answered for him and added for my benefit: "The Prime Minister wishes to thank you for your letter of January 19 and he has instructed me to say that he certainly smoked a great many excellent cigars sent from Cuba during the War."

That huge and splendid size of Havana cigar, such as he smoked, has, since the war, had the trade name of "Churchills." This places Sir Winston in the same class as that "mighty man of valor," Jeroboam, who gave his name to the outsized wine bottle.

The Conservatives had come back to power with the 1951 elections. Once again, it was time for a change. There had been a rejuvenation of the Tory party machine under Lord Woolton. The ideas were provided by R. A. (Rab) Butler, who was also a brilliant example of brains as well as character. So Britain had thirteen years of stable, moderate, undistinguished Tory government except for the one astonishing deviation which I mentioned before. This was the attempt by Britain, France, and Israel to seize the Suez Canal and overthrow the Nasser government in 1956. President Eisenhower, Secretary Dulles, and Dag Hammarskjöld, then Secretary-General of the United Nations, saw to it that the adventure was an ignominious failure. Nasser seemed such a menace to the West, as well as Israel, that we handled the attack on Egypt editorially with kid gloves. Looking back, it did seem to be a very rash and foolish move on the part of Anthony Eden, then prime minister. However, it did not shake the fabric of the British nation or even cause a political crisis.

Britain's foreign policies are hardly ever affected by partisan politics, except in minor ways. In the United States it makes little difference to foreign affairs whether there is a Democrat or a Republican in the White House. In Britain it is the same with the Tories and Socialists. Power politics have no party. I believe that Britain would enter the Common Market whichever party is in office.

In 1964 Labor returned for six more years of moderate and undistinguished government under Harold Wilson. Now the Conservatives are back again, this time under Edward Heath.

It does not matter much to the nation which side wins a given election, but it is healthy for the pendulum to swing and prevent either side from remaining in power too long. Men of one party supplant men of the other party, none of them outstanding leaders. It was said of Harold Wilson, "He's the best Prime Minister we have." Ted Heath is proving more original but not revolutionary in his policies. The oft-cited dictum of the nineteenth-century French historian and statesman, Louis-Adolphe Thiers, that British governments always tend to be left-center is as true today as when he wrote it more than a century ago.

It was my lot, from the time I joined the Editorial Board late in 1949 until I retired in October 1967, to write a great many editorials about Britain. I waxed lyrical in my obituary editorial for Winston Churchill, for I considered him a very great Englishman. Biographers since he died seem to have stressed his mistakes and weaknesses, of which there were many, but this is no way to judge a man.

There was plenty to censure in British affairs, but criticism of Great Britain is like swearing to oneself. The British simply do not care what is said and written about them, and they hold no grudges. They feel just as unmoved by praise. There is the utmost in urbanity and supercilious toleration, the product of centuries of power and diplomatic training. At only one period in my career was I bitterly critical of the British. I despised them —by which I mean their statesmen and politicians, not the people; I have never despised any people in any country except for the Germans during the Nazi regime. My period of harsh and virulent criticism, mixed with contempt, of the British was during the appeasement era, especially from 1936 to 1939. Britain was at her feeblest and most inglorious in those years. The foreign policy was out of character, but none the less reprehensible. It was a satisfaction to criticize prewar Britain, but the process was quite ineffectual. One normally gets an effect—and I had some great effects in my editorial days, thanks to the power and influence of *The New York Times*—but not with the British. Their statesmen do not care; they know they are always right, but if they should be proved wrong, it is nobody else's business, and they won't let on.

The basic elements of British life have rightly been taken for granted for generations. There is a sublime trust in the virtues of the British parliamentary system, under a hereditary constitutional monarch, with universal suffrage. The two-party system (formerly Conservative and Whig or Liberal, now Conservative and Labor) is operated within this democratic framework. The Socialist party even assumes a capitalistic society. State control is greater under Labor governments, but not enough to change the way of life. Debates in the House of Commons over political and social issues often sound fierce, but the verdict on a given government usually comes from the people through a general election, not from a vote of no confidence in the House. Class consciousness remains, but it is less acute now that university education and the higher ranks of the civil service are open to all.

So government runs smoothly, with no basic changes exclusive to whichever of the two big parties is in power. In four years the Laborites may well supplant the Conservatives once again.

The editorials on Britain that I was writing from 1949 to 1967 were as unexciting as British events and politics.

Amusingly and unexpectedly, it was London that set a whole new tone and appearance for youth everywhere in the 1960's. The New Look could not be enjoyed when it began, because of clothes rationing. Now, more sensibly and cheerfully, the British invented the mini-skirt and made London's Carnaby Street world famous. The young men let their hair grow long and wore fantastic clothes. The Beatles came down from Liverpool and started a new, joyous rhythm that the whole world copied as hundreds of Beatle-type groups and songs flowered from New York to Melbourne in Australia.

It was so sensational that everyone started writing about "swinging Britain," as if every city, town, and hamlet from John O'Groats to Land's End was swaying in short skirts and long hair to Beatle music. After my wife and I got back from a trip to England in 1966, I wrote an editorial column, published by *The New York Times* on August 22, ridiculing the reports. We went back in 1968, 1969, 1970, and 1971, and I would still consider a picture of "swinging Britain" ridiculous.

Britons are the most solid, stable, democratic, politically sophisticated, sensible, and bourgeois people in the world. There are plenty of young swingers. Some students—as the London School of Economics has shown—were as unruly as in Berkeley, Columbia, or the Sorbonne. A vicious, fascistoid reaction has come along from the young "skinheads." There is racial strife, which Enoch Powell and his extremist followers have blown up to sensational proportions. These are like the froth on England's ale, bubbling on the top of an excellent, trustworthy product. In the more than fifty years since I walked on Salisbury Plain during World War I, I have seen and studied every part of the United Kingdom. Britain, after 1918, was to go through economic crises, World War II, and lose the greatest of empires —and remain herself. I have seen New York, Rome, Paris, and Madrid altered out of all recognition—for the worse, incidentally—but in some magic way London does not change. At least, it has not changed for me in any fundamental way.

The British are bored with, and generally tolerant about, their politics, but when they are called upon for a considered electoral judgment they confound the pessimists. This was so true in the election of June 18, 1970 that all the opinion pollsters were fooled. The change that swept Harold Wilson and the Laborites out of power was like a ground swell which came from the unseen, unruffled depths of British life.

During our summers in the late 1960's, visiting seaside resorts like Brighton, Eastbourne, Bournemouth, and Porthcawl in Wales, we found the real England taking its holidays. The weather was usually—perhaps I should say, normally—bad, but the beach chairs were full, and the younger people actually enjoying the bathing. The older folk were strolling or sitting around talking, and then drifting into tearooms and pubs. The great majority were dowdily dressed, leaving the plumage to the brightly colored young. One sensed that the mini-skirted girls and the long-haired boys would be like their parents some day. A few years have passed and the mini-skirts are becoming old-fashioned; the long hair is commonplace; the skinheads will go into history with the mods and rockers; the dances will become less frenetic—but there is a traditional quality to British life and character, which nothing will change, a quality that places Britons in the highest ranks of citizens of the world. One feels this most of all on trips away from the coasts, in towns and villages, in the quiet and lovely downs of Sussex, Dorsetshire, Wiltshire, and Hampshire, where history was made by Romans, by King Alfred the Great, by William the Conqueror.

We spent a summer once at Lyulph's Tower on Lake Ullswater, just above the field where Wordsworth saw the daffodils and wrote one of his most famous lyrics:

> I wandered lonely as a cloud
> That floats high o'er vales and hills,
> When all at once I saw a crowd,
> A host, of golden daffodils. . . .

One can go on up to the lochs of Robert Burns' country, and down to unpronounceable Welsh villages where heavenly choruses are heard at an eisteddfod, and to many other places, so obvious, so famous that there seems nothing fresh to write about them. Yet this is the point. This is why one reads a thousand times that "there'll always be an England." One cannot say, in the same sense, that "there'll always be an Italy," or a France, or a Spain, or a United States. These countries are in transition or in some process of revolution. Not Great Britain. In this revolutionary world she stands like a beacon, shining with a steady light.

When I left the London bureau in 1949, an old and very great era had ended for Great Britain. The world was shaken by the approaching collapse of her Empire. Power vacuums were being created; new forces were set in motion in the United States, which had to fill some of the vacuums, and in Africa and Asia where movements for independence were becoming irresistible. India, Burma, and Ceylon had just been lost; the fleet that had "ruled the waves" all through the nineteenth century and until World War I, was being reduced to a skeleton. The City of London had ceased to be the financial heart of the world. What had been the greatest of all creditor nations was now a huge debtor, unable to balance her trade. Geography, which once assured Britain's security, was now a handicap, leaving her uniquely vulnerable to atomic destruction and even to starvation in time of war. One could see the once-great British Commonwealth fading away.

It was the irony of history. If the Empire dissolved, it was largely because Britons had taught their colonies what independence meant; had trained their citizens to be governors and civil servants; had built up their armies and inculcated principles of justice and civic rights. Curiously—at least, it seemed curious to an American—there was no popular discontent in Britain over the decline of the Empire. The painful results were economic, not imperial.

Britain had become an ineffective economic unit, lagging a

generation behind the United States in practices of standardiza-
tion and mass production. British genius was in quality, but
today's world was demanding necessities in large quantities, not
luxuries. It was the time of Churchill's pungent jest: "The inherent vice of capitalism is the unequal sharing of blessings; the
inherent virtue of socialism is the equal sharing of miseries."

Even that wonderful instrument of British government, the
"Mother of Parliaments," was changing character. Scholars like
Prof. Arnold J. Toynbee were beginning to wonder whether
Parliament had not outlived much of its usefulness and become
an anachronism. After all, it was an institution evolved in the
thirteenth century. In its present form it dates from the Civil
War period of the seventeenth century. I had come to feel that
it was still functioning only because of the British genius for
somehow muddling along with old, traditional, outmoded machinery.

I still think so in 1971. The practice of acting through administrative Orders in Council, most of which are never discussed in Parliament, is used as much as the U. S. President's
powers to bypass Congress. The permanent bureaucracy, responsible primarily to government leaders, not to Parliament,
has become ever more powerful.

The British are a slow, stodgy, cautious people, middle class
in heart and soul, inclined to compromise and adapt, rather than
to alter and abolish, steeped in traditions, determined to move
by evolution, not revolution, always keeping their feet on the
ground. The wonderful sense of humor—"one-quarter cynical
and three-quarters kindly"—the incurable optimism, the robust
zest for life, the assurance, complacency, self-righteousness, the
stoicism in the face of hardship and danger, the political wisdom, the tolerance, the good manners, the world-weariness—
these are now an inalterable heritage of a great past.

But a revolution in British history approaches, for it can be
taken as certain that she will join the Common Market. England
will again become a part of the European continent after centuries of separation. The Atlantic Community—based on the
bridge between Great Britain and the United States—will disap-

pear in its present form. The Commonwealth, already only a feeble remnant of the empire, will virtually cease to have meaning. Yet the event, whenever it occurs, will not be a defeat; it will be a new adventure.

We go back every year, Nancie, who is English, and I, who am an American, and we are both at home. So are our children. Everything and everybody seem so familiar. They all talk of the weather, of course; and of business, sports, families, rising prices. Nobody talks politics or Vietnam or the Middle East. The things that Britons take pleasure in are astonishingly simple to Americans.

One must not be starry-eyed. There are serious pockets of poverty, especially in the big cities. The economy is always precarious. The people are complacent; they are satisfied with themselves; they feel superior; they persist in enjoying life when so many foreigners think they should not do so.

In 1949 I felt—as I still do today—that anyone who wrote off a nation like Britain as a has-been of history was running counter to common sense. In a series of articles written toward the close of my London assignment, I quoted from Ralph Waldo Emerson's famous speech, made in Manchester in November 1847, during the terrible economic crisis of the "Hungry Forties." "In prosperity," he said, "they were moody and dumpish, but in adversity they were grand. . . . with a kind of instinct that sees a little better in a cloudy day, and that in storm of battle and calamity, she has a secret vigor and a pulse like a cannon."

Chapter 7

LATIN AMERICA

Latin America is a subject that belongs to the editorial-writing stage of my career, although I wrote many news articles, some books and made innumerable lectures on the region. From 1950 to 1967 almost every editorial in *The New York Times* relating to Latin America was written by me. This was a wide-open secret in Washington and below the Rio Grande. It was so far taken for granted that any editorial on the subject was mine that even when I was on vacation or on a trip to Europe, I would be credited or blamed.

It used to be said (the one-time Acting Managing Editor, Frederick Birchall, often said this) that "nobody reads the editorials in *The New York Times.*" Before the 1940's, and especially during the life of Adolph Ochs, this must have been the case. It was generally a waste of time to read our editorials on anything important or controversial because they were always cautious, innocuous, on-the-one-hand and on-the-other-hand pronouncements. Of course, in the case of elections *The Times* had to come out for one candidate or another, although even there, the paper's long-range line was so discreet that *The Times'* political policy was labeled as *"independent* Democratic."

Those were the decades of the "good grey *Times.*" They began to change soon after Arthur Hays Sulzberger became publisher and Charles E. Merz editor of the editorial page. Merz was a liberal but he allowed individual editors to express their personal opinions in the editorial columns. If the editorials were liberal—or in my case almost radical by historic *Times'* standards —the newspaper's editorial policy on a particular subject would reflect the writer's liberality.

All editorials were kept within a certain range or limit that did not violate what might be called "*Times* style." Merz had an uncanny ability to place himself in the mind of Arthur Sulzberger. He knew what the publisher thought on any given subject and whether he would agree or disagree with an editorial line. Since editorials are the expression of the newspaper's policy, this had its justification. Moreover, Arthur Sulzberger trusted Merz's judgment and usually decided that what was good for Merz was good for *The Times.*

When the publisher balked against any given line, Merz would not, so far as I knew, put up a fight. The first editorial of mine that was rejected (I remember it because I was shocked) was one I wrote after Marshal Tito's defection from the Soviet bloc, in which I argued that the United States should now support Tito and give him aid. Sulzberger vetoed it on the grounds that it seemed to run counter to State Department policy, and we should wait until the Truman government had taken a position. I was in close touch with State Department thinking at that time, and happened to know that both State and the White House were in favor of such a move and would have been grateful for a lead. But I was not given a chance to explain.

Another and more understandable example—although I thought it poor judgment—occurred at the beginning of the Cuban Revolution. I sent an editorial from Havana that condemned the kangaroo-style trials and the mass executions that were taking place. I explained why Fidel Castro was carrying them out, how the Cuban people felt, and how the bloodletting by the Castro government was preventing a more sanguinary, popular revenge such as Venezuela had seen the year before, when mobs slaughtered 2,000 Pérez Jiménez followers in the streets of Caracas. It was enough for the publisher to be shocked; he never acquired sophistication in the art of politics. Considering the simple-minded American reaction to the Cuban executions, I am sure that many *Times* readers would also have been shocked. This would have been an adequate, businesslike excuse for killing—or postponing—such an editorial, but the real reason was a lack of understanding.

The final transformation from a "good grey" editorial page to a courageous, hard-hitting, sharp, and colorful outlet for opinions came when John B. Oakes succeeded Merz in 1963. The improvement has been striking; the influence of the page has soared. It is now more personalized than institutionalized, for it bears the imprint of John Oakes, but it remains within limits suitable to the traditions of *The Times*.

Fortunately for me, my own ideas on foreign affairs were much the same as Oakes'. He respected my opinions and would almost always accept a suggested line—and I felt the same way about his opinions. Where we disagreed, someone else would write the editorials.

Even on Castro and the Cuban Revolution, it was possible for me to write editorials all through the years when the News and Sunday departments recoiled in horror at the idea of printing anything under my by-line. I do not mean to say that I could freely and fully put into *Times'* editorials my ideas and opinions on Cuba. They were heterodox, minority opinions, which I could not and did not ask *The Times* to share. However, I was at all times able to praise where praise was due, as well as to criticize where criticism was warranted. I tried to keep a balance, to explain Cuba to the United States and (for I knew how closely my editorials were read in Havana) to explain the United States to Cuba. There was a great deal to criticize about the Revolution, and Fidel knew he was being criticized by a friend, although he had a tendency, which I argued against, to believe that I was critical only because *The Times* forced me to be so.

I think we were the only important newspaper in the United States that consistently tried to be fair to Castro and his revolution. It took courage to print my editorials. In another chapter I will have much to say about Cuba, *The Times,* and myself that is not so agreeable, but it would be unfair to withhold the praise that is due.

When I joined the Editorial Board late in 1949, I discovered very quickly that the editorial page was not only read, but had enormous impact and influence.

My field was foreign affairs, although not exclusively. I had served *The Times* in Europe, Africa, and Asia and could draw on my experience and acquaintanceship with many statesmen and public figures. Furthermore, my sources at the State Department were a great help in furnishing information and, at times, guidance. That institution does hold a wealth of knowledge and experience in its huge staff about every country on earth. It was never possible, for instance, to keep all the details about all twenty of the Latin American countries in my head or my files. I came to know just about all the department heads and desk men, not to mention the assistant secretaries of the Inter-American Bureau as they came along.

On the other hand, the old belief about *The Times* being a mouthpiece for the State Department must surely have died a well-earned death after our editorials during the Kennedy, Johnson, and Nixon administrations. Our editorials on Cuba and Vietnam alone have been the despair of the State Department.

Soon after I was settled in New York in 1950, I noticed an important Latin American news story and asked Merz who wrote our editorials on the region. He blandly replied: "No one." This, incidentally, was a measure of the lack of interest in the United States in Latin American news. I said to Merz: "I speak Spanish and understand Portuguese. I'll be glad to take it on." He agreed, and I went down to Washington to see Assistant Secretary Edward G. Miller, Jr., about it. Eddy Miller, who was to become a good friend, nearly jumped out of his seat for joy to learn that the most important newspaper in the United States was going to turn its attention toward Latin America. He and all his associates had been working in a wilderness.

It was the beginning of a long quest for knowledge and understanding. The Inter-American Bureau was put at my disposal, so to speak, and for some years I had to rely on it heavily. Another very valuable source was the late Professor Frank Tannenbaum of Columbia University, one of the outstanding Latin Americanists of the United States, a superb teacher and a wonderful friend. He ran a weekly seminar to which visiting celebrities from Latin America were invited, first to make a talk and then to conduct a discussion. I hardly missed a Thursday afternoon session over ten or more years, and a time came when I conducted some of the seminars myself.

Then there were the Latin American diplomats in Washington and, as I made trip after trip to the area, a growing list of Latin statesmen, politicians, newspapermen, and businessmen. For much of the time, I knew nearly all the Presidents, some of them on first-name terms. Even dictators, who were always strongly attacked in *The Times* and who knew I wrote the editorials—Trujillo, Batista, Pérez Jiménez, Stroessner, Duvalier, Odría—would see me because of the importance of *The New York Times.* The one exception was General Perón. There was always a welcome in American embassies, for obvious reasons.

I found the Inter-American Press Association (IAPA), on which I represented my newspaper, very useful and interesting, for it kept me in touch with all the leading newspaper publishers of Latin America and many in the United States. Meetings were held semiannually in different countries, offering the opportunity for fruitful trips. This went on for eleven or twelve years until I was pushed out over Cuba—but that is a story to tell later.

On the whole, I was fortunate. No one wanting to learn about Latin America could have hoped for a better, easier, and more pleasant schooling. The reason, of course, was not—as the French would say—*mes beaux yeux;* it was the magic name, the power, and the influence of *The New York Times.*

I was frightened when I first realized the impact of any editorial I wrote about a Latin American country or personality.

The Associated Press and United Press International would pick up the text from our first edition and send parts or all of it to the capital of the country concerned. It would be published as a story in the local press and often commented upon editorially. Every Latin American diplomat in Washington and everyone in the State Department's Inter-American Bureau would watch for the editorials and transmit them to their foreign offices and, in the case of the State Department, to our embassies.

I was told by people who knew whereof they spoke that our editorials contributed significantly to the overthrow of Perón in Argentina, Pérez Jiménez in Venezuela, and Rojas Pinilla in Colombia. To a considerable extent the dictators were responding to vanity and sensitiveness. In their own countries they were either immune to criticism or could and did put critics in jail. An attack in *The New York Times* would come as a shock. It would lower a dictator's prestige in Washington and would hamper or embarrass the State Department's almost invariable policy of favoring the dictators who were pro-American and hospitable to United States investors and who maintained stability and the status quo—until they were overthrown by a "palace revolution" or a popular uprising. They all made believe that they were anti-Communist because this was the way to the State Department's and Congress' hearts.

When the then Vice-President Nixon made his famous trip to South America in 1958 and was spat upon and stoned, he drew the right conclusion. We must confine ourselves to a formal handshake with the dictators, he said, and reserve an *abrazo* (an embrace) for the democratic leaders. Evidently this was considered idealistic but impractical. President Nixon seemed to have forgotten his own experience when he sent Governor Nelson Rockefeller of New York to embrace all and sundry in 1969— with catastrophic results.

Actually, *The Times'* strong editorial attacks against dictators, and against military coups overthrowing elected presidents, were often privately applauded and even encouraged by my friends at the State Department. They appreciated the fact that the most important American newspaper was giving expression to the way the American people felt.

A simple, trite lesson is that journalists consort with strange bedfellows. I always kept on good terms with General Fulgencio Batista of Cuba, for instance, even after I had done him what proved to be irreparable harm by my interview with Fidel Castro in the Sierra Maestra and my editorials criticizing his regime. He was sophisticated enough to act friendly and receive me cordially in the Presidential Palace whenever I visited Havana, taking care to have a photographer present and sending pictures of us shaking hands to newspapers and magazines. Yet I knew at the time that he would gladly have paid a henchman a million dollars to bump me off and stop those editorials in *The New York Times* if he thought he could get away with it. Personally, Batista was an important journalistic source for me, and that was enough. The last years of his brutal counterterrorism appalled me, as his venality disgusted me, but it was always professionally satisfying to see him.

There were occasions when my aggressive attacks on a dictator cost *The Times* money in canceled advertising. Each year a man is sent around to gather contracts for our New Year sections on different parts of the world. One year our representative, who happened to be the son of our vice-president, General Julius Ochs Adler, had just concluded a $10,000 contract with the Venezuelan government when a hot editorial, attacking the infamous dictator, Marcos Pérez Jiménez, appeared in *The Times.* The contract was promptly canceled. Young Adler wrote a complaining letter to his father, who passed it along to me for comment. I replied angrily that the editorial was fully justified and asked since when was *New York Times'* editorial policy supposed to be adapted to our advertisers' desires? The next time I saw General Adler he chuckled and said: "You certainly told Julie, Jr., off!"

Latin America is, technically, a formidable problem for a North American newspaperman. Without counting the newly independent, formerly British Caribbean colonies, there are twenty traditional Latin American republics, each one differing from the other as much as one Asiatic country from another. Everybody who writes about Latin America starts by conceding that he has embarked on an impossible task. Then he embarks upon it. The region tempts experienced journalists into the well-known technique of writing all about a nation and its current situation after a sojourn of a day or two. Even to spend one week in each of the countries would take up five months. However, by building up a good background of knowledge, revisiting familiar ground, and knowing the political leaders and academic figures—plus help from American embassy staffs—it is remarkable what a seasoned newspaperman can accomplish. In this he is like an artist who turns out a sketch in minutes but has spent many years learning his profession and developing his style. I was once asked how long Picasso would have taken to do a drawing that fetched thousands of dollars. My answer was, "Forty years." In any event it is always better to spend at least a few hours or days in a place one has to write about than not to go there at all.

Thomas Ybarra, who was a Latin American specialist for *The Times* many years ago, was, I believe, the first to paraphrase Kipling: "North is North and South is South and never the twain shall meet."

When Willard L. Beaulac was U.S. ambassador in Santiago, Chile, in 1955, I made a note after a talk with him that could have applied to every country in Latin America and, for North Americans, anywhere else in the world except England, Australia, and Canada. Beaulac was a very experienced career officer.

"One's first impressions of Chile are deceptive," he said. "Chileans talk as we do; appear to see things as we see them; feel that they are like us Americans and understand us. In reality, their mentality and logical processes are different. They do not act as we would act, and do not draw the same conclusions from similar sets of facts. Without realizing it, they deceive themselves and us. The important thing is not to take them at face value."

Here is a passage from a note I made for *The Times'* editors on returning from a trip to Colombia in August 1965:

"Colombia never was the White Hope that Washington foolishly thought it was several years ago, making it the fair-haired boy of the Alliance for Progress and the main target of the Peace Corps, which has 500 people there. This was another evidence of how poorly the higher ups in Washington understand Latin American countries and people. The Colombians, in fact, are as hard for North Americans to understand as Zambians and Cambodians. They are very special, and even U.S. Ambassador Covey T. Oliver, as shrewd and knowledgeable as they come, is baffled by them."

Yet we must try. President Kennedy, in his short term, had shown more understanding of, and sympathy for, Latin America than any American President since Franklin D. Roosevelt. "I regard Latin America as the most critical area in the world today," he said in a press conference on February 7, 1963.

The best way I can think of, both to give a broad and varied picture of this fascinating and vitally important region, and to sketch some of my own experiences and present-day ideas, is to offer a series of vignettes about a number of the countries.

ARGENTINA

Argentina is a nation that has not been able to find herself. She is in constant crisis, but a country where there is no hunger, no great poverty, no racial problems, no ideological struggle (except dying echoes of Peronism), no overpopulation, and where Nature has been as bountiful as anywhere on earth. She has had no revolution of the Mexican-Cuban type, no civil war or war devastation, and no proletariat until recent times. Argentina should be one of the happiest lands on earth, but she is living as if under a self-pronounced curse.

Before the military clique led by Colonel Juan Perón seized power in 1943, the picture from the outside was of a wealthy, relatively satisfied country in a feudal sense. Its *oligarquía*, of pure, early Spanish descent, has been world-famous for its wealth, exclusiveness, and cosmopolitanism. Alberto Gainza

Paz, publisher of Argentina's best-known newspaper, *La Prensa* of Buenos Aires, once told my wife and me about his grandfather who not only sailed to Europe with his chef, valet, and other servants, but who also took along a cow so that he would have fresh milk on board. My wife and I stayed once at the *estancia* of an Argentinian friend, which was 85,000 acres of the incredibly rich *pampa* land. The estate was one of three owned by the family.

In the small oligarchy there is a snobbishness generally directed against Argentinians belonging to the great immigrant wave—mostly Italian and Spanish—around the turn of the century. However, what matters most in society is a certain breeding: people must not be vulgar; they must "belong." This leaves room for the Anglo-Argentines, a remarkable ethnic group descended from the English who once controlled the land around the mouth of the River Plate. (W. H. Hudson, their most illustrious son, wrote a superb novel about the region called *The Purple Land that England Lost.* The Welsh, who still speak their native language and who are an even more closely knit community, live down in the bleak sheep lands of Tierra del Fuego. By Argentine social standards they are "non-U.")

Juan Perón, who was of partly Italian descent, did not "belong." His wife, Eva, even less so, as she was a small-time actress of dubious morality when she became Perón's mistress. He and the great following of "shirtless ones" (*descamisados*) were, to use a special Argentine word, *guarangos,* which put them beyond the social pale. Class consciousness existed from the immigration waves of the 1890's, but there was little Marxism or revolutionary sentiment from below to bring out a class struggle until Perón and Evita came along. The latent antagonism, whose embers he fanned, must still be there today, smoldering under the relatively calm surface.

It is a tragedy that the oligarchy, allowing for many honorable exceptions, ran things in pre-Perón years with a certain heartlessness and selfishness. It was and still is, on the whole, a reactionary class, clinging to its wealth and privileges. The old families did not divide the land—not even Perón made them do that—and no real middle class grew up until the immigration and the twentieth-century industrialization. Politicians came from a professional elite—doctors, lawyers, engineers, professors—but they ran the country for the oligarchy until Perón arrived.

Argentina always had the Spanish-Latin tradition of the strong executive, even in their liberal 1853 constitution. They never fought for democracy, even in overthrowing Perón. The oligarchy let individuals looking for power seize it. They despised army life and the "best" families did not let their sons go in for it, nor did they receive officers socially. Hence, in crises —such as 1943—they did not necessarily have the military on their side.

Argentinians permitted their demagogues, tyrants, and strong men the freedom to destroy freedom. Their chief objection to Perón was not that he was a dictator, but that the methods he used were bad. They seem to have the same instinctive and traditional opposition to government that the Italians, French, and Spanish have. They, themselves, talk of a destructive trait in their character—that they more easily tear down than build up. The man in the street, who has seen corruption in government, politics, and business all his life, is cynical. In a civic sense they are a divided, weak people, a frightening example of the difficulty of maintaining a middle-of-the-road democracy, one that is prepared to fight for its existence. Eternal vigilance has not been there.

Politics in Argentina is not an art; it is a disease. The people are apathetic and the politicians intolerant. Argentinians are incomprehensible to all foreigners, and especially to North Americans. Presumably, politicians and military officers understand each other, but certainly they do not trust each other—and with good reason. An American ambassador said to me: "It is a nation without heads; you couldn't have a French Revolution to chop off the heads of the rulers because they have no heads." An Argentine newspaper publisher, the night before I was to see Acting President Guido, warned me: "Don't believe anything that he—or for that matter any Argentine leader—tells you.

They say just what you want to hear—and then do something else."

On one of my visits, in October 1962, just after a military coup that overthrew President Arturo Frondizi, I wrote in my notes: "There is a lack of political and fiscal rectitude, a lack of patriotism in the sense of wanting to serve the country and not oneself, a lack of unity and civic sense. I feel once again what I felt during the Perón dictatorship, and which I then blamed on Perón—a moral or spiritual corruption, a sort of original sin which pervades political, economic and civic life. The oligarchy—economic and social—are good people with good intentions, but they are like the aristocracy before the French Revolution—they are living in a world that does not conform to the 1960's, defending wealth and a way of life that are anachronistic."

In Argentina, as in all of Latin America, it is often wrong to look for economic and social causes for revolutions or political unrest. The real motive for action is usually personal ambition for power or wealth or both. Juan Perón was a case in point. As a military attaché in Rome, he admired and studied the techniques by which Mussolini came to power. Then he copied them with remarkable fidelity in Argentina.

His definition of government was a classic one, whether Fascist, Communist, or just dictatorial. "We claim as a fundamental truth of our doctrine [*Justicialismo*]," he said in a speech on March 11, 1951, "that true democracy is one in which the government does what the public desires and defends a single interest—that of the public." Rousseau would have approved; so would Lenin; so would Fidel Castro; so would any authoritarian ruler however differently they put their theories into practice.

Perón was always underestimated by his enemies. In his heyday he was one of the most formidable demagogues of modern times. Argentina, it must be kept in mind, is a great, naturally wealthy nation of white, educated, politically conscious people. It took intelligence to rule them for twelve years, as Perón did. He knew how to use men—and women, as he used Evita. He never trusted anyone except, perhaps, her. Even as a young officer of twenty-two or twenty-three he worked with his door open all day so that his industry could be appreciated. He courted popularity from the ranks, as well as from his superior officers, and kept himself in fine physical shape. He would never get into debt, for it would have made him dependent on others.

Juan Perón achieved greatness on his own. But, of course, the idol had clay feet—young girls, soft living, vanity, overconfidence, a failure to protect his lone position. He said: *"Al pueblo, los tangos los cantos yo"*—a good Argentine way of saying, "For the people, I'll call the tune." But power never rests in the people. A military dictator is vulnerable to military enemies—and for good measure, to these he added the landowners, the industrialists, the intellectuals, the Roman Catholic Church, and the middle classes who were the greatest enemies. Since the nineteenth century, the army was almost entirely middle class at the officer level. They destroyed the budding democracy of the 1920's, paved the way for Perón, and when they kicked him out, again destroyed the burgeoning efforts to build a democracy.

Perón made a fatal mistake that his model, Mussolini, cynically avoided—he antagonized the Church. His "religion" was to make a secular goddess, alive and dead, of Evita. Eva Perón was an astonishing phenomenon in a continent (Spain is the same) where woman's place is in the home and never in politics. She was a very strong character with passionate hates, ruthless, daring, determined, ambitious, astute, indefatigable, and physically attractive. She never forgot a slight or an insult, and was especially vindictive against the women of the oligarchy, who would never have anything to do with her.

People argued about whether she or he ran things, but after watching and studying, I decided that Perón was the boss, even before Evita became fatally ill of cancer. They were two dynamic, explosive characters, trying to pull the chariot of state as a tandem, but they did not always pull together, or in the same direction. The situation was completely new for Latin America, and rare in any country any time. Evita's handicap was that the men did not like it, and the army was run by men.

But how did Juan Perón really feel about Evita? The enigma

closes in on us. She died on July 26, 1952. Here is a true story that may throw a little light on the subject. It was told to me by an eyewitness, one of the officers present on guard duty at the end of the third day that Evita's body had been exposed to a worshipping populace.

The bier had been taken back to a room in the building of the General Confederation of Labor. General Perón walked in with the doctor who had originally embalmed Evita for the ceremonies. The doctor was protesting. Perón had evidently asked that the body be fixed up for three days more, since the ceremonies were proving such a success, but the physician said that he could guarantee nothing. The General ordered him to do his best and watched impassively as the doctor prepared his instruments and injected the embalming fluid into Evita's body.

When finished, the doctor stumped out. Perón halted for a moment at the bier, gazing critically down at the face of his dead wife. Then he reached into his uniform, took out a pocket comb, and carefully combed and set Evita's hair.

With Perón, Argentina passed through a crisis of which he was a result and an episode, more than a cause. Argentinians got Perón because of errors and political and economic sins before he seized power. However, his overthrow in 1955 did not solve the crisis, partly because he corrupted and fragmented the whole structure of Argentine society. Unlike Hitler, Mussolini, and Stalin (but like Franco), Perón had no system to perpetuate. Peronism was formless, amorphous, opportunistic. It was a regime without a future although it left a residue that has been bothersome and, at times, dangerous. There really was no viable alternative to Juan Perón, and no successor. A Peronist was a man who had something to gain from the regime.

A famous anecdote, used by Italians in Mussolini's last years, applied to Perón in 1955. Il Duce sends a party official to a town whose loyalty is reported dubious and asks him to report. When the official returns, he says to Mussolini: "I found 20 percent of the people were Socialist; 15 percent were Liberals; 40 percent were Populists; 10 percent were Communists, and 15 percent were Republicans." "But," Mussolini protests, "what about the Fascists?" "Oh, of course, Your Excellency, they were all Fascists."

Such a regime relies on the army and police to stay in power. When the military split, and the navy, air force, and part of the army turned against Perón, he was finished.

Argentinians have an apt label for their right-wing, interventionist military officers—Gorillas. They had been pro-Axis in World War II until they saw that Hitler was going to lose. Afterward, the State Department foolishly issued a "Blue Book" on Argentina, which was damning from our point of view and very irritating to the Argentinians. Spruille Braden, our first postwar ambassador, made things worse by openly quarreling with the then upcoming Colonel Perón. In the presidential elections of February 1946, Perón campaigned under a very successful slogan: *O Braden O Perón.* Then Washington went to the other extreme and in 1947 started sending some fulsomely pro-Peronist ambassadors—George Messersmith, Stanton Griffis, Alfred Nufer—but rancor and resentment remained. Argentine nationalism is a sense of pride, plus fear of "Yankee imperialism." The only attitude that would not have been resented was one of strict, hands-off neutrality, which neither favored nor opposed the wartime government or Perón. Only Norman Armour, early in World War II, and Ellsworth Bunker in the 1950's, followed that policy.

The stream of editorials I wrote about Perón and Argentina from 1950 to 1955 were intensely annoying to the dictator and —on the evidence—very effective. I was able to get three or four of his liberal opponents out of jail simply by writing editorials mentioning their plight.

My chief exploit in that field—and one of my most rewarding adventures—occurred in March 1955, at the end of a two-months' assignment in Buenos Aires. It was later televised in the United States in an adventure series. I would rather, immodestly, let Alberto Gainza Paz, owner of *La Prensa* of Buenos Aires, relate the story as he told it at the annual conference of the Inter-American Press Association in October. Dr. Paz's intervention was published in the proceedings of the IAPA for 1955.

"I must admit that the establishment of a journalistic 'supreme court' with jurisdiction over human rights is no more than a remote hope," he said. "However, I do believe that a supreme court in fact exists and I should like to relate a story in connection with my country that, perhaps, you are not familiar with.

"Dictators are the principal, perhaps the only, violators of human rights. In Argentina, as you know, we have had years of a tremendous dictatorship. A distinguished colleague of ours, here in this hall, heard that the dictator had, for more than six months, held in prison a large group of students, perhaps a hundred or more, whose only crime had been their refusal to submit abjectly to the Perón regime. These students were imprisoned in the jail of Villa de Voto and had no way of regaining their freedom, because not even the right of *habeas corpus* existed under Perón.

"Not one line of information had been published on the matter because the dictatorship prevented all media, national and international, from using this horrible item of news. Only the students' relatives knew what had happened.

"This North American newspaperman, representing a great newspaper, went to Argentina and tried to enter the jail. He succeeded, by using a false Argentine name, and he managed to interview the students. The next day, on the airplane that took him to Chile, he drafted a despatch, a detailed story on what was happening. He also sent an editorial which was published next day in his newspaper. [Actually, I arranged for the editorial but did not write it.]

"That newspaperman was Herbert Matthews, and the newspaper that sent him to Buenos Aires and published his reports was *The New York Times*.

"Mr. Matthews is such an able man, as intelligent as he is modest, that I thought it our duty to render him this tribute.

"The case I have related also proves that the supreme court in cases of this sort is public opinion."

Juan Perón was thrown out in the autumn of that same year, 1955. He had salted away a great fortune in Europe, including Evita's fabulous collection of jewelry. Argentinians estimated that his wealth in exile in Spain could be counted in the hundreds of millions of dollars—enough to permit him to make a great and continuing nuisance of himself for years. His end will be Biblical: "and he that had driven many from their own country into strange lands perished himself in a strange land."

The military "Gorillas" were never happy with civilian governments. In 1962 they struck again and are still running an unpleasant, ugly dictatorship in 1971. The pendulum has swung to the extreme Right, but nothing has been solved, and one of these days it could swing back toward the Left—but not to Peronism. It is Argentina's tragedy that she seems to have nowhere to go.

BRAZIL

Like virtually all observers, I used to write of Brazil as a sane, healthy, tolerant nation with a dazzling future. Brazilians, I said, were a gentle, easy-going people who had shed the hardness of their conquering forebears. It would have seemed incredible that Brazil, of all countries, should become a place to be branded with unassailable proofs of the bestial torture of hundreds of political prisoners and of murders by "death squads," whose members came mostly from active and retired police officers. These misdeeds, and the worldwide condemnation of them, have shattered illusions about happy-go-lucky Brazil. One should never say of evil things and any country: "It can't happen here."

Brazil is overwhelming. In size she covers nearly half of the South American continent. Her population of ninety-four million is almost half the total for Latin America. In natural wealth she is potentially as rich as, or richer than, the United States or the Soviet Union. She is the largest Roman Catholic nation in the world. Brazilians claim that they are the only people to have conquered and built a civilization out of the tropics.

Everybody who writes about Brazil, I think without exception, says she is "a future giant of the world." One means that when her economic potential is fulfilled, and when her fast-growing population soars to—let us say—150 million, she should be in a class with the United States, Russia, and China.

Brazil is handicapped by a huge area in the northeast, which is one of the poorest regions on earth. Sixty-three percent of the nation's population in the 1960's depended on agriculture, but half the farmland in Brazil is in the hands of 1.6 percent of the owners. The massive misery of a large proportion of the people remains. Except for an unusual stretch of five years—1963 to 1968—Brazil has been badly and extravagantly governed. There is now (1971) a reign of terror. The idea of a Brazil with a fair distribution of wealth, efficient, honest governments, and education and public health for all, is a dream of a far-distant future.

I could feel all this coldly when I got away from Brazil. While there, like all visitors, I succumbed to its charm and extraordinary vitality.

"The value of periodic trips to Brazil," I wrote John Oakes after a visit in 1962, "is to restore one's faith in that unique and astonishing country. You, perhaps, did not grasp on your recent visit how unlike other Latin American countries Brazil is, since you don't know the others, but some of the remarkable optimism, zest, faith and drive of the Brazilians must have rubbed off on you. It is the United States a century ago. There is no question whatever that they are at the moment making a grand mess of things; that they have no leaders worthy of running the country; that they have no unity, no national parties, and that if the inflation is not soon stopped, they will run into something very grave."

Two years later, President Joao (Jango) Goulart was overthrown by a military coup. He had been outrageously extravagant and inefficient. Although a great landowner, he was flirting with the extreme left. The inflation I mentioned was of the order of 85 percent that year. Washington was so overjoyed at the coup that it rushed exuberantly to recognize the successor, Marshal Castelo Branco. It almost looked as if the United States had engineered the revolt. When our editorial mildly pointed this out and also, pro forma, criticized the fact that a duly elected President had been overthrown in the midst of his term, Kennedy's White House assistant, McGeorge Bundy, was furious.

All the same, it is never either wise or right for the United States to flaunt its power and loudly proclaim its likes and dislikes in Latin America. Brazilians, like all Latin Americans, are very nationalistic, and it is impossible to be nationalistic without being anti-Yankee. The Brazilian officers needed no help from the United States.

Marshal Castelo Branco was a remarkable and, for Brazil, a unique leader, courageous, incorruptible, and firm. He had a brilliant economic and financial minister in Roberto Campos. It seemed as if the miracle had happened, but his successor, Marshal Arthur da Costa e Silva, was uncertain and inefficient. Castelo Branco had started a ruthless repression against opponents in the political and academic fields. (Costa e Silva abolished constitutional guarantees in March 1967, and because of torture, terror, and army rule, things are no better in 1971 under his successor, General Garrastazú Médici.) Many of Brazil's best-known politicians have been deprived of their civic rights; many of her most famous professors have been driven into exile; the jails are crowded with political prisoners.

On my first visit to Brazil in 1951 I wrote that there can be no country in the world easier to dictate to. Getúlio Vargas was then an elected President after having been a benevolent dictator from 1930 to 1945. I saw him for a long talk. (I always speak Spanish to educated Brazilians, which they understand, and they speak Portuguese to me, which I understand). My impression was of a round ball of a man, shrewd, forceful, humorous. I did not sense the tragic morbidity that must have been there, for he committed suicide three years later as a result of a scandal which was not his fault, leaving a bitter testament accusing the United States.

Brazilian politics until 1969 reflected the mildness and tolerance of the Portuguese character. They had no history of violence, as in Spanish America. The political backwardness of the mass of Brazilians lies in indifference, apathy, and cynicism. So long as his personal liberties were respected, a Brazilian did not care much about civic rights, nor did he care to perform his duties as a citizen.

Politics are highly personalized; parties have little meaning. The most successful politician takes the middle way. Perón would have been laughed out of power by the worldly, cynical, humorous Brazilians, with their keen sense of the ridiculous. They say of themselves that Brazilians spend six days undoing the work that Bountiful Nature performs for them, but fortunately at night and on Sundays, while they rest, Nature repairs the damage and adds a little more.

The ordinary people are like the Portuguese, but on the whole more relaxed, more tolerant, more sophisticated, and with a much more developed sense of fun. Carnival time in Rio de Janeiro is madness, an explosive release from a year of meager living.

Brazil solved the problem of absorbing the great numbers of Negro slaves brought in for the sugar and rubber plantations by the simplest of methods—miscegenation to begin with, then intermarriage. There is a small element of pure Portuguese descent who occupy the top level of society, army, landowning, and business; otherwise it seems hard to find a Brazilian outside the Indian jungle areas who does not have some Negro or Indian blood. I was much struck during the Italian campaign in World War II, to which Brazil, alone in Latin America, had sent a division, with the great gap between soldiers and officers. General Mark Clark, who commanded the Fifth Army, used to groan about the Brazilians to me. They had to be given easy tasks because, as he and others explained it, they were poorly led. The officers were Portuguese-Brazilians; the rank and file were of mixed Portuguese-Negro-Indian blood. They were brave, hardy soldiers, but the officer class was made of softer stuff.

The rule I mentioned at the beginning of this chapter—that one must not take literally what is said—applies in full measure to Brazilians. I am sure they understand each other, and with effort a North American on his guard can get the knack of it—at least, up to a point. On a visit in April 1958, I spoke to Foreign Minister Negrão de Lima in his office. He said, on parting, that he wanted to go to my hotel and pay his respects to me the following afternoon, but he emphasized that I was not to wait for him, as he could not be sure. This was a typically Brazilian way of giving me to understand that a visit from the foreign minister would be a proper act of courtesy which he would like to perform. In that way he paid his respects without having to pay the visit.

Since I have been stressing the delightful Brazilian sense of humor, and since I think that the present sadistic madness is a passing phase, I would like to end with a favorite Brazilian story —which is also one of my favorites. It concerns the *amigo de tigre* —the friend of the tiger.

A man asks his friend: "What would you do if you were out in the countryside and a tiger attacked you?"

"Well, I guess I would run away."

"But you are standing on the edge of a cliff and cannot run away."

"Then, I would climb a tree."

"But there are no trees around."

"I'd shoot the tiger."

"But you have no gun."

"Look," says the man in exasperation, "whose friend are you, mine or the tiger's?"

CHILE

Chile is the most democratic of Latin American countries. This is one of the reasons why she was able to startle the world by electing a radical left-winger, backed by the Communists, as President for the years 1970 to 1976. If Salvador Allende, the new President, who is a Socialist, gets legislative support, Chile will be the first country in the world to elect a revolutionary government by a scrupulously honest, secret ballot.

Even a peaceful revolution is a great strain on a nation. This one will have profound repercussions throughout South America. I would not dare to predict what is going to happen in Chile, but nothing can erase the fact that Chileans voted for an extreme leftist government, first by a popular plurality and then by a congressional majority. Allende's program includes more nationalizations (another blow for the American copper and nitrate companies), much-needed agrarian and tax reforms, and, in the international sphere, restored diplomatic and trade relations with Cuba (Allende is a friend and admirer of Fidel Castro) and with other Communist countries put beyond the pale by Washington—North Vietnam, North Korea, Communist China, East Germany.

Chile is the oddest country, geographically, in the world—a beanstalk on the map, 2,600 miles long and only 100 miles wide on the average. It is what Indians called "the land where the earth ends," as far "down under" as Australia, and as isolated from the Northern Hemisphere, hugging the western slopes of the Andes along the Pacific Ocean. You can have a wonderful deep-sea fishing holiday off the coast, or go skiing in winter time in very beautiful Andean resorts—that is, you can if you are wealthy enough to pay the fare up and back.

Chile, like Australia, is "out of this world" when you look at the map. Yet a European or a North American with cosmopolitan tastes will be more at home in Chile than in Anglo-Saxon Australia—so long as he sticks to Santiago, Valparaíso, and other towns and resorts, where the people he meets will be of European stock, middle class, educated, sophisticated, with a highly developed political consciousness. Go into the countryside where most Chileans live, and you will find misery and social injustice as bad as anywhere in Latin America.

Despite the imbalances, Chile is one of the most advanced nations of Latin America. She has an exceptionally good university and engineering school, the best army and the best police force (*Carabineros*) south of the Rio Grande. The agrarian situation—large landowners and wretched peasants—is shameful, but Chile, at least, does not have the immensely wealthy land-owners and businessmen one finds in Argentina and Brazil. The Church (always Roman Catholic in Latin America) is socially progressive. The left-wing parties are so strong that a coalition led by Senator Allende, including the Communists, first came within an ace of winning the 1958 presidential elections, and it has now won the 1970 election.

On one of my trips to that country in October 1958, when the old General Carlos Ibáñez was ending a six-year term as President, Raúl Prebisch, the noted Argentine economist who was then head of the United Nations' Economic Commission for Latin America (ECLA), made an analysis of the Chilean situation for me. ECLA's headquarters are in Santiago. (I wished the eighty-year-old General *"buena fortuna"* when I said good-bye to him. He chuckled. "You know what Fortune has in store for me." He died a year and a half later.)

"Chile needs a social revolution," Dr. Prebisch said prophetically. "If it comes from the Left—Socialist or Communist—it would result in great ferment, not only here but throughout South America where Chile is often a leader of social and political trends. The strongest social pressures come from the agricultural districts where there is latifundism, absentee land-lordism, and extreme misery among the people. In some respects, Chile's land system is feudal. The maldistribution of wealth, common to Latin America, is accentuated here by the decades of inflation from which the organized industrial workers are protected, and which the high-income classes manipulate profitably, but which oppresses the rural workers and the middle classes. Taxation hits the low-income brackets who cannot escape, but for others there is a great deal of evasion.

"The agrarian problem and maldistribution of wealth are centuries old, but they have a new urgency for two reasons: Chile is going through a population explosion and, nowadays, there is a greater awareness of social injustices and of the fact that they are not the natural order of things.

"The future choice is either reforms or a violent, revolutionary reaction from the Left."

(I have quoted Dr. Prebisch because what he said not only applies to Chile, but to the large majority of Latin American countries.)

When Eduardo Frei, the Christian Democrat, was elected President in 1964, a wave of hope swept over Latin America and up to Washington. Frei was liberal, progressive, and a strong character, who had promised reforms. He tried hard, but he has ended his six-year term with little accomplished except "Chileanization" of the copper industry, and this will now be wiped out by nationalization if Allende has his way. His land reforms were blocked by a conservative and partly reactionary Congress. More than a decade has passed since Raúl Prebisch made his analysis for me—and it is as valid today as in 1958.

Yet when I spoke to President-elect Jorge Allessandri on that same visit (it was only ten days before he took office), he was contemptuous of "theoreticians who work out plans on paper that are not feasible and are too radical"—meaning Prebisch. He was also contemptuous of Eduardo Frei, then a senator and head of the Christian Democrat party. "I understand Chile's problems. I have been trained in economics and business. Frei hasn't. I know what I am talking about, but he doesn't."

Alas! does anyone know what he is talking about in this complex, unpredictable world? Allessandri really didn't, either. When I saw him again four years later he was sour on the world and all its inhabitants, including the United States and North Americans, a grim, bitter, suspicious, complaining man, and a very reactionary one—although he denied it vehemently. "Christian Democrats are Catholic in theory but Communist in their actions," was a typical remark. "Frei plays the Communist game"—which was nonsense. Allessandri knew that he had not been a success—and he failed in his attempt to be re-elected in 1970.

For Americans, Chile was a rich source of natural nitrate (until the Germans perfected a synthetic nitrate in World War I), and it is one of the greatest copper producers of the world. Anaconda and Kennecott were the American firms who put hundreds of millions of dollars into Chilean copper—and got more dollars out. Now, control is, perforce, passing into Chilean hands. This is a trend throughout Latin America.

The Americans built fine towns, paid higher wages than the Chileans, and were paternal in taking care of the health and education of their miner families. However, I did get a shock one day at the Braden (Kennecott) copper mine of Sewell near Santiago.

It seems that in the early decades, miners were dying of silicosis after working for seven years—or were leaving work to die. On a visit in 1955, the doctor in charge of the hospital and of safety precautions in the mine said to me that up to 1945, it cost the company nothing for the miners' illnesses and there were plenty of Indian miners to take the place of those who dropped out. So there was no problem for the Braden Company. However, in 1945 Chile passed a law forcing all mining companies to pay compensation to silicosis victims. Braden officials figured out that it would cost the company $1 million a year, at the rate miners were getting silicosis. So they decided to introduce safety measures which cut the disease down to a minimum—presumably for much less than $1 million a year.

Virtue has its rewards. This is what Fidel Castro calls "Yankee imperialism," but I am sure that Latin American-owned mining companies were no better. It should be chalked up to original sin.

COLOMBIA

Unhappily, Colombia's distinguishing mark for more than two decades is the appalling violence that, so far as I know, is unique in the world. Yet Bogotá, the capital, has been called "the Athens of Latin America" for the high degree of culture its leading families display. Some of the finest human beings I have known in any part of the world are Colombians. Some of the most bestial criminals—thousands of them—are also Colombians.

The phenomenon of violence, Minister of War Alberto Ruíz Novoa said to me on a trip in the early 1960's, seems to have begun in 1903 shortly after a devastating series of civil wars. It died down in the 1930's and flared up again in 1948, when the two political parties—Liberal and Conservative—waged a virtual civil war in the countryside. Nineteen forty-eight was the year of the *Bogotazo*—the great explosion of violence in the capital when a Liberal leader, Jorge Eliécer Gaitán was slain on April 9. The Ninth International Conference of American States was meeting there at the time. One of the young hotheads running around with a gun, irresponsibly and futilely, was the twenty-one-year-old Fidel Castro. The uprising was a result of Liberal-Conservative hostility, not a cause.

In recent years *la Violencia,* as it is called, has been reduced but not eliminated. Estimates of the dead range from 200,000 to 300,000 in less than twenty years. Colombians have been fighting each other with religious ferocity since 1830. The Liberals stand for political decentralization, separation of Church and State, and universal suffrage. The Conservatives, backed by the strongest Church influence in Latin America, stood for centralized government, and traditional class and clerical privileges; they tried to block voting rights for all citizens.

Each side has felt itself to be morally right and the opposing side oppressors or heretics. The fighting has a fanatical quality which can be idealized, or it can be condemned as inhuman. The late Professor Hubert Herring in his *History of Latin America* quotes from a well-known work, *Latin America, Its Rise and Progress,* by the Peruvian scholar, F. García Calderón:

"In Colombia, men have fought for ideas; anarchy there has had a religious character. . . . A Jacobin ardor divides mankind; the fiery Colombian race is impassioned by vague and abstract ideas. . . . These sanguinary struggles have a certain rude grandeur. . . . In Colombia, exalted convictions are the motives of political enmities; men abandon fortune and family, as in the great religious periods of history, to hasten to the defense of principle. These hidalgos waste the country and fall nobly, with the Semitic ardor of Spanish crusaders. Heroes abound in the fervor of these battles. Obedient to the logic of Jacobinism, Colombia perishes but the truth is saved."

There is some truth in this, but it is mainly romanticism. I heard and read too much on a number of trips to Colombia to see the violence as anything but criminality and insane bestiality. Perhaps 25 or 30 percent of it is political—mainly Liberal and Conservative, with a little Communism, and less Fidelism in it. Some of it is personal feuding, or a heritage of the fierce rivalries between villages and regions. Some of it is pure banditry. In some respects it is simply a way of life that has existed for generations.

What is inexplicable is the ferocity and cruelty of the violence —for instance, the cutting off of old women's or of children's heads, and even more horrible acts performed as if by pathological sadists. Yet it is too widespread and prolonged for that. The minister of war, in the conversation I mentioned, coined a word —"thanatomania," a mania to kill, from the Greek, *thanatos*— death.

Moreover, there is generally a lack of law and order by normal standards, much thievery, and such a degree of impunity that— almost literally—one can get away with murder in Colombia. "In our country," Ruíz Novoa said, "laws are made to break, not to obey, and it starts at the top."

This was an exaggeration, especially as Colombian political leaders on the whole are men of the highest integrity. Alberto Lleras Camargo, secretary of the Organization of American States for ten years and afterward President of Colombia, is for me the outstanding political mind of Latin America, the one with the widest vision and the greatest prestige. He is a rare figure —a patriot of his country who thinks in terms of Latin America.

Lleras is a Liberal, as are most of my Colombian friends. There are Eduardo Santos, founder and publisher of *El Tiempo* of Bogota, one of the best newspapers in Latin America; Germán Arciniegas, the noted historian and diplomat; President (from 1966 to 1970) Carlos Lleras Restrepo.

Certain names—like Restrepo, for instance—crop up in politics, business, finance, and landowning. The Colombian elite is small and closely knit, and it has not allowed the internecine violence to affect its wealth or social connections. At the height of *la Violencia* leading Liberals and Conservatives would be playing golf on one of the three courses of the most magnificent golf course I have seen anywhere in the world. It is outside of Bogota. As in other Latin American countries, there is a crying need for agrarian reform. The misery of the peasants and the great gap between the poverty of the masses and the wealth of the small elite is a natural breeding ground for the violence.

Like so many friends of Colombia, I feel ungrateful at having to be critical. No country of Latin America has been more friendly to me, from a decoration to encomiums in their press and to the warmth of the many friends I made there. Although a liberal newspaper with a natural policy of anti-Communism and anti-Fidelism, *El Tiempo* continued defending me editorially in the midst of the worst period of attacks on me because of Cuba. So did the rival Bogota newspaper, *El Espectador.*

In some ways Colombia is the greatest enigma in Latin America—a mixture of the best and worst. The finest emeralds, the finest coffee, the finest Castilian Spanish to be heard in the Americas, the worst violence, the typical social injustices—such is the mixture.

The United States has not known how to handle its relations with Colombia, which is understandable. All the same, the anti-Yankeeism of the ruling classes is understandable, too.

I made a note in Bogota in October 1962, after wholesale dealers in the United States cut the price of roasted coffee by four cents a pound. Coffee then represented 80 percent of Colombia's exports (less now, but still the major export). Every cent that the wholesale price dropped in New York cost Colombia between $7 and $8 million annually.

I wrote: "This is why there are revolutions. In New York, the price cut in roasted coffee represented a small item on *The New York Times'* financial pages. Here in Colombia it means something close to national disaster. The very Americans who have been howling about Cuba—our big business interests, for instance—are the ones who callously cut the throats of the Colombian people, and if the end result is revolution, they will again start howling about Communism. Sometimes these North Americans remind me of the swarm of lemmings we once saw in northern Canada doggedly moving on to their suicidal doom in the Arctic Ocean."

In cases like that, the State Department is helpless. It always does its best to protect the Latin American exporters of raw materials when lobbies for agricultural or mining interests succeed in inducing the American government to impose higher tariffs or reduced import quotas. Now and then it succeeds; more often it fails, and this is one reason for anti-Yankeeism in Latin America.

CUBA

I had the best of reasons to feel (and by some am accused of creating) the shock to history, economics, strategy, ideology, and Latin American affairs caused by the Cuban Revolution. I discuss its importance to American journalism in general and to me and *The New York Times* in particular in other chapters. Meanwhile, to look at the Latin American scene and leave out Cuba would be to present Hamlet without the Dane.

The Revolution brought some permanent consequences. Communism was introduced into the Western Hemisphere; the Monroe Doctrine was forced to develop a blind spot if, indeed, it has not suffered a mortal illness; United States hegemony in Latin America can never be recovered in the form in which it operated before 1959; and whatever anyone thought and thinks about him, a figure of worldwide fame stormed on to the Latin American stage for the first time in modern history—Fidel Castro.

A library of books has already been written about him and his revolution (I think the Che Guevara phenomenon is a passing fancy), and there is no reason why the flow of new volumes should stop for decades to come. I have contributed my share.

Instinctively, one wants to place Cuba in a well-worn Latin American category, but it will not fit. A social revolution is a dynamic process. The Cuban Revolution is an anomaly in the Western Hemisphere and—fortunately for the United States and other countries—there is only one Fidel Castro. It seems clear, in 1971, that the Cuban experience will not be repeated elsewhere in Latin America. This is different, however, from saying that Cuba and Castro will not have a great influence on the region. The French Revolution was not repeated in detail anywhere after 1815, nor has there been another Napoleon, but all of us, everywhere, are the heirs of 1789.

Issues are never "settled" nor are historic problems ever solved while the history is being made. A journalist, like a statesman, works while options are open; while events are unfolding; while judgments are subjective; while the inevitability of the past is still the uncertainty of the present.

From the beginning, my arguments about Cuba have been based on certain simplicities that are embedded in the complexities that always confuse a great historic development. A lot of chickens came home to roost in 1959—the shabby and threatening treatment of Cuba in the nineteenth century; the cavalier way in which the Cuban patriots were treated in the misnamed Spanish-American War which, in reality, was a Cuban war of independence; the economic and political grip clamped by the United States on independent Cuba and held there for six decades of corruption and economic colonialism; the emergence of a nationalistic patriot with an almost mystical popular appeal. The stage was set. Cuba in 1959, in Arthur Schlesinger's now well-known phrase, was "ripe for revolution." What very few Cubans or Americans foresaw was how drastic the revolution was going to be.

American efforts to overthrow the Revolution have failed. Fidel Casto is still there, as strong as ever. Despite Washington's brave words that the United States would not accept a Communist government in the Western hemisphere or negotiate with it, we are living with a Marxist-Leninist regime ninety miles from Florida and have done so for a dozen years. Latin American guerrillas have done badly, but they exist in a number of Latin countries. Right-wing military reactions in half a dozen countries are either oppressive and tyrannical or, as in Peru, are standing Castroism on its head. The appeal of the Cuban David who defied the Yankee Goliath will be a permanent feature of Latin American history and mythology.

Cuba is ostracized and isolated, but there is an empty chair for her in the Council of the Organization of American States where Fidel sits like Banquo's ghost. The most that can be said for Washington's policy is that it has thus far helped to prevent Castro from achieving economic viability. He is further than ever from prosperity as 1971 ends because of his rash and foolish effort to harvest ten million tons of sugar in the 1969–1970 *zafra.*

Fidel agreed with me in 1959, when he first took power, that his revolution would succeed in the long run only if he could make it an economic success. I thought (and wrote in my biography of him in 1969) that he had learned enough and had enough shrewdness and common sense not to put all his eggs into one basket—meaning the ten-million-ton sugar crop. He did just that, with the disastrous results he described with astonishing frankness in his *mea culpa* speech of July 26, 1970. It will take years to repair the economic damage. I often thought and said that Castro seemed to be driving the Cuban people to limits that were dangerous to his revolution. This is such a period.

A social revolution is devastatingly costly and, in many ways, a tragic phenomenon in any country. Who pays the Cuban bill? Many thousands of Cubans of the middle classes, many American investors, and the Russians who may be spending as much as a million dollars a day for the luxury of seeing a member of the world Communist bloc in the Western hemisphere. The Kremlin at least gets political and strategic dividends. Millions of Cuban peasants, workers, blacks, mulattoes, youth, children, and old folk are either better off or living an exciting and often rewarding, although very hard, life and one without civil liberties. One thing is certain: prerevolutionary Cuba is gone forever. Historians must write about it as they would about Cuba as a Spanish colony.

Like so many others in the early years of the Revolution, I argued long and earnestly with Castro and his associates against the steady progress toward Marxism-Leninism. At first Fidel assured me that he had no intention of turning Communist—and I believe he was sincere. Then he set about demonstrating —again, in all sincerity—that Communism was the best possible answer to Cuba's problems. Moreover, he argued, it was a *Cuban* answer because his Communism was going to be different from Moscow's, Peking's, or anybody's. So it was—and is.

With hindsight one can see that all the elements in the Cuban situation made an authoritarian socialist solution a virtual certainty. The choice was between a capitalistic democracy with a constitution and a congress, or a social revolution. There was no middle ground, least of all for a leftist intellectual like Fidel Castro whose whole adult career was oriented toward revolution.

I stopped arguing with him, President Dorticós, Raúl Castro, and (the hardest man of all to argue with) Che Guevara. Fidel, it is clear, is neither going to succeed nor fail because of what he calls Marxism-Leninism. He—and all of us—almost came a cropper in the missile crisis of September–October 1962, the maddest adventure in Castro's wild life, but that is a nightmarish memory. There will be no repetition.

The Cuban Revolution has to be accepted by the United States as an irreversible fact. This looks like a truism, but it is yet to win official or popular acceptance in the United States, although Washington has obviously given up any idea of using military force to overthrow the Castro government.

The American government may think that Castro and his Revolution are on the way out. Anything is possible in the dynamic process of a social revolution, particularly with such a volatile people as the Cubans. The chances are that the Revolution has a long run and time to make up lost ground. Fidel's charismatic appeal is still phenomenal. His revolution was necessary and it has done more good than harm. It is the greatest historic event in Latin America since the Mexican Revolution of 1910, and it has had a much wider impact than Mexico's upheaval. Fidel Castro is not only one of the two or three greatest figures in Latin American history since the wars of independence 150 years ago; he is the first to achieve worldwide fame. I am glad that my newspaper career was, for a period, so closely linked with his.

DOMINICAN REPUBLIC

No example of Washington's favoritism toward Latin American dictators was more flagrant or outrageous than the years of toadying to one of the most monstrous dictators of the century on our side of the Atlantic Ocean—Generalissimo Rafael Leónidas Trujillo of the Dominican Republic, who blandly had himself called "Benefactor of the Fatherland."

He was a pathological megalomaniac, coldly cruel, lecherous, insatiably greedy for himself and his large family, and withal a "good friend" of the United States, highly praised by senators like James O. Eastland of Mississippi and Allen J. Ellender of Louisiana; businessmen like Edwin and William Pauley; diplomats like Phelps Phelps; churchmen like Cardinal Spellman. At best this was out of ignorance and naiveté; at worst it was a reflection of a callous cynicism.

I made the first of a number of visits to Santo Domingo in 1953 at a time when Trujillo's fortunes were at their height. (The "Benefactor" had changed the historic name of the capital in 1935 to "Ciudad Trujillo" but, of course, it was changed back after he was assassinated in 1961.) U.S. Ambassador Phelps Phelps earnestly and sincerely argued with me that Trujillo should be supported by Washington because he maintained discipline, was anti-Communist and pro-American. This was the policy that Phelps was urging upon a receptive Eisenhower regime. Phelps Phelps, in fact, never lost his admiration for Trujillo, which suited Washington for many years. He was an example of how badly Washington was, at times, served by its political appointees in Latin America.

I calculated that the Dominican Republic under Trujillo had the most dictatorial pattern in the world, for it was a small, backward country which could be wrapped up into a neat package and kept under control.

Trujillo made everyone believe that he did much for education, public health, housing, and agriculture. His paternalistic pose was part of his megalomania, not of his nonexistent kindness; it fed his vanity—and it was a fraud. After he was killed, the veil was lifted and the world could see that Trujillo was not only one of the worst tyrants on earth; he was one of the greatest shams. Those American senators and representatives (I suppose the businessmen knew better and were simply being "realistic") who fooled themselves and the American public about Trujillo's virtues should have gone back to see the reality behind the phony façade that the Generalissimo had erected.

He "eliminated" unemployment by denying its existence. Few countries of Latin America had a higher degree of poverty and illiteracy while Trujillo was proclaiming their well-being and issuing statistics to prove it. One year he exported some $20 million of cattle to the United States for personal gain, while his people ate no meat and almost starved. When the census-takers said they found a population of three million, Trujillo said it had to be four million—and four million it was, for the official record.

There was a capriciousness and willfulness about existence in the Dominican Republic that paralleled in its little way the despotisms of the Roman emperors or the Renaissance city-state tyrants of Italy. Favorites were made and unmade overnight. Suspects were quietly killed—without torture if they were fortunate, but with torture if they were caught and jailed first. Others would fall into temporary disgrace and be told that if they behaved, they might come back into favor—which many did. Property would be given, taken back and, sometimes, restored. No one could become too popular or too much admired. When he wanted to, Trujillo's long arm reached into New York to kill an opponent or, as in the case of Professor Jesús Galindez of Columbia University, to kidnap him on a New York street and, it must be presumed, have him killed back in the Dominican Republic.

Machiavelli would have approved of Trujillo without being fooled by him. He was eased into power by the American Marines, who did the same favor at about the same time for "Tacho" Somoza in Nicaragua. The key to Trujillo's success was his use of terror as a method of governing—what Hannah Arendt would call "an instrument to rule masses of people who are perfectly obedient." Hitler had a good phrase for it in *Mein Kampf:* "The one means that wins the easiest victory over reason —terror and force." Hitler's extermination of the Jews and Stalin's massive purges came after internal opposition in Germany and Russia was either eliminated or so unimportant that it held no threat.

Trujillo's rule was never threatened by a mass, or popular, uprising. He used terror to cow any possible rival and forestall any plot to assassinate him. Considering what a loathesome tyrant he was, he was lucky to last as long as he did.

Like all dictators and many (most?) politicians, he worked on the theory that every man has his price. Where fear cannot be instilled, the appeal must be to ambition, power, greed, flattery, vanity, or temptations of the flesh.

Thereby hang some of the hazards of being a newspaperman. On arriving in Ciudad Trujillo in mid-March 1953, I found that a big cocktail party had been arranged for me under the patronage of the man who was then—not for many years longer— Trujillo's right hand and manager of the dictator's private fortune. He was Anselmo A. Paulino who also happened to be president of the capital's main newspaper, *El Caribe*. A well-printed invitation was sent around to a number of the leading lights of Ciudad Trujillo, who showed up at General Paulino's sumptuous house on the afternoon of March 18. Germán Ornés, editor of *El Caribe* and a member of the Inter-American Press Association, had obviously been ordered to take good care of me. He could not have been more attentive. I think he spent half his time trying to persuade me to join him and others for dinner and gaiety at one of the main night clubs. We were expected, and Ornés was so upset I could see that he had his orders to get me there. Since cameras were popping and flashing every few minutes at the cocktail party, I could envisage the same thing happening at the night club without the saving presence of ambassadors and high government officials.

The next morning's *Caribe* had a full page of photographs taken at Paulino's house and a friendly, but cleverly restrained, story by Germán Ornés. The photos would make a possibly embarrassing record for some of those shown and mentioned. However, photographs can be misleading. The last time I saw General Batista in Havana he had a photographer present who snapped us shaking hands cordially. The photos were duly published in the next morning's newspapers. It was part of my job, and the same for Fulgencio Batista.

Five days after the cocktail party, the Generalissimo received me in his office, with one of his aides carefully present. I had preconceived ideas—in fact, knowledge—about the "Benefactor," which, I suppose, accounts for the fact that he seemed as coldly monstrous as he was. Certainly, he radiated no warmth, although he was trying to please me. He actually gave me a present, which was so worthless that I had no hesitation in accepting it, although I was puzzled. They were two secondhand books, one a propaganda job about the country and the other a school textbook on Spanish literature. He handed them over with the nearest thing to graciousness he could assume, as if he were conferring something truly precious upon me. He spoke banalities, and gave me no opening to draw him out, so that I did not even make any notes about our talk when I got back to my hotel. Yet, he did succeed in conveying a sense of ruthless power and cruelty—or was that subjective on my part?

Back in New York I wrote an article about the extraordinary extent of Trujillo's holdings in land, industries, banks, and so forth. I had secretly gathered quite a list in Ciudad Trujillo although, as it turned out, I was far short of the total. Whereupon the distressed Germán Ornés, in the same *El Caribe*, published a scathing attack on my "lies." Ornés later fell out with Trujillo and took refuge in the United States until the Generalissimo's death when he returned and got his newspaper back.

Such is life in Latin America for a newspaperman who has to work with—and against—dictators. I never saw Generalissimo Trujillo again. He was shot down on the night of May 30, 1961, like the beast he was. The beast I mean is the lone wolf. Are all dictators lone wolves? They seem to be. Perhaps they have to be.

The Dominican Republic figured sensationally in the American press in the spring of 1965, when a liberal uprising was mistakenly identified as communistic. The fault lay in bad and frightened intelligence from the American ambassador in Santo Domingo, W. Tapley Bennett, Jr. There were supposedly fifty-two or fifty-seven Reds involved—a false and exaggerated figure. President Johnson lost his head and reacted in panic, sending 30,000 Marines to defeat those fifty-seven Reds and forestall "another Cuba." The President was also being badly advised by Assistant Secretary for Inter-American Affairs Thomas C. Mann, whose unrivaled knowledge of Latin American affairs was stunted by his almost religious anti-Communism and pro-American-type capitalism.

I admired Mann over many years, especially during his first stint as assistant secretary when he was invariably helpful to me and a good friend. He changed his mind about me over Cuba, as I shall point out in a later chapter. However, Mann had an open mind on the Cuban Revolution in its early period, and was not taken in by the misinformation that the Central Intelligence Agency was handing out which led to the fiasco of the Bay of Pigs. When Fidel Castro embraced Marxism-Leninism, Mann naturally and rightly turned strongly anti-Fidelista.

Mann was then Johnson's ambassador to Mexico and we had some sharp arguments about Cuba as I went to and from Havana. By then Mann was fiercely emotional against Castro. When I remarked that he (Mann) was "fanatically democratic," he exploded, and would not give me a chance to explain what I meant. I believe that there is a type whose commitment to liberal democracy and capitalism is so fanatical that it parallels the fanaticism of the dedicated Communist or Fascist.

Mann was too intelligent to have been misled by the panicky reports about the Communists taking over the Dominican Republic, but he was in favor of preventing a leftist revolution and, especially, of "teaching" all of Latin America that the United States would not permit "another Cuba" in the hemisphere. The enormously disproportionate forces that Johnson threw in naturally brought a sullen peace after several months of fighting. Since the Dominican landowners, banking and business interests, high military officers, and the Roman Catholic Church were against revolution or even drastic reforms, and since the impoverished country is heavily dependent on the good will of the United States, it has been possible to keep the lid on. Relatively few Dominicans, thanks to the thirty-year paralysis of the Trujillo regime, are socially or politically mature. A natural apathy returned under President Joaquín Balaguer who got himself re-elected in May 1970, with the customary techniques of bribery and corruption.

Johnson, Mann, and Co. calculated well and had a lot of luck. All the same, what they did was inexcusable. The shock to the whole of Latin America, and the long-range effects on relations with the United States add up to a high price. Our editorials— which I wrote, of course—were strongly critical of the Johnson policies. We pointed to the phoniness of the President's statements about the Communists and about the dangers to Americans. We called attention to the fact that a major element in Latin America's persistent anti-Yankeeism came from the bitter resentment against just such military interventions as the United States was now perpetrating. The falsity of the whole episode was well documented by a number of newspapermen and by scholars like Theodore Draper who did a notable hatchet job for *The New Leader.* Senator J. W. Fulbright made a first-rate speech in the Senate on September 15, 1965, which attacked the Johnson administration for intervening "forcibly and illegally against a revolution which, had we sought to influence it instead of suppressing it, might have produced a strong popular government without foreign military intervention."

The economy has been slowly decaying since 1965; hardly anything has been done to correct the old, glaring inequalities of wealth and privilege. The Dominican Republic is little better off in 1971 under Trujillo's son-in-law, President Balaguer, than it was under the "Benefactor." Johnson and Mann, in the Dominican affair, perpetuated the bad old policies of Yankee interventionism in Latin America. The anti-Yankeeism that poor Governor Nelson Rockefeller found when he went pathetically around Latin America in 1969 for President Nixon showed that Latins are more worried about United States policies than they are about Washington's hysteria over Communism.

GUATEMALA

Guatemala was an earlier example of Washington's reactionary policies, based on exaggerated fears of Communism and a determination to protect American investments. However, the American intervention had more justification in Guatemala than in the Dominican Republic—if Washington's judgments were correct. This is another case where it will never be possible to prove who was right, since Washington's *diktat* cut off any other solutions.

I thought and wrote and still believe that John Foster Dulles' policy (as usual, President Eisenhower left foreign affairs to Dulles' mercies) was wrong. It certainly lacked understanding and imagination—and I would also say, courage. It is always easier to wield Teddy Roosevelt's "Big Stick" than to be patient and let Latin Americans work out their own problems.

Guatemala had had a relatively easy dictatorship under General Jorge Ubico for fourteen years from 1930. Typically, it suppressed all freedoms and deliberately held down the standard of living of the masses, who were Indian and mestizo (mixed Indian and white). Before Ubico there had been four more ruthless dictatorships interspersed with periods of anarchy. Ubico was "good" for the United States because he kept law and order, and especially good for the United Fruit Company, which owned the only railway and controlled the only good port and the whole banana industry.

In 1944 Ubico was overthrown in a revolution which naturally resulted in a violent swing to the left. To many Guatemalan intellectuals and young army officers, socialism, Communism, and/or a radical liberalism seemed to provide the doctrinal answers. Washington and United Fruit were very unhappy.

They became more so when Lieut. Col. Jácobo Arbenz was elected President in 1950. He was not a Communist, but he was pro-Communist, seeing the Reds as "social reformers" who would help him carry out a radical reform program. Arbenz, unfortunately, was weak, inexperienced, unintelligent. The job was too big for him, and he seemed always flustered and bewildered by the drive of events. Although he began his term in 1950 with nothing, by 1952 he was a large property owner with five homes—which shows how little of a Communist he was.

I felt that he was hopeless and that it was right to get him out, but to me (after an intensive study on the spot in March 1952) the way to do it was secretly to help the army and the police (whose officers were mostly anti-Communist) to stage a palace revolt.

We had a very amateurish ambassador when Arbenz began— Richard Patterson, a businessman and political appointee, with the most naive ideas on Communism and a complete ignorance of Latin Americans. He was understandably declared *persona non grata.* Patterson had been God's gift to the United Fruit Company. So were two *New York Times'* correspondents sent in to do some articles—Will Lissner of the City staff and Sydney Gruson, then our correspondent in Mexico City. They unintentionally saw and wrote exactly what the State Department wanted to see.

The reasons being given by the American embassy and State Department for calling the Arbenz regime communistic were not what they seemed to be. The President's secretariat did not have a single Communist member. It was not true that Reds controlled the labor unions. When the Tiquisate banana workers on the Pacific coast wanted to go on working for the United Fruit, instead of striking, all it needed was for a shyster lawyer to go down there and induce them to break away from their union. The railway union, once the strongest in the country, was broken by dissensions. The Communists had been unable to get the labor code they wanted.

Names of top Communists were being uttered in alarm. The head of the railway union, Pinto Usaga, had lost control. Although a supposedly dedicated Communist, he had sent his daughter to school in the United States. Another Communist leader was an opportunist; still another an inexperienced young bungler.

The indigenous, traditional emotion of nationalism, which made the Guatemalans anti-Yankee, was being interpreted as Communist machination.

No one will ever be able to say whether Guatemala would have fallen under Communist control if the United States had not intervened. My guess is that the Guatemalan army and police officers could have handled the matter better than the CIA.

And what of the United Fruit Company? At this time, they were doing about $6 million annually in banana exports from Guatemala and—without counting their railway monopoly—they owned property and equipment worth about 25 million. This was a big stake, worth pulling off a good, old-fashioned, "dollar diplomacy" coup.

I will now tell a story that has been superconfidential but need no longer be so. Edward G. Miller, Jr., assistant secretary of state for the Inter-American Bureau, who told it to me over a luncheon table on September 25, 1953, is dead now. I give it here verbatim from the note I made afterward.

"Early in the summer of 1952 [Anastasio]Somoza [President of Nicaragua] came to Washington. At the State Department, in the presence of Miller and a few others, he said: 'Just give me the arms and I'll clean up Guatemala for you in no time.' They all laughed. A few days later, at a luncheon given by Truman, Somoza was sitting opposite the President, with Acheson on one side and [Undersecretary of State] Lovett on the other and he repeated the remark. Again, everyone took it as a good joke.

Also at the table was General Vaughan, Truman's aide, and his aide, a Colonel Marrow (?).

"Somoza was suddenly taken ill, flown to a hospital in Boston, and after his recovery he was flown back to Managua in an American Army plane, always with Marrow attending him. On the way down to Managua he sold Marrow on the idea, so they got together in the plane and worked out how much arms would be needed. On his return, Marrow made a report which went directly to Truman who, for the first time in Miller's tenure, acted without consulting the Inter-American Bureau of the State Department. Truman initialed the report and passed it along to [General] Bedell Smith to put it into effect.

"In August 1952, Tacho Somoza made a trip to Ciudad Trujillo where he told the *Jefe* [the Generalissimo] about it, and then to Caracas where he told [President] Pérez Jiménez, and to Havana where he told Batista. Batista was wary and uninterested, but the other two were enthusiastic.

"Part of the scheme was to do in José Figueres and prevent him from becoming President of Costa Rica, so a part of the large sums of money raised were to be applied to backing Figueres' opponent, Castro Cervantes.

"Meanwhile, the United Fruit got into the picture in the person of Zuleta Ángel, now Colombian Ambassador to Washington, and a lawyer. Zuleta enlisted the enthusiastic cooperation of Acting President Urdaneta Arbeláez of Colombia. He then made a trip to the Central American countries, the Antilles and Venezuela, ostensibly on behalf of the coffee industry of the United Fruit Company. Gálvez of El Salvador appears to have joined the conspiracy, and perhaps Honduras, but the main actors were Somoza, Trujillo and the United Fruit.

"Miller and the State Department were at all times ignorant of what was brewing, but Bedell Smith was going right ahead and the CIA had been called in to help. It was decided that the man to back as the winner in Guatemala was a notorious exile named Castillo Moreno, who lived in Honduras. Miller was being asked about these arms and when they would be available and kept saying he knew nothing about them—they thinking that he was being cagey. In October, Miller was in Panama for the inauguration of Remón, and Somoza sent his son, Tachito, to represent him. Tachito got hold of Miller and kept asking vainly about the arms.

"The arms were gathered. A representative of the United Fruit in Nicaragua was assigned to receive them. The United Fruit turned over one of its freighters which it had specially refitted for this purpose. Two leaders of the stevedores in New Orleans had to be told about it. The arms were then loaded into the ship as 'agricultural machinery' in cases, and the ship sailed for Nicaragua.

"A day or two afterward, a CIA representative went to Miller and asked him to initial a paper on behalf of the Munitions Department of the State Department (not knowing that the ship had sailed). Miller refused and showed the document to Doc [Freeman] Matthews and David Bruce, Undersecretary of State, both of whom hit the ceiling, went to Acheson, who went to Truman and a message was sent redirecting the ship to Panama, where the arms were unloaded and where they still remain in the Canal Zone.

"Miller points out, to add to all this, that Nicaragua is not contiguous to Guatemala (Honduras being between) and Somoza could not attack it."

Instead, Dulles (who followed Acheson as secretary of state) arranged to arm and send in a Guatemalan exile, Colonel Carlos Castillo Armas, who was in Honduras. A few planes dropped bombs. Castillo, with a small force, put his foot over the border into Guatemala in June 1954. Arbenz was deserted by his army and police; a "pistol-packin'" American ambassador, John E. Peurifoy, flew into Guatemala City and swashbuckled around for a few days—and it was all over. An unknown, unimportant young Argentine doctor, named Ernesto Guevara, who had offered his services as an army medico, fled over the frontier into Mexico.

Castillo Armas was made President and tried a few cautious reforms. However, he did nothing so daring as to permit any of the democratic freedoms allowed by his predecessors, Arévalo and Arbenz, to continue. His regime was corrupt, officer-ridden, and weak. He was assassinated on September 29, 1957.

The clock was set back. Guatemala remained a banana republic (although her chief export is coffee). The Indians, with their wonderful artistic sense, are as poor and land-hungry as ever. Two percent of the population own about 70 percent of the land. I took some figures from the official Guatemalan budget for the fiscal year 1961–1962 when Miguel Ydígoras Fuentes was President. (Incidentally, there was no personal income tax in Guatemala.) Ydígoras' salary was $72,000; his "representational allowance" $72,000; his personal confidential fund was $244,000; the confidential expenditures of the President's office were $852,000; office operating costs were $628,488. Pity the poor President of the United States!

I am conscious of the argument that American policies toward Guatemala have already gained seventeen years of "peace" for the security of the United States. It is also argued that what happened was better than a slide into amateurish, anti-Yankee, and possibly communistic rule. In the same way, it is asserted that six years of Dominican "peace" have been good for American business interests and the Pentagon.

This is *realpolitik* of the sort that any imperial power can and does exercise. The policies may or may not be good for the United States; they are bad for the countries and peoples who are exploited. They go counter to professed American ideals of democracy and of the freedom of people to change governments and regimes—if necessary by revolution. Progress and reform are prevented in the name of anti-Communism, law, and order.

The United States, in short, is basing its Latin American policies on maintenance of the status quo in a fast-changing hemisphere. The reckoning began in Cuba in 1959, but the worst is yet to come—that is, if the policies of the last two decades are not changed.

So far as Guatemala is concerned, there was a military *coup d'état* in 1963. The army arranged, in 1966, for a moderate conservative, Méndez Montenegro, to be elected President. In January 1968 two senior American military officers were murdered by terrorists, and in July 1968 the American ambassador met the same fate. The election of March 1970 brought in a President with an earned reputation as a ruthless killer of the rebellious—Colonel Carlos Araña Osorio. The country faces adamant repression (kidnappings are frequent) or civil war. Is Washington happy?

HAITI

Haiti is a dismal example of a Negro republic—which is why Black Power advocates skip over her to Africa in their propaganda. Nowhere did Negro people have a better chance to show what they could do, and nowhere have they made such a tragic failure.

Haiti was the richest of all French colonies in the eighteenth century, primarily thanks to sugar. It is now one of the poorest nations on earth. Sugar exports alone in 1791 exceeded in value the total foreign commerce of the country in any modern year. The French were driven out in 1804, and Haiti became the first independent republic of Latin America and the only black, French-speaking one. Actually, the language of the people is Creole—a sort of simplified seventeenth-century Norman French with African, Indian, Spanish, and English words mixed in.

The black man, during his unhappy history, has impoverished the land, denuded the forests, thus bringing erosion, and he has failed to develop the soil by proper methods or to exploit the natural beauties of the land with roads. Tourism in modern times brought foreign investments to build fine hotels in the capital of Port-au-Prince and its upper suburb of Pétionville; otherwise there is little development.

Overpopulation, malnutrition, disease, illiteracy, wretched housing, few public works, few new industries, unskilled labor, a small internal market, few opportunities or incentives for foreign investments, a caloric intake of food that theoretically should starve almost everyone—these are the abiding curses of modern Haiti.

Her one great asset is the people—friendly, surprisingly hardy in the rural areas, gay, gentle, warm, and swarming, so that labor is the cheapest commodity on the quarter-island of Hispaniola which Haiti occupies. Haitians are very much alive. There is stamina and an adjustment to what is literally a bare subsistence. They do not even look emaciated or apathetic, as the Andean Indians do. The human element defies statistics. Their remarkable artistic gifts, which rank with Mexico's and Peru's, have never been lost.

The veneer of the twentieth century and the West is thin in Haiti. The spirit of Africa survives; so does the seventeenth-century atmosphere of fear, repression, and slavery—and yet Haitians do not have a slave mentality. If they have any sense of inferiority, it is because of the white man—early French and late American—not because of their own tyrannical, bloodthirsty, corrupt, and inefficient leaders.

Nowhere in Latin America is the difficulty of bridging the gap between minds greater. I always left Haiti baffled, frustrated, and sad. It is not a question of color. I do not believe that an American Negro can understand Haitians any better than can a white man. There is an unattainable, unreachable, impenetrable depth—perhaps a heritage of the African mind with its roots in (to us) ancient superstitions and fears.

These words would not apply to the small mulatto elite, who speak Parisian French—the men suave and sophisticated, the women so chic in their Paris clothes and often so beautiful that Anglo-Saxon women feel like sparrows amidst birds of paradise.

The mulatto sector has been going through difficult and even dangerous times, for recent Presidents have been blacks and have taken some revenge for the long stretch of mulatto control. Unhappily, the mulattoes, over the generations, were selfish and callous, doing little for their country and much for themselves. A price is now being paid.

In the beginning, King Christophe killed off the mulatto *aff-ranchis* in the north, but later rulers favored them. There was a long, bad period from 1843 to 1915 during which there were twenty-two rulers, who misruled atrociously. In 1915 American Marines landed, put an end to the chaos and bloodshed, re-stored order, controlled customs and finance, funded the debts, and gave Haiti stable government until Franklin D. Roosevelt pulled them out in 1934.

It was American interventionism at its best—but with one fatal flaw. The Americans—white men, of course—were race con-scious and showed it. They naturally favored the mulattoes, who were educated and sophisticated and who were—more for social than religious reasons—good Roman Catholics.

It is estimated that only 1 or 2 percent of the population belongs to the upper reaches of Haiti's elite. A good 90 percent of the people are independent farmers with one or two acres, or farm laborers. They, too, go to their dances on Saturday night. Sunday morning, the men will watch cockfights while the women go to church. But all of them go to their voodoo ceremonies. Haiti's state religion is Roman Catholicism, but its base is voodooism. An American priest told me that the young are no less devotees of voodoo because "we lose them after a few years."

From 1957 to 1971 Haiti had a President who was a scientific student of voodoo—and who perhaps practiced it for political or personal reasons—Dr. François Duvalier. He was a black, who succeeded two black Presidents—Dumarsais Estimé and Paul Magloire.

I had several long talks with Magloire on early trips to Haiti and praised him editorially. Others thought well of him, too, including American envoys and the State Department. Then he was ousted in December 1956, after five years in office, and fled to New York with a reputed $5 million—an enormous sum for his impoverished country. It was also revealed that there had been an unusual degree of corruption in his government.

After a succession of provisional Presidents and sharp infight-ing, Dr. François Duvalier came out on top, with no inkling from his mainly medical record of what a monster he was to become.

In a letter he wrote me during the electoral campaign on May 22, 1957, he said: "Before going any further, I do wish to state that I have been consistently faithful to the Hippocratic oath that I took when I became a Doctor of Medicine, and that instead of killing people—as I have been accused—my mission has been to save lives and to alleviate suffering whenever possible."

Apropos of the election to come on June 16, 1957, and of alleged attempts by his opponents, Déjoie and Fignolé, to fix it, he added: "Haitians have paid too dearly for their liberty to relinquish it easily. The right to vote—an expression of Democracy [his capital letter] is to them a symbol of that hard won liberty."

His indignant self-righteousness in these and other respects, such as his refusal, as he put it in his letter, "to foment class and color strife" were extraordinarily ironical, considering what a bloodthirsty tyrant he was to be as President of Haiti.

I had a long talk with him in November 1962, by which time he had been President for five years. Absolute power had corrupted him absolutely. I have met some sinister characters of modern times, but of them all I would say that two were the most chilling and the most able to make me feel the depths of evil to which human beings can descend. One—already noted—was Generalissimo Trujillo of the Dominican Republic, and the other François Duvalier of Haiti.

My interview was the first he had given in a year. It was a carefully staged performance, attended by the Secretary of Commerce Clovis Desinor (who curiously had the same post and influence under Magloire) and a white American who came straight out of an Eric Ambler novel—Dr. Elmer Laughlin. The good doctor was reputed to be making great amounts of money in strange ways. At that period the only channel to Duvalier was through Dr. Laughlin.

In the President's office, the three of them worked on me as if I were the subject of a voodoo ceremony. Duvalier was silent for a long time, his marble eyes staring at me fixedly. I wondered if he was going to say anything, but he finally responded to a question of mine and then talked at length without stopping. There was no animus toward me or toward *The New York Times*, despite our very critical editorials. Otherwise, I would not have been granted the interview. François Duvalier was either insensitive or impervious to criticism. The object was to impress on me the allegedly disinterested friendliness of Haiti for the United States; how anti-Communist the Duvalier regime was; and how misunderstood, unappreciated, and unrewarded Haiti was. (Washington had cut off all economic and military aid.)

I could not ever decide whether Duvalier was pathological or experiencing an atavistic throwback to African savagery. After all, he was a medical doctor, American-trained, who had a fine record working with the United Nations before being elected President in 1957. Later, he arranged to get himself elected "President for Life." It is still not clear—and I suppose never will be—why or how he turned into something so corrupt and cruel.

In order to stay in power against formidable enemies, he quickly surrounded himself with tough, gangsterlike characters whom he armed and allowed to acquire immunity, to carry out arbitrary arrests and torture, and to seize properties. They became known as the *Tontons Macoutes*— Creole for bogeymen. In addition, Duvalier had the regular Palace Guard, plus the regular army and, after 1959, a personal militia and a "secret" police corps. It is no wonder that he stayed in office until his death in 1971. I need hardly add that all those forces were armed with American matériel and, to a considerable degree, trained by Americans—a fact that many Haitian families do not forget, although it is hard to see how this could have been avoided.

I often wondered why some patriotic Haitian officer had not assassinated Duvalier. Haiti has some Olympic-class marksmen. But this is always a stupid question to ask of life and history. Why was Stalin allowed to die in bed and John F. Kennedy assassinated?

In a report to *The New York Times'* editors on a visit to Haiti in 1962, I could not refrain from a rather malicious aside. I was ending a trip to twelve Latin American countries, made for editorial background.

"Believe it or not," I wrote, "I was treated almost as a hero by the Haitians I met, or who tried to get in touch with me, for there is a strong current of intellectual, not pro-Communist, *Fidelismo* in Haiti. It may also be hard for you all to realize that, aside from the normal recognition of the importance of *any New York Times'* editor in Latin America, I would not have been gladly received by every Latin American President in the countries I visited (except Valencia in Colombia who had pneumonia) if it were not for my personal reputation—Cuba not only included, but Cuba as a decided asset."

This was at the height of the criticisms I was getting in the United States because of Cuba. The different attitude toward Fidel Castro in Latin America was partly a result of the omnipresent anti-Yankeeism.

Before his death, Duvalier named his twenty-year-old son Jean-Claude to succeed him as President. The transition was suprisingly peaceful. The fat, woman-loving, fast-driving Jean-Claude began with the necessary support of the military and the *Tontons Macoutes.* He also began with one great asset: He could not help being a better President than his father.

MEXICO

All modern social revolutions, starting with the French Revolution, are irreversible in the sense that the clock can never be turned back to the prerevolutionary situation. However, they all follow a roughly similar pattern, or in Crane Brinton's word, they have a similar "anatomy." As the years pass, the destructive, radical, violent phase levels out, moderates, moves to the right, stabilizes—and the revolution is over. This is what has happened in Mexico, but the mystique of *la Revolución* persists and colors political and social life. Communism had nothing to do with it. As Mexicans never cease pointing out, their Revolution antedated the Bolshevik one by seven years.

Most authorities in recent years, and today, consider that the Mexican Revolution "went wrong." By this they mean that the peasants profited little; that poverty in rural areas remains severe; illiteracy is about 50 percent; agriculture on a large scale, mining, and banking are once again heavily infiltrated and often controlled by American investors; a new class of Mexican politicians has replaced the old aristocracy as latifundistas; and a new Mexican capitalist class has supplanted the old. Politics are corrupt; the press is controlled through government subsidies and by a firm hand on the supply of newsprint. The press is venal and generally uncritical of governments—not a free press by American or European standards.

In a talk I had with President Ruíz Cortines on May 9, 1955 (he said he was not speaking as President of Mexico, but as a man and a sociologist), he said that one million Mexicans still lived in caves and that twenty million are not "much above the subsistence level." (His Minister of Education Gilberto Loyo told me on that trip that 80 percent of Mexicans earned no more than thirty-five to forty dollars a month.)

Speaking of the notorious custom of the *mordida*—literally, bite—which is the Mexican word for the ubiquitous system of graft, Ruíz Cortines said: "A man who is ignorant and starving cannot be expected to have the morals of the well-fed American." However, he was speaking of petty graft. The real, deep corruption of the *mordida* lies in the large-scale graft of politicians and businessmen. Honest men—and there are plenty, of course—have to take two or three jobs to keep themselves and their families going.

I saw President Ruíz Cortines a second time in 1957 when he lamented that Mexico is not homogeneous. "There are 3,000,000 Indians who do not speak Spanish," he said. "All we can do in the countryside is give them a little more food, a little more to wear, little better homes." He was still complaining to me a year later of the gap between the many poor and the few rich, and of the dismaying population explosion. It was running at 3.2 percent, or a million souls, a year. Mexico City, with five million people, he ruefully noted, was one of the largest cities in the world, with a steady wave of peasants moving in from their rural misery.

By the 1968 census, there were forty-seven million inhabitants in Mexico of whom 60 percent were under twenty years of age. Three times as much money is allocated to education as to defense—and still illiteracy is 50 percent.

Yet Mexico is the most stable and one of the most prosperous nations of Latin America. The Revolution did tackle land reform, health, education, housing, taxation—but the problems were so huge that results were uneven and superficial.

There have been five civilian Presidents in a row now. The end of military rule came with Miguel Alemán (1946–1952) who made millions out of the presidency, as did many of his cronies. Ruíz Cortines, his successor, reduced the enormity of the *mordida* at top levels of government and army, but all Mexicans were convinced that his wife and her relatives helped themselves generously. The *mordida* is a permanent feature of Mexican life and politics.

After talking to President Alemán in May 1951, I made a note: "He, most of all, gives the impression of how conservative Mexico has become." Six years later, I made this note: "One can say that the days of militarism and *coups* are over. Mexico has ceased to be revolutionary. She is as peaceful as any country in the hemisphere. Her political system has been likened to a constitutional monarchy with a king who is changed every six years."

In the last thirty years or so, Mexicans have worked out a unique political system, which baffles observers like myself who like to attach labels. One can say that Mexico has a one-party dictatorship or that she is a democracy—and both these contradictory labels are correct. The secret of Mexico's political stability—unrivaled in Latin America—lies with the PRI (*Partido Revolucionario Institucional*), which embraces the whole political spectrum from left to right. The President has enormous powers, controls patronage all the way down, as well as a rubber-stamp legislature and a judiciary that is not independent by Anglo-Saxon standards. However, the President has to satisfy every source of power in the country, so he is really a prisoner of a system in which he must achieve near unanimity. He controls all branches of the federal and state governments through the machinery of the PRI; and also the economy, by playing a major role in credits, imports, and public works. His crowning privilege, as his term nears its end, is to choose the man who is to succeed him.

Where, it may be asked, is the democracy? There is the fact, mentioned above, that the President must satisfy all elements in the PRI. If any important part of the machinery breaks down, the whole structure becomes vulnerable. Mexicans in the capital and other cities are politically conscious in a demanding way; they are not apathetic subjects. While the press is hampered, it is by no means inarticulate. Mexicans as a race cannot be prevented from saying what they think—the Romans called it the *jus murmurandi*. The trade unions have a degree of power. The legal structure, while far from perfect, provides a fair degree of justice. Normally, there is complete freedom to hold public meetings.

Democracy is not like pregnancy; there are degrees of it. A nation does not have to copy the United States to be a democracy. Besides, as Fidel Castro once asked me, "Can you say that Negroes in Mississippi have democracy?"

Perhaps the best evidence both of Mexican democracy and autocracy is to be found in the student movement. Just before the Olympic Games were to be held in Mexico in October 1968, university students in Mexico City rioted. Mexico is, in some ways, a harsh, cruel country, more Indian than Spanish. Life is relatively cheap and violence always close to the surface.

President Díaz Ordaz took no chances. He realized that the Olympics, on which Mexico had spent so many millions and which were to bring prestige and tourists to Mexico, were in jeopardy. "States are not ruled with prayer-books," Machiavelli has Cosimo de' Medici say. That goes in a big way for Mexico. To choose a native authority on what is to be done in doubtful circumstances, there was Pancho Villa's macabre decision: "Shoot him for the time being."

On October 3, 1968, during one of the bad riots, Díaz Ordaz turned army and police on the students and civilian bystanders with orders to shoot. At least twenty-five and probably as many as sixty civilians were killed and many wounded. It was a method of governing that all Mexicans understood. The ruling classes applauded. The unruly were cowed, and the games went off peacefully.

But the students now had a popular slogan: "Down with Díaz Ordaz!" and they had won many sympathizers from extreme left and right elements within the PRI. The man whom Díaz Ordaz had chosen to succeed him in July 1970, his Minister of the Interior Luis Echevarría Álvarez, was responsible for handling the student disturbances. His chances were badly "burned," as the Mexicans put it, but he was duly elected.

The students had, at least, delivered a warning. The healthiest development in Mexico in decades lies in the aspirations of the student leaders for a rejuvenation of Mexican democracy, a return to the ideals of the Revolution of 1910. The students, themselves, are not revolutionary; they seek changes by constitutional means. Their protest movement may yet shake Mexico's long stretch of stability, which has masked a great deal of governmental cynicism, corruption, and inertia. Mexican youth is on the move—a potentially massive force that will become still stronger when, as planned, the voting age is brought down to eighteen.

The Mexican Revolution was not as dead as it seemed; it was dormant and it appears to be awakening.

NICARAGUA

Anastasio (Tacho) Somoza, whose idiocy about Guatemala has already been recounted, was a typical Central American dictator. American Marines put him in power in 1932 when they left, and there he stayed for twenty-four years until an assassin's bullet finished him on September 29, 1956. Tacho, as everyone called him, was one of the beneficiaries indirectly referred to in a famous passage from an article in the magazine, *Common Sense* for November 19, 1933, written by U.S. Marine General Smedley D. Butler: "I helped make Mexico safe for American oil interests in 1914. I helped make Haiti and Cuba a decent place for the National City Bank boys to collect revenues in. I helped purify Nicaragua for the international banking house of Brown Brothers. . . ."

My wife and I once drove down from Managua, the capital, to the west coast where Somoza had one of his many homes and many properties, in this case a plant to make salt from sea water. It was late afternoon when we arrived and it soon got dark. We sat with the President on the porch of his house, which was completely surrounded by troops. However, we were under a strong electric light and all about was pitch-black undergrowth. We both remarked later how easy it would have been for an assassin to creep up and take a pot shot. It was not yet Tacho's time.

When Trujillo was killed one said: "Three cheers!" With Somoza, one could not help thinking: "Too bad!" He was a typical example of the benevolent despot and, personally, was a hearty, jolly, *simpatico* character. Besides, killing him did no good, for he had created a dynasty. He was succeeded by his oldest son, Luis, who was President for a term and tried to make a few reforms. Next in line—today's President—came Tachito, a tough, hard, reputedly cruel army officer. The two brothers kept the immense family fortune intact. Nicaragua was just one huge plantation for the Somozas and all their relatives, as the Dominican Republic was for the Trujillo family. Somoza owned coffee, cotton, and sugar plantations, cattle ranches, salt plants, aviation and shipping lines, banks, and an assortment of industries.

A 1952 report of the International Bank for Reconstruction and Development said that more than 25 percent of Nicaraguan national production went to about 1 percent of the population and within that 1 percent there is a further concentration that included the Somoza and Debayle (his wife's family) clans.

One day Tacho Somoza was driving in the outskirts of the city when he saw a fine *quinta* (estate), neatly fenced, beautifully kept, and luxurious. His eyes gleamed, and he ordered his car to be stopped.

"Go in there and find out who owns that *quinta*," he said to his aide-de-camp. The aide went in and returned in a few minutes, looking embarrassed.

"Well," said Tacho impatiently, "come on, tell me who owns it."

"*Mi general,*" the aide replied, "you do."

PANAMA

Machiavelli could have been writing about Panama in No. 17 of his *Discourses on the Decades of Titus Livius.* "I assert then, that nothing that befell Milan or Naples, however grave and however violent in character, could ever bring them freedom, since their members were wholly corrupt."

One of the paradoxes of Latin American history is that the two countries most closely connected to, and controlled by, the United States have been the most corrupt. Cuba ceased to be connected, controlled, or corrupt when Fidel Castro came along —but Panama has the Canal Zone and no Fidel Castro. Theoretically, Panama has been Washington's best chance to show what American "colonialism" can do for a country and its people to make them more prosperous and democratic. What the United States has done is to make the proverbial "forty families" of Panama wealthy and powerful, while the people are poor and—led by the university students—belligerently anti-Yankee.

In mitigation, one has to admit that the material was poor. In Panama the response toward politics is from the purse, not from the mind or heart, and certainly not from an unselfish patriotism. There is what Westerners call an "Oriental conception of government," whereby the holding of office is a means to make money, a source of personal profit, and an opportunity to favor and enrich one's family down to remote cousins.

Districts and villages are run by bosses *(caudillos)* who control and deliver the votes. The counting is fair enough once the votes are in; the real juggling is done by a central *jurado,* or electoral council, in Panama City. The government party has the council chairmanship and the largest representation, backed by the chief of the National Police, Panama's only regular armed force, although every man seems to carry a revolver. If a vote is close —say, a difference of 1,200 or 1,300 votes—the ballot boxes are stuffed to get the desired result. If there is a wide margin against the strongest man, a *coup d'état* is in order and usually forthcoming.

The Arias family is a leader among the ruling "forty families." Dr. Arnulfo Arias has been one of the most colorful politicians of the last three decades. His first term was in 1940–1941 when he was an extreme nationalist, pro-Nazi, and completely dictatorial. He was ousted when he made the mistake of flying to Havana to visit his oculist. However, he returned from exile amid popular acclaim in 1945 and ran once more for President in 1948. From what I was told soon afterward, he really won, but enough votes were thrown out to defeat him.

On November 24, 1949, the Panamanian kingmaker, Colonel José Antonio (Chichi) Remón, commandant of the U.S. trained and armed National Police, put Arnulfo back in the presidential seat. It was an insecure regime, beset with plots, blasted with criticisms and consumed with venality and political blunders.

I first met Arnulfo Arias in 1951, at which time he looked the part of a very handsome Hollywood film villain (and really was the equivalent, I kept being told in Panama City). Before he was thrown out again, the following year, Arnulfo (in Latin America public figures are always called by their first names) tried to get control of the Panama Trust Company, a banking-investment firm, and the hotel El Panama, the newest and most luxurious. He was thwarted, but there was a near crisis from which he was temporarily saved.

It was a period when Dr. Arias, who was pro- or anti-Yankee as it suited him, happened to be pro-American, anti-Communist and even, to hear him, pro-democratic although he wielded absolute power. So Washington sat back. Arnulfo had put relatives in as ministers of foreign affairs, finance, government and justice, and education. He had his own political party, called the Authentic Revolutionary party. And he had friends. Just to be safe—he hoped—he also had his own little army of secret police who were not much better than thugs and gunmen.

When I was there in 1951 and 1952, Panamanians estimated that Dr. Arias was making as much as $100,000 a month, aside from his presidential salary and perquisites. His subordinates were equally corrupt. There was technical incompetence, ignorance, irresponsibility, and chaos in all branches of government. People said Arnulfo was relying on spiritualism and astrology.

Chichi Remón decided that he wanted to be king and not just a kingmaker, so he arranged to win the election of May 15, 1952. His genius, politically, was that of a Tammany ward heeler, doing little things for little people year after year until he had built up strong, popular support. He was shrewd, not intelligent.

I saw him two months before the election and asked him what sort of a program he had. He began eagerly: "My program can be summed up in three words—work, justice. . . . justice? Ah—er—what was the third one?" (turning to Acting President Fulgencio Arosemena, who frowned in puzzlement. Then the word came to Remón). *"Pan,"* he said triumphantly, "bread! Work, justice and bread." Aside from mumbling that it would be necessary to better the lot of the people, he had no ideas. It probably never occurred to him that he should have any; certainly, he did not need any.

Poor Chichi Remón did not last long. He was killed on January 2, 1955, with a fusilade in the back while he was at the race course. The man everyone took for granted had engineered the assassination was acquitted and, fifteen years later, assassinated in his turn.

In May 1967 Arnulfo Arias made still another comeback and was elected President for the third time—and was ousted again on October 12, 1968, eleven days after assuming office, through a military coup by the always decisive National Guard. In the name of democracy they established a military dictatorship. Ar-

nulfo embarrassed the Americans by taking refuge in the sacrosanct Canal Zone.

A week before this, Peru had also had a military takeover.

PERU

There are experiences that tell more about a country than a
library of books.

One evening in October 1962, my wife and I dined with some
friends belonging to the Peruvian aristocracy in Lima—champagne and Strasbourg *pâté de foie gras* to begin with, as we waited
for a superb dinner, with three men serving the four of us in a
grand old colonial house. The next day, outside of Cuzco, two
miles high in the Andes, we saw ragged, wizened, bare-footed
Indians, their clothes falling off them, the women with babies
slung on their backs and primitive bobbins in their hands as they
trudged along weaving, for there was not a minute to lose. The
picture would have been the same centuries before. These were
the typical Peruvians—ten of them for each white Peruvian like
our friend of pure Spanish descent. In between would come 45
percent mestizos, or *cholos* as the Peruvians call them (mixed
Indian and white) with a wide social and economic range.

The 5 percent of whites from the oligarchy are, no doubt,
good people on the whole, many of them well meaning and
wanting to help to bring Peru up from its Inca age to the 1970's
—provided their wealth and privileges are not severely dimin-
ished. The enlightened among them are doing the best they
know how, and, meanwhile, they ask why should they be blamed
for living in a fine house, with many servants, and starting a meal
with champagne and *pâté de foie gras*?

What has saved Peru from a popular revolution is the historic
accident that the Indians have lived under a land system since
the seventeenth century which has held them in rural communities (*ayllus* is the Indian word). Most are outside the money
economy, completely apolitical, illiterate, and beyond knowing

or caring if a general or junta of generals throws out an elected President in Lima, as happened with Fernando Belaúnde Terry on October 3, 1968.

While we were in Cuzco, the administrator of a *hacienda* (the owners were doubtless in Lima, New York, or Paris) went to court complaining of violence and theft by Indians. He administered a latifundia of 140,000 hectares (350,000 acres) of which only 700 hectares were being cultivated. The news item telling about the case said that the *hacienda* "possessed 4,000 families." While the verb, *poseer,* in Spanish can mean simply that it contained 4,000 families, in this case "possessed" is the right word, because those Indians were tied to the land. They were literally serfs. Often, when land is sold in Peru, the Indian families are part of the price, since they provide the labor.

Peru has had the most colonial, feudal, paternalistic pattern in Latin America. Nowhere is the Spanish inheritance stronger, even in religion, for the Church has retained her privileges and wealth. The country has been run by a small group of families who possess an inordinate proportion of the wealth. One and three-tenths percent of the farms make up 63 percent of the land devoted to development. The German-descended Gildemeister family have had a virtual kingdom of their own inside the republic with their own police corps, curfew, and paternalistic feudalism. They "possess" their peasants, but at least they do keep up with the times in social betterment and wages. They are careful not to display their wealth or flaunt their power.

All this, from the point of view of the white ruling class and the American investor, has been too good to last. There is a growing middle class and a growing awareness among a small minority of Indian workers and peasants. Their radicalism was stirred up by a brilliant, but flawed, character named Víctor Raúl Haya de le Torre, who founded a movement which was powerful until recent years—APRA (*Alianza Popular Revolucionaria Americana*). It owed more to Don Quixote than to Karl Marx, but it was radical, and had the virtue of appealing to intellectuals and of seeking to aid the downtrodden Indians, thousands of whom were flowing desperately into the slums of Lima and other cities.

I have had to be careful in the tenses I am using for my verbs, because the quaint old picture of anachronistic Peru may, at last, be changing. The possibility was ruled out during my two decades as an editor because of the ignorance, disease, poverty, and political inertia of the great mass of Indians and *cholos*. They could not be organized, armed, and led into a revolution. The terrorism and corruption of the Odría regime (1948–1956) kept the nation cowed. No one could have expected a social revolution to come from army generals, who have always belonged to the ruling classes. Yet that is what seemed to happen with the palace revolt of October 1968.

General (now President) Juan Velasco Alvarado astounded Peruvians and dismayed foreign—especially North American—investors by setting out to make drastic, Nasser-type social and agrarian reforms—even affecting the Gildemeister plantations —and to nationalize the big industries, including American oil, mines, and landholdings. He proposed a new, liberal constitution and talked of "a new path and the new feeling in Latin America."

"This is not a Marxist revolution," he said in a speech in the summer of 1969. "The new society will not be Communist, but we are not going to maintain the traditional status quo. It is a nationalist revolution."

If President Velasco goes ahead and the economy can stand it, he really will be blazing a new path in Latin America. The nearest thing to a militarily directed social reform movement was General Perón's *Justicialismo* in Argentina, but it was half-hearted and never did touch the great landholdings of the oligarchy. Perón used much of his power to enrich himself and a clique of followers in an atmosphere of corruption and fraud.

It will take a near-miracle to transform Peru from a feudal into a modern state. It is clear enough why Peru needs something approaching a revolution—hopefully, a peaceful one. What is not clear is whether she is going to get it.

VENEZUELA

The richest country in Latin America is Venezuela, flowing with oil and heaving up incredible quantities of iron ore. It is a country where orchids are cheap and bread is dear; where the United States has invested a few billion dollars, enriching the government and a handful of Venezuelans, and giving employment to some thousands of workers, while millions of peasants live in poverty, and the slums of the capital are as bad as any in Latin America. The flour for the bread eaten in Caracas and other towns is imported from the United States; the potatoes come from Idaho, the meat from Chicago. Nature intended Venezuela to be an agricultural country, but oil was discovered in 1920, and then iron. Wealth was created at a rate never before equaled in Latin America.

But, as elsewhere in the hemisphere, there is a population explosion—a rate of about 3 percent annually, with 70 percent young. This means that even the process—in a famous phrase invented in the 1920's—of "sowing the oil" is not good enough. Per capita income now runs above $1,000 a year—much the highest in Latin America—but most Venezuelans are hardly better off than in colonial times. As is always the case, per capita figures are deceiving. The great majority of Venezuelans have to live on about $200 annually with the highest cost of living in the hemisphere.

Things have been better since the second presidency (1959–1963) of Rómulo Betancourt and his Acción Democrática party, but imbalances of this magnitude take a long time to correct.

No country has had a bloodier or more despotic history than Venezuela, from its independence in 1810 until the revolution of 1958, except for a brief interregnum of Acción Democrática from 1945 to 1948. In 1948 one of the worst of the modern Latin dictators, Marcos Pérez Jiménez, a military officer, rose to power and kept it by cruel, ruthless, reactionary methods.

Pérez Jiménez had an influential American friend, Ambassador Fletcher Warren, a career officer surprisingly, who was an even closer friend of Venezuela's "Himmler"—Director of National Security Pedro Estrada. In October 1958, after Pérez Jiménez was overthrown, *Coronet* magazine reproduced a warm and fulsome letter written by Warren from Turkey, where he was then U.S. ambassador, to Estrada. It was dated January 10 (a few weeks before the revolution) and was reproduced at a time when Estrada's cruelty and the corruption and tyranny of Pérez Jiménez were the sensation of Latin America.

Perhaps Fletcher Warren brought them hard luck—at least, in Venezuela. Pérez Jiménez and Estrada were soon basking in exile in the Florida sun, spending the millions they had deposited in American banks.

I had two long talks with Pérez Jiménez while he was still in power. He reminded me of Chichi Remón of Panama, being tubby, unattractive, uncultured, unintelligent. It was the all-powerful military machine that kept "PJ" in power for a decade, much to the satisfaction of the American oil interests who thrived on the status quo. They were frightened by what they thought might happen when the 1958 revolution brought in Rómulo Betancourt and the Acción Democrática. To them, Betancourt was a radical leftist. In fact, he was a liberal, with much too much sense to upset an industry on which Venezuela depended.

New and exorbitant royalty demands have only now, in 1971, been made on the American oil companies, which are dominated by Standard Oil of New Jersey (Creole Petroleum).

Betancourt was a good friend of mine and my wife's from the years when he was an exile in the United States and Puerto Rico. He was a rare figure for Latin America and especially rare for Venezuelan politics—scrupulously honest, a superb administrator, a clever politician, and extraordinarily brave. He had to be brave to hold back the military hawks and face the constant menace of assassination. Generalissimo Trujillo, who hated him, almost managed to have him killed and permanently crippled his hands. Fidel Castro kept doing his best to overthrow the regime through the guerrillas whom he armed and financed.

Rómulo Betancourt became the first elected President of Venezuela to serve out his full term in office. His successor, Raúl Leoni, also of the Acción Democrática, also served out his, and so will the Social Christian party's present President Rafael Caldera (incidentally another fine personality, and a liberal).

It would seem as if Venezuelans should be thanking their lucky stars, but human beings, Venezuelans included, are not as logical or sensible as they should be. Pérez Jiménez, having been extradited from the United States and jailed for five years in Venezuela for embezzling $13.4 million while in office, and then having gone to Spain to live on his millions, ran for the Senate in absentia on December 1, 1968. He was elected with massive support from Caracas and its surroundings, along with members of the political group he formed.

There is nothing so fickle or forgetful as a voting public. It reminded me of a sentence I saw painted on a wall in Rome in 1943 a few months after the Allies moved in and life became more difficult for many easy-going citizens. It read, in the Roman dialect: *"Arrivolemo il puzzone"*—"Let us have the stinker back." As a New Yorker who saw the egregious Adam Clayton Powell elected again and again to the House of Representatives with huge majorities from Harlem's black community, I should not feel surprised. Nothing Powell could do—financial irregularities, absenteeism, superluxurious living, expulsion from the House of Representatives—made any impression on his Negro constituents.

I can see Powell's appeal, which is purely racial; I cannot see P.J.'s. He did not even have the charisma of a Vargas, or Perón, or Arnulfo Arias. There were no good times for ordinary people during his dictatorship. There must be something in the Venezuelan psyche that eludes the Yankee mind. My wife and I have a number of Venezuelan friends who seem perfectly understandable. Perhaps they really aren't to us—or we to them. In Latin America I often feel as if I am groping across a chasm which I cannot bridge. I have to keep reminding myself that the area, each country and its people are *sui generis*. How can I understand them? But how can they understand each other?

REVOLUTION

Perhaps, as the Mexican economist, Víctor Urquidi has written, there must be "a new evaluation" of contemporary Latin America. When Adlai Stevenson came back from a long trip of exploration around Latin America on behalf of President Kennedy, he said: "The underprivileged have been caught up in the winds of change." Celso Furtado, the Brazilian economist, coined a word for his country's situation that became famous and is applied to all of Latin America—"prerevolutionary."

Urquidi put the problem succinctly: "Latin America is in a state of disquiet and tension that is bound to last for some time, because social and economic needs cannot be met—in any kind of society, but much less in one with a rate of population growth of over 2.7 per cent annually—through overnight action."

My own ideas changed over these last two decades of close study of Latin American affairs. I began with a natural sense of bewilderment and hopelessness over the complexity, range, depth, and seriousness of the problems. During the late 1950's and early 1960's I had some hopes, because there was a genuine antidictatorial wave, which I interpreted as a sign of a democratic trend. During that period I used the phrase: "Evolution not Revolution" as the title of an editorial. That day, President Eisenhower wrote a letter to Arthur Sulzberger saying that the editorial expressed the ideas of his administration. He did, in fact, formulate a program similar to the Alliance for Progress before President Kennedy coined the phrase and made the ideas the basis for a hemispheric campaign whose emphasis was as much, or more, social than it was economic.

Kennedy was responding to the impact of the Cuban Revolution, so much so that all through Latin America the Alliance was credited to Fidel Castro. Since the ideas of the Alliance conformed to what we had been proposing for many months, *The New York Times* backed it enthusiastically and kept on doing so even when the hopes gradually faded. My argument was that the Alliance might not be working well, but nobody could offer a better idea. By the time Nixon, who did not believe in it, became President, Congress had been cutting down on appropriations for the Alliance.

Fidel Castro had once said to me of the Alliance for Progress: "You can put wings on a horse, but it won't fly." Unfortunately, he was right. Even more unfortunately, there is still no better alternative, which leaves me in a state of anxiety and depression where Latin America is concerned. There have been at least eighteen *coups d'état* since the Alliance was launched in 1961.

A recent study by the International Monetary Fund (IMF) is alarming. In 1950, 11 percent of the world's exports came from Latin America; in 1967 the figure had fallen to 5.7 percent. While total global exports grew at a rate of 7.4 percent annually in the 1950–1960 period, those of Latin America were only 2.9 percent. And so forth.

The failure of the Alliance for Progress is nowhere more dangerous than in the key agrarian sector. An estimated 90 percent of the cultivated land is owned by 10 percent of the landowners. This is an average; in some countries the situation is much worse. For instance, in Argentina, Chile, Brazil, and Peru, about 2 percent of landowners possess more than one-half of all the farmed land.

The antidictatorial trend was reversed in the 1960's. The decade ended with military dictatorships in half the countries and civilian dictatorships in Cuba and Haiti.

Latin Americans—and foreign students of the area—are always haunted by a famous and bitter judgment from their first and greatest leader, Simón Bolívar: "America is ungovernable," he said just before his death as he was on the way to exile. "He who serves a revolution ploughs the seas."

Many authorities blame the heritage of Spain—the psychological characteristics of the old Spanish elite, which is still dominant, even though Latin America is ethnically more mestizo than Spanish. (In Brazil, it is the Portuguese inheritance.) The weary round of palace revolutions goes on, with little change from the old classic pattern with its Spanish legalistic formula. A military group in a capital seizes power. Then it engineers a so-called democratic election and so becomes a "constitutional government" by the "will of the people." The same men—or their puppets—are involved at the top all along. However arbitrary a dictator may be, he likes to have a legal status and act under laws, even if he manufactures laws after the event to suit his particular case. As a rule, there will not only be a constitution (usually modeled on that of the United States) but also a Congress. Form comes before substance.

The outstanding exception, of course, is revolutionary Cuba where Fidel Castro has swept the heritage aside to introduce his own special brand of Marxism-Leninism. Perhaps Peru and Chile will provide other exceptions.

Cuba, however, is a dramatic example of the price that has to be paid in the underdeveloped countries for development through a radical form of socialism (although Cuba was only relatively underdeveloped). When the choice of evils—as it may be called—is such that a drastic social revolution offers hope for a better life, as it did in Cuba, and before Cuba in France, Mexico, Russia, and China, the price is considered to be worth paying, especially to the young.

The contrast between the few rich and the many poor in Latin America is outrageous. It is estimated by the United Nations to be greater than that of any developing region. Youth demands changes, humanistic as well as economic, but unconsciously the young are choosing between totalitarianism and anarchy. Since anarchism is a method, or technique, of protest, not an answer, sooner or later they will get totalitarianism in some form.

It is ironical that our North American ideas are more truly revolutionary than those of the Communists will ever be—especially the idea of equality of opportunity. We are setting an example that is a constant incitement to revolution in Latin America. We have a standard of living ten times higher than theirs. We planted revolutionary ideas in Latin America—"life, liberty, and the pursuit of happiness," for instance—long before Marx was born. And revolutionary ideas have a tendency to express themselves in revolution.

Even the post-John XXIII Roman Catholic Church—and

remember that Latin America is more than 90 percent Catholic —is revolutionary, despite the brakes put on progressivism by Pope Paul VI. "The economic wealth of a people," Pope John wrote in his great encyclical *Mater et Magistra*, "arises not only from an aggregate abundance of goods but also, and more so, from their real and efficacious redistribution according to justice, as a guarantee of the personal development of the members of society, which is the true scope of a national economy." Thousands of young priests in Latin America are taking these revolutionary ideas seriously.

"The disease of liberty," as Thomas Jefferson called it, is infectious. This is a world seeking answers that no one can yet give, because they are not going to be found in the books or in the past. Men and women in Latin America—mostly young men and women—are going to venture their careers, even their lives, in the quest for the right answers.

I am too old, myself, to abandon rationalism, or common-sense solutions, but as a newspaperman, I am too close to what is happening to believe that one can hope for rational conduct in an area like Latin America—or at least, in all parts of it. More real social revolutions are undoubtedly shaping up, although we are going through a relatively calm period, which may last for years. The hijackings of planes and the kidnappings and murders of diplomats (especially by the Tupamaros of Uruguay) are ominous signs.

THE YANKEES

As I have said earlier, Latin American politicians thrive on anti-Yankeeism. To be branded popular in Washington is the kiss of death to a Latin statesman. "Poor Mexico," said Porfirio Díaz, dictator of Mexico for thirty-four years until 1910, "so far from God and so near to the United States!" So say they all. But often in my work I thought: "Poor United States! whatever we do is too little or wrong."

The problems are easy to formulate. The power and wealth

of the United States is such that everything we do or don't do has a profound effect on Latin America. Our hemispheric policies have always—and naturally—been based on the continental security of the United States, plus the economic and strategic benefits of trade with Latin America.

It was never possible to achieve a *Pax Americana*—and less so now than in the past. Rome could rule, Tacitus wrote, "by the terror of the Roman name." The exercise of power has great restraints in our age, which is why a vulnerable Fidel Castro can defy the United States.

Anti-Yankeeism in Latin America was not invented by Castro or by the Cubans. It is a complicated phenomenon with deep roots in our long historic relationship with the region. The past is haunting us—"dollar diplomacy," our brief imperialistic fling around the turn of the century, and the interventions in Central America and the Caribbean with the use of American Marines —shockingly resurrected in 1965 by President Johnson in the Dominican Republic. On the Latin side is an aggressive political and economic nationalism and a feeling that the United States "neglects" them in favor of Europe and Asia.

Latin Americans accuse us of exploiting their natural wealth, employing cheap labor, and making high profits that we withdraw. Many times in the past we made and unmade governments, either by force or by bribing officials. We still can exert such formidable pressures on the ruling classes that governments we favor can be kept in power and revolutionary trends held back.

Much of the Latin American reasoning and many of their complaints are exaggerated, illogical, unreasonable, unfair, emotional. There is envy, self-pity, and buckpassing. One could draw up a long list of abuses by the Latins, such as defaulted loans and expropriations. It is legitimate to ask: who is exploiting whom?

If there is injustice in their complaints, there are also many just causes of resentment. I have mentioned how much they resented Washington's favoritism toward Latin dictators. Our trade practices were by no means always fair or beneficial.

Our sales of arms to Latin countries that never could afford them and did not need them except for internal security; our training of Latin officers; our ubiquitous and always overswollen military missions—these have been Washington's encouragement to Latin American military dictators and to the armed forces of every Latin nation. History provided a basis for the fact that almost every government in Latin America can be made or unmade by its army officers, but Washington (i.e., the Pentagon) perpetuates this state of affairs.

"We are creating armies," the wise Eduardo Santos of Colombia once said, "that carry no weight in the international scales, but are monstrous destroyers of each nation's internal life. Each of our countries is being occupied by its own army."

When Honduras and El Salvador fought in the summer of 1969, what could the U.S. military missions—ridiculously large ones in their capitals of Tegucigalpa and San Salvador—do? Sit back and egg their protégés on? Wring their hands? I trust that they simply felt foolish.

The North American obsession about Communism is, of course, behind our policy. Latin America is not looking to the United States to lead a crusade against the Communists, for they do not feel the way we do about Communism. There have been no Communist parties in Latin America strong enough to take over a country. The Cuban Reds sabotaged Castro's Sierra Maestra guerrilla operation until they saw that he was going to win. When he decided to lead the Revolution into Marxism-Leninism, it was a personal decision and the United States could not stop him.

In 1953 President Eisenhower enunciated a policy which was later violated by himself in the case of Guatemala, by Kennedy in Cuba, and by Johnson in the Dominican Republic: "Any nation's right to form a government and an economic system of its own choosing is inalienable. Any nation's attempt to dictate to other nations their form of government is indefensible." This was either hypocrisy or naiveté. The United States also violated Article 15 of the Charter of the Organization of American States which reads: "No State or group of States has the right to intervene, directly or indirectly, for any reason whatsoever, in the internal or external affairs of any other State."

No one country is to blame and all are to blame for the dangerous mess in which Latin America and the United States find themselves. Any authority can draw up a list of the things that ought to be done by both sides, but there is no easy or quick solution. It surely is clear that the answers—if or when they are made—will have to be radical. The world we live in is not listening to the conservatives. Anyway, what do the masses in Latin America, Africa, and Asia have to conserve?

Those who work in the field of Latin American studies often, in Bolívar's phrase, feel that they are "ploughing the seas." Bewilderment, pity, anger, frustration—these are stronger than hope. There is so little room for optimism when the region as a whole and its relations with the United States are considered!

I, personally, have no complaints—very much to the contrary. What I wrote of anti-Yankeeism does not apply to Americans as Americans. I can stand, figuratively, on the banks of the Rio Grande looking south, and count my friends by the dozens and remember warm hospitality everywhere. I wish I could be optimistic.

Chapter 8

CUBA

I have been the principal journalistic scapegoat for the rise to power of Fidel Castro and for the success of the Cuban Revolution. Owen Lattimore was assigned a similar role in the case of the Chinese Revolution in 1949. As the *Hispanic American Report* of Stanford University wrote of this interpretation of my role in Cuba, "This is as absurd as blaming a meteorologist for a thunderstorm."

I suppose that I have been asked hundreds of times in the past decade: "What do you think of Fidel Castro now?" My replies varied in details as the years passed, but not in substance. Like all overpowering historic figures, Castro has a character of such complexity that no portrait can be definitive. *My* Fidel Castro is poles apart from a Cuban exile's, an American congressman's, a student's, or a Wallacite's. At least I have the advantage of knowing him well—and liking him.

His ideas and policies changed with the years; his performances in social, economic, and political fields ranged from admirable to awful. When I first interviewed him in the Sierra Maestra on February 17, 1957, he believed that he could work within a democratic system.* By mid-1960 he had converted himself to a belief in socialism, which inevitably led him into "Marxism-Leninism"—his own special brand of Communism. His attitude toward the Russians changed from admiration and gratitude to anger and distrust and now (in 1971) back to friendly cooperation. His feelings about the United States—not about Americans as persons—were always hostile.

I disliked and disagreed with a number of the things he did, and told him so, and wrote critically, especially in *New York Times'* editorials, about many of his activities over the years. I also wrote favorably about him and the good things he was doing for Cuba and the Cubans. I think I understood the problems he faced, his feelings as a Cuban, and the reasons that rightly or wrongly impelled him to choose specific policies. I have always given him credit for sincerely wanting to do what is best for his island and its people. Insofar as the differences in our ages, nationalities, and characters permitted, we have been friends, and I see no reason on my part why I should ever cease to be one.

I would not be greatly surprised, although I would be sorry, if Fidel Castro (as Theodore Draper once predicted) turned against me. He is a rash, passionate, arrogant, moody creature, and he has accepted more verbal and written criticism from me than from any of his associates or friends. I think it speaks well for his character that, so far as I know, he has said nothing worse than to complain petulantly that "this old man treats me as if he were my father." Fidel is not the type cynically to consider that I do him more good than harm and therefore had better not be antagonized. He is too emotional and short-tempered to restrain himself if he felt the urge to attack me.

He is no longer the wide-eyed, innocent, amateurish revolutionary I watched floundering around when he first took power in January 1959. For one thing, he was thirty-two years old then and is forty-five now. Power has corrupted him, as it does all men, but in a very human way. It has made him so in love with

*See Appendix for my *Times* article about this interview.

power, so addicted to it as if it were a drug, that he has never relinquished an iota of it once he achieved complete personal power early in 1959. The biography I wrote about him* begins and ends with the thesis that the Cuban Revolution is Fidel Castro's revolution. In his discouraged July 26, 1970, speech, he talked of broadening the Cuban power base, but I do not believe that he is temperamentally capable of sharing the supreme power.

To an overwhelming degree, he has that almost religious popular appeal now labeled as charisma. This is of paramount importance in all of Latin America where personalism is a major feature of politics. Such an appeal is Castro's greatest "treasure." Unlike the typical Latin dictator—Perón, Pérez Jiménez, Trujillo, Somoza, Batista—Fidel has no interest whatever in money. If he is driven from power he will have no millions salted away in Swiss banks or, like Batista, in Florida real estate. He is scrupulously honest and has given Cuba its first honest administration since Columbus discovered the island.

Fidel Castro's place in history will be marred by his mistakes, his willfulness, his fanaticism, his ruthlessness, his blindness to what freedom for the individual means. These are great flaws in a great character whose solid virtues and ideals far outweigh the weaknesses. In the fourteen years I have known him he has not changed in the fundamentals by which a man's character should be judged. He adjusts himself, as any statesman of our time must, to the irresistible forces of today's stormy world, and to the limits that Cuban traditions, geography, and economy impress upon him, but he stands, in Dante's phrase, "four square to the winds of fortune." He is no man's puppet; he takes orders from no one and, unhappily, he takes nobody's advice. He learns by making mistakes.

His technique has been to exercise autocratic rule through a group of remarkable young men and women, nearly all of whom were with him since his wild attack on the Moncada Barracks in

---

* *Fidel Castro* (New York: Simon & Schuster, 1969).

Santiago de Cuba in 1953 and the Sierra Maestra guerrilla insurrection of 1957 and 1958.

Of them all, by far the most famous was Ernesto Che Guevara. There is already a library of books about him—with few exceptions, idolatrous. His death in the mountains of Bolivia in October 1967 made him a legendary figure. He became the ideal revolutionary to rebellious youth everywhere in the world.

I was in the Cabañas Fortress of Havana to greet Guevara when he first entered the capital in triumph at the beginning of January 1959, and I came to know him fairly well until the time he disappeared on the quixotic quest that was to fail but, as with the hero of Cervantes' story to whom Che likened himself, was to immortalize him. Our meetings were always long arguments in the small hours of the night when he would defend Marxism and the measures that the Castro government was taking—while I disagreed. In two of his books which he autographed for me, he expressed friendship despite our "ideological differences."

His role in Cuba, although important for a few years in the economic and financial fields, was never decisive. Castro made the decisions. Guevara may have influenced him at times, but the policies failed and Che became bored. He earned his niche in the history of our times, but Cuba was only one act, and not the climactic one, of the drama he played. Che would have been a rarity at any time because of his almost religious dedication to his high ideals. I thought he took the wrong road—the road of hatred and violence—to achieve a better life for the disinherited masses. He paid his price. I would never worship him; I admired, respected, and liked him. Che Guevara was one of those people who bolster a man's faith in the value of the human race. Perhaps, after all, that is the highest compliment one can pay an individual.

The other important figures in the Cuban Revolution deserve —and will in time get—their biographies in book form. They are a remarkable lot. Raúl Castro, Fidel's younger brother and closest associate; Celia Sánchez, the faithful and charming companion since Sierra Maestra days, with a shrewd mind and a tough core behind her gentle manners; President Osvaldo Dorticós, a servant of great ability and intelligence; Haydée Santamaría, who fought with Fidel in the Moncada Barracks attack and in the Sierra Maestra; her devoted (to her and to Fidel) lawyer husband, Armando Hart; the Negro guerrilla fighter who became commander of the Cuban Army, Juan Almeida—these and some others make up the Cuban pantheon, each with his special place and all of them followers of Fidel. They were young amateurs, all of them with charmed lives, for they risked everything in their time. There has been nothing comparable to this loyal group in any of the major revolutions of the last two centuries except, perhaps, Napoleon's marshals.

They are all, I like to think, my friends, At least I know them all, and they have acted as friends. A social revolution is a rare event in history. Only Mexico has had one in the Western hemisphere. Fidel Castro and the Cuban Revolution provide a unique case in contemporary American journalism. They also form a colorful episode in the history of *The New York Times*. From my personal point of view, the Cuban story was exciting and rewarding although, as I once said to Fidel, I am afraid I will have to wait fifty years for my reward. Meanwhile, I must put up with a fair amount of abuse.

A good deal of the sound and fury came from senatorial hearings where I was given no opportunity to reply and did not, indeed, know what was said until many months had passed. I can now tell aspects of the story that I had kept to myself.

The loudest noises were being made between 1960 and 1962 when Fidel Castro moved into the Communist fold and the Cuban Revolution turned out to be a bitter business for the United States, economically and strategically. There was a series of congressional hearings between August 1960 and August 1964 of the pompously named "Subcommittee to Investigate the Administration of the Internal Security Act and Other Internal Laws of the Committee on the Judiciary, United States Senate." At each of the ten or more hearings my name and supposed misdemeanors figured more or less prominently. Not all were open hearings and even when they were, there was always a good deal of "discussion off the record." My knowledge of the times and extent to which my name was under discussion is, therefore, incomplete. I must presume that the published material, of which there is a good deal in the *Congressional Record,* was typical.

The hearings on Cuba were, with a few exceptions, held by only three or four of the nine members then belonging to the subcommittee. The ones who attended most of the meetings were the extremist, Red-baiting demagogues—Senator James O. Eastland of Mississippi, chairman; Thomas J. Dodd of Connecticut, vice-chairman; and Roman L. Hruska of Nebraska. Senator Kenneth B. Keating of New York, a right-winger, and Senator Hugh Scott of Pennsylvania, a liberal, attended a few of the meetings. The others—Everett M. Dirksen of Illinois, Olin D. Johnston of South Carolina, and John L. McClellan of Arkansas, washed their hands of the proceedings. I was told that the liberal and moderate Senator Sam J. Ervin, Jr., of North Carolina was at times ashamed of his colleagues' intemperance but could do nothing to stop them. The counsel throughout all the hearings was J. G. Sourwine. He played a role comparable in every way to that of Roy M. Cohen in the notorious McCarthy hearings.

I expected to be called before the subcommittee, and should have been, if only to defend myself, but the members were playing a political game. It was never serious and will not be taken seriously by any historian of the Cuban Revolution, except to show the prevailing hysteria about Cuba—but a permanent record was made.

I had believed that the subcommittee might have been afraid to tackle so formidable an adversary as *The New York Times,* but when Harrison Salisbury made his historic trip to Hanoi in 1964 and wrote articles that the extremists who dominated the subcommittee considered to be pro-Communist, they summoned him to testify.

"Did the Matthews' visit to Cuba induce you to try to make a scoop in North Vietnam?" Senator Frank J. Lausche of Ohio asked Salisbury in a hearing on February 2, 1967.

"No, I do not think so," Salisbury replied. "It never entered my mind."

There was no reason why it should have, but the questioning, which went on to try to pin responsibility for Castro and the Cuban Revolution on me and *The Times,* was typical of a widespread and still-existing opinion.

I thought that one reason why the subcommittee never called me might have been a realization of the futility of doing so. The FBI and later the CIA must have been amassing formidable dossiers on me ever since the Spanish Civil War. It was their business to do so. My wife and I were certain that our home telephone on East Seventy-Fourth Street in New York was tapped during the Cuban period. We had constant and unmistakable troubles with the instrument which the New York Telephone Company said that they could do nothing about.

My career has been an open book. When *Time* magazine turned against me as a result of the Cuban business, and built up a critical article about my mistakes and changes of mind, every fact that they offered was taken from my own writings—without ascription, I should add. I never belonged to any party —Communist or otherwise—or even to a club or association listed as a Communist front or as left wing by the House Un-American Activities Committee. There were no secret friends, no secret meetings, no suspicious connections—nothing, in fact, that could have been dug out of my past and triumphantly presented to the Senate, the House of Representatives, or the world. This did not protect me from abuse, or from labels of Communist, pro-Communist, fellow traveler, and so on down to the mild terms of leftist and radical.

The name-calling was annoying, amusing, and interesting— but essentially inconsequential. The columnists who abused me were always ones whose praise would have been embarrassing. I generally found myself in good company. The testimony before the Senate subcommittee, the texts of senatorial speeches, and the articles inserted into the *Congressional Record* were another matter. They do not, as I said, make "serious" history because of the errors, bias, exaggerations, and, in one notable case, lies, but they are on record, now and forever. Had I been called before the Judiciary Subcommittee, my side of the story would, at least, also have been in the *Congressional Record.* I do not suppose that Senator Dodd and the others had figured out that they could do me the most harm by not calling me; this would have been Machiavellian and much too subtle. In any event, I have always given the senators credit for being sincerely misguided.

"In much of the blather dispensed by the Senate Internal Security Subcommittee about the causes of the unhappy events in Cuba," the *Washington Post* wrote in an editorial on February 27, 1961, "a deeper purpose has been evident. That is to hang someone for the loss of Cuba. In a release last fall the Subcommittee stated its own prejudgment quite frankly: Cuba was handed to Castro and the Communists by a combination of Americans in the same way that China was handed to the Communists."

When I said that there had been a case of lying, I had in mind the testimony of Arthur Gardner, chairman of the board of the Bundy Tubing Company and U.S. ambassador to Cuba from 1953 to 1957. He perjured himself—quite deliberately—in order, I presume, to do me the greatest possible harm. If so, he was clever, because the lie he told struck at the aspect of my career on which I am most sensitive—that I never wrote anything which was untrue or which I did not sincerely believe to be true.

As Gardner was ill at the time, his testimony was taken at his home with Senator Dodd presiding and doing all the questioning. It began harmlessly.

"I feel very strongly," Gardner said at one point, "that the State Department was influenced, first, by those stories by Herbert Matthews, and then it became a kind of fetish with them."

Some time later there was this exchange:

SENATOR DODD. Mr. Gardner, do you regard Herbert L. Matthews as an expert on Latin American affairs?

MR. GARDNER. I do not.

SENATOR DODD. Or Cuban affairs?

MR. GARDNER. Any affairs. I think his history, if you look it up—I am sure you know of it—I mean in Spain —is indicative of his character.

Then came the big lie.

SENATOR DODD. Did Herbert Matthews ever contact you while you were the Ambassador in Cuba about—

MR. GARDNER. I made every effort, and saw him a good many times, tried to get his friendship, because he and a man named Dubois who worked for a Chicago paper—both of them were considered by us to be radicals. And I even arranged meetings for him. And I made it possible actually for Herbert Matthews to go down and have his interview, because he asked me.

SENATOR DODD. Yes. I wanted to ask you about that. He did ask for your assistance in arranging an interview with Castro?

MR. GARDNER. He did.

SENATOR DODD. And this was arranged.

MR. GARDNER. Yes.

SENATOR DODD. How did you arrange it?

MR. GARDNER. Only under the condition that when he came back he would tell me his reactions.

SENATOR DODD. Yes. But how could you arrange a meeting with Castro?

MR. GARDNER. Well, I mean in those days Batista was all for the U. S. Ambassador, no matter who he would have been. And he was very loath to do it, but he said, all right, if you think it won't do any harm, it is all right, and he let him go down.

SENATOR DODD. This would indicate to me that Batista knew where Castro was, all right.

MR. GARDNER. Oh, they all knew where he was. But they couldn't put their finger on him. He was moving every night.

SENATOR DODD. But certainly they knew how to get in touch with him if they wanted to.

MR. GARDNER. There isn't any doubt about that. But I think Batista was afraid he would make a martyr of him if he dragged him out.

SENATOR DODD. How soon after Castro landed in Cuba did Herbert Matthews seek an opportunity to see Castro?

MR. GARDNER. I would say, offhand, 4 or 5 months after. It wasn't immediately.

SENATOR DODD. And I think you started to say that you agreed to help him—or help arrange for him—to see Castro. But you made him promise that he would come back and see you and tell you—

MR. GARDNER. Tell me.

SENATOR DODD (continuing). About his meeting with Castro.

MR. GARDNER. Senator, to be perfectly clear about this, the only thing I could do was help him, so that he would have a pass to go down the island, so that he could make this trip.

SENATOR DODD. I understand—whatever it was that he thought you could do, he wanted you to do it to help him get there?

MR. GARDNER. That is right.

SENATOR DODD. And in return for this he promised he would come back and tell you about this conversation with Castro?

MR. GARDNER. That is right. And to this day I have never seen him.

SENATOR DODD. He never did return and never did tell you?

MR. GARDNER. No. It was a big shock to me, as a matter of fact.

(302)

The phony shock that Arthur Gardner said he received was nothing to the real shock that I got, six months later, when the Gardner testimony was published. Every word in Gardner's account about how I asked for his help, how he helped me, what Batista said and did, what I promised Gardner—every word, I repeat, for there was no exception, was a lie. Had Gardner's version been true, the whole story of my historic interview with Fidel Castro would have been a fake.

It was the most extraordinary thing of its kind that happened to me in my long career—and in its way it was the worst. Arthur Gardner had reason to congratulate himself gleefully; he had had his revenge.

I took what measures I could, giving the Washington *Daily News* (edited by a friend of mine, John O'Rourke) a strongly worded rebuttal, which was printed on February 3, 1961. In it I said: "Ex-Ambassador Gardner lied 100 per cent in his testimony that he had helped me to get the interview with Fidel in February 1957." Representative William F. Ryan of New York, whom I knew, read the article into the *Congressional Record* of February 15.

When I thanked Ryan he said that if I wanted him to do so, he would suggest that the Internal Security Subcommittee give me a chance to rebut Gardner's testimony. I wanted to very much, but Louis Loeb, *The New York Times'* counsel whom I consulted because Gardner had denied the truth of a *Times* story, advised me to wait and see.

Meanwhile, Thomas Mann, who was then in his first term as Assistant Secretary of State for Inter-American Affairs and who was very friendly at the time, did some discreet investigating at my request. He advised me—and this would have borne fruit if I had been called to testify—that "there is nothing in the records that should bother you and no reason, from the State Department's angle, why you cannot go ahead." By this he meant that there had been no message from Gardner to show that Gardner had ever played the role that he described—which, of course, there would have been for the official record, considering the sensation that my interview with Castro caused. Also, the State

Department must have asked the embassy for comment.

In writing Louis Loeb about this, I said that there were two reasons why I wanted to take action: "In the first place, I will not stand for my probity as a journalist being denied by someone whose statement was entirely false. I think this is also important from *The Times'* point of view since the story in question—my original interview with Fidel Castro—was printed in *The Times.* In the second place, since this story was one of the very rare occasions on which a correspondent makes history, I consider it important to set the historic record straight."

I would have obtained sworn statements from our Havana correspondent, Ruby Phillips, Ted Scott of the National Broadcasting Corporation in Havana, and Felipe Pazos, president of the National Bank of Cuba, all of whom took part in the very secret and dangerous adventure. Batista, himself, at the time, and in his memoirs, written in exile, clearly stated that he thought Castro was dead and that my interview came as a rude shock to him—and a costly one.

Gardner, of course, perpetrated a deliberate and calculated lie and took a risk in doing so, because he was under the customary oath. He perjured himself, knowing that he was doing so.

Did he know that he would be protected by the Senate subcommittee? When I publicly called Gardner a liar, and thus challenged the subcommittee, they were faced with the knowledge that testimony from me would have meant that either I or Gardner had committed perjury—and I most strongly suspect that they knew which one it was. Such being the case, one of their star witnesses—ex-Ambassador Arthur Gardner—would have been discredited, and the Senate witch hunt, which was off to such a promising start from their point of view, would have been undercut before it got off the ground.

Gardner, of course, knew better than to sue me for libel or slander. He had achieved his purpose, and I must suppose that I will come out the loser since many future historians of the Cuban Revolution will find it hard to believe that a man considered distinguished enough to be named an ambassador, and testifying under oath, would commit perjury out of spite.

I did have a small measure of revenge. When Eisenhower began his second term of office in January 1957, all American envoys—*pro forma*—sent in their resignations. During the sub-committee hearing there had been this exchange:

> SENATOR DODD. Mr. Gardner, do you feel that your
> expressed attitude with regard to Castro had a part
> in bringing about your replacement as our Ambas-
> sador to Cuba?
> MR. GARDNER. Senator, I don't know. I only know that
> I was very anxious to stay. I felt that if I had stayed
> it was encouraging to the Batista regime, which
> was through.

The State Department did not share Gardner's opinion of himself. On the contrary, it was embarrassed by his close friendship and support of General Batista at a period when the Cuban dictator was being so cruelly oppressive and corrupt.

I saw Secretary of State Dulles around the time that appointments and reappointments of envoys were being considered, and I asked him what was going to be done about Arthur Gardner. He laughed.

"He is desperately anxious to keep the post," Dulles replied, "and when we told him that his resignation was being accepted, he hopped the first plane for Washington and went to see the President to plead with him. The President is accepting our judgment."

Dulles, of course, knew my opinion of Gardner, whom we had criticized editorially in *The Times*. I am sure that was why he laughed when I questioned him. I do know that Gardner blamed me for his recall because he said so to someone who passed the information along to me. I presume that this was why he wanted to do more than give the Senate committee his genuine, although simple-minded and muddled, ideas about me.

Unfortunately, Gardner's successor as Ambassador to Cuba—Earl E. T. Smith—was no better as a diplomat and no less ama-

teurish. In fact, he was worse, because he failed to perceive that
Fidel Castro could not be stopped and as a result, Cuban-Ameri-
can relations started off very badly when Fidel triumphed. Smith
never appreciated a simple diplomatic axiom—that one does not
ostentatiously back a losing side.

Smith also figured in a Senate subcommittee hearing—three
days after Gardner—which was more sensational, so far as I was
concerned, and inexcusably damaging in the way it led to the
wreckage of the career of two loyal and innocent State Department officials—Roy R. Rubottom, Jr., the Assistant Secretary of
State, and William A. Wieland, head of the Caribbean desk of
the Bureau of Inter-American Affairs.

My name and misdeeds came up often and extensively in
Smith's hearing, but for present purposes the new and important feature was the so-called briefing which I gave to Smith in
New York over a luncheon table just before he went to Havana
to take up his post as ambassador in June 1957. One side remark
of Smith's is worth quoting because it became historic.

"Senator [Eastland]," said Smith, "let me explain to you that
the United States, until the advent of Castro, was so overwhelmingly influential in Cuba that. . . . the American Ambassador was
the second most important man in Cuba; sometimes even more
important than the President."

Smith never did realize that he was giving one important
reason why there was a Cuban revolution.

Here is the main passage regarding the "briefing" from the
exchange between Smith and the committee's counsel:

> MR. SOURWINE. Is it true, sir, that you were instructed
> to get a briefing on your new job as Ambassador
> to Cuba from Herbert Matthews of *The New York
> Times?*
>
> MR. SMITH. Yes; that is correct.
>
> MR. SOURWINE. Who gave you these instructions?
>
> MR. SMITH. William Wieland, Director of the Caribbean
> Division and Mexico.
>
> MR. SOURWINE. Did you, sir, in fact see Matthews?

MR. SMITH. Yes; I did.

MR. SOURWINE. And did he brief you on the Cuban situation?

MR. SMITH. Yes; he did.

MR. SOURWINE. Could you give us the highlights of what he told you? . . .

MR. SMITH. We talked for 2½ hours on the Cuban situation, a complete review of his feelings regarding Cuba, Batista, Castro, the situation in Cuba, and what he thought would happen.

MR. SOURWINE. What did he think would happen?

MR. SMITH. He did not believe that the Batista Government could last, and that the fall of the Batista Government would come relatively soon.

MR. SOURWINE. Specifically, what did he say about Castro?

MR. SMITH. In February 1957, Herbert L. Matthews wrote three articles on Fidel Castro, which appeared on the front pages of *The New York Times*, in which he eulogized Fidel Castro and portrayed him as a political Robin Hood, and I would say that he repeated those views to me in our conversation.

MR. SOURWINE. Did he, sir, call your attention to those articles?

MR. SMITH. No; he did not.

MR. SOURWINE. Did the State Department call your attention to them?

MR. SMITH. I don't believe anybody called attention to them. At that time I recall that I was going to be Ambassador to Cuba, and I read them with great interest.

MR. SOURWINE. What did Mr. Matthews tell you about Batista?

MR. SMITH. Mr. Matthews had a very poor view of Batista, considered him a rightist, ruthless dictator whom he believed to be corrupt. Mr. Matthews informed me that he had very knowledgeable

views of Cuba and Latin American nations, and
had seen the same things take place in Spain. He
believed that it would be in the best interest of
Cuba and the best interest of the world in general
when Batista was removed from office.

(Gardner had also said I had compared Castro to Robin
Hood, and so did others. Smith added Abraham Lincoln for
good measure. Dodd once expanded the list to Jefferson and
Washington. I never, in writing or speech, used any of these
names. Actually, it was Jules Dubois of the *Chicago Tribune,* in his
1959 biography of Fidel Castro, who called him "the Robin
Hood of the Sierra Maestra.")

The truth about the notorious "briefing" came out during
one of the many brutal and ruthless hearings to which William
Wieland was subjected over a period of two years—1961 and
1962. A report summarizing the testimony, insofar as the subcommittee wanted it to be known, was published on October 16,
1962. This is the pertinent passage:

"The second time he appeared before the committee, Mr.
Wieland had this to say about arrangements for the briefing
of Ambassador Smith by Herbert Matthews of *The New York
Times*:

" 'MR. WIELAND. . . . Ambassador Smith told the committee
that I had arranged for him to be briefed by Mr. Herbert Matthews of *The New York Times* for his new position as Ambassador
to Cuba. I believe the facts are as follows:

" 'In May 1957, Mr. William P. Snow, who was then Deputy
Assistant Secretary for Inter-American Affairs, suggested to
Ambassador Smith that he get in touch with Mr. Matthews in
New York for an informal "off the record" conversation on
Cuban matters. Mr. Snow did this at the request of Mr. Rubot-
tom, Assistant Secretary for Inter-American Affairs, in line with
a suggestion made by Senator Javits of New York to Under
Secretary Herter. . . . He [Smith] replied that he knew several
people on *The New York Times* and thought it would be a good

idea to meet with Matthews on the clear understanding that nothing would be said for publication.' ''

Therefore, Smith's statement before the committee that his "instructions" to see me had come from Wieland was wrong; Wieland was simply acting under orders from above. That this harmless talk with Smith should have become historic was silly, but there is no reason to doubt that Herter, Rubottom, Snow, and Javits, as well as Wieland, thought it was a good idea—and so did Ambassador Smith.

Certainly, he was cordial and appeared interested during this so-called briefing, and it was equally certain that it made no difference to his policies in Havana. Had he followed my advice, the United States would not have started its relations with Castroite Cuba on such an unfriendly basis.

"Concerning his association and contacts with Mr. Herbert Matthews of *The New York Times,*" the Senate report states, "Mr. Wieland testified, on the occasion of his second appearance before the committee as follows:

" 'MR. WIELAND. Mr. Matthews is, as Ambassador Smith said, the leading Latin American editor for *The New York Times.* He is an important newspaperman. He would telephone me from New York when there were important developments in the Caribbean area, and he came to my office a total of perhaps two or three times when he was in Washington. These conversations with him were conducted with the knowledge and approval of the public affairs adviser or the Assistant Secretary. Nevertheless, my connections with him were certainly no closer than they were with the newspapermen who work in Washington and deal with developments affecting the countries with which he was concerned in the Department. In every conversation that I can remember having with Mr. Matthews he was critical of our attitude toward Cuban matters. I know of no basis for the remark by Ambassador Smith that Mr. Matthews was more familiar with the Department's thinking regarding Cuba than our Ambassador was.' ''

In testimony of February 8, 1961, under questioning by J. G. Sourwine, there was the following exchange:

MR. WIELAND. I disagreed with Mr. Matthews' reporting
on Castro. . . .

MR. SOURWINE. You never told him that you disagreed?

MR. WIELAND. Yes sir, I told him that I did not share his
views on Castro. . . .

MR. SOURWINE. You knew Mr. Matthews fairly well, did
you not?

MR. WIELAND. Only through the meetings we had, sir,
when he would come down and talk, or on the
telephone. . . .

MR. SOURWINE. And your dealings with him were not on
a social basis but wholly in line of duty?

MR. WIELAND. Yes, sir.

Every word of this published testimony was true. I was critical
of State Department policies toward Cuba from 1958 onward—
and still am. It was a disgraceful job of McCarthyite witch hunt-
ing to blame either Wieland or Rubottom for following my
opinions and actions regarding Cuba. I would have told any
Senate committee or subcommittee as much—and more—if
they had had the courage of their convictions and called me to
Washington to testify. It will always be a source of wonder to me
why they did not do so.

An injustice was being done. I was steadily being attacked by
speakers with immunity, whose testimony was being published,
but I was given no opportunity to reply.

The crucifixion of William Wieland was one of the most
shameful examples of witch-hunting that occurred during my
career. It is a source of profound regret to me that I inadvert-
ently and innocently was used as an instrument to destroy the
careers of Wieland and his superior, Roy R. Rubottom, Jr. The
hatchet job by the Senate subcommittee was not quite as crude
as those perpetrated by Senator McCarthy, but it was as effective
and as unjust.

The case built up against Wieland was a mass of innuendos,
hearsay, misinformation, malice, and hysteria. Mixed in with
these, of course, was much correct information which laid Wie-

land open to the accusation of "unsuitability" made by the Senate committee. That is a debatable matter of opinion which Wieland's superiors obviously did not share.

The subcommittee was politely put in its place as a wasteful, destructive, witch-hunting group whose efforts served no useful purpose. President Kennedy and Secretary of State Rusk went though the testimony twice and decided that Wieland "could not be considered a security risk." After Kennedy's statement, a State Department spokesman told the subcommittee that Wieland "is not a security risk, a loyalty risk, a suitability risk, or any other kind of risk." Robert J. McCarthy, security officer of the State Department, read all ten volumes of the testimony to see "whether there is any indication that the Wieland reports concerning Castro and Cuba were slanted." His conclusion was: "I did not see anything that was slanted." William O. Boswell, director of the Office of Security, and other officials from the Office of Administration, from the Department of Justice, and the FBI (which did a "full field investigation"), came to the same conclusions, exonerating Wieland.

When the committee persisted in its persecution, Robert Kennedy, then Attorney General, studied the case during the autumn of 1964 at the request of Secretary Rusk. As the official record states, Kennedy "indicated that there was no reason for him to reopen the case or to recommend that the case be reopened."

Therefore, Wieland could not be suspended or dismissed—but his career was wrecked. He was given minor posts. The other officer, Roy Rubottom, although nothing was proved against him, felt constrained to resign from the Foreign Service in 1964.

(Incidentally, another victim of the witch hunts was the very able career diplomat, Philip Bonsal, who was the first and only American ambassador to Havana after the Revolution. He was by no stretch of the imagination sympathetic to Fidel Castro—very much to the contrary—but he came under criticism for the "crime" of being a diplomat in the true sense of the word and not a rabid, fire-eating, anti-Communist, America Firster. In the emotionally charged atmosphere of 1959–1962 nothing less would have done.)

What was especially shameful in the Wieland case was to question his "integrity." The committee's disclaimer that Wieland's "loyalty" was not in question was meaningless, since all the proceedings against him and, especially, the baiting by the committee's counsel, Sourwine, indirectly and clearly impugned Wieland's loyalty.

It is impossible to read the harshly worded introduction to the committee's publication summarizing the Wieland case and not get a black impression. Selected passages from Wieland's appearances are given with tendentious introductions before each extract. The passages were all chosen carefully to show Wieland in the worst light.

Ironically, his case before history, his ideas and beliefs about Fidel Castro, his doubts about the CIA and FBI reports, were all logically arguable opinions. Wieland was condemned as much as anything because he did not, between 1957 and 1960, accept the charges that Castro was a Communist or a tool of the Communists. Wieland was right. He was in the American embassy in Bogota, Colombia, on April 8–9, 1948, when the historic uprising occurred. He therefore—and rightly—could not agree with the false report which the Senate committee took as gospel— that Castro "was a leader of the *Bogotazo.*"

If Wieland had been in a real court of justice, undergoing a fair trial and with a competent defense lawyer, the case of the Senate Internal Security Subcommittee and its counsel, J. G. Sourwine, would have been torn to shreds and thrown out of court.

In all the hearings on Cuba by the Senate subcommittee there was no instance of the group calling in any authority on Cuba to get an impartial view, let alone one contrary to their predetermined position.

One of the published hearings was held on July 19, 1962, under the heading: "Attempts of Pro-Castro Forces to Pervert the American Press." The title was a giveaway and typical of the committee's prejudices and prejudgments. This one, at least, had Senator Keating as chairman and Senator Scott as a member, both of whom tried to be fair to the accused who were not present.

The main witness was Carlos Todd, a Cuban businessman in exile who had been a political columnist for the English language *Times of Havana*. He was one of the middle-class Cubans who were understandably disturbed, deeply and emotionally, over the radicalism of Fidel Castro and the growing influence of the Cuban Communists.

Carlos Todd's testimony was of some interest because it was about the newspaper coverage of the Revolution up to that time. He was entitled to criticize since all press coverage of the Revolution contained errors of details and judgments—his own included. What was inexcusable was his imputations of bad faith and deliberate misrepresentation by those newspapermen and television correspondents who wrote anything favorable about Castroite Cuba.

"The intention," Todd said at one point, "is to condition the people of the United States to accept the proposition that Castro and Communism are in Cuba to stay; that this historically inevitable process should be understood by all Americans; and that, therefore, it is advisable to enter into a policy of peaceful coexistence with the Cuban Communists."

The offensive phrase was: "the *intention* is to *condition* the people of the United States." The intention, of course, was simply to present a description of the situation in Cuba as the correspondents saw it. One is entitled to ask, in 1971, what was wrong about the analysis that Todd ridiculed?

Senator Scott, at one moment, blandly remarked: "I was pointing out that only those reporters who were acceptable were permitted to travel in Cuba." His questions showed that by "acceptable" he meant "favorable." Even in the Todd hearing it was shown that many American correspondents, who were "accepted," came back and wrote very unfavorable copy. Todd ignorantly implied that if a correspondent "received a visa from the Czech Embassy [which acted for Cuba in Washington], the Czech Embassy must have thought that he would have written something favorable to Cuba." This was complete nonsense; the Czech embassy was simply a channel for Havana; it had no authority to act for Cuba.

Todd was asked by Senator Scott to comment, one by one, on a list of American newspapermen who wrote on Cuba. My name, like Abou Ben Adhem's, "led all the rest." Todd mentioned a meeting during a reception in Havana given by Paul Bethel, then press attaché of the American embassy. (Bethel later left the Service and became a professional anti-Fidelista.) Todd's testimony indicates that he was baiting me at the cocktail party in Havana, but since the conversation left no impression on me, I cannot say whether Todd's version of my unsatisfactory—to him —answers was correct or not.

Senator Keating, in the interest of fairness, stated at the end of Todd's testimony: "The staff will advise those whose names have been brought out in the hearing that they will be given every opportunity to appear and testify before the committee." According to the counsel, Sourwine, such notification "went to all of those whose names came into that hearing." I never received any such notification.

One of the sharp attacks on me and *The New York Times* during the hearing came from Robert C. Hill, a former U.S. ambassador to Mexico, who also included an inexcusably nasty onslaught against William Wieland. Hill, who had political ambitions at the time, is now, suitably, the U.S. ambassador in Madrid. I had known him in Mexico. When he visited *The Times* on December 1, 1961, about six months after his committee appearance, he came down to my office to see me. I suppose that Hill's testimony was, among other things, a case of telling the senators what was good for his political image. At least he assured me at great length that while he disagreed with my ideas on Cuba, he always took the line that I was an authority on Latin America and was entitled to my opinion. He claimed that he had said this in his testimony before the Senate subcommittee, but it did not appear in the printed text. Afterward, he added, he complained to Senator Dodd about this omission, but it was too late.

The situation was hopeless where Dodd and I were concerned. The senator, from his high position of morality and patriotism, had many a field day discharging arrows at me and *The Times* over a period of years.

One of Dodd's speeches in the Senate, on September 10, 1962, was entitled: "The Problems of the Soviet Quisling Regime in Cuba and the Future of Latin America." Senator Dodd was one of those who swallowed whole the often naive and mistaken beliefs of American envoys and intelligence officers. For instance, Dodd talked in this speech of "the leading role he [Castro] had played in the Bogota riots of 1948." At the time the senator spoke, there was ample proof that Fidel Castro's role in the *Bogotazo* was a very minor one.

"Unfortunately," said Senator Dodd, "there were those in the State Department [1958] who were prone to accept as gospel the evaluation of the Castro movement which found its way into the staid columns of *The New York Times* through the pen of Mr. Herbert Matthews.

"Mr. Matthews assured the American public that Castro was not a Communist and that the Castro movement was not Communist-dominated; and Matthews built up a hero image of Castro in which all the virtues of Robin Hood and Thomas Jefferson, of George Washington, and Abraham Lincoln, were contained in a single man."

Mr. Dodd's mistaken ideas, alas, were typical of prevailing American opinion. Truth was a major sufferer; I was a minor one.

Unlike newspapermen and television and radio commentators in the Nixon administration, I cannot complain over the way the White House under Eisenhower, Kennedy, and Johnson, or the State Department under Dulles and Rusk, treated me over the Cuban story or, indeed, over anything else. I met unfailing courtesy and helpfulness, although I was giving the various administrations a good deal of pain. When I needed passport and Treasury authorizations to go to Cuba and spend American dollars, they were always forthcoming without delay. When I phoned assistant secretaries or desk chiefs at the State Department, I invariably met with cheerful cooperation. There was a time—the first three years or so of the Cuban Revolution—when I heard what must have been confidential off-the-record information. This was more than I could ask or hope for by the time President Johnson came along, but for a long time the State Department and the CIA (as the Bay of Pigs invasion proved) were getting little worthwhile information out of Cuba and believing much which I knew to be incorrect. This was still true when I retired in 1967. It was a not uncommon case of a newspaperman having knowledge that was not available to diplomats or security agents.

I have no doubt now, with Richard Nixon holed up in the White House, shut away from newspaper contamination, with Spiro Agnew flailing away abusively, with the general atmosphere of suspicion and criticism of the mass media throughout the administration, that I would not have cooperation or even tolerance in Washington. At no time in my career did the Attorney General's office try to subpoena reporters' notes or seek to force them to divulge their sources of information.

My talks with Cuban leaders, for instance, were at all times confidential. I would never have surrendered my notes while the material in them was still off the record. They are no longer confidential because of the passage of time, and I have given all my Cuban notes and documents to the Columbia School of Journalism for the use of students and historians. No administration tried to curtail freedom of the press during my career. My difficulties were never with the executive branch of the government. They were with governmental aberrations like the Senate Internal Security Subcommittee, the House Un-American Activities Committee, and demagogic congressmen like Senator Dodd. While these organizations and individuals did me some harm, they could not directly curtail my freedom to write and say what I pleased. They smear a man's reputation under the shield of congressional immunity, without leaving him recourse for an adequate reply.

Given a clear conscience (which rightly or wrongly I had) and a loyal organization like *The New York Times* to backstop me, the superpatriots became nothing worse than painful nuisances. They made me angry at times, and in the case of Arthur Gardner rather bitter, but they will not be the judges of my career.

For a young man entering the journalistic profession in the United States today, there are risks and pitfalls, but they are worth taking, if only to make officials like Agnew and Mitchell realize that American newspapermen will not be muzzled by their government.

The misconceived and mischievous gloating of my enemies when Fidel Castro publicly proclaimed that he was a "Marxist-Leninist" nearly two years after taking power were no problem to me once the facts were available. The hard thing to take, in circumstances like that, is the sympathy of friends: "Anyone can make mistakes. . . . It is easy for people to be smart after the event. . . ." and so forth. There were those who pitied me—which was excruciating.

As it turned out, I had been right, but for forty-eight hours after Fidel made his famous "I am a Marxist-Leninist" speech on December 1–2, 1961, I went through the worst period of my career. I was on record, again and again and quite positively, as saying that Fidel was not Communist in the Sierra Maestra or during the first year and a half in power. But now the United Press International was quoting him from his December 1 speech as saying that he had been a Communist since his university days. At first I thought that Castro was boastfully lying for political purposes.

A few days after the speech, I was due to appear at the Overseas Press Club, to which I belonged, for a seminar discussion of my just-published book, *The Cuban Story*, in which I had stated that neither Fidel nor his close associates were Communists at the time I was writing the book. Herminio Portell Vilá, a noted Cuban historian, then a bitter anti-Fidelista exile, was invited to do the hatchet work. The session was intended to be a crucifixion—always a great pleasure for the mob, and there was an overflow attendance.

I would have been in a journalistically desperate situation but for a lucky break. On that same afternoon of December 4, the CIA documentary service in Washington, which I received, contained a fairly complete, although unofficial, monitoring of the Castro speech. It was a long, rambling, confused oration, which had to be read carefully to be understood, but there was enough in the text for me to defend myself with some assurance. The American journalists in the audience were so hostile, and Portell Vilá so emotional, that I spent a very rough evening.

In fact, the Overseas Press Club, like the Inter-American Press Association at much the same time, contained enough enemies of mine over the Cuban affair to make it too uncomfortable for me to remain a member. I should add that when I did resign from the OPC, many friendly members tried to get me to stay, and were ashamed of the way the organization was acting.

The full official text of Castro's speech soon became available, and it was quite clear that far from saying that he had been a Communist all along, he was apologizing for *not* having been one and for being so slow in appreciating the virtues of Marxism. The speech had been monitored in Florida for the UPI in the middle of the night by an excited Cuban exile who picked some passages out of the address which seemed to say what he and others wanted to believe.

The UPI never corrected what proved to be a monumental error. When the text was circulated, authoritative scholars like Theodore Draper; serious newspapermen like the *New York Post*'s editor-columnist James A. Wechsler; academic publications like the *Hispanic American Report* of Stanford University and the quarterly of the Columbia School of Journalism, all called attention to the fact that Fidel Castro had said the opposite of what he was supposed to have said.

"Thank you, Fidel Castro," the New York *Journal American* wrote in its editorial of December 3, 1961, "Herbert L. Matthews, of *The New York Times*, was another who insisted on giving you the benefit of almost every doubt. Seven months after you took power Mr. Matthews said: 'This is not a Communist revolution in any sense of the word.' You have just proved, Mr. Castro, that Mr. Matthews was in error."

The Times (Orvil Dryfoos was then president) got a flood of letters along the same line, and so did I. I know of no better contemporary example of the persistence of a journalistic error than this. A myth was perpetuated—that Fidel Castro had always been a Communist and had fooled his admirers. I wonder how many readers of this book—a decade later—know that the story was wrong. Months afterward, Eleanor Roosevelt and Adlai Stevenson in a United Nations TV broadcast accepted the false version as gospel.

I could give other examples, which merely prove a journalistic adage—that denials never catch up with false reports. The episode, incidentally, is one more piece of evidence to bear out my indictment of the disgracefully poor coverage of the Cuban Revolution in the American press.

The Marxist-Leninist speech was a case of Castro letting his oratorical gifts run loose. He has his periods of euphoria and of depression. This one was euphoria; the July 26, 1970 speech was depression. Fidel takes a certain childish pleasure in shocking his enemies. The year, 1961, was a period of acute conflict with the United States (the Bay of Pigs invasion occurred in April) and of gratitude to the Soviet Union. December was the climax of an agonizing transition from the capitalist structure Castro found on entering Havana in January 1959 to the Communist system he had just finished installing.

I never could or did expect Fidel to take my feelings or those of *The New York Times* into account. He knew how critical I was of his journey into Communism. On my next trip to Cuba I complained to him and everybody I met, not that the embrace of Marxism-Leninism was now open, but that his December 1 speech was so badly constructed and confusing that his enemies could pick sentences out of it here and there to give the impression that Fidel was confessing he had been a Communist since his college days. He agreed with me that, of course, he had not meant to imply this, since it was not the case, but he never did care much what his opponents said of him. My Cuban friends commiserated with me over the way Fidel had made his startling announcement, but the damage was minor and it could not be undone.

I had been going through a stormy period over Cuba during all of 1961. Cuban exiles who, during the Sierra Maestra period and in 1959, had picketed *The Times* to demonstrate what a wonderful character I was, were now picketing in protest. As late as February 2, 1964, a group marched up and down Forty-third Street with signs like this: "Matthews Number One Enemy of Cuba's Freedom" and "Down Matthews [*sic*] and all Communists of The New York Times." An exile group in Caracas sent *The Times* a letter with a penny pasted to the page. "Enclosed you will find one U.S. cent," it read, "as our contribution for the 'Send Herbert Matthews to his Communist Cuba Paradise Fund.' We are sure that thousands will join us to pay for his one-way ticket so that he can be reunited with his true comrade, Fidel Castro."

Naturally, I had my supporters, among them Ernest and Mary Hemingway. For old times' sake, and knowing their passionate interest in Cuba, I sent them a copy of my book *The Cuban Story* when it was published in September 1961. Ernest was already getting caught up in the illness that was to lead to his suicide, but his sympathetic attitude toward Fidel Castro can be gleaned from the references in Carlos Baker's biography. On November 29, 1961, Mary Hemingway wrote me a letter from Ketchum, Idaho, which she has given me permission to reproduce.

Dear Herbert:

Thank you so much for the book and forgive me for not acknowledging it earlier. I wanted time to read it and now I have read every word and hope you will forgive the endless marginal drawings and exclamation points with which I decorated this copy.

I think it is a wonderful and courageous book and admire you very much indeed for the hard work and good judgment you have put into it and agree-agree-agree with every single point you've made. But I am afraid that perhaps, in spite of this great effort of yours, you are a voice crying in the wilderness. I wish I could provide for you a loud, Greek chorus. There were only two words I would have added to the entire performance and they would have been at the end of the second paragraph on page 203, [about the "magnitude" of the demands being made on the ruling classes of Latin America "and their resistance."] You are so very right, page 243, that we are behaving as a dowager aunt preventing students and teachers—or indeed anyone else interested—from going to Cuba to study and observe. As you know, or will have surmised, the Cubans individually, as you've pointed out in the book, could not have been more gracious, kind and loving to me when I went there in July to retrieve stuff from the Finca. This was true not only of the village beggar who used to sell lottery tickets, but of local police who saw I was obviously not Cuban even not knowing me, but also every single individual—bankers, lawyers, businessmen—I had to deal with, including Fidel who saved our French pictures for me and helped me get them shipped north in spite of the fact that it is now, as in all Communist countries, an offense against the state to take away from the Island any art treasures.

Being never in my life of any political party, but an interested observer of many, I am really appalled that there appear to be inside the United States so few people who are not afraid to open their eyes to the facts of change that are happening to all the hemisphere south of us. If anything can help them to see more clearly and wish to understand, it will be your book.

I hope to finish my work here and to get to New York in February and perhaps to see you and Nancie both.

Very best wishes,

Mary Hemingway

P.S. Fidel's revolution continued last July and August, as interesting as you'd found it before.

Newspaper work in a field like the Cuban Revolution inevitably brings up a problem of ethics—the extent to which a journalist or a newspaper is obliged to support the policies of the government when issues of national security can be invoked. The incident made famous by Clifton Daniel, *The Times'* managing editor, of suppressing a story about the Cuban Bay of Pigs invasion was an example. *The Times* was wrong not to print the story, as President Kennedy himself acknowledged after the fiasco. Publication by *The New York Times* of the secret Vietnam file in June, 1971, is going to be the classic example in American journalistic history of how far a newspaper can and should go.

Joseph Alsop has long been an exponent of the my-country-right-or-wrong school, especially if there is a real or suspect Communist angle.

"When the going gets rough," Alsop wrote in a column on May 10, 1965, during the American intervention in the Santo Domingo uprising, "so the rule runs—think twice or even three times about what you say; for what you say will always be used to embarrass or obstruct your government's policy, if this is at all possible. . . .

"The question raised here is of extreme interest and importance nowadays. Curiously enough, it is of even more importance to the newspaper business than to the professional politicians, for the rather simple reason that the politicians cannot do as much damage. No Wayne Morse-like series of Senatorial utterances has ever had the unfortunate impact of the famous Herbert Matthews series on Fidel Castro, or of the innocent but highly biased reporting from wartime China, or of some of the more self-satisfied reporting in the earlier period of Vietnam."

To me, this is dangerous nonsense. At the time Alsop wrote this column, my newspaper was printing critical editorials on President Johnson's intervention in the Dominican Republic— which I was writing, incidentally. The Johnson policy was palpably wrong and harmful to the United States' long-range relations with Latin America. We would have been derelict in our duty as a responsible organ of opinion not to say so. The early reporting on the Vietnam War—especially in *The New York Times* —not only provided some of the best journalism of recent years, but in its realism and soundness gave the reasons why our Vietnam policies were so tragically wrong.

Joseph Alsop on Cuba and China needs no answer except to point out that he bases himself on the untenable and ridiculous premise that China would not have gone Communist or Cuba Castroist if the American newspapers and some senatorial spokesmen had kept quiet.

The point where freedom of expression and national security clash is incapable of definition in peace time. In war the censor decides; in peace it is a matter of opinion and judgment. A right-winger like Joseph Alsop would naturally have a different border line from a liberal like myself, or a leftist.

Alsop, Jules Dubois of the *Chicago Tribune,* and I were panelists in a symposium on "What Happened to Castro" at the annual meeting of the American Society of Newspaper Editors (ASNE), April 21–23, 1961. Fidel was then in very bad repute. It was a hostile audience for me in that respect. Dubois and Alsop were strongly anti-Fidelista in their talks. When Lee Hills of the Knight Newspapers introduced me he said: "He was among the first to beat the drums for Castro, and perhaps he may be among the last to surrender his confidence in Cuba's man on horseback."

I did not rise to the bait and, in fact, reiterated beliefs that I continued to hold and still hold. I mention this incident because at the end of my talk I repeated a judgment which, as it was made this time in such an exalted American editorial milieu, caused a mild sensation. The proceedings were published by the ASNE as "Problems of Journalism."

"Finally," I said, "if it is of any interest, all of us being newspapermen, I will repeat what I have said often in the last 15 months, which is that in all my 38 years on *The New York Times* I have never seen a big story so misunderstood, so misinterpreted, and so badly handled as the Cuban Revolution."

I am willing to leave that as a final, unchanged judgment, so long as I am allowed a number of individual exceptions. Some journalists and professors have done outstanding work on the Cuban Revolution.

The ignorance of Latin America in general and Cuba in particular in the United States had tragic consequences when the Cuban Revolution came along. I explained the situation then obtaining in an article I did for *International Affairs* of January 1961. This is the organ of the Royal Institute of International Affairs (Chatham House) in London. What I wrote then of the Eisenhower administration applied to succeeding administrations with one exception—President Kennedy interested himself keenly in Latin American affairs, although he could not be an expert and was led into the Bay of Pigs fiasco.

"Few of our Congressmen know anything about the area and none is a specialist in Latin American affairs," I wrote. "For the past eight years there has been no expert in the area at the White House to advise President Eisenhower. . . . Our State Department, to be sure, is reasonably well provided with Latin American specialists. We also have a number of first-rate Latin Americanists in the academic world, although not nearly enough.

"The Cuban Revolution has come upon us and there is not a single North American professor in any of our universities who had specialized in Cuban affairs. As a journalist, I have to confess that little attention has been paid to Latin America in our mass communications media, few newspapermen know the area, and there is very little interest amidst the general public.

"We are ill prepared as a government and as a people for the crisis that has now come upon us. Ignorance in the conduct of foreign affairs is dangerous, and when it is compounded with emotionalism, as is the case with Cuba, there is reason to be frightened."

I can give many examples of how that emotionalism affected me, personally. None is better than the episode that began when Agent James Kenny of the Federal Bureau of Investigation walked into the office of John Oakes, editor of the editorial page, on the afternoon of September 14, 1964. What he said brought an alarmed call from Oakes for me to come into his office. Since I was asked to keep mum at the time, this is the first that I have written of the incident.

The FBI, said Kenny, had learned from one of their informants in a Cuban exile organization (he never would identify it), that the group "has decided that you are to be killed by a hired professional killer and they are now looking around for someone to do it." In time, I learned that the Cuban outfit was in Miami, but since there were more than a hundred such organizations, there was no use trying to guess which one. The plot, according to Kenny, was still "in a very preliminary stage" and they were watching the group. The New York police, he went on, were being notified and told to get in touch with me and advise me what to do.

Oakes immediately got hold of Punch Sulzberger, who was by then president and publisher of *The Times.* Punch asked if I wanted a private guard for which *The Times,* of course, would pay. I said to wait until the New York police said what they wanted, if anything. Meanwhile, the plant security guards, headed by Eugene Zaccor, were told to keep a special watch for any odd characters. I was to turn over, unopened, any packages which I received.

Kenny was a tall, blue-eyed, handsome young chap—a good movie version of an FBI character. He asked if I had done anything recently or heard anything that would have aroused the Cubans or pointed to such a decision, but the answer was, No, nothing special. My first reaction was to say that it would, if successful, make a good story. My last, to Kenny, was: "Hope you can keep me alive."

Zaccor got me on the phone that night at home, after getting a call at his apartment from *Times* Vice-President Andrew Fisher. "This doesn't happen unless it is something urgent," Zaccor said, but since I was keeping the matter secret from my wife, I told him to come up and see me in my office the next day, which he did. He had just talked to Agent Kenny who told him that the

Cuban group was trying "to make a contract" with someone to assassinate me and was still talking about doing so.

My wife and I being devoted TV fans ("The Untouchables" was one of our favorites), and I having read a great deal about the Mafia and Cosa Nostra in the course of my work, that word "contract" was a chilling one. I believed—and I am more than ever convinced by what has come out since 1964—that once a professional group makes "a contract," the victim is sooner or later dead. I pinned my hopes on the fact that, so far as the FBI knew, no such contract had yet been made, nor had anything been said about beating me up, throwing acid in my face, or other such gangster pleasantry.

Zaccor asked if I wanted protection. He said that *The Times* was prepared to give me the maximum—a man who would meet me at our apartment house on East Seventy-Fourth Street and ac- company me to the office, hang around during the day, and then accompany me back, always discreetly and in civilian clothes. I said that on the basis of our present knowledge this seemed unnecessary. We had to hope that the informant whom the FBI was using was a good one and was on the ball. He might not be able to get word to Kenny in time, but this was a risk we would have to take. Kenny engaged himself to notify *The Times* and me immediately, day or night, if anything developed one way or another. Zaccor was unhappy about the ease with which anybody could get by the editorial reception desk and how poorly the tenth floor was protected, but for the time being we had to let that go.

The next day, September 16, I received a visit at the office from Detective Jack Corfield of the New York Police Bureau of Special Services. He had been put *au courant* by Kenny, with whom he had worked on other Cuban affairs. He wanted me to have the name, address, and telephone number to be called "if anything happens, however silly or unimportant it may seem to you, if it is out of the way; we are open 24 hours a day." He gave me both the direct line to his office and the switchboard number of the Special Services. If I telephoned, he said, someone would be with me in a half hour. He wanted to meet *The Times'* security officer, and I asked Zaccor to join us. Corfield said that the Cuban colony in New York had dwindled almost to nothing so far as demonstrations were concerned—no life in them. He said that he had orders from his superiors to give me any protection I desired. I told him what I had told the others—that in present circumstances I could see nothing to do. He took our home address and telephone number. I learned from him that Kenny's information came, as I suspected, from Miami.

My efforts to keep the affair from my wife broke down when Detective John Justy of our district police precinct called me at home in the evening and said he wanted to come around to see me. He settled for talking to me on the phone, but since Nancie was sitting there, the cat was out of the bag. Justy gave me more numbers to call and said that he was notifying the building help and giving them the phone numbers "in case they saw anything suspicious." The next day I called Justy to say that this seemed unnecessary, but he told me that he had already been around.

He had seen the doorman, Denis Walsh, and given him all the information and told him to tell the building superintendent, Wente. The latter was to advise all the help. Justy left a typewritten memo with all the necessary phone numbers. He told the doorman that if anyone came to see me, they were to get one of us on the intercom and ask if it was all right, but to allow no one up unless they did this. Justy said that he was "quite emphatic" with the building staff and if they saw anyone loitering around they were not to hesitate to call the precinct, and especially to watch out for Cubans and Puerto Ricans. I called Justy's attention to the fact that the house intercom was broken, but he said to insist that the superintendent get it fixed quickly. He agreed with me that the information did not yet warrant guards, and he gave another reason—that guards would draw attention to me and let it be known that I was being protected. This seemed like an invitation to make me a sitting duck. However, Justy assured me that the official setup was sufficient, as the FBI would "cut into the people" in Miami as soon as anything got more definite.

I "vibrated," as Samuel Johnson would have said, "in a state of uncertainty" as the weeks dragged on and nothing happened. On Monday morning, November 2, seven weeks having passed since Agent Kenny first came to *The Times* to warn me, I telephoned him. I hoped that he would let me off the hook. However, all he could say was that there was nothing new, but the fact that there were no new developments "looks good." So far as the FBI knew, the exile group had not "carried its plan or inclination" any further. He assured me that the FBI was following the situation and did not want me to think that they had dropped it. "We have continued the contact with our sources who, in turn, were in touch with the Cuban exile sources," he said. "We did and do follow the situation." He still would not name the Cuban exile group who was after me, but, as he put it, "the fact that nothing has happened seemed indicative that they have gone no further. . . . The calendar is certainly on our side."

On December 2 I called Kenny again to tell him, as requested, of my movements, and specifically that I was going away the next day for three weeks. The "thing we talked about," he told me, was "as dead as it has been." I said that it certainly seemed obvious that they had given up the idea of killing me. He agreed that this was "a fair inference" as "the thing has not gone ahead," but when I said that this business could not go on forever, he argued that "proving a universal negative" was not possible. He assured me that at the time when he had first spoken to me, the events were really as he had said they were —that there was the "intention or inclination" to get me assassinated, but it "had not gone forward at all" since then. He asked that I get in touch with him when I got back.

I did so on December 28. "It doesn't look like it has been going any place recently," Kenny said. "The imminence of anything is rather remote. I can hardly say that no one is ever going to do anything in the future. That would be foolish—but you should put it out of your mind."

I will never know what frustrated the Cuban exiles, but I should guess it was a matter of expense. From what I have read about the Cosa Nostra, I should think that the going price for killing an editor of *The New York Times* would be at least as high as $15,000.

I was much in demand for lectures on Cuba in universities around the United States, particularly after the Revolution took its Communist turn. The almost invariable pattern was for the American students to be attentive, open-minded, and liberal, but every university had its group of Cuban exile students and a minority of Birchites. This meant picketing, heckling, and—on one occasion—a bomb scare that stopped me in the middle of my lecture.

This was at the University of New Mexico in Albuquerque, where I spoke on March 11, 1964. I opened a series on "New Thinking about the Cold War." The visit was made spectacular by the bomb scare, but in other respects was so typical of the popular reaction that it can pass as an example of the sort of problem Cuba brought into my career.

When I was met at the airport by Professor Edwin C. Hoyt, head of the university's Department of Government, a television reporter who had come to photograph and question me warned that the lecture was going to be picketed. Hoyt said that if so, it would be because the local Scripps Howard newspaper had been printing inflammatory pieces about me and also about the university for inviting me to lecture. I learned the next day that a radical rightist disc jockey, who was on the radio all afternoon, had continually called on his listeners to picket me and do everything possible to make things difficult. Hoyt said that the man was a Birchite, and while the Birchites and the Cuban exiles—by no means all students—were small minorities, they were noisy and vocal.

The pickets were there all right, carrying a number of placards including two reading: "Cuba si, Matthews no!" and "Matthews Go Home." However the lecture hall in the Student Union Building was full and the audience quiet and attentive. It was a written lecture, as the university was planning to publish the series. I noted later that I was reading page sixteen of the twenty-seven page lecture when Dean Sherman Smith of the university came on the platform. I could hear him talking to Hoyt, but not the words. In a minute, Hoyt put a paper in front of me on the rostrum saying: "You must finish your talk now."

I finished the paragraph and then said to the audience, in puzzlement: "I have been asked to stop my talk here." Many cried, "No"—"Go On"—and so forth, but when I turned to Dean Smith he told me what had happened, and then announced to the audience that the police had received a report that a bomb was planted in the hall and it would have to be cleared immediately.

"City police, University of New Mexico police, and city firemen combined in an immediate search of the Union," the *New Mexico Lobo* stated the next day. "Sgt. C. J. Martin of the Albuquerque police told the *Lobo* that the call sounded as if it came from 'an elderly Spanish lady' because of her accent. He said she was 'incoherent and almost hysterical,' and mentioned a bomb in the Student Union at the University and 'something about a Cuban speaker.' Three police units in the area were despatched to the Union, plus the Fire Department and a rescue squad. Other police units in the nearby area were told to stand by." The *Albuquerque Journal* (which, like the *Lobo,* printed a very fair, accurate, and friendly account) said the woman had called at 8:53 and warned that the bomb would go off in fifteen minutes. The hall was cleared by 9:05.

When I stepped down from the platform, a number of students came up to me, all of them friendly and complimentary, and it was suggested that we go to a nearby dormitory lounge where I could finish the lecture and answer questions. As no announcement was made, only 100 of the 1,000 in the audience followed me there.

The Cuban students came along and had their innings after the lecture, asking the usual questions such as how could I say that Castro had not been a Communist on taking power when he, himself, admitted having been one since his university days —citing the famous "I am a Marxist-Leninist" speech. As is always the case with Cuban exiles, the truth about that speech made no impression.

When Hoyt put an end to the questioning, there was much applause, as there had been in the lecture hall, but the Cuban students kept hectoring and shouting. One asked, in Spanish, if I knew how many Cubans Fidel had killed. The din increased. A well-dressed woman stood in front of me as Hoyt and his wife were ushering me out and tried to block the way. She was white with anger. Other students—Americans—crowded up to shake my hand and thank me. Two policemen, who had been detailed to guard the meeting, escorted me out of the building.

The episode as a whole was encouraging. The great majority of the students—and the faculty—were interested, friendly, and open-minded. The Albuquerque press, with one exception, could not have been more fair. In fact, the respected *New Mexico Lobo* even went to the trouble of getting the text of my lecture and printing it, a week later, on two and a half pages "for the benefit of students who were unable to hear the speech in full" due to the bomb scare. In an editorial the day after my lecture, the *Lobo* blamed the *Albuquerque Tribune* "for the bomb scare, picket line and sundry other stunts that turned U.N.M. students and townspeople out into the cold."

"Getting word from local right-wingers that Matthews did not adamantly favor sending in the Marines to turn on the water," the *Lobo* continued, "the Trib began calling up Cuban exiles resident in Albuquerque asking them what they were going to 'do' about it. The Trib then began running stories which might be called malicious if it were not for the unfathomable ignorance displayed in their content. The net effect of the articles, however, was to incite an unbalanced local denizen to phone in a bomb threat and to move local Cuban exiles to picket the famous journalist's speech.

"The bomb threat, augmented by the picket line and the bitter emotionality displayed by some of the Cubans, could very well have produced a panic in the lecture hall, possibly resulting in deaths and injuries."

A letter to the editor of the *Albuquerque Journal* put the basic issue well.

"Eternal vigilance is the price of freedom," the reader wrote. "It seems that in New Mexico even vigilance can't protect freedom of speech. We have witnessed the incredible sight of a university intimidated by one person with a phone. Not a gun was fired nor a blow struck; just a simple threat.

"The first speech in the University of New Mexico series on the cold war had begun well. A large crowd had assembled to hear a nationally known speaker discuss a topic on which he was an expert. In the face of a threat, the speaker, the university and the interested audience were helpless to act.

"The shocking thing was how easily freedom of speech was destroyed."

I have given this whole Albuquerque incident in detail because it epitomizes both the good and the bad of the American reaction to the Cuban Revolution in general, and to me in particular.

A letter I received in June 1965 from someone in Vermont, put forward an ingenious hypothesis.

"The following," my correspondent wrote, "was in a quotation from the broadcast of Fulton Lewis Jr. at seven P.M. radio station WOR on Monday, May 24:

"And Senator Dodd criticized *New York Times* correspondent Herbert Matthews who sold Castro to the State Department in advance of the overthrow of the Batista regime, as a modern George Washington of Latin America and who two weeks ago had undertaken to lecture the Administration and the American people on the non-Communism of the Dominican revolution and the wickedness of American intervention.

"Mr. Matthews—haven't you done enough damage to this country? Why don't you just shut up and be thankful you have a job? As a matter of fact, I can't understand why *The Times* retains you unless the explanation is that you own a huge block of stock." (At the time, unfortunately, I did not own any *Times* stock.)

For some years I kept a file of the uncomplimentary oddities that came my way, partly for amusement and partly as examples of the tribulations of a dissenter, but one day I threw them in the waste basket where they belonged. A few have survived somehow. There was the anonymous postcard writer, on November 30, 1962, who said: "After all, Judas hung himself, why not you?" Another persistent writer, from whom I got at least a dozen letters, suggested that I "take an overdose of hemlock and be a real hero."

Naturally, there were innumerable blasts from Cuban exiles and their organizations. I especially liked one statement issued in Miami by the Cuban Liberation Committee on November 6, 1963, while I was in Cuba on a trip.

"Through diplomatic sources accredited in Havana," it read, "we have been advised that Mr. Herbert Matthews, reporter of *The New York Times,* apparent public relations manager of the Castro regime, recently had several high level meetings in Havana with Soviet and Cuban government officials.

"Although we do not have details of the secret conversations, there are indications that a plan is being concocted to introduce apparent changes in the Castro regime, probably through a Soviet-controlled internal uprising and a well-rehearsed split in the Soviet bloc.

"This plan is called Operation Judas.

"Our diplomatic sources believe Mr. Matthews was acting as a non-official representative of the U.S. State Department, thus continuing the secret mission entrusted to him when Earl E. T. Smith was U.S. Ambassador to Cuba. The purpose of this pressure is to provoke collapse of Cubans' resistance, ease pressure of American public opinion prior to the election, and pave the way for U.S. recognition and economic support of the Cuban regime disguised as neutralists and without the Castro brothers."

Cubans were not the only ones. There was a United States Information Agency press conference while I was in Cuba which Meyer Handler, a *Times'* reporter, attended. He told me when I got back that some Latin American journalists asked in all seriousness: "Is it true that Herbert Matthews is now President

Kennedy's man in Havana from whom the President takes advice and is getting his policy?"

The USIA, in fact, has at all times taken great care to keep my books on their proscribed list. An article in the *Philadelphia Bulletin* of October 10, 1969, by Paul Grimes, referring to my three books on the Cuban Revolution, said: "An agency spokesman stated it was felt that they 'did not represent a balanced view or would be suitable for non-American audiences.' "

This virtuous policy, however, did not prevent the USIA from circulating thousands of copies of the strongly anti-Fidelista and far from "balanced" books of Theodore Draper and others on Fidel Castro and Cuba. I do not blame them, since the USIA is a propaganda organization and my books, directly and indirectly, were indictments of American policies and critically sympathetic to the Cuban revolutionaries, but I would feel better if the USIA directors were more honest about their motives.

There has been a form of censorship by Washington on the Cuban Revolution from a very early period. I once wrote an editorial headlined "The Cuban Wall," which was an attack on the State Department's policy of preventing any but accredited American journalists from visiting Cuba. This meant that university students, professors, even scientists were prevented from studying the most important Latin American development of modern times, and also from witnessing the rare political phenomenon of a social revolution in process.

The trade embargo keeps Cuban books out of the United States, and it has restricted Cuban newspapers and magazines to a limited number of subscribers who, for years, had to notify the American authorities each time a shipment arrived that the material was wanted. The policy was successful in contributing to American ignorance of what was happening in Cuba, and thus giving much wider scope to the often false and distorted news given out in Washington and in most of the American news media. After some years Fidel, on his side, began making it difficult and, recently, almost impossible for American journalists to visit Cuba—which was just as reprehensible.

Censorship has a boomerang effect. Both Cuba and the

United States were harmed by their news restrictions. I used to argue with Fidel about that, and I kept on criticizing the American government for its efforts to surround Cuba with a wall of ignorance. In recent years Washington has eased up on its regulations; the more difficult problem since 1969 is to get a Cuban visa.

Being an old-fashioned liberal, I have always drawn comfort from John Stuart Mill's essay *On Liberty*. "If all mankind minus one were of one opinion," he wrote in Chapter II, "mankind would be no more justified in silencing that one person than he, if he had the power, would be justified in silencing mankind."

Not, very obviously, that I can complain of having been "silenced." Hampered, at times, pressured, vilified, called all sorts of names like "the Alger Hiss for Cuba"—these, yes, but they are annoyances, not prohibitions. "If you cannot answer a man's arguments," William Hazlitt wrote in his essay on Mr. Jeffrey, "you may at least try to take away his character." Many have tried, since the Spanish Civil War days.

It is a satisfaction to be criticized by certain people and organizations. When the John Birch Society listed me in a manual they put out in May 1968, called "Men of the Left," I felt that something would have been wrong if they had left my name out. It was much more disturbing when Assistant Secretary Thomas Mann referred to me as "an extreme leftist" at a banquet given by the Venezuelan Embassy in Washington for about a hundred guests. A friend of mine who was there told me that his Latin American diplomatic colleagues thought the remark in *muy mal gusto*—very bad taste—in which case Mann, not I, lost out.

A *New York Times'* reporter who followed George Wallace around the country during the 1968 presidential campaign said that Wallace never lost a chance, in repeating his speeches, to attack me and *The Times* over Cuba. It was much better for us to be attacked by George Wallace than praised.

I saw a review by Clare Boothe Luce of a book called *The Experts*, written by Seymour Freidin and George Bailey.

"Two seasoned journalists boldly take to task the newspaper pundits and foreign affairs amateurs inside and outside of government who become Kremlinologists, China-watchers and instant experts on Asia, Africa and Latin America," Mrs. Luce wrote. "The reader is warned by the authors: 'There are few heroes in this book; there are a few more villains, and a great many fops, dupes and dolts.' The main villains, Harrison Salisbury, Herbert Matthews, Senator Fulbright and the up-to-now sacrosanct Walter Lippmann, are certain to squirm, if they read it."

I have not read the book, but why I should "squirm" at being put in a category with three such admirable men is a mystery. It would be terribly upsetting to me if men like Salisbury, Fulbright, and Lippmann opposed and criticized me. They could hurt me. Men like Freiden, Bailey, Joseph Alsop, William F. Buckley, George Sokolsky, Fulton Lewis, Jr., George Wallace, and others like them can do me no harm, and I would rather have them attacking me than agreeing with me.

I am not arguing that it is a pleasure to be a dissenter. The years from 1957 to 1959 when everyone agreed with me on Fidel Castro and Cuba, and when I was a sort of "hero," not a "villain," were very pleasant ones. The years since have been difficult and, in some respects, unpleasant. The price that had to be paid was not high; the rewards have been great.

The attacks, incidentally, have been confined to the United States. During years when I was a constant target of attack in the United States, I was honored abroad wherever I went. Even when the American hostility was unspoken and unwritten as, for instance, in our favorite southern town of Asheville, North Carolina, I and my wife could know that everyone felt critical. The atmosphere was not happy for us. This did not, as I have mentioned, apply to academic communities around the United States where there is a sophisticated understanding of Communism and foreign affairs.

The chief sufferer (I almost wrote "victim" but that was not the case) was *The New York Times.* Cuba and I were a trial to this greatest of newspaper institutions—and *The Times* was, on occasions, a great trial to me.

Chapter 9

CUBA AND
THE TIMES

Nothing in my forty-five-year career gave *The Times* so much trouble, so many complaints and doubts and fears, as my work on Fidel Castro and the Cuban Revolution. It can be—and has been—argued that no other American newspaper would have kept me on its staff, not only doing my regular work on Europe, Africa, and Vietnam, but also writing our editorials on Cuba. I will grant that, but add that considering the policies, ideals, and the role that *The New York Times* plays in American and world journalism, it would have been inexcusable for *The Times* to have done anything else. I believe that it should have done more.

My feelings, therefore, are a mixture of gratitude, admiration, and resentment. I worked, during nearly all my career, on a different *New York Times* from the present one. Like all the old-timers of my generation, I profited from its paternalism, but also gave it respect and loyalty, which helped to build *The Times* into a unique institution, as if one were part of a team, or even a family. I considered *The Times* to be strong and idealistic enough to live up to Adolph S. Och's boasts of publishing "all the news that's fit to print" and doing so "without fear or favor." I do not believe that it lived up to those slogans in the case of Cuba.

My position was inescapably unique. Because of the way my first interview in the Sierra Maestra had helped Fidel Castro and the revolutionaries, and because I retained a great deal of sympathy for the regime after the Revolution started and even after it turned Communist, I always had an entrée into Havana and the charmed circle of Cuban leaders which no newspaperman of any nationality could remotely equal. Cuba was an open book to me during all the years when it was closed to everyone else. I was in a position to get *The New York Times* information from the highest Cuban sources which nobody could duplicate.

Here was the most important development in Latin American history since the wars of independence a century and a half ago. Here was one of the rare phenomena of modern history—a social revolution of the most drastic kind on which I, and I alone, could report from the inside, as it went along. It was a golden opportunity for *The New York Times.* But I was muzzled!

Concededly, *The Times* would have had to pay a price in facing up to the truly furious attacks and criticisms from Cuban exiles and sympathizers and from Washington. Admittedly, my copy would have given the Cuban side of the story with sympathy and understanding, but the paper knew that with my long experience as a correspondent I would have written without editorializing, "without fear or favor," presenting the bad as well as the good, sticking to facts for the news columns and keeping opinions for editorials adjusted to *Times'* policies.

The problems would have been a question of degree. Having launched Fidel so sensationally in February 1957, and having covered the triumph of Castro in 1959, *The Times* could never escape unreasonable but understandable criticism. What little it saved by preventing me from providing the firsthand coverage that I, alone, could have given, was not worth the amount of criticism that was saved by keeping not only my name—but what was infinitely more important—my information out of the newspaper.

The Times, which all my life had represented an institution of historic, documentary information, failed of its mission in the case of the Cuban Revolution. It was a disappointing, as well as frustrating experience. I am happy that I got as much as I did into the paper, but I am sorry that I was not permitted to do the job that I could have done.

I began to feel critical of *The Times* and of the American press in general early in 1959 when I saw how blindly and emotionally the question of the execution of the Batistianos was being handled. It was legitimate and necessary to condemn the way these summary trials and executions were carried out, and to express dismay over their number; it was wrong not to explain that an overwhelming majority of Cubans approved of what Fidel was doing, and that by his swift justice he had prevented the kind of mass slaughter that took place in Caracas, Venezuela, the year before when the dictator, Pérez Jiménez, was overthrown.

After a visit to Cuba in March 1960, I wrote a confidential memo for the editors.

"One of the basic feelings I have come away with," I said, "is that there is an abyss of misunderstanding between the United States and Cuba. We do not have any comprehension of the way they feel, or even, to a considerable extent, what is happening there. The Cubans do not have any comprehension of why we feel the way we do or why we act the way we do, and they are also ignorant of American politics, press and public opinion. . . .

"In conclusion, I would say that I found the trip a necessary one to have made. The coverage of Cuba in the American press, and I am sorry to say that I include *The New York Times,* has been most deficient. In my nearly 38 years on *The Times* I know of no other story of major importance on which *The Times* has done such a poor job. I am referring, of course, to the period from January 1, 1959. Through her emotional and technical insufficiencies, Ruby Phillips [our correspondent in Havana] has been most incapable of sending a clear and detached and understanding picture of the Cuban Revolution. The information given out in Washington is often deliberately misleading or quite simply incorrect. Yet, because of the fact that nobody on our Washington staff knows or understands the Cuban situation, this information has to be accepted and it is giving an incorrect picture."

I could give many examples of the American government's ignorance of what was happening in Cuba in addition to the notorious CIA disaster of the Bay of Pigs operation. One of the most striking in my experience happened while I was in Havana on April 28, 1966. The assistant secretary in charge of the Inter-American Bureau of the State Department, Lincoln Gordon, made a public statement that there was dissension in high Cuban government quarters and that there had been a demonstration in the streets of Havana with the protesters carrying a coffin.

The story was completely false. The next day I lunched with a group of foreign diplomats in Havana and several expressed a sense of shock (one ambassador said that he was "appalled") at so high an American official making such a statement. It showed an astonishing depth of ignorance, but unfortunately a typical one. Gordon must have believed what he said.

I saw Fidel on May 2 and he asked, wonderingly, whether it was a case of Gordon's ignorance or of lying? I said ignorance. He thought it incredible that there could be such a lack of knowledge of the true facts in Cuba as there was in the United States.

This, incidentally, gave me one of my frequent opportunities to insist that if *The New York Times* were allowed to send a regular correspondent back to Havana, it would make an enormous difference to the information that the American public, at least, received. We had had three excellent correspondents after Mrs. Phillips left—Tad Szulc, Juan de Onis (in my opinion the best), and Richard Eder, but unfortunately the last regular correspondent, Paul Hofmann, had done a mischievous as well as poor job in 1965, not only sending out incorrect information, but also what Fidel characterized as *"cosas odiosas"*—hateful things. Richard Eder was allowed in for a few weeks in October 1965, but from Hofmann's stint until today (mid-1971) no *New York Times'* news staff correspondent has been permitted to stay in Cuba. I was the only *Times* staffer allowed in. As I told Fidel when I was in Havana in October 1967, the greater loss was Cuba's.

The bitterly hostile press that Castro and Cuba faced in the United States began with those executions early in 1959, and it has never ended. It has become less virulent in recent years as Vietnam absorbed American attention and as Fidel concentrated more and more on his internal problems. The height of the hostility was in the years 1960 to 1963. I became more and more uneasy for *The Times,* which was under constant attack because of me. On May 18, 1961, I wrote Arthur Hays Sulzberger, then chairman of the board and still active, a note that I hoped would be reassuring.

"I have just completed a long series of lectures, seminars and such in a number of colleges and universities around the country, responding to requests that I tell them about Cuba and the revolution," I wrote. "I had many more requests than I could satisfy, but accepted enough to keep me very busy and very tired.

"As I believe I indicated some time back, I felt this was the best possible answer to the continual criticisms coming from the right-wing organizations and publications and from those responding to the current emotionalism about the Cuban situation. To give you a partial list of the places I went to, there were Yale, Dartmouth, Columbia, Trenton State, Patterson State, Rutgers, Sarah Lawrence, C.C.N.Y., Oberlin, Michigan, Princeton and Wesleyan.

"Almost without exception, I found audiences that were at least open-minded and usually enthusiastic. There was surprisingly little criticism or hostility. I believe that the reactions since the Bay of Pigs invasion from universities like Harvard, Princeton and California show that my ideas on Cuba are getting acceptance among many professors and teachers. The outcome of the invasion fiasco last month exactly fitted what those to whom I spoke would have expected.

"I am writing you simply because as I remarked before, I realize the problem that *The Times* faces on this Cuban issue and I wanted you to know that so far as the academic world of the

United States is concerned, I and *The Times* have a very consider-able body of support on the Cuban issue."

The problem, however, never lay with the American academic community. In New Mexico the trouble had not been with stu-dents or faculty. An ill-informed, emotional, unsophisticated public, led by an equally uninformed body of columnists, com-mentators, congressmen, and nationalistic superpatriots—all driven by a fanatical anti-Communism—provided the mass of maneuver.

In cases like this, it is a general rule that ridicule is more effective than sledge-hammer blows. William F. Buckley got off a few thrusts in his *National Review* that deserve preservation. One was a cartoon showing Fidel Castro sitting happily on his island of Cuba waving a rifle. The caption underneath was our famous advertising slogan: "I got my job through *The New York Times*." I thought this was so clever—despite its exaggeration—that I described it in my book, *The Cuban Story.*

Another clever one was a piece of irony based on the fact that in July 1959 I had written that neither Castro nor any of the top Cuban leaders were Communists—which was true at that time.

In the May 20, 1961 issue of the *National Review*, Buckley printed a column composed like a news despatch. The headlines and opening went like this:

"No Communist Threat Seen in New Russian Regime

Dynamic Young Bolshevik Administration Is Reforming Country by Trial and Error

---

Inquiry Shows Lenin, Trotsky, Others are Anti-Communist

By SHERBERT MATTHEWS

MOSCOW, May 7, 1918—Communism played no part in last November's Revolution here, and no Commu-nists, of any size or stripe, hold power in the new gov-ernment. . . ."

Irony, as all writers learn to their cost, is a blundering weapon because there are always some readers silly enough to take it seriously. Although in this case the irony was heavy, a number of readers found it credible. One well-meaning individual ended a letter to the editor of *The New York Times* in these words: "If it is authentic, you ought to explain to the National Review how you happened to publish such a silly thing. If it isn't authentic, you ought to sue them for libel in attributing such a thing to you."

As late as February 1964, we received a letter from a James R. Taylor, president of the Committee of Christian Laymen, Inc., of Woodland Hills, California. The two-sentence text read: "Some 45 years ago a 'Sherbert Matthews' wrote articles for your paper. By any chance does he today write under the name of Herbert Matthews; if not and they are two different persons, are they related?"

It was not fun and games like Buckley's which disturbed *The Times* publishers but the violent attacks and the sensationalism that sometimes accompanied them. I generally ignored the attacks, but felt constrained to try, at least, to put the record straight on Castro's supposed prerevolutionary Communism. I also resented the unfair accusations that *The New York Times* was approving the outrageous things Fidel was doing and saying, or that we were denying or ignoring the growing strength of the Cuban Communists. Both for *The Times* and for the book I was writing in mid-1961, *The Cuban Story*, my wife compiled a list and summaries of forty-three editorials on Cuba that I wrote between January 3, 1959 and August 10, 1961. This compilation permitted me to say, with truth, that there was not a single editorial praising the Cuban Revolution or Fidel Castro in well over two and a half years. The same could be said of succeeding years, with the proviso that when there was good to be said as well as bad, it was at all times included in my editorials and editorial columns.

The atmosphere was getting so hot for *The Times* that late in the summer of 1961, Orvil Dryfoos, then president and publisher, called me to his office. He was cordial and pleasant, but also upset and worried. The gist of what he said was that somehow a truce must be called in the battle between me and my critics, as it was proving too embarrassing to *The Times*. I fully agreed, and gave him all my sympathy, but asked how we could achieve a truce in view of the fact that the attacks on us were a reaction to Castro's and Washington's policies? He agreed, but argued that if I stayed out of the public eye and kept quiet the heat would simmer down somewhat.

The main result of our talk was that I did not try to visit Cuba again for two and a half years, thereby losing touch—which was bad for *The Times* as well as for me, and I also cut down on my lecturing. Dryfoos, whose tragic death at the age of fifty as a result of the prolonged newspaper strike of 1962 was a great loss to *The Times* and a great personal sorrow to me, could not have been more understanding or friendly.

When *The Cuban Story* was published, Dryfoos told me he had "read every word of it with fascination"—although it was a pro-Fidelista book. He always defended me in answering critics who wrote letters to the publishers. Several letters were about my book, and in each case he replied in the same terms sending me copies, one of which I kept. This one was dated October 6, 1961.

"Your letter of September 28th concerning Herbert Matthews and his recent book on Cuba has come to my attention," Dryfoos wrote. "I appreciate your comments. However, what Mr. Matthews or any other staff member writes in a publication other than *The Times* is an expression of his own point of view.

"*The Times* believes in freedom of thought and expression. Its news columns endeavour to present the news objectively, and its editorial columns express the newspaper's opinion rather than that of any individual writer. All editorials and news dispatches are written under the supervision of the editor.

"Mr. Matthews has been with *The Times* for thirty-nine years and we respect his integrity and honesty.'

"Thank you for taking the trouble to write. I hope that *The Times* will continue to have your respect and confidence."

Dryfoos and *The Times* were given a prime example of how

impossible it was for me or the newspaper to avoid controversy when the Inter-American Press Association (IAPA) held its annual conference in New York in October 1961. On Tuesday, October 17, some Cuban exile editors attacked me and *The Times* and, according to our reporter, Tad Szulc, who was present, suggested a vote of censure against me. I was there the next morning at a session during which the Vice-President, Andrew Heiskell of Time-Life, was chairman. Jules Dubois of the *Chicago Tribune,* who headed the Freedom of the Press Committee, had done some spade work and started the proceedings by saying that it was not the intention of the Cuban editors to ask the IAPA to censure me. It was then my turn.

"I was naturally glad to hear Jules Dubois' explanation of what happened yesterday afternoon," I said. "I accept the fact that today this is to be considered a misunderstanding and that it was not intended as a censure against myself. . . .

"I am sorry that you are being subjected to a dispute which, in spite of what was said this morning, was given a personal aspect and was certainly, by implication, an attack on *The New York Times,* on just one member organization out of 643. This dispute is not of our choosing. It will not do the IAPA any good, but now we must face it and in so doing face issues that greatly transcend myself and *The New York Times.*

"I could not be here yesterday afternoon, but *The Times* was represented by a registered member, Tad Szulc. As I understand it, there were three interventions yesterday about me and *The New York Times.* Jules Dubois protested that we had an editorial saying that the IAPA has been driven by the Cuban issue from journalism into politics. I certainly do not contest Jules' right to protest against what we said, any more than he, I know, would contest the right of *The New York Times* to say what it thinks.

"The question of what is journalism and what is politics is not easy to define. Perhaps it is impossible to define precisely. I submit that there is quite a difference between the way that the IAPA handled the struggle against Perón, Pérez Jiménez and Rojas Pinilla, and the struggle against Fidel Castro. It is partly a matter of degree. In my opinion. . . . the IAPA has been obsessed by Cuba. It was, and is, important, but it should not be allowed to absorb the work of the IAPA to the point of almost exclusivity, as well as one of intense emotionalism. . . .

"I think it was wrong to inject personalities of any sort into this issue as was done yesterday, but since it was brought up, Manuel Braña's statement that I had been decorated by Mussolini is a case in point. The decoration to which he refers was the Italian War Cross—the *Croce de Guerra.* It was given by the Italian Government 'for valor in the field.' I should not have to make this explanation. Personalities should have nothing to do with the subjects of debate.

"The real issues are much greater, and I ask you to face them. The issue is not me, or *The New York Times;* it is whether an individual has a right to hold and express in his writings ideas that differ from those of a majority in the IAPA, and whether a newspaper has a right to express editorial opinions that differ from those of the majority. It is not a question of personalities, but of the right to dissent.

"On principle, no one quarrels with the denunciation of the killing of freedom of the press in Cuba. We have had many editorials in *The New York Times* attacking the Castro Government on that subject.

"No one needs to tell me, or *The New York Times,* about the evils of Communism. We have done our part in this conflict and we are still doing it. No one needs to lecture me, or *The New York Times,* about dictators in Latin America, anywhere in Latin America, Cuba included. If any of you had taken the trouble to read my book on Cuba, you would find that the description of it in the proposed Cuban resolution of yesterday was a travesty. These are things I should not have to tell you, on behalf of myself or *The New York Times.*

"We have a different concept of the historic phenomenon taking place in Cuba than most of you have. We have different ideas about how to combat it, and we are opposing it in the way we think is best. These, essentially, are our only differences. . . .

(346)

"Those who are trying to separate me from *The New York Times* are wasting their time. The editorials that appear in *The Times* —all editorials, including the one on Cuba yesterday—are expressions of the newspaper's opinions. They are discussed, passed upon and edited by the Editor. They are seen by my Publisher. They are checked for accuracy in the News Department. You have every right to disagree with what we say in *The Times*, but *The Times* has a right to say what it believes, and the editors have the same right. . . ."

There were some heated interventions after I finished, but more defensive than accusatory. I came back at the end for a brief, final word:

"It is not true, as has been implied, and even said here, that we have been justifying Fidel Castro or what he does. We are not supporting him. We are opposing him. This does not mean that we have to agree with everything that the opponents in exile, or the majority in the IAPA, say and believe about the Castro regime.

"In conclusion, I want to make it very clear that neither I, nor *The New York Times*, can accept accusations that we favor the Castro regime or that we favor Communism."

I should have qualified what I meant by "favor." I did not "favor" the strong trend toward Communism in Cuba, the unrecompensed seizure of American properties, the suppression of freedom of the press and speech, military justice, political prisoners. I favored a radical social revolution for Cuba, and I gave Fidel Castro credit for wanting to do what was best for Cuba and the Cuban people as a whole, with idealism and an incorruptibility unique in Cuban history.

I sent a copy of my interventions at the IAPA conference to Orvil Dryfoos, who heartily approved. But my days as one of the principal figures in the IAPA were over. I was soon dropped from the Executive Committee. Pressure was brought to bear on Dryfoos to have my name withdrawn and another *Times* man nominated for the next board of directors. Dryfoos told the person who approached him that the IAPA would take me or nobody.

It was nobody. Dryfoos died early in 1963. Before the next meeting that October, Punch Sulzberger, who succeeded Orvil, asked me if I would mind if his sister, Marian, Dryfoos' widow, were nominated by *The Times* as a director of the IAPA. He wanted to give Marian a new interest. I was enthusiastic. The result, after Marian attended some meetings where she saw much of Andrew Heiskell, was that they fell in love and were married. So my career in the Inter-American Press Association had a happy ending.

The reactions to my Cuban coverage among my colleagues on *The Times* and in the American mass media generally were much less marked than during the Spanish Civil War. When it came to Spain, I had a flood of sympathetic support, which reflected the prevailing American opinion in favor of the Spanish Loyalists. With Cuba there were the complicating factors of Communism, the generally hostile attitude toward Fidel Castro, and—perhaps most important of all—the ignorance, misinformation, and confusion that characterized American ideas about Castro and what was happening in Cuba.

The journalistic world was divided on the subject. There was no general hostility, as was the case with public opinion, government, and business. However, newspaper publishers reflect public opinion and belong to the so-called Establishment, which meant an almost universal condemnation of the Castro revolution in American publications. Most of my colleagues on *The Times* were either with me or not against me, but there were some, especially in the key editing positions of the foreign news copyreaders, who were antagonistic. I received much verbal support and sympathy on the paper, but occasions did not arise for staff members to have to take an open stand in my favor. On the whole, I had the warm feeling that the news staff was with me and was critical of the policy from on high to muzzle me.

I had no way of gauging general approval or disapproval, but I retired with the feeling that a goodly majority of my journalistic colleagues approved of my Cuban coverage. I hope I am right. I have, now and then, been called a newspaperman's newspaperman. To me, this is the highest praise that anyone in my profession can earn.

What was potentially the best news story that *The New York Times* could have got out of the Cuban Revolution was blocked by the publishers. I almost surely could have flown into Cuba and been there during the missile crisis of October 1962. I would doubtless have been under detention in Havana—probably in jail—but sooner or later I would have been out with a hell of a story, which would have had considerable historic value, because the Cuban side of that incident has never properly been described.

My wife and I were then completing a swing around Latin America. Before leaving New York I had arranged for Cuban visas. On arriving in Mexico City I booked places on what turned out to be the last *Cubana de Aviación* flight to Havana after President Kennedy made his "quarantine" speech. The following letter, if he reads it, may come as a shock to Fidel Castro although he, himself, told me a year later when I was in Havana that he was glad I had not shown up during the missile crisis since, being an American, he would have had the painful duty of arresting me.

Mexico City, Oct. 23, 1962

Private and Confidential
His Excellency,
Ambassador Thomas E. Mann,
Embassy of the United States,
Mexico City, Mexico.
Dear Tom:

This is for your records and for any disposition you want to make of it for Washington.

Accompanied by my wife, Nancie, I have been making a swing around Latin America gathering background information for editorial work. This is the ninth country and the tenth is scheduled to be Cuba. I visited Washington early in July, primarily to keep an appointment made for me by

Pierre Salinger with President Kennedy for a private, off-the-record talk. My itinerary had then been worked out, and I told the President of my plans to visit Cuba. During our talk, and again on saying goodbye, Mr. Kennedy asked me to come back to see him after I returned from my trip. Pierre Salinger, Dick Goodwin and others at the State Department expressed the same desire.

I am writing you because it is our intention to go through with this trip to Cuba despite developments of the last twenty-four hours. I do not want my motives to be misunderstood by you or anyone in the Government. To go to Cuba now and speak to the government leaders will obviously have great value journalistically. Aside from that, I want to go on record in advance to say that the circumstances being what they are between us and Cuba, I will break a normal rule and keep nothing confidential that may be said to me or that I see in Cuba. If the trip goes through as planned, I will be at the disposal of any U.S. Government authority that wants to know what I saw and heard. I do not need to remind you that because of past events it may well be possible for me to have talks with Fidel Castro, Che Guevara, President Dorticós, etc., which no other American could hope to have. However, I do not know what to expect, the way things are now going, or whether—indeed—we will be able to get to Havana on October 26th, as planned. As of now, we have the State Department authorization in our passports, the Cuban visas and the plane tickets—so we hope for the best.

Let me inject the personal note that I and my Nancie had been looking forward since before we left New York to seeing you and your Nancie [his wife] here in Mexico. We realize how busy you are, but at the least, if there is a chance, I will drop in at the office for a chat.

I did, in fact, drop in at Mann's office because I decided to take the letter to him. He read it carefully and not only said that it was all right with him, but that he would arrange for me to talk to the CIA men at the embassy before I left. The day before the *Cubana* plane was due to go to Havana, John Oakes, the editor, telephoned me with orders from on high that I was not, under any circumstances, to go to Havana. In a final report to *The Times* at the end of my Latin American trip, I inserted this bitter comment:

"So far as the planned stopover in Havana was concerned, I would not be honest if I did not go on record as saying that I think it was a pity to rule it out so hastily. I was in the peculiar position of being trusted by the White House and the State Department, but not by my own newspaper. President Kennedy and Secretary Rusk knew that I planned to visit Havana and had asked to see me afterwards and tell them what I found. In Mexico City, when I still hoped to go, Ambassador Thomas Mann was going to arrange for me to get a briefing from the CIA as to what they wanted to know.

"Thus, *The Times* would have had it as a matter of record that we were cooperating with the White House, State Department and CIA, even though this could not be divulged quickly. And this would have been aside from a journalistic scoop for *The Times* that no other correspondent in the United States—or anywhere, for that matter—could have got."

The moral is that journalism is sometimes too important to be left to editors and publishers. I presume that there was some element of concern for my safety in the veto from the New York office, but I suspect that it was much more a case of the embarrassment that would have been felt—and the criticisms from obvious quarters—at *The New York Times'* having an editor in Havana—and me, of all people—during such a crisis. There would have been a price to pay, but as in other aspects of the Cuban coverage, I felt that *The Times* was—and should have been —strong enough to face some temporary criticism to get a very big news scoop.

I helped the News Department, over the years, to get *Times* correspondents into Cuba—which was an embarrassment to Managing Editors Turner Catledge and Clifton Daniel. In my last years on *The Times,* when I offered to help, they politely declined, as they felt that it was demeaning for *The Times* to have to resort to an intermediary when Castro should have been glad that we wanted to send a correspondent to Havana. I kept a copy of a letter that I wrote to Turner Catledge, then the managing editor, and John Oakes, from Mexico City, November 4, 1963, on returning from a trip to Cuba.

"I feel just about certain," I said, "that I have persuaded Fidel Castro and President Dorticós to permit a *New York Times* correspondent to operate in Cuba again. It took a lot of argument with both, but I was with them both on different occasions for a long time.

"I confess that it had never occurred to me why, exactly, Fidel would deny a visa to a *Times* correspondent of all papers—until he explained. The reason, as he put it, was that he did not care what any other newspaper or magazine in the United States printed about Cuba, but *The Times* is so important, so influential, so intelligent that whatever it wrote about Cuba had profound effects. He did not feel (and the others—I spoke to many, including Che and Raúl Roa about this—seemed to agree) that Cuba could run the risk of having a *Times* correspondent in Cuba. It isn't, Fidel insisted, that they had anything to hide or were looking for someone who would be especially sympathetic, but that wrong information in *The Times* could do the Cuban Revolution much harm—or 'great damage' would be a better translation of his phrase.

"I explained—and I don't know how often I've tried to explain this to Fidel and others—the difference between our news columns and our editorial page. This is a concept that Cubans (and not only Cubans) find difficult to grasp and accept.

"Naturally, it is fully understood by all of them that *The Times* must be entirely free to choose what correspondents it wants to send. Dorticós assured me, for instance, that they never dreamed of anything else. 'We don't want a correspondent who sends only favorable news,' as he put it. 'No one would believe him. We simply want a man who will be fair and will send a complete picture, the good as well as the bad.' Of course, I told them that this is our practice at all times in all places. . . .

"We simply must try to cover the Cuban Revolution as well as possible—and I must say, it is beyond question the hardest assignment for a correspondent to do a good job of any I have seen in my long career.

"My own position in respect to Cuba is unique, as I wrote Arthur Sulzberger way back in 1957. I can't help it, but every time I go back to Cuba I am treated like a Founding Father or an elder statesman. This time, Nancie and I were treated like visiting royalty. We were met by five high officials of the Foreign Ministry and it was 1:30 in the morning. I discovered to my dismay that, although I had cabled for reservations at the Habana Libre Hotel, they were putting us in a super-de-luxe, ex-Batistiano house as guests of the Government. In view of the time of night, and our fatigue, and out of courtesy, we accepted twenty-four hours of this but, of course, I explained that this could not be, and we moved over to the Habana Libre the next day and paid all our expenses.

"However, what I did accept for working reasons, was a car put at my disposal; Fidel's Ilyushin plane to take us to Oriente to see the flood damage for two days; an Army helicopter to fly over and land in the affected areas, etc. Taxis are scarce in Havana now, communications to Oriente still difficult, and so forth.

"In other words, professionally I had entrées, information, trust, facilities, a concentration of people high up who saw me, a chance to go to places and do things that no other correspondent anywhere can remotely duplicate. It is trite to say that since history is being made in a big way in Cuba, and journalism is day-to-day history, this has a unique value.

"A *Times* correspondent will get some benefit from all this, but he mainly will be on his own—and it will be hard to get news and uncomfortable to live. I don't mean creature comforts. There is plenty to eat, although it is dull stuff, and children are especially favored. Fidel told me that it could be arranged for a correspondent to receive food packages. The great difficulties will be journalistic—gathering the news, and the censorship. A revolution is a very special historic phenomenon. A correspondent will be working in some respects as in war time. He must, of course, know Spanish. It would be utterly impossible for the most expert journalist to understand what is happening unless he can speak the language and, I would hopefully add, have some understanding of the Latin character. . . .

"Fidel referred to me in a big speech while we were there, but he is much too intelligent not to have spoken very carefully, and it was quite harmless. I have the passage in the text of the speech for whoever is interested."

My intervention was successful so far as getting a *Times'* correspondent in—and even for the American press in general during 1964. However, I was evidently naive in believing that Fidel's reference to me in his speech was "harmless."

The pervading American emotionalism about Castro and the Cuban Revolution seemed to me to affect Lester Markel, the Sunday editor, more than anyone on *The Times.* He was quite upset about Fidel's reference to me, as I learned when I got back to New York, both from what Markel said to me and what I was told. Markel was an editor who always wanted contributors to the Sunday paper to write what he thought should be written in the way he would have written it. This was a great weakness in a generally remarkable editor. Since he knew nothing about Cuba, but felt very strongly about it, a barrier was raised that I could not surmount. This was too bad because my by-line was not automatically barred from the Sunday Magazine and Weekend sections, as it was in the News Department.

Here is what Fidel said about me in his speech before a typically huge crowd in front of the Presidential Palace in Havana:

"We spoke recently with a newspaperman who has been an objective and honest newspaperman; I do not mean a Marxist-Leninist newspaperman, but a man with liberal ideas, who is the journalist Herbert Matthews, who is on a visit to our country. . . .

[Someone in the crowd asked if I was present.]

"No" Fidel replied, "he is not here at this moment; he is in

Oriente. Last Sunday it so happened that he was with a group of students who were doing voluntary work. He naturally has his conception of society, which is distinct from ours. And he said [to me]: 'I asked them, "How is it that you do not note a lack of freedom, that you do not miss your freedoms?" ' Then Matthews said to me, 'It was as if they had not thought of it.' I said to him, 'No, it is not that they haven't thought of it.' "

Fidel went on, at length, to argue that before the Revolution a peasant possessed nothing and was oppressed by the power of the army and government. Now he has land, schools, medical care, credit, and a rifle as a militiaman.

"He *is* the Power [el Poder]. He does not see any difference between the Power and himself."

Castro continued for some time along these lines, referring to the students and how differently Negroes are treated in Cuba and the United States, the conclusion being that Cubans have freedom and North Americans do not.

His logic was hardly acceptable to me, but, as I said, the personal references were harmless. They were picked up by the Associated Press and United Press International in Miami in a typical 80 or 100 word news item on an address of many thousands of words. It was as if Fidel had made a speech about me.

I wrote a long memorandum to *The Times'* editors on Cuba when I got back to Mexico City, sending a copy to Markel and expressing a willingness to do a magazine article for him. He wired back that we could discuss the matter, adding: "Situation as you must realize is delicate." I wrote back:

"I was glad to get your cable about possible magaziners because, frankly, I could not understand the pall of silence which suddenly descended after all the trouble I took to do a report for the editors and send you a copy with a letter. I know better than anybody the 'delicate,' as you put it, nature of the problem of writing on Cuba, although I think it is exaggerated and beneath the dignity of *The Times*. I was not expecting to write anything, but now I think we should have something, and I will be glad to do it. I just don't like to be treated as an untouchable."

Back in New York, I suggested either a roundup on the mass of original and journalistically unique and important information I had gathered, or an interview with Fidel Castro—or both. At Markel's request, I wrote a magazine article. His only reply to the long report and the article I sent him was: "I have read the piece and I do not think it adds much in the way of light on Cuba, and so I feel we should not print it."

I could understand reasons not to publish an article by me on Cuba, but not the one he gave. No United States correspondent had been in Cuba for a year. As I have said, no newspaperman of any nationality could go to Cuba, as I did, and see every Cuban revolutionary leader of importance from Fidel Castro down. *The Times* relied on meager agency copy from Havana and slanted news from our correspondent in Miami.

The daily News Department likewise refused to print a word from me about my trip. It was this experience that made me realize how far *The New York Times* had strayed from Ochs' motto to print all the news without fear or favor. Anything I wrote would, of course, have made a big commotion and there would have been protests. But it was fresh news from the highest Cuban sources on the biggest of all Latin American stories.

However, I did not own *The New York Times* or direct it. (Let me say, in partial mitigation, that a little of the information and a number of the ideas did get into editorials passed by the editor of the editorial page, John Oakes.) I was always willing to accept a decision by the men who owned *The Times* and ran its departments, but I never allowed them to muzzle me in what I wrote outside of *The Times,* or what I said in lectures or conversation. I had written Oakes from San Juan on November 16, before my return, warning him that if *The Times* refused to publish anything from me on Cuba, "I will publish my findings in the *Hispanic American Report* of Stanford University." I did exactly that. It was a purely academic, unpaid service. Professor Ronald Hilton, editor of the Stanford review, made a pamphlet out of my report and sold many thousands of copies in colleges and universities around the country, the proceeds going to his institute. John

Oakes protested when he learned that I had sent my material to Stanford for publication.

"I was disturbed and a bit shocked by your evident desire that I publish nothing about my trip to Cuba," I wrote Oakes on January 8, 1964. "It surely ought to be clear that I cannot go through the rest of my life saying and writing nothing about Cuba and what I learned there.

"What more could I have done for and about *The Times* after the trip? I wrote a full report intended for all the editors and clearly leaving it open for a request to write something for the news or Sunday columns if that should have been desired. I had no expectation of doing so, but the news I got was so clearly sensational and timely that I thought it possible there would be a request. At every point—Mexico, Puerto Rico, the Dominican Republic, Haiti and back in the United States, I refused to talk to reporters or even students and professors about my trip because I was protecting *The Times*. This was very difficult and sometimes embarrassing to do, and it was only because I did so that the Jean Daniel interview with Castro [a French journalist whose piece was front-paged by *The Times*, a month after my trip] still was 'news.' Markel cabled me even before I left Cuba that he was interested in a magaziner. I discussed the matter with him and actually wrote a magaziner at his request—which he rejected.

"Only then did I arrange to publish my findings in the *Hispanic American Report* of Stanford University—the most dignified and non-commercial outlet I could think of. To have suppressed information of considerable historic and scholarly interest and value—and it was and is that—would be an astonishing and unprecedented example of *New York Times* censorship and suppression of the news.

"Let me also get it on record that I am as certain of anything in my very long career on *The Times* (this sentence is getting mixed up) that the record, the reputation and the prestige of *The New York Times* will in the long run prove to have been enhanced by the work I have done from the beginning on the Cuban Revolution. It would have been better for *The Times* to have published something by me on the trip which, after decades of experience, I could easily have written quite objectively and without any editorializing. It is not immodest to say that thousands of people in the United States and Latin America have been waiting to read what I learned in Cuba and what I think about the situation. It is not going to harm *The Times* for me to publish a serious and scholarly paper for Stanford University—on the contrary."

A few days later I received a note from Punch Sulzberger:

"John has forwarded your memorandum of January 8 in which you state your position on writing an article on your recent Cuban trip and concluded that it would *not* be harmful to publish something for Stanford University.

"I think I owe you a clear explanation as to why there is some hesitancy on the fourteenth floor [the executive offices]. The hesitancy is no reflection on your ability, nor is it intended as any expression of lack of confidence in you. If there were a lack of confidence, you would not be writing editorials for *The New York Times*.

"I always realized that in your going back to Cuba we took some chance of adding fuel to the controversy, but because of my belief in your integrity I was ready to take that risk. I thought, and still think, it is essential that our editorial writers travel freely in places and countries about which they write, and your case is no exception. I was also perfectly aware that you were bound to run into some news stories. The purpose of the trip, however, was—and to my mind remains—for background information, and there was a clear understanding that you were not going to write news articles about it for *The Times*.

"As regards pieces for the Magazine, Mr. Markel informs me that he did ask you whether or not you had any material that might be suitable. He has, as you know, come to a negative conclusion on the merits of your material.

"Because of the nature of your travel to Cuba and the understanding that we had prior to your departure, I think it unfair for you to put us on the spot at this time by citing *The Times*'s rule that when an article is offered and rejected, the writer then has the option to offer it to another publication. I understand the Stanford material is gone, but for future guidance I wish you would bear in mind that the entire trip was of an unusual nature and it would be far better for *The Times* if it were kept for the purpose that it was intended—gathering background information."

I did not continue the argument at the time but, so far as I was concerned, Punch Sulzberger missed the point. I came back from Cuba with uniquely valuable material. Either I published it somewhere—anywhere—or it was lost to historians and future students of the Cuban Revolution. *The Times* had the right to refuse to publish my information; it did not have the right to suppress that information for all time—which was clearly the Publisher's desire. The paper could copyright what I wrote and published in *The Times;* it could not copyright my mind.

Punch Sulzberger and I had another exchange of notes about Cuba in August of that same year, 1964. In forwarding copies of the notes to John Oakes, I said: "When Punch wrote me after the Stanford piece came out I was shocked at his misunderstanding of the situation but decided not to get into an argument. This time I am much more shocked, because he has a complete misconception of the situation—100 per cent complete—and I therefore felt it must be answered and straightened out."

"Herbert," Punch wrote, "while I sympathize with your determination to defend your ideas, it is obviously impossible to separate yourself from *The Times.* Prolonging the Cuban debate, as reflected in the July and August issues of *Encounter,* is harmful.

"The irritations of this situation should have long since been healed to the good of you and our newspaper.

"I do wish you would give this matter the serious consideration I do, and quietly give time a chance to work."

"Dear Punch," I replied, "I hope you can find the patience to read what will have to be a longish note on this Cuban business because you are clearly laboring under a misconception.

"In the past several years I have written only two papers on Cuba—both of them long, serious and, if you will forgive my saying so, historically important pieces. In each case, I picked serious publications in order to reach academic and informed readers.

"The first piece, for Stanford University's *Hispanic American Report*, was written only after *The Times*—given every opportunity and two months' time—refused to publish any of the important and, in some respects, remarkable information that I got out of my trip to Cuba. Many thousands of copies of the pamphlet that Stanford printed were distributed and read, and it has become a document in the history of the Cuban Revolution. I must add, although I know the reasons, that it shocked me almost beyond belief that *The New York Times*, when offered such an important news break would have rejected it. This was not in *The Times* tradition.

"The *Encounter* piece was written fully a year and a half ago, and it was not written to 'prolong the Cuban debate,' as you say. It was written for a book of essays on Latin America, but since the project fell through, I chose *Encounter* as the best outlet. They held it for six months, incidentally. I had something to say there that needed to be said and that was an important contribution to the Cuban question. This was the reason for publishing it.

"I do not engage in debate with anybody on Cuba, as you say. I never answer the innumerable attacks and criticisms that continue. They will never stop, nor will the attacks on *The Times*. I can also add that I receive many testimonials of praise and encouragement for myself and for *The Times* on Cuba, as well as the criticism. I am as sure as I am of anything in my career that in the long run, and even today with the people who really count, the record of *The Times* on Cuba is going to be highly rated.

"I don't know if you realize the amount of praise that has come to *The Times* for our news coverage of Cuba this year—or if you know that I was responsible for it. It was my visit to Cuba and my insistent arguments with Castro and Dorticós that got them to agree to let a *Times* correspondent in. When they stalled, I intervened for Juan de Onis and he got the visa. I did the same for Dick Eder and helped him to get his sensational interview with Fidel. (He thanked me in a letter for my intervention.) It was because Castro realized the value of *The Times* coverage, as he said, that he invited 25 newspapermen to Cuba in July, so that the whole American press and public has benefited. Let me say in passing that I never had a word of thanks from Turner [Catledge] or Clif [Daniels], which I thought strange, but it was of no importance.

"*The Times* has nothing to be ashamed of, and nothing to be afraid of on the Cuban Revolution. I have played a very special journalistic role in that revolution and what I write is eagerly read by every Latin Americanist in the country and it becomes part of the historic record. This is the only reason I write anything. I turn down innumerable requests to talk or to appear on the TV or radio. All that I accepted were a half-dozen or so invitations to lecture at universities—without pay.

"I do not need to defend myself, and this was not the purpose of either of the two papers I wrote. Those papers stirred up controversy, of course, but such controversy cannot hurt me or *The Times*. I was careful in both these papers to defend *The Times'* position.

"*The Times* is really hurt when it refuses to print important news from a staff member, and *The Times* would really be harmed if it muzzled a staff member who has something important to say and who chooses the most dignified and non-commercial way of saying it."

Whether through despair or a recognition that his note to me was unfair, Punch Sulzberger made no comment. When I next visited Cuba from April 18 to May 7, 1966, and *The Times* refused to print any news story or, even, an editorial column from me, there was even more of a hullabaloo, but it was a public one, and not of my doing.

It was my first visit in two and a half years. Fidel had not seen a newspaperman since his interview with Richard Eder in November 1965. *The New York Times* had not had any staff coverage of Cuba in nine months. It was still a fact that no newspaperman had been able to match the contacts I had with the Cuban leaders, or to win their cooperation. The Cuban government has always remained a charmed circle, a club, a closed corporation into which it is almost impossible to break. The American news photographer, Lee Lockwood, is the only American who has won the confidence of Fidel and some of the other leaders in recent years. Aside from him—and being a latecomer he is somewhat handicapped—there have been no gate-crashers in the Cuban club since the earliest period of the Revolution.

In the first of the magazine articles (*Esquire*, November 1967) that Gay Talese wrote about *The New York Times* he referred to the newspaper's refusal to use my material from Cuba in 1963 and 1966. In his book, *The Kingdom and the Power*, published in 1969, there is an expanded version of the affair.

"*The Times*," Talese wrote in the *Esquire* piece, "is quick to denounce the suppression of news and ideas, even when such may be contrary to its own editorial policy, and yet in recent years its News Department has refused to print anything by Herbert L. Matthews, who now sits rather quietly in Room 1048 along a corridor of editorial writers. . . .

"In the Spring of 1966, Herbert Matthews returned to Cuba, again representing *The Times* Editorial Board, not its News Department; while there he reacquainted himself with Fidel Castro and Cuba, amassing 25,000 words of notes. The News Department again, upon his return to New York, declined his offer to write for it. So now Matthews writes anonymously for *The Times* editorial page on Latin American affairs, including those on Cuba—about which he has often been critical; other than that, he devotes himself to his books and to his belief that history will finally absolve him. But at the age of sixty-six, he is not counting on a clearance during his own lifetime."

That sad picture of me in semiretirement led *The Nation* to print an editorial headed: "The Penance of Matthews." Talese became worried that he had done me some harm with the powers that be on *The Times* and wrote me apologetically.

"I appreciate your concern about the *Esquire* article reference to me," I replied, "but your letter still shows a complete misunderstanding of my position on the paper. It was not in the slightest affected by what you wrote, nor could it be expected to have any effect. . . .

"I have been on *The Times* forty-four and a half years and am much too much a part of it from the point of view of the Publisher's office, and most everybody else, for anything to affect my position. Iphigene Sulzberger [Adolph Och's daughter], for instance, is our son's godmother and he is now nearly thirty-five years old.

"In the case of the Cuban problem, it was purely what you might call a family quarrel. I disagreed strongly and openly with the attitude that *The Times* has taken about it and will continue to do so, but this does not mean that either my attitude toward *The Times*, nor theirs to me, could change because of Cuba. . . .

"I only felt badly because your article depicted me as sitting rather forlornly in my ivory tower writing editorials only about Latin America, whereas I am not forlorn and, on the contrary, write a great many editorials on Europe, Africa, the Middle East and Vietnam."

Before leaving Havana in 1966, I telephoned in a Monday editorial column that, I learned later, was killed by Punch Sulzberger. It was a generally favorable piece, but also critical and certainly balanced. I mailed a copy of my notes—25,000 words of them, as Talese had written—to Abe Raskin, assistant to John Oakes, who was away, and asked him to circulate them. The rest was silence. I used the material in my biography of Fidel Castro, along with notes made on another trip in October 1967.

I confess to feeling bitter after the 1966 experience. It reminded me of how I felt at the end of the Spanish Civil War, as I described it at the close of my section on Spain in *The Education of a Correspondent* (and in my chapter on Spain in this book). It told how sick at heart I was after sending my last dispatch on the lost cause.

"But the lessons I had learned!" I concluded. "They seemed worth a great deal. Even then, heartsick and discouraged as I was, something sang inside of me. I, like the Spaniards, had fought my war and lost, but I could not be persuaded that I had set too bad an example. . . ."

I xeroxed the page from my book and sent it to John Oakes with this note:

"When I called Abe from Havana the day after sending a hopeful Monday column and realized from the way he talked that it was all going to happen again, my mind went back to this page and I gathered some wry comfort.

"I thought you might be interested. In any event, I am signing off on Cuba for *The Times* except, of course, for any required editorials, although my last one was so mutilated that I wished I hadn't written it. I am sending this simply as a way of saying: 'the incident is closed.' "

So it was. I wrote about Cuba in editorials (usually not "mutilated") and in a few editorial columns, but because of its refusal to print any news piece from Cuba by me, *The New York Times* to this time of writing (mid-1971) has had no firsthand information by a staffer since 1965. I submit that this is a poor record for the greatest newspaper in the world on one of the greatest—if not *the* greatest—news stories in Latin American history. Our "special" news about Cuba has, for a number of years, come from a stringer in Miami whose copy is at all times an expression of Cuban-exile hostility and, contrary to *Times'* policy, is always editorial. I called the attention of the Foreign News Desk to this on several occasions. The undeniable evidence was, and still is, in the files of *The Times'* morgue. It is a fair deduction that the foreign news editors were content to print slanted news on Cuba in violation of the old and basic *Times'* rule that news must never contain editorial opinions.

After I retired in October 1967, there was a subtle but noticeable switch in *The Times'* editorial policy with regard to Cuba. I had always been critical, but tried to be understanding and fair. Certainly, my editorials could not help being authoritative. I never was emotional in the Cuban editorials because I wanted, insofar as possible, to counteract the extreme emotionalism regarding Cuba in the United States.

The editorials on Cuba after I left, starting with a tenth anniversary one on January 3, 1969, were rather hostile. The tone had changed—and tone means a great deal in editorials. This showed how much individuals do affect *New York Times'* editorial policy, despite anonymity and the fact that editorials express the newspaper's opinions.

This was true of all the editorials on Latin America over a period of eighteen years. I made *The Times'* policies because I was the only one who knew the subject. On Cuba I faced a natural and understandable handicap. Castro's words and actions and the fact that he led his revolution into Marxism-Leninism meant that there was no reason why *The New York Times* should not be consistently critical—as we were. However, the picture was by no means all bad; there were many good features about the Cuban Revolution for which, it seemed to me, Castro deserved credit. There were also mistakes, misunderstandings, and wrong policies by the American government which deserved criticism.

Above all, there was the need, as I saw it, to present a sophisticated, fair, and authoritative picture of what was happening in Cuba. I come back to what is, for me, the key to good newspaper work—understanding based on personal experiences.

Chapter 10

CHINA–VIETNAM

The future center of world power is surely going to be Asia. Already Western Europe has lost its predominance to the United States. American supremacy—an extension of Europe's —is unlikely to last a historically long time. The East, with its vast, rich territory, its more than a billion people, and its ability to draw on the technology and know-how of the West into which, indeed, it extends through the Soviet Union, contains the promise of ultimate pre-eminence.

Time must pass, but what is time to the immemorial East? Part of the unresolvable conflict between East and West is due to a different attitude toward the passage of time. We Westerners go at a faster pace and transfer our sense of time into policy. Where the Chinese Communists, North Koreans, and North Vietnamese patiently face the need to accept a situation for an indefinite number of years, Americans impatiently act to put a quick end to a state of affairs that they find intolerable. The six years since President Johnson escalated the war in Vietnam have seemed unbearably long to us, but to the Vietnamese they are a brief passage in a conflict with foreigners that began when the French occupied Indochina more than a half a century ago and that will end at some time in an unforeseeable future.

Nothing is accomplished in a hurry in the Far East. The planners in the White House, State Department, and Pentagon should have based their calculations on this when they began operating in South Vietnam. Americans thought that poor, weak little North Vietnam must, of course, yield to our overwhelming power and wealth. This is what would have happened in the West. We did not understand. If ever the Far East is devastated by nuclear bombs in a third world war, this is the epitaph that historians will write over the grave of Eastern civilization—"The West did not understand."

Yet Rudyard Kipling's inescapable dictum that "East is East and West is West, and never the twain shall meet" is only partly true. Wisdom lies in sensing the degree to which Kipling was wrong as well as right. In this era of change, what used to be called the "unchanging East" is moving as fast as, or faster than, the West. The semblance of lethargy comes from the fact that the East is starting from far back and has a long distance to go. A great mass has the appearance of moving slowly. Japan moved quickly for special reasons, but what she has done, the mainland and the other islands will do in their good time. In my college days, Sir Edwin Arnold's famous lines were a standard classification of the Orient: "The East bowed low before the blast in patient, deep disdain; / It let the legions thunder past, then turned to thought again." Those days are gone forever.

I spent five months in Japan, Korea, and China in 1929 with a small group of newspapermen from all over the United States. We were sent by the Carnegie Endowment for International Peace to foster good will and peace by our contacts. Not one of us could sense the war aims already taking root behind the charming Japanese hospitality. In Peking where the recently triumphant Chiang Kai-shek entertained us, no one could sense that not the Kuomintang, but the Communists, who had suffered many defeats and were beginning to build up a base area around Juichin in Kiangsi Province under a young leader named Mao Tse-tung, were going to conquer and transform China.

Why I was chosen by Adolph S. Ochs to go on that most

wonderful of newspaper junkets has remained one of the mysteries of my journalistic career. At the time I was the second man on our new little Cable Desk. The other dozen or so newspapermen on the trip were all important and well known.

Needless to say, our group did not foster peace, and any good will engendered was not to last long. Ironically, I am sure that every one of us much preferred the Japanese we met to the Chinese.

Japan was so efficient and so clean, and the Japanese were charming hosts. We were dined, wined (with saki), and loaded with gifts. Mikimoto, the inventor of the culture pearl, then an old man, gave us a luncheon in Fukuoka which started with a dozen oysters from his culture beds. Any pearls we found were ours. I found four, one of which turned out to be a natural pearl.

I was often to think during World War II when these same Japanese, including friends I made, behaved so cruelly to American prisoners, that the hospitality must have been a veneer. I do not now think so. The Japanese are a naturally friendly people. Some of them—the government officials especially—had a compulsive sense of duty. Just before Pearl Harbor the Japanese ambassador in Rome invited all the American correspondents and their wives to a most delightful dinner. As we realized later, he and all Japanese diplomats around the world had been ordered to make friendly gestures to Americans—undoubtedly as a smoke screen for the blow being prepared.

The hospitality we received in Japan in 1929 was genuine. It was Oriental courtesy to guests, among other things. When the time came, the same Japanese would have treated us cruelly— quite as naturally. I do not believe that any of us were so simple-minded as consciously to equate the treatment we received, and the characteristic virtues of the Japanese, with political virtues. Yet when the former are the only criteria to go by—and I for one was completely ignorant of Asian affairs—they were bound to exert a strong influence. This is a journalistic pitfall in all times and places, as well as a trap for politicians. Reject hospitality and you miss a lot of contacts and information; accept hospitality and you are under obligation, aside from the temptation to feel that your host is a good fellow.

China—when we went over there from Japan—was different. It was inefficient, materially backward, slovenly, and rather clumsily hospitable, at least to us. This may have been simple disorganization, or it could have been suspicion of foreigners who had just been guests of the Japanese. We generally got a poor impression of the Chinese compared to the Japanese. Our criteria were appallingly misguided and our ignorance colossal. Fortunately, none of us wrote anything of the slightest importance. *The Times* did not expect me to send despatches, and the only story I can recall doing was an interview with Rabindranath Tagore, the Indian poet, who was on our ship going over.

The Times' correspondent in Peking in 1929 was Hallett Abend. I was not competent to judge his work, but he seemed knowledgeable and had a good reputation. I was a bit disturbed by his attitude toward the Chinese, especially his servants. He had No. 1, 2, 3, 4, and 5 boys, in a descending scale of importance, and he was very strict with them. If the boy who washed and ironed his clothes took a button off his shirt, for instance (two clean white shirts a day), Abend fined him. Since the servants were very poor and wages were very low, a fine was harsh punishment.

This was the typical white foreigner's attitude toward Chinese servants, tradesmen, and workers. The Chinese were considered inferior. It was a nasty form of colonialism. If the white man has now been put into his place by the Chinese and Japanese, there is no cause for surprise.

The memory of Peking in 1929 is a nostalgic one. The city was still the lovely, ancient capital of one of the oldest civilizations and highest cultures in the history of mankind. The palaces, the gardens, the art treasures, the superb food were as they always had been and are not now, or ever will be again. Yet these were the façade of the living city. I remember, as a rickshaw-man trotted us along a wide, dusty street, asking Abend why an old man was lying alongside the curb, in the street. He told me that the man was undoubtedly dying and his family, in order to save funeral expenses, would have put him there. Bodies found in the streets had to be taken away and buried by the municipal authorities. Considering how Chinese families revere parents and elders, the need to do this meant the direst sort of poverty.

If ever a nation was ripe for a social revolution it was China. A real revolution never would or could have come under Chiang Kai-shek and his venal, corrupt, reactionary, incompetent clique. It was China's tragedy that only the Communists could have made a revolution.

Mao Tse-tung was an invisible speck over the horizon when I first visited China in 1929. In fact, he was dismissed as a defeated leader because two years earlier Chiang had slaughtered his tens of thousands in the terrible "Kuomintang repression." (To be sure, Mao, in Fut'ien, Kiangsi, had previously killed 2,000 or 3,000 of his opponents. He was never a man to give or ask quarter.)

The shadow of events to come were easier to see in Kunming and Chungking in central China during World War II. I flew "over the hump" of the Himalayan chain from Assam in India in December 1942—a famous, tricky, and spectacular air service, provided by the American Air Force of the China-Burma-India theater. Brooks Atkinson, normally our drama critic, had dropped his regular work to be *The Times'* correspondent in Chungking. Whatever he did, he did well.

Chou En-lai (later Mao's minister of foreign affairs and prime minister) came down from Mao's headquarters in Yenan to Chungking, where Chiang had his wartime Government. Some of us correspondents interviewed Chou through an interpreter. He spoke cautiously but confidently of a "Chinese victory over the Japanese." He had a right to speak. It was the Communists in their famous "Hundred Regiments Offensive" who had fought the Japanese. Chiang and the Kuomintang, with American arms and money, did nothing. They were saving their resources for the inevitable postwar conflict with Mao's Red force.

General "Vinegar Joe" Stilwell, the American commander, launched into a typical string of expletives when we discussed Chiang, his wealthy family, and his useless army at that time.

It was possible to buy a railroad ticket from Chungking through Japanese-occupied territory to Canton on the east coast. There was a regular traffic by Chinese traders and other privileged persons at the time. Since the Communists were also biding their time up in Yenan, and since the Japanese were not looking for trouble, it had become a "phony war."

When the mainland went completely Communist in 1949, I agreed with Secretary of State Dean Acheson, with whom I discussed the matter several times, that nothing the United States could have done would have saved Chiang Kai-shek. "The unfortunate but inescapable fact," Acheson pointed out in a White Paper issued by the State Department in 1949, "is that the ominous result of the civil war in China was beyond the control of the United States. Nothing that this country did or could have done within reasonable limits of its capabilities could have changed that result; nothing that was left undone by this country has contributed to it. It was the product of internal Chinese forces which this country tried to influence but could not."

The lesson of Vietnam ought to make Americans realize today that a Communist victory in China in 1949 could only have been postponed by a war of far greater proportions than the Vietnam War. Acheson, General Marshall (who was an ambassador to China before Chiang's collapse), and President Truman had the wisdom to see that, but the myth of a "China betrayed" persisted.

It was especially strong in that upcoming McCarthy era and, I regret to say, *The Times'* editorial policy was consistently on the side of reaction, then and throughout the 1950's, on the subject of the Far East. The reason was that our Asian editorials were written mostly by Robert Aura Smith and, for the remainder, by Otto Tolischus. Both men were extreme conservatives who believed that McCarthy was doing some good. The other writers on foreign affairs—and I include myself—were on the liberal side.

Charles Merz, who was editor of the editorial page in those days, was very easy-going and believed in letting the editorial writers make their own policies. The theory was that we were all "specialists" in our fields and knew our subjects better than he did. This may have been so, but it ignored the desirability of there being a *Times'* editorial policy. John B. Oakes, who succeeded Merz in the post in 1961, did not make that mistake. Moreover, where Merz was only mildly and ineffectively liberal, Oakes was—and is—a strong, courageous, and determined liberal.

The idea, during the Merz-Arthur Sulzberger period, was to "balance" the Editorial Board, just as the coverage of the Spanish Civil War was supposed to be "balanced." It was argued that the Board should be neither all liberal or all conservative, but a mixture of both. This, it seems, was calculated to ward off criticism that *The Times* was biased, prejudiced, bigoted, one-sided, or anything definite. As a result, it was nothing in those days—or everything—conservative on Asia, liberal on Latin America, and so forth.

In any event, neither Robert Aura Smith nor Otto Tolischus really were specialists or authorities on the Far East. They were not alone in their ignorance. Americans, as I have said, did not understand and did not know the Chinese. Our Orientalists were in the universities, not in government or journalism, and anyway they were not, with a few notable exceptions, equipped to analyze politics, peasants, and "wars of liberation." This was the period when the "China Lobby" was doing its mischievous work. My inglorious role on the Editorial Board while Smith and Tolischus were writing about the Far East was to protest in vain. When Oakes took over, it was different. We saw eye to eye, and especially so when it came to the Vietnam conflict. Before then, our editorals on the Vietnam War were pro-administration.

It fell to my lot, during 1964, 1965, 1966, and 1967 to write nearly all of *The Times'* editorials on Vietnam. Oakes tried unsuccessfully to get me a Pulitzer prize for my Vietnam (as well as

Dominican Republic) editorials. The policy that he and I worked out, and that other editors had to follow, was a bitter one for President Johnson, Secretary of State Rusk, the Pentagon generals, and all the hawks to swallow. One very determined—and very unhappy—hawk was on *The Times* Editorial Board. He was our military editor, Hanson Baldwin, certainly the best writer on military affairs in the United States for thirty years and more. He understood how a nation—or half of one in this case—could be wiped out, thus bringing "victory" to the United States. Baldwin did not make allowances for the feelings of a people struggling for their country against foreigners; he underestimated the problems of defeating guerrillas with regular forces, and overestimated the effect of material superiority in a "war of national liberation."

He was tragically wrong. So were the White House under four presidents, the State Department under Rusk, the Pentagon under McNamara, the American army in Vietnam under General Westmoreland. This had become so clear to Johnson after the Tet offensive of February 1968 that in March he gave up and announced his decision to reduce the bombing of North Vietnam and not to run for the presidency in November. It was so clear to Nixon when he became President that he immediately began working to extricate the United States from its military commitment in Vietnam.

President Nixon's "Vietnamization" is a disguised continuation of the final Johnsonian policy, devised by Clark Clifford, Johnson's secretary of defense. It will extend the war for years if allowed to run its course, but it has made the conflict much less costly in American men and matériel, and it will give the illusion of an undefeated United States. Yet nothing will disguise for future generations and for all the world outside the United States that the Vietnam War was lost in the Tet offensive of February 1968. Like Blenheim, the Tet was "a famous victory" for the Americans on the battlefield, but it proved to President Johnson that the war could not be won militarily, and it meant that politically, Hanoi was probably going to win sooner or later. The questions became: how much can be salvaged for the South Vietnamese, and how long will it take? The key date probably is November 1972, when Richard Nixon intends to be re-elected as President, Vietnam or no Vietnam.

Nixon's most successful move from the American point of view was the invasion of Cambodia. This time the Pentagon guessed right. Militarily, the invasion succeeded beyond all hopes. The North Vietnamese and Vietcong were set back for many months; the Mekong delta was freed from immediate danger; vast quantities of war matériel and food stocks were captured; the South Vietnamese army fought competently on its own.

But something was terribly wrong from any viewpoint except that of the United States and the Thieu government of Saigon. Nixon saved American lives at the cost of bringing Cambodia into the war, devastating large areas of the country, destroying the homes and properties of poor Cambodians, and bringing death to thousands of Cambodian civilians as well as soldiers. It was Richard Nixon, ironically, who proved the "domino theory" to have been right. Whatever the price Prince Sihanouk had had to pay, Cambodia was neutral under his rule and Cambodians were left in peace.

Should Nixon, Agnew, the generals in the Pentagon, or the American people care? There was little evidence, after the initial shock of dismay, that Americans did care. Cambodia was far away and Cambodians were not like Americans; their lives were not so precious; they were only "Oriental human beings."

The military success may prove to be a short-term one. The North Vietnamese, despite the setback, will go on fighting as long as they want to. Nixon won; Cambodia lost. The war may —or may not—have been shortened for the United States, but not for Indochina, and probably not for South Vietnam.

The Cambodian invasion proved again that war, as Clausewitz wrote, is "of all branches of human activity, the most like a gambling game." Nixon's gamble paid off—but the game was not over, and he still had to go on gambling. On October 7, 1970, he put down another bet—a standstill cease-fire proposal with a concession on the withdrawal of American troops. Hanoi,

understandably, rejected the offer. There will be other proposals and other rejections. The emphasis in 1971 is on the release
of American war prisoners. One day there will be an agreed
basis for "peace." The Americans will presumably withdraw,
having avoided defeat, at least on paper. But the North Vietnamese will still be there. So will Communist China, and so will
the Soviet Union. Hanoi will not have been defeated, either.

As 1971 draws to a close, the North Vietnamese do not show
signs of any hurry to end the war. In October 1970, President
Nixon had proposed his cease fire from a position of strength,
asking the North Vietnamese to negotiate from a position of
weakness. His proposals ignored what has seemed to be Hanoi's
long-range objective—to achieve Vietcong political supremacy
in both parts of Vietnam. If that takes another twenty-five years
—well, there is no hurry. Hanoi could even meet—or partly
meet—American terms, and wait until the Americans withdraw
and then start up again. There is no way in which the United
States can insure a victory for so-called democratic forces in
Saigon. There never was. Only the Vietnamese can do that, with
American help, and if enough South Vietnamese want to
do it.

The Americans may avoid the appearance of defeat, but the
Vietnamese—all of them, and one can now add the Cambodians
and Laotians—have been terribly punished in the process. The
American people have also paid a tragic price. More than 54,000
dead, an untold outpouring of treasure, the deprivation of funds
for American domestic needs, a divided United States—what
possible gain could there have been to compensate for such a
price? In Churchill's phrase, it was "an unnecessary war."

We said all these things in *The New York Times* from the moment President Johnson began escalating the war and long
before we knew the information contained in the sensational
secret McNamara study. The editorials are there for any student
to read. I helped formulate the policy in accord with John Oakes.
Two or three members of the Editorial Board did not agree with

us. President Johnson was in a constant state of anger and resentment.

The Times argued as early as August 17, 1964 that the problems of Vietnam "cannot be solved by smashing North Vietnam." An editorial I wrote on January 11, 1965 ended as follows: "President Johnson has an opportunity to work toward the only goal that seems to remain open: negotiations from a sufficiently strong position to seek a genuine, internationally guaranteed neutralization of the whole South East Asia area." On January 28, 1965, we warned that "the policy of drift is getting more and more dangerous, carrying with it, as it does, the possibility of falling by inadvertence and indirection into a major war."

There were many critics—so many that on March 11, 1966, I drew up a long memorandum for Oakes and other editors on our ideas and editorial policies on Vietnam. The newspaper was under heavy attacks from hawks and superpatriots. The report outlined ideas that later became acceptable commonplaces and government policy. There were, of course, many other doves in the United States—especially in the academic world and some in the mass communications media—who were expounding the same ideas.

It was clear enough that Johnson was on the road to a greatly escalated war in which there could not be a military victory except at the cost of almost destroying South, as well as North, Vietnam. The price, I wrote, was "going to be prohibitively high for whatever results can be achieved." We had never argued for a "cut-and-run," complete withdrawal unless there were adequate defense guarantees. The Chinese threat was being vastly overrated, we thought. Peking was talking tough but acting cautiously, and her whole history showed that she was not a military aggressor. It was General MacArthur's folly in driving to the Yalu River in Korea that forced the Chinese to act there. Otherwise, they had avoided a United States counteraction, as they did in Quemoy and Matsu, in India in 1962, and Sikkim in 1965. We feared that if President Johnson's policies were steadily pursued, China would be provoked into intervening militarily in

North Vietnam. The Middle East later became the potential flashpoint of world conflagration, but in 1965–1967 Vietnam was the danger. The hawks were ignoring the fact that there is a built-in antagonism to China in all of Vietnam, so that even a Communist government in Saigon would most likely end up with a relationship somewhat like that of Rumania to Russia.

It was easy to foretell "a very long and costly conflict."

"The objective," as we on *The Times* saw it, "is extrication with honor for the United States and peace for an independent Vietnam—divided or united, Communist or coalition." This should be achieved, we argued, by negotiation leading, inescapably, to a coalition government, to begin with, in Saigon.

My report pointed out that the United States could not be driven from South Vietnam nor the South Vietnamese army be defeated.

"If there is—as there seems to be—a more flexible attitude on the part of Washington and the possibility of a compromise solution," I concluded, "it has surely come about through pressures brought upon the White House by *The New York Times,* among others. The offer of unconditional discussions, the bombing pauses, the more open attitude on the National Liberation Front, the determination not to bomb Hanoi and Haiphong and, in general, a more restrained policy than the White House seemed to have in mind at given periods in the past year—all these are, in part, results of *The Times'* editorials and the reactions they brought.

"Thus, it has now come about that the Johnson Administration's policies—in theory and in form—do not show a wide variation from the editorial policy of *The New York Times*—except in the all-important field of extension. *The Times* would like to see the bombing of North Vietnam stopped, the Vietcong accepted as a belligerent entitled to a delegation at peace negotiations, a coalition government recognized as a desirability, if necessary, during an interim government, and the limitation of men and arms to the minimum point needed for a safe defensive posture. Within possibilities, there should be a general pause or plateau and not the steady escalation of men and arms."

These policies and ideas were not adopted by President Johnson until March 1968, when, except in a few unimportant details, they became American policy.

Of course, the hawks can and do claim that they, the United
States and the "free" world were let down. One school says that
had Johnson given General Westmoreland the troops he demanded, the Vietcong would have been rendered ineffective and
Hanoi so exhausted and discouraged that Ho Chi Minh would
have surrendered. Another school fastens on our "failure" to
use American air power to its full, although nonnuclear, extent.
Admiral U.S. Grant Sharp, who retired after serving four years
in Vietnam, called this "perhaps the most serious error made in
American history." We could have "achieved victory with relative ease," he wrote, by destroying Hanoi and Haiphong as
economic centers.

This, for one thing, is a reminder of MacArthur's folly in
provoking the Chinese to enter the Korean War. Admiral Sharp,
and all who thought like him, were operating in a one-sided,
one-dimensional world, blandly ignoring what Communist
China and the Soviet Union might have done. For another thing,
this policy overlooked the fact that, at best, the conflict would
then have turned into an interminable guerrilla war.

Furthermore, the dramatic betterment in relations with Communist China, which is to lead to a visit to Peking by President
Nixon, could not have been foreseen during the dangerous
Johnsonian escalation in Vietnam, when there was a justifiable
fear that China might be goaded into intervening. The irony,
looking back, is that the United States, not the Peking government, was aggressive.

The hawks will go on believing their theories. There is no way,
ever, to prove that something that was not tried would have
failed. It was the same way with those who argued in 1949 that
if the United States had increased its aid to Chiang Kai-shek, the
Communists would not have won.

Neither history, common sense, nor military judgment will
support the hawks in the cases of China and Vietnam. When
President Nixon told a unit of American soldiers in Vietnam on
July 30, 1969, that they had taken part in the United States'

"finest hour," Senator Albert Gore of Tennessee sensibly remarked that Vietnam was one of America's "most historic mistakes and surely must be one of its most excruciating hours." In one of my valedictory editorial columns for *The Times* I wrote: "Historians of the future will surely rate the Vietnam War as the greatest blunder in American history."

One of the most bitter and terrible aspects of the Vietnam War is the inescapable thought that so many American youths were sacrificed in a bad and easily avoidable cause. Only too many parents and wives and children of those who died or became addicted to heroin or were wounded, will realize this, and it will be an intolerable burden. This is not to say that those who died or were maimed deserved anything but a full measure of esteem and pride. They obeyed orders; they usually believed what they were told about the righteousness of the American cause and the necessity of the war; they responded to the eternal urge to show courage and to an *esprit de corps.* They earned the highest possible tribute of honor.

They were not to blame; the Presidents, the Secretaries of State, the generals, the hawks—these must bear the historic stigma of a tragic folly. War can be necessary. World War II was an example, once events had reached the conjuncture of 1939. War, even the Roman Catholic Church tells us, can in some circumstances be "just." The Vietnam war was neither necessary nor just.

One may respect President Johnson's courage and despair when he finally realized the hopelessness of the American commitment, although he had deceived the American people.

> When I peruse the conquer'd fame of
> heroes and the victories of mighty
> generals, I do not envy the generals,
> Nor the President in his Presidency,

Walt Whitman prophetically wrote.

As a presidential candidate, Richard Nixon spoke like a hawk. As President Nixon, he immediately accepted the fact that there could be no victory, but he was determined that there would be no defeat, either. "This is the most difficult war in American history," he ruefully conceded. In theory, the United States has never lost a war, although it is stretching historic reality pretty thin to claim that the Americans won the War of 1812. Nixon, the consummate politician, is not going into history books, if he can help it, as the first United States President to lose a war. The major reason for continuing intervention in Indo-China is the defense of the power, influence, and prestige of the United States.

The basic fault, surely, was a miscalculation, due to misunderstanding, of the human factors involved. The Vietnamese has a natural sense of pride in being Vietnamese; the Chinese in being Chinese; the Indian in being Indian. How obvious and trite that seems! Yet for more than three centuries Westerners have been trying to turn Asians into good Europeans. And here is the United States trying to turn South Vietnamese into good Americans.

Asians will generally deny that there is an "Oriental mind" different from the "Western mind." Semantics, they say. It is true that Chinese or Japanese, born and educated in the United States, can be, and usually are, indistinguishable from older or European-American stock if one's eyes are closed to their looks. Each Asian country is different from the others, but the concept of racial particularities is useful when applied to Asiatics in Asia and Westerners in the Western world. Centuries of history, traditions, social customs, and religion create basic differences in "mind."

The greatest of all mistakes on both sides is to assume an attitude of superiority, as if an American were a better, more civilized person than a Chinese, or a Chinese than an American. For many American soldiers, Vietnamese "gooks" were not human beings.

It may be human nature to feel superiority and to believe that what is good for Americans is good for Asians. Applied to politics, this belief meant that democracy, American style, would be good for Vietnam, and Communism, or whatever was shaping up, would be bad. Insofar as this meant "bad for the United States," there was a nationalistic justification for intervention in Vietnam—if the belief that we had the right answers for our national security was a valid one. It was not, especially when the futility and cost of intervening were considered.

The reason the intervention was going to be futile and the cost monstrously high was, I repeat, the human factor. I could not claim to know Vietnam or the Vietnamese from personal experience with the country and the people. I could claim to have some understanding of the Asian mind from the little I knew of China and the much more that I knew of India. I had also seen, at firsthand in Spain, how human beings react to intervention by foreigners. I saw, in Cuba, how helpless Batista's large, well-armed, well-trained regular army was against handfuls of fanatical guerrillas under inspired leadership.

The necessity, as I keep on saying, is for empathy. This goes for politics and military strategy, as it does for journalism. Had American leaders been able to put themselves in the place of the Vietnamese—or accepted the advice of those who knew—they would not have embarked on the Vietnam adventure, or if they did, they would have known what to expect. The tragic *reductio ad absurdam* of the Vietnam war was that in 1969 and even 1970 all that mattered to the American military commanders in the field was the "kill ratio." Yes—they killed many more Vietcong and North Vietnamese than Americans and South Vietnamese killed by the enemy. So what?

The horror of My Lai gives us a terrible answer. The hysterical reaction of so many Americans when Lieutenant William Calley was condemned by a court martial shows the depths of callousness and false patriotism to which millions of Americans can descend. A murderer became a national hero. A day will come when those Americans—or certainly their children—will feel a deep shame for their reaction and for the twisted mentality which can regard Vietnamese men, women, adn children as less than human. Germany had its Lidice and South Africa its Sharpeville. The United States has its My Lai.

Chapter 11

A WORLD IN REVOLUTION

The year of my birth, 1900, marked not only the beginning of a new century but of a new world. We who have lived the Biblical span of this century have no right to complain that the world has changed; it has never ceased doing so and never will. But do we not have a right to say to the young that it is *our* world which they are revolutionizing and on whose foundations they must build their new one? A few billion people, including myself, made this world, and if I believed that what I saw and did and chronicled in my forty-five years on *The New York Times* was wasted, lost, worn out, and fit for the scrap heap, I would be a fool. Obviously, the youth of today do not like what we have done. I am willing to try to understand why, especially as I agree that in many respects we did do a bad job of it. But not wholly bad; not as bad as they say. Furthermore, is what they are offering us so much better?

One gropes in a fog with few guideposts for help. Revolutionaries (Fidel Castro is my prime example, for he was a forerunner and is typical) are impelled by their temperaments and emotions, more than by logic, reason, doctrine, or ideology. This makes them hard to categorize and harder to predict, while they are at work. To an older generation, their world seems irrational.

One should add, I suppose, that to the younger generation our world seems irrational and hypocritical when they observe the gap between our principles and our acts. Fidel Castro is so fascinating to watch, among other reasons, because he was so young—thirty-two years old—when he seized power in 1959. He followed the sage advice that the minister of Genghis Khan's son, Ogdai, is supposed to have given his master: "You conquered your empire on horseback, but you cannot rule it from the back of a horse." Fidel learned quickly, dismounted, and ruled his "empire" very much from the ground up. More literally, he had to come down from the remote and romantic peaks of the Sierra Maestra and grapple with day-to-day realities. No head of state in the world ponders over his problems more agonizingly or works harder. His companion, Che Guevara, on the other hand, as he said in his touching farewell letter to his parents, rode off as if he were Don Quixote on Rosinante, and came to grief. Yet he, not Fidel, became the idol of revolutionary youth.

There is another famous judgment in equine terms—Ralph Waldo Emerson's: "The horseman serves the horse. . . . Things are in the saddle and ride mankind." This seems more true today than when it was written. Someone said acutely of the Vietnam conflict: "The weapons are running the war." A computer tells what villages to bomb and what people to kill.

The technological wonders of our century—electronics, telephones, wireless, computers, automobiles, airplanes, radios, television, atomic energy, space rockets—are no more astonishing in themselves than were the invention of the wheel or the telescope or steam engine in their day. For new weapons and new machines are but extensions of old weapons and old machines. With an antipersonnel bomb, an American helicopter can kill every man, woman, and child in a given radius. The armies of Tamerlane and Genghis Khan were as effective in killing in their time. The millions of Jews consumed in Hitler's ovens were preceded by many thousands killed in Russian pogroms of the nineteenth century.

Yet, some of these changes have helped to bring in a new age comparable in its impact, let us say, to the Renaissance. For a newspaperman, the technological advances were easy to chronicle and useful as tools with which to communicate and to travel from one place to another, but how does one describe a world that is, for the first time in history, entirely in the midst of a revolutionary process? Are we not seeing the social emphasis shift from the individual to the masses? Where are the humanistic traditions that guided, however haltingly, all the generations since the Renaissance? How different living conditions are today than they were between the wars, not to speak of the beginning of the century!

I am alive today because some doctors discovered what causes pernicious anemia and how to relieve it. The pill is more than a convenience; it is a revolution in women's lives. The computer will revolutionize lives as well as work. Having isolated the gene, biologists will soon be able to control the inborn traits of humans. These are qualitative changes affecting all humanity. They represent more than a continuation of the nineteenth century into the twentieth.

My career focused my attention to an unusual degree on wars and revolutions. In this transitional period of world history, where democracy and totalitarianism preach an equality that cannot be achieved, there is a revolutionary potential which causes such ferments as racial strife, student rebelliousness, urban violence, political crises. Poverty or deprivation, per se, do not—or did not in the past—cause revolutions. Today, it is the gap—a growing one—between the few rich and the many poor in the underdeveloped or developing countries, such as those in Latin America; the difference between what an individual or a family believes it is entitled to and what it gets; rising expectations compared to the daily reality; social injustices that no longer are accepted fatalistically—these breed a revolutionary atmosphere.

The British in India used to argue (as I heard many do during my year there) that the masses did not feel rebellious against their lot and took it passively as the natural state of affairs. So they did, and still do—but by no means all, and the result, in 1947, was that the Attlee government had to grant independence. On the other hand, the desperately poor Andean Indians of Peru and Colombia live outside politics, as they do outside a money economy, with no arms, no organization, and no leadership. They do not know enough to rebel and could not do so successfully. Even Bolivia, which had a real but short-lived and abortive revolution in 1952, does not contain the human material for a sustained social revolution, as Che Guevara discovered. But this is a matter of time. The question in Latin America is not whether there will be revolutions, but when. Dr. Milton Eisenhower said so when his brother was President. John F. Kennedy realized it, and vainly sought to remove the obvious causes of insurrection with his Alliance for Progress.

All through the underdeveloped southern half of the globe there is a revolutionary ferment. It is one of the ways in which the world is changing. Social injustices have been accepted as normal throughout history—until this postwar age. The tide is rising almost visibly, as more and more millions of those in ignorance, poverty, and disease learn that neither God, Allah, destiny nor the sins of previous incarnations have condemned them to misery. I know that this is so; I learned it and felt it in China, India, Africa, and Latin America.

This is not where the fog of confusion lies. The problems of bridging the gaps between the poor and the rich people and the developed and underdeveloped nations are enormously difficult, but they are technical problems which any economist or statesman can solve—on paper. The same is true of the racial conflict in the United States. One knows what should be done, but not how to do it.

The baffling problems today lie in the so-called generational gap; in the weakening of parliamentary, or liberal, democracy;

in the adjustment to depersonalized economies and the monster cities of modern times. A newspaperman, starting a career which will last into the twenty-first century, will have to deal with a very different world than the one I worked in from 1922 to 1967.

I remember something that the French statesman, Aristide Briand, wrote or said when I was a correspondent in Paris. It went like this: "If a young man of twenty is *not* an anarchist, there is something wrong with him. If a man of forty is an anarchist, then there is something wrong with *him*." One has to struggle against the temptation to say that the world-changers of today are anarchists. There is no form. The feeling that there is nothing worth living for is commonplace among thoughtful youth. One extreme that can get them out of their despair, apathy, or melancholia is the appeal to rebellion or, as the case may be, to religion, Communism, or Fascism. The reaction is always more emotional than rational, which is why I say that an observer like myself gropes in vain for a consistent direction or a definitive ideology.

The rebelliousness and destructiveness are only too clear. The phenomenon has been noted innumerable times throughout history. In the Cox Commission report, "Crisis at Columbia," on the April–May 1968 disturbances, there is this passage: "Six thousand years ago an Egyptian priest carved on a stone the lament: 'Our earth is degenerate. . . . children no longer obey their parents.'"

Perhaps it is romanticizing, but I believe that the youth of today, with their thrashing about on worthy causes like opposition to the Vietnam War or unworthy ones of sheer destructiveness and anarchy, are like those who went to Spain in 1936–1938 to join the International Brigades and fight for the Loyalist cause. At least in this way, an old man like myself can feel (is it imagination?) a rapport, a measure of understanding and a sympathy for the generation that rebels against my generation. The "alienated" young seek to relate to each other.

Dorothy Parker, in an introduction she wrote for an anthology of stories, poems, and articles on the Spanish Civil War, called *The Heart of Spain,* had an apt passage. "I stayed in Valencia and

Madrid," she wrote, "places I had not been since that fool of a King lounged on the throne, and in those two cities and in the country around and between them, I met the best people anyone ever knew. I had never seen such people before. But I shall see their like again. And so shall all of us. If I did not believe that, I think I should stand up in front of my mirror and take a long, deep, swinging slash at my throat."

We are seeing such men, but they have no cause like Spain to fight for, only causes like Vietnam to fight against. As Genevieve Taggard wrote in her beautiful poem, "To the Veterans of the Abraham Lincoln Brigade":

> And what they knew, they know,
> And what they dared, they dare.

But those who "know" are old; the young are having to learn all over again.

The generational gap has always been with the human race, but why, as today, are there times when it takes so acute and violent a form? One might say that in our times the typically destructive, senseless, unreal aspect of modern life, in its literary form, was first described by Franz Kafka in the 1920's.

"Human nature," he wrote in his extraordinary evocation of the building of the Great Wall of China, "essentially changeable, unstable as the dust, can endure no restraint; if it binds itself it soon begins to tear madly at its bonds, until it rends everything asunder, the wall, the bonds and its very self."

The mood was one of despair, emptiness, and hopelessness, which is no longer characteristic of our times. When Samuel Beckett wrote *Waiting for Godot* in 1952—two derelicts waiting vainly in a vacuum of nothingness for someone who was not going to come—he seemed to have caught the mood of an age, but today it strikes one as the end of an age. There is nothing lifeless or hopeless about the world of the 1970's. If anything, life is too boisterous and hectic. One can argue (to keep on a literary tack) with Dostoevsky's Grand Inquisitor that the frantic struggle for something called freedom is unbearable and doomed to failure: "What though he [man] is everywhere now rebelling against power, and proud of his rebellion? It is the pride of a child and a schoolboy. They are little children rioting and barring out the teacher at school."

So they did at Berkeley, the Sorbonne, Columbia, but I find it impossible to believe that the rebellion was in vain. It was a disappointment to those of us who knew André Malraux in the quixotic days of the Spanish Civil War to see him turn contemptuously on the French students in the *événements* of May–June 1968 when he was a minister in De Gaulle's Cabinet.

As mentioned earlier, he told *New York Times'* correspondent Henry Tanner in an interview in November 1968 that he saw the Spanish Civil War as important "not only as a struggle, but also because it was a most profound experience of brotherhood." Yet this, if I understood it aright, was exactly what the French students were experiencing—and not only the French and not only the students, but the young everywhere.

Malraux complained—with more reason—that "the universe, our concept of it, is independent from man. It is extremely difficult to envisage a civilization which accepts a complete rupture between man and the universe. Humanity, I believe, is conscious of this, and so there is this extraordinary malaise, especially among the young."

The young may not be trying to bridge the gap between "man and the universe." They are probably not conscious that there is such a gap, and if they were, I doubt they would care. However, they seem to be groping for a common ground where intellectuals and workers, white and black and all nationalities can meet, where the individual is not isolated but becomes a part of a harmonious society. I do not say that the youth of today formulate their goals so simply or clearly, but when one tries to make sense out of what is happening, one can come up with something hopeful.

In my career, in many countries, I often saw the students as the conscience of their nations. They were rebellious against societies that perpetuated social injustices in fossilized institutions. They often succeeded in their work of upheaval, and sometimes won reforms, but human nature is stubborn and "establishments" have roots that cannot easily or quickly be torn up. And one still has to say that the aims of youth are vague and impractical. They seek a world where all men are brothers; where there is equality and the freedom to live without taboos of custom, sex, or behavior; where the government exercises a minimum of restraint; where the high moral and ethical principles of religion and philosophy are practiced and not just preached. This is a dream world—a beautiful dream in many ways, but it is one that can never come true.

The young accuse my generation of being like so many King Canutes trying to stop a tide of liberty, honesty, and equality. Most elders would turn the image against them. Establishments will change with the flowing tides of history; it is to their advantage to do so. Youth is told to be patient—but youth is never patient; it is in such a hurry to make a revolution that it hampers the process of evolution. However, I would also argue that the young are forcing the pace, which is a good role for youth to play.

I began writing editorials in 1949 with a feeling that I, too, was waiting for Godot and never going to see him. I had, after all, come from Europe, a Europe whose predominant role in the world was ending after thousands of years of history. Although born in the New World, my roots and those of all Americans of European descent since the colonies were settled were in the Old World. I have lived to see my children grow to maturity without such roots. They are as much at home in Australia or Africa, as they are in France (where they were born), or in Italy, England, or the United States. This would have happened if they had been born in New York. My children are half-American and half-English, but they are citizens of the world.

Cannot one say the same of the international hippy fraternity, which, at one time, was finding its way from all over the world to Katmandu in Nepal? It was a phenomenon different in more ways than that from the pilgrims who once wended their pious ways from all over Europe to Rome and the Holy Land. Brotherhood, not religion, was the guiding hippie sentiment. Perversely, they did not seem to note today that social injustices in Nepal were as bad as anywhere in the world.

My eyes were opened to the changing world when I started learning about Latin America. Its traditional links to Spain and France had all but disappeared. The revolt against the hegemony of the United States was one of the strongest of Latin emotions. Then came Fidel Castro and a Cuban revolution that not only broke with the United States, but launched itself into economic, social, and political fields so new that Russian Communism as well as Yankee capitalism were left far behind. Castro, whether he succeeds or not in the long run, is a phenomenon of today's kind of world.

The air has been full of diatribes, warnings, and sage advice that violence defeats its purpose. Yet Fidel won power by violence. When the turbulent school year of 1968–1969 ended, *The New York Times* printed an editorial headed: "The Failure of Violence." It was not a convincing argument. The upheaval at Columbia University, however ugly, had not failed. Important reforms followed, which would not otherwise have been made, or at least made in a foreseeable future.

The methods by which revolutions are carried out are almost always violent, and usually brutal and even cruel. They are accompanied by much suffering and much injustice. Yet no one with any sense of history, progress, or justice can argue that revolutions should not take place. "The American Revolution is intended for all mankind," Thomas Jefferson said. "The right of revolution is a most sacred right," Abraham Lincoln asserted, "a right which we believe is to liberate the world."

Those who seek to destroy and subvert, as revolutionaries do, are always a tiny minority, but they would be ineffectual without the broadly based support of discontented, moderate, middle sectors of society. Student violence is relatively new in the United States, having started with Berkeley in 1964. French students did not revolt until 1968. Italian students, quiescent since the Fascist revolution of 1919–1922, accompanied the French. The phenomenon is a recent one in Japan. There was no worldwide conspiracy. Something was in the air. It was as if a conjuncture of historic events and social pressures had heated the atmosphere to cause a chain of explosions. The students were dramatizing far more than their educational grievances, and they were not alone in their revolt. In France, intellectuals, men from every liberal profession, became active participants in the protest movement. Workers joined the French students in the uprising with a disciplined general strike that almost destroyed the Gaullist regime. The massive American "moratoria" against the Vietnam War in 1969 were much more than student protests. A *generation* is rebelling.

It is a dangerous and frightening phenomenon, but not unwholesome or unnatural. History is not an inevitable process of causes followed by foreseeable effects, but there are times when historic forces are irresistible. I can see, looking back over my career, how I was being swept along by forces that I only dimly understood, and sometimes did not understand at all. I had a sense of being driven toward an unknown destination. There has been no rest and no stability for my generation, and it is obvious that there will be even less for my children and children's children. Yet, as I said before, I feel that I have arrived at a new world.

I am not sorry; only worried at the painful process of gestation. Benedetto Croce, the Italian philosopher, once said to me during one of our long conversations in Capri as he waited for his beloved Naples to be "liberated" (he was quoting his favorite author, Goethe), that the worst thing in the world is "active ignorance." I am certain that he would be critical of his young compatriots today if he were alive, but youth, surely, either accepts an established system or strikes out blindly and ignorantly toward a new way of life.

The process, if it continues and is not blocked, will "rend everything asunder," as Kafka wrote. This was why conservative France, the so-called party of fear, rallied to De Gaulle in 1968. The "silent majority" is never revolutionary. It had seen an abyss open in front of the French nation during four days—May 27 to May 30, 1968—when the regime was very nearly overthrown. The spectre of Communism was raised—an imaginary ghost, but it aroused fear. The great mass of bourgeois France —workers and peasants—had not bargained for a new social order. Yet the government was so shaken, and the price of pacification was so high, that De Gaulle, despite his triumphant counterrevolution was, himself, to become a victim of the *événements*.

When George Orwell wrote his *1984*, I shuddered along with everyone else, for it seemed prophetic. What I wrote for my newspaper in the early postwar years reflected a fear that Orwell might prove right. Yet in 1968 the French students and workers showed, on the contrary, how vulnerable our governments and capitalistic system are to the new and powerful currents of our mass industrial societies.

The American "revolt of youth" has not been so strong or so widespread. Workers are not involved, except as part of the racial strife, or as flag-waving, superpatriotic hawks. When the student riots began in Berkeley, I do not believe that any of us on *The New York Times* realized that much more than student unrest was involved. By the time the Columbia University upheaval came in 1968, the situation was clear enough. Since then, we have come to worry about Black Panthers, Weathermen, bomb throwers, hijackers and kidnappers.

It is significant that students today are, in many respects, striking out at the right targets. My generation vividly remembers the notorious resolution passed by the Oxford Union and many other British university debating societies, "That this House will not fight for King and Country." This was during the Spanish Civil War, but a few years later these same students fought and died bravely for king and country.

The British students then did not know what offended them; the French students, workers, and intellectuals do, and so do the American students.

In Italy the student rebellion was originally directed toward educational reform. Italy, like other countries, developed serious student troubles toward the end of the 1960's, and she still has them, but the movement has broadened into political and economic fields and has been joined by workers.

Education is a great social weakness in Italy. The son of a poor workman or farm laborer cannot hope to get a higher education unless he is a genius. University education is for the privileged. Schools are overcrowded; there are ten times as many students as thirty years ago; the students have no say in how the universities are run or what they should teach; there is not nearly enough technical training; professors hold chairs for life; curricula are old-fashioned. The whole system is antiquated—but the students are modern, with a new radicalism and rebelliousness, perhaps caught from neighboring France. Reforms are now promised, but as Amintore Fanfani, the Christian Democrat leader and a former teacher, said to me, reforms have a tendency to increase revolutionary sentiments by a process of rising expectations. Moreover, the tidal waves of worker unrest manifested in innumerable strikes in 1969, and still continuing, have heated the Italian atmosphere. As in France, but more slowly, what started as student protest is spreading into a *crise de structures.*

Except for Russia and China, where the leaders were already Communists, all social revolutions in my experience began on a minor key. The leading politicians, the vested interests, the middle classes, never realized that they were starting or supporting a venture that was bound to destroy their world if it succeeded. In Latin America foreign interests can be deluded by false concepts and hopes, as was notoriously the case with Fidel Castro and the Cuban Revolution. Peru and Bolivia are showing that army generals can be leftist as well as rightist.

The liberals who cheer for leftist revolutions and the conservatives who help finance Fascist or military revolutions are the ones who generally end up bewildered and dismayed. A revolution cannot adjust or submit itself to a liberal constitutional system. Leftist revolutions become authoritarian in their forma-tive years, while even rightist revolutions must generate and hold a mass support, which means higher pay, shorter hours, government subsidies, better social services—all at the expense of the business and propertied classes. The hardest thing to accept or realize is that a structural change is being forced upon a nation, and that a new edifice is going to be erected by revolutionaries—generally young men—with different ideas and desires. A revolution unleashed is like a genii let out of a jar who cannot be coaxed back or commanded to return by an Aladdin's abracadabra. The French sensed this in 1968 and drew back in the nick of time.

The young say with Shelley: "The world is weary of the past." They will not listen to an old man like me who has been through it all before, even though I was in other places in other times. They have a true sense that much is wrong, but without recognizing the complex reasons for the wrongness. They have discovered sin and blame us for it without accepting the age-old wisdom that there has always been what theologians call "original sin." This is their strength and weakness. The future, as Renan said, belongs to those "who are not disillusioned."

The anti-Americanism of young Americans is bewildering to Europeans who remember some of the grand gestures like the Marshall Plan, and who recall so vividly their own tragic years between the wars and during World War II. So few of these young Americans seem to know anything of other countries. Stalin is almost as dim a figure to them as Nero. Trust in liberalism cannot be restored in them by expressions of faith à la John Kenneth Galbraith or Gunnar Myrdal that Americans will somehow at some future time solve their problems.

The youthful temptation to reject the past—to which every new generation yields and which ours seems to be doing in exaggerated form—is unacceptable to someone like myself who sees from experience the links between today and yesterday. History has fascinated me all my life, and in my newspaper work I never ceased to perform what has been called "the marriage between the present and the past." Yet it would be stupid for anyone of my age to offer advice; it is hard enough to try to understand. I have a feeling that the last people the young want to hear are those of us who have been there before. All we can do is to say that this is the way it was; these are the mistakes we made, but we did not always build badly.

What we, who are old, cannot see is what the hippies—or their equivalent—of today are going to be and do when they are forty years old. The very exaggerated types—dirty, slovenly, ill-kempt, and ill-mannered—remind one of the Yahoos and of Gulliver's land of the Houyhnhnms. Dean Swift was positively prophetic—but this is modern youth reduced to its absurd extreme. The vast majority are serious and idealistic; one quarrels with their ideas and methods, not with their goals.

This is true of the whole New Left, which embraces far more than the young. I feel regret, even sadness, against what is rightly being called "the revolt against the West," which is such a disturbing feature of contemporary life, but I accept its inevitability. If we are going to have "One World," as Wendell Willkie foresaw a quarter of a century ago, "Western" values have no more validity than Oriental; Christian values than Mohammedan or Buddhist. I cannot extend the list to say that Marxism-Leninism is as valid as liberal democracy, although Communism is a Western political system, not a Russian-Asiatic-Chinese invention. I am critical of the totalitarian systems for pragmatic, not religious, reasons.

In a microcosm, as at Columbia University, or in a macrocosm, as in France, youth can paralyze an institution or a nation, but it is a process of destruction, done in blindness and intolerance. Academic life without rational discourse, national life conducted with passions, emotions, violence, and unreason brought chaos and an inevitable "counterrevolution." The truism that destruction can be immediate but creation takes time is hard to learn. I suppose that in a generation that has seen Hitler's Auschwitz, Truman's Hiroshima, the My Lai massacre, and a flight to the moon, disorientation, anarchy, nihilism—anything but orthodox and traditional reactions—are to be expected.

At my age one clings to one's roots and at the same time looks around with what tolerance and philosophy can be mustered. When youth says that it is more intelligent and wiser than we were, I know that they are deluded, but if they thought otherwise the world would stand still. Social change is a process of renewal, not collapse. Even a nuclear war would not wipe out all humanity and, anyway, that would merely start a new process of change.

On August 11, 1945, the day after the Japanese sued for peace, I saw the philosopher Santayana in Rome. "How true the prophets were," he exclaimed, *"solvet mundi cum favilla* [the world goes up in a flash]. What is the difference whether the Last Judgment comes exactly as they envisioned it, or through the atomic bomb? Leonardo, Jules Verne, H. G. Wells missed the truth because they dealt imaginatively with the relations of specific facts to man. The prophets dealt in fundamental truths."

As a newspaperman, I always dealt in "the relations of specific facts to man." I am not religious in the sense that Santayana—fortunate man— was. A nuclear destruction of humanity, in my opinion, would be man's last judgment on man. In the meantime, there is change.

"Germany and Japan committed suicide, and it is a pity," Santayana said in that same conversation. "In the name of liberty you destroy the liberty of others to think as they please and have the government they want."

What Santayana overlooked was that Nazi Germany and militaristic Japan were out "to destroy the liberty of others." So was Stalin's Soviet Union. Nazism was evil because of its racism, not because of its political system. In 1945 I was shocked at Santayana's tolerance of Fascism because Fascism seemed to me to be inherently evil. I felt the same way about Communism for many years after the war. It seemed to me that militaristic aggression was built into Fascism and Communism. I had a quasi-religious emotion about individual liberty in the Western liberal-democratic sense.

My ideas changed. The aggressiveness of the Axis and, later, of Stalinist Russia, was a disguised form of nationalism or, to use a favorite Communist word, of imperialism. Fascism, Communism, and other forms of totalitarianism are different political systems that I consider technically bad, but certainly not evil. I would hate to live under a totalitarian regime. I could not follow my profession of journalism because I believe passionately in freedom of the press. I would end up in jail or exile. I could not live and work in the United States if Agnewism were carried to its logical conclusion. Yet I would still say that if this is what the great "silent majority" of Americans want, it is their privilege. I would not like it and I would oppose it to the best of my ability, but I would recognize it as another—if to me terribly wrong—point of view for the United States.

I do not pursue the argument to say that Fascism, Communism, or other types of totalitarianism are wrong or necessarily bad for other countries and other people. I do not say that the Anglo-Saxon system of liberal democracy is the best and the only moral and ethical political system and that, therefore, we North Americans must force it down the throats of Latin Americans or destroy Vietnam, Laos, and Cambodia to "save" them from Communism.

One can reject Communist ideas and still recognize the fact that hundreds of millions of people the world over hold such ideas—ordinary, humane, and perfectly decent people. It stands to reason that if Communism were nothing more than an ideological disguise for Russian national interests, it would not have won such a long and wide and powerful following throughout the world. It has been argued (by such authorities as Professor Geoffrey Barraclough, the English historian who has been teaching at the University of California) that Communism, far more than the ideas of the French Revolution, has become a world-wide ideology. Barraclough traces today's "drastic rejection of gradualism" back to the beginning of the century and especially to Georges Sorel, whom I have mentioned as having such an influence on my generation of university students. Sorel's *Réflexions sur la violence,* which was published in 1905, was a pre-Leninist appeal for direct action by an "audacious minority."

The line from Sorel led to Fascism; Lenin's to Communism, and in both cases the "enemy" and the chief sufferer was progressive liberalism.

It was no accident that Fidel Castro, at first unconsciously and then deliberately, took Lenin as his model and called his government Marxist-Leninist, not Communist. It is also obvious that the Cuban Revolution would never have occurred without the powerful and extraordinary personality of Castro himself.

Robespierre, Lenin, Mussolini, Mao Tse-tung, Castro, and a host of lesser revolutionaries have been such powerful enemies of liberalism because of their conviction that they must bring about a new order, discarding the laws of the past, sweeping opposition aside as criminal. The result is a form of authoritarianism in which individual liberties are submerged. To us, who are liberals, this is deplorable. I would argue, however, that we should not, in our turn, look upon Communists and Fascists as criminals. No American can forget Huey Long's priceless remark that it would be possible to establish Fascism in the United States, only it would have to be called anti-Fascism.

It is valid to defend liberal democracy as the best method of government in an imperfect world; it is foolish to say that other methods of government are not only bad, but evil. What we have seen in the postwar world are two very complex ideologies, which can be labeled as democratic capitalism and Communism, spreading geographically and politically to make two global, alternative systems. It is false history to say that democracy is old and Communism is new. They are both as old as the hills; only the Communist label is new.

The new factor is the way the whole world has been dividing into blocs of nations which call themselves democratic or Communist. (Communist countries, incidentally, also call themselves democratic—a better distinction is capitalist and socialist.) That this division should have led to the cold war during the Stalinist regime was a result of aggressive power politics and not an inherent ideological combativeness. Of course, Communists— Russian, Chinese, and all nationalities—seek to convert humanity to Communism, but equally, of course, the United

States wants to convert the whole world to democratic capital-ism. "The Declaration of Independence," as Henry Steele Com-mager has written, "is more subversive than the Communist Manifesto."

Much of the world has not accepted our belief that liberal democracy and capitalism offer the best solution to the prob-lems of modern society. We make an especially doubtful claim in the case of the underdeveloped countries. No one can im-merse himself in the politics and economics of Latin America, as I have done, and argue that a United States form of demo-cratic capitalism is best for those countries. Considering how far Castro still is from demonstrating that he can make a viable economy out of his peculiar brand of Marxism-Leninism, one cannot argue in favor of Communism, either.

One can argue for coexistence while different countries try out different ways of solving their particular problems—and this is what is happening, even in the case of Cuba. It is what will happen when the United States gets out of Vietnam. Every na-tion is groping toward a satisfactory political, economic, and social response to the problems of our new mass industrial society. The result is going to be different from the liberal democracy in which I was born and brought up, and also differ-ent from the Marxist-Leninist system which Moscow introduced.

No one can predict what will evolve, but it is as wrong for the United States to seek to impose its particular solution by military and economic means as it is for Moscow and Peking to impose their particular solution by forcible subversion or, as in Czecho-slovakia, by military intervention. President Nixon is showing a realization of this.

"I think we must save poor America from the missionary idea that you must get the whole world on to the American way of life," the Swedish sociologist Gunnar Myrdal said in an inter-view given to the Cowles magazines toward the end of 1968. "This is really a big world danger. You will have to live with people who have other ideas. We Swedes are not out reforming

Russia, and I think we are wiser there. It would be a healthy thing if the Americans did not feel this tremendous responsibility to remake the whole world in the American image. You will never succeed. You did not succeed in petty little Vietnam."

I have thought, during this period when I have been trying, in simple terms, to analyze and synthesize the ideas with which I ended my newspaper career, that a good motto for United States foreign policy in this revolutionary age would be: "Live and let live." This, to be sure, could only be the roughest of philosophies, for United States power and wealth are such that it cannot avoid entanglement and global responsibility. Isolation would be dangerous and stupid. Leadership with restraint, tolerance, and understanding is the ideal. How easy it is to formulate such a generalization and how hard to put it into practice! In writing editorials, nothing would have been more futile than to offer sage advice, which could not have been followed by American statesmen dealing with harsh realities. Praise or blame had to go for specific policies.

The cold war and anticolonialism, which dominated my early years as an editorial writer on foreign affairs, took specific forms —for instance, a general policy of supporting the status quo in Latin America would be expressed in Washington's tolerance, or even support, of reprehensible dictators like Perón, Stroessner, Pérez Jiménez, Batista, Somoza, and Trujillo. In such cases *The Times* could slam away at the State Department, as well as at the dictators.

United States foreign policy during the height of the cold war, and even to a large degree today, was based on the theory that revolutions are communistic (Soviet- and, later, Chinese-inspired and directed) and hence they must be opposed for the sake of the security of the United States. Starting with the Truman Doctrine of 1947 to "save" Greece and Turkey from Communism, there has been a string of American interventions to quell real or threatened revolutions. Witness Korea, Lebanon, Laos, Vietnam, Cambodia, Cuba, the Dominican Republic and, in a more general way, our post-Cuba Latin American policies. The military containment policy served its purpose briefly, but it is an anachronism in the 1970's which, I suppose, will not prevent the United States from trying to block or hamper leftist revolutions, especially in Latin America.

History has decided that the United States must carry out its foreign policies on a global scale. For that we have needed statesmen—especially Presidents and Secretaries of State—qualified by training and character for tremendous and frightening tasks. During my writing career, I would say that Roosevelt, Truman, and Kennedy performed adequately, but not Eisenhower or Johnson, while Nixon belongs in a doubtful category, at least on the basis of his first two and a half years.

Of the Secretaries of State whom I came to know (Hull, Acheson, Dulles, and Rusk), Acheson was the one whom I admired most. Dulles, with his narrow, moralistic religiosity and belief in exercising and imposing American power up to the point of "massive retaliation" against the Soviet bloc, and Rusk, with his tragically stubborn Vietnam obsession, were historic misfortunes for the United States. Hull played a grievously mistaken role in the Spanish Civil War. Acheson was much the most intelligent, able, and understanding.

Of the many talks that I had with Acheson in his office at the State Department, the one I remember best was a farewell visit on the eve of his retirement. He was unhappy at relinquishing power and influence, and when I would see him later in his law offices, he would sigh ruefully at being unable to stop Dulles from doing things he thought were wrong. Acheson admired types with clear ideas and forcefulness, like Washington and Wellington, the "Iron Duke." Lincoln was not his ideal.

Acheson's technique was to concern himself with a problem from its beginning, unlike his predecessor, General Marshall, who allowed Acheson and a few other undersecretaries to summarize problems and make suggestions. Acheson kept in touch with every officer at the Department and decided every problem of importance. His delegation of authority to Edward G. Miller, Jr., on Latin American affairs was an exception due to his inability to devote enough time to hemisphere policies.

We discussed, for the umpteenth time, the most controversial

of Acheson's decisions—to stop pouring aid down the Nationalist Chinese drain in a vain support of Chiang Kai-shek in 1949.
"It might have been better to keep on helping Chiang even
though one knew it was hopeless," Acheson conceded. "Then
I could not have been blamed for the collapse."

Despite Senator Joseph McCarthy's charges, Acheson said,
there were very few of what McCarthy called "bad eggs" in the
State Department. "Alger Hiss—and what I said about him—
was an awful case. That started everything." (What he said was
that he would not turn his back on a friend, which I thought at
the time was courageous as well as honest.)

Dulles had already been named as Eisenhower's Secretary of
State.

"He is a terribly worried and nervous type, and too old,"
Acheson said. "He cannot work the way I do until midnight
every night. It is a matter of training and temperament. I drink
a whiskey, read for five minutes, and sleep like a log until the
alarm rings. A program like that would kill Dulles in a year; he
wants to work like Marshall."

When I remarked about how much Dulles loved publicity and
how much he wanted to be praised and not criticized, Acheson
said about the knocks he had received: "Oh, you just can't pay
any attention. You can't let such things bother you."

Out of office Acheson, in my opinion, lost his sure touch. His
legal training supplanted his diplomatic acumen. In the Cuban
missile crisis his analysis of why President Kennedy should have
bombed out the Russian bases then being built in Cuba was
logically flawless. He wrote an article for the February 1969
Esquire concerning Bobby Kennedy's account, which he subti-
tled: "Homage to plain dumb luck." His advice to President
Kennedy had been to destroy the missile sites, for he did not
believe that the missiles would be peacefully withdrawn. From
the lawyer's point of view of the danger to the security of the
United States, his conclusion seemed inescapable.

The President, advised by his brother and by Theodore So-
renson, although forced to make the decision himself, refused
to be stampeded by the Pentagon with its obvious reactions, or

by advisers—some unexpected ones like Douglas Dillon, John McCloy, and Senator Fulbright—and fixed his mind on avoiding, at all costs or risks, the bloody, dangerous military response which could have led to the unthinkable horror of nuclear war.

I think that Kennedy's decision was an outstanding example of wisdom, intuition, and humanity against logic and what superficially seemed to be reason. Acheson was "right," but the world can thank its stroke of "dumb luck"—if it was that—when the President did not do the obvious, logical, and apparently almost necessary thing. His aim was higher.

In writing this I am defying a gnawing doubt in the back of my mind, for Kennedy was taking the fate of the world, not just the United States, in his hands, and doing so without consulting any of the United States' allies. If posterity decides that the President had no right to take such a chance, I would understand, but I would still think his decision a better one than Acheson's proposal.

All the same, Acheson was in many ways the American civil servant at his best. All four of the Secretaries of State I knew were ignorant of Latin American affairs, which they, at least personally, neglected. Acheson was fortunate in having a brilliant Assistant Secretary for Latin American affairs in Edward G. Miller, Jr., and he had the judgment to give Miller considerable authority. Of the Presidents, only Franklin Roosevelt and Kennedy concerned themselves, understandingly and sympathetically, with the hemisphere.

"No one would argue for the mandarinate of Whitehall or the Quai, but the United States still has a very amateur public and political service for a power of its appalling responsibilities."

The man who said that was Henry A. Kissinger—but while he was still a professor at Harvard. Today he would not say as much out loud, now that he is in the White House with Nixon, but I cannot believe that he has changed his mind. The policy that Kennedy followed of drawing upon the academic world for brain power was admirable. Eisenhower, a man of limited intelligence, was almost anti-intellectual. Nixon is the politician *par excellence,* and he cannot be happy with intellectuals, but he has chosen some good ones—enough to bring fierce denunciations against his as well as Johnson's "mandarins" from Professor Noam Chomsky of M.I.T.

An American who shows a propensity for theoretical generalization, or for using history to develop philosophical as well as practical conclusions or general principles, is regarded with suspicion. *Vide* President Kennedy or Senators Fulbright, Mansfield, and Eugene McCarthy. The United States does not have many politicians steeped in the culture of the humanities. To an Italian, a Frenchman, or a German it is amazing that men so devoid of theoretical discipline as Harry Truman, Dwight D. Eisenhower, Lyndon Johnson, or Richard Nixon, can become Presidents of the most powerful nation on earth. The reputation for naiveté and amateurishness that Americans have earned in Europe is largely due to this lack of formal education and intellectual discipline, and the sophistication and maturity that go with it. West Europeans, who could produce a Hitler or a Franco, are in no position to throw stones but it is argued that these men are not typical Europeans. "Ike," "LBJ," and "Dick" Nixon are typical Americans.

The streak of moralism that runs through American history is, if anything, a heritage from cultured men. "I know but one code of morality for men, whether acting singly or collectively," wrote Jefferson to Madison. The most cultured President of our century—Woodrow Wilson—"regarded morality as a guide in foreign policy and thought that moral duties between nations were the same as those within a nation, that the United States used moral standards in its judgments, and that all nations were coming to be judged by morality," according to Harley Notter in his book, *The Origins of the Foreign Policy of Woodrow Wilson.* Notter wrote of Wilson's "general ideal of the world mission of America as leadership not in empire, but in trade and ideas and ideals."

Alas! this, as much as anything, led us into Vietnam. Our Department of State had the complacency to proclaim the United States' purpose was "to shape the course of history . . . in our favor." This can be found in a 1963 "Report to the

Citizen" put out by the Department. It was this sort of folly that got us embroiled so deeply in Southeast Asia. We did not understand the convulsive period of change brought on, in part, by technological developments at a time when European imperialism was weakening and worldwide events were making it impossible for any nation, even the richest and most powerful in history, to impose its will.

"History and our own achievements have thrust upon us the principal responsibility for protection on earth," President Johnson said in a speech on February 12, 1965, just before he began escalating the war in Vietnam. Kennedy harbored the same illusions about the United States' duty to preserve global freedom and to oppose revolutionary "wars of liberation" everywhere, regardless of their justification.

The policy has never worked both ways. For the United States to plant atomic missiles in Turkey on Russia's frontier is legitimate; for the Russians to plant missiles or establish a submarine base in Cuba is criminal. For us to use the CIA to arm and direct an invasion of Cuba and to go on harrying the Cubans with guerrillas and sabotage is also legitimate, but think of what would happen, as Fidel Castro once said to me, if he did likewise in Florida! Might makes right, and the premise is that the United States is a "good" country and Castroite Cuba is a "bad" one.

Besides, Cuba is a Communist country. Future historians will surely stress American preoccupation with, and misunderstanding of, Communism as a major factor behind such mistaken policies as Vietnam and the interventions in Guatemala, Cuba, and the Dominican Republic. Communism is not, and never has been, the cause of the fantastically rapid social and political changes of the postwar era. It is an important factor, with a logical appeal to the underdeveloped half of the world, but Communism, itself, has evolved into a viable, relatively stable, and even conservative order in Russia and Eastern Europe.

Eurasia and Latin America are in process of revolting against the traditional, hierarchical, feudal and colonial rule of recent centuries, but the evolution of these more or less developing countries cannot duplicate England's—and Western Europe's—industrial revolutions, or the United States' road to capitalism and democracy. Some two-thirds or more of the world, containing billions of people before the end of this century, is going to go along different roads. Because nationalism is still the most powerful political emotion in the world—particularly in the underdeveloped areas—the giants of the developed world, and especially the United States, will be the targets of animosity and blame. Even if the United States could succeed in helping backward nations out of their abysses of misery, the phenomenon of rising expectations will foster revolutions. We are likely to see some of these developing countries choose Communism or another form of collectivism as the only road to modernization for them.

"I believe it must be the policy of the United States to support free peoples who are resisting attempted subjugation by armed minorities or by outside pressure," President Truman said on March 12, 1947, when he inaugurated his policy of helping the Greek and Turkish governments to resist an attempted Communist takeover. Using hindsight, it seems most unlikely that Stalinist Russia would have dared to invade Turkey, and so far as Greece is concerned, is the present ugly military dictatorship really better than a Communist regime, which, being geographically detached from the Soviet bloc, would have been as harmless as Yugoslavia, supposing it survived to this day? Now we are afraid of Soviet penetration into the Middle East, the Mediterranean, and the Indian Ocean.

The Truman Doctrine started the United States on the road to Vietnam and to the attempt, under President Johnson, to be the world's policeman. As Denis Brogan wrote in his famous article on "The Illusion of American Omnipotence" for the December 1952 issue of *Harper's* Magazine: "Probably the only people in the world who now have the historical sense of inevitable victory are the Americans." How prophetic he was, and what a price is being paid by Vietnamese and Americans so that the

United States can say that it was not defeated in Vietnam!

The specific "illusion" to which Professor Brogan referred (and which has made his article especially precious for me) is "that any situation which distresses or endangers the United States can only exist because some Americans have been fools or knaves."

Senator Fulbright also had a now-famous phrase about Johnsonian policies: "the arrogance of power." George F. Kennan, in an article for the *Atlantic Monthly* of June 1954, which he entitled "The Illusion of Security," wrote of "that peculiar form of American extremism which holds it possible that there should be such a thing as total security, and attaches overriding importance to the quest for it."

"We took it upon ourselves to judge the political systems of other nations and the right to alter those systems if we found them wanting," Senator Eugene McCarthy said during the 1968 presidential campaign. "We spoke of making the world safe for diversity while we were damaging, even destroying, diversity when it failed to meet our specifications."

Senator Mansfield, another of the intellectuals from the upper House who in my opinion express what is best in American political thought, has called attention to the fact that the United States had far greater fear of the Southeast Asian countries' being invaded by China than the countries themselves. "The independence of Asian countries would be hollow indeed," he said after a trip to the area in September 1969, "if it involved merely an exchange of a past colonial status for the indefinite prop of United States support."

As 1969 was drawing to a close, thoughtful Americans learned with a shock of dismay, and even horror, what the result of our policies—the Vietnam War—was doing to the United States and to the young men sent over there to fight and kill Vietnamese, and destroy their country in order to save them from Communism. The motives appeared to be sincerely idealistic by standards that see liberal democracy as a moral imperative, and the intentions were couched in moralistic terms—but we know now from the revelations of the McNamara report that the basic reasons were national prestige, power, and security. We have not only made Vietnam pay a terrible price for a policy that is American, not Vietnamese, but the inevitable brutalizing effect of a prolonged war under heartbreaking conditions is corroding American society, and destroying the illusion of the humane American soldier versus the Communist beast. My Lai—or "Pinkville"—taught the United States that Americans can, and do, commit atrocities.

The knowledge should not have come as a surprise, but the American public was constantly fed nonsense by military leaders and by such Hollywood idiocies as John Wayne romanticizing the Green Berets. Anyone who has seen men subjected to the physical and emotional strain of war knows how callous they become to suffering and how cheaply life is valued. I saw this on many a battlefield. Americans who learn in school that Sherman said, "War is hell," do not absorb the meaning of what he said —or even know what he did. Those Americans honest and intelligent enough to face the true significance of the My Lai massacre and the other atrocities, which they finally learned about, must realize, if only dimly, what a high price the United States is paying for the Vietnam folly.

This aspect of the Vietnam conflict was always in my mind when I was writing editorials attacking Johnson's escalation of the war. I felt a horror of the indiscriminate bombing, the napalm, and the wanton defoliation of so much terrain that would have fed thousands of innocent Vietnamese, as well as a relatively few Vietcong. The only disagreement I can remember with John Oakes on our Vietnam editorials was over the use of napalm, which I wanted to condemn. He felt that this would be going too far, although he agreed to a strong editorial against the first use of nauseating gas.

I make a distinction between the acts of bombardiers, who killed their thousands of innocent civilians, and the soldiers who faced women and children and killed them as if they were not human beings. I saw too much of bombing in three wars (and participated as a correspondent on bombing raids) not to realize how impersonal it is to drop bombs on unseen people and houses.

I made a note after a talk with Santayana on August 11, 1944 at his last refuge in the nunnery of the Blue Sisters in Rome. "We discussed the possibility of neutralizing the atomic bomb," I wrote, "as had been done with poison gas, because every country will have the bomb in time. But we also talked of the way feelings have hardened. He told me of a visit he had just received from an American bombardier grand-nephew. He said that he asked him: 'What do you do?' 'I wait for a signal', the young man replied, 'and I press a button.' "

So it has been with the B52 bombardiers in Vietnam and the soldiers in helicopters who spray the ground with the terrible new antipersonnel weapons that kill every man, woman, and child in range; they press buttons. No one will—or should— have them up before courts-martial because they kill many "Oriental human beings" (to use the horrible American official phrase) who are innocent of anything except being on the spot. The moral condemnation—and there should be one—goes for those high-up officials and generals who made the war and kept it going over the months and years.

But even in their case, one must make a distinction. What the soldiers did at My Lai was to stand in front of old men, women, children, and babies and slaughter them. There is all the human difference in the world between doing that and pressing buttons in the air. I can understand how Americans can do things like My Lai, for I have seen the madness in men's eyes in the furnace of war, but if bestiality is understandable, it is not excusable.

How could Hanoi hurt us more than we have harmed ourselves? As *The Times* of London said editorially: "The feeling grows that the war is too often being waged by methods and under directives which dishonor a civilized and an idealistic nation."

The anguished mother of one of the soldiers involved in the My Lai massacre said: "I gave my baby to the Army and they sent me back a killer."

This was a terrible indictment, but if it were taken as a condemnation of the hundreds of thousands of American youth
who were sent to Vietnam, or of the minority who saw action in
the field, it would be wildly unjust. I did not have to see American soldiers fight in Vietnam; I had seen their fathers fight in
World War II in India, Africa, and Europe. They were good
soldiers—brave, effective, and extremely tough. I remember
how often that toughness and hardness struck me. From one
point of view, this was why they were such good soldiers. They
were, of course, no better than British, Russian, German, or,
taking the partisans into account, the Italian or French soldiers,
but as an American, I could be proud of the American soldiers.

I see no reason not to be equally proud of the children of
World War II's soldiers who have fought in Korea and Vietnam.
This is not the point that distresses and embitters every thinking
American who reads of the rape, murder, and massacre perpetrated by some American soldiers in Vietnam. The point is that
American soldiers should not have been sent to fight in Vietnam
in the first place or, above all, be kept there for years fighting
a maddening war with cruel, inhuman, and impersonal methods,
for objectives that had long before lost what little justification
they seemed to have.

In our times one takes nationalism for granted—and calls it
patriotism. I have had an unusual life and career, living and
working in so many different countries. After a while, it became
impossible for me to feel that Americans were better than other
people, or the United States a morally and ethically better country than other countries. I could be, and am, grateful that the
wealth and power of the United States give me a privileged
status as I go around the world, but if I were a wealthy man, I
would be grateful in the same way for my riches and the privileges I could buy.

I feel pride in American democracy; in the freedoms that
know-nothingness, McCarthyism, and Agnewism can never take
away; in generous acts like the Marshall Plan; in ideals that are

true and valid, even when they are mistakenly interpreted. Because of Vietnam, the United States is in a mood to subject itself to a healthy catharsis.

In my school days in New York we all recited, with fervor, those lines of Sir Walter Scott's poem:

> Breathes there a man with soul so dead
> Who never to himself hath said:
> "This is my own, my native land."

The world is now full of displaced persons, exiles, refugees, emigrants, expatriates—but, still, one wants to belong. I have never lost a sense of satisfaction in saying: "I am an American," and I am sure I never will. What I will never say is: "My country, right or wrong." Few of those who quote Stephen Decatur's line know, or remember, that he added that if she is wrong, she must be put right.

There have been few more stupid and harmful governmental institutions in the United States than the Un-American Activities Committee of the House of Representatives. Many Communists, especially during Stalin's "Socialism-in-one-country" era, were bad Americans, but they were Americans.

It should be obvious that one is not un-American or anti-American if one criticizes government policies, or an Establishment that seems deficient and unjust, or a war that seems tragically mistaken. The friend of my enemy is not necessarily my enemy. He may be looking at the two sides of the argument; he may be partly critical and partly sympathetic; he may, with Pope John XXIII, say that one must condemn the error, not those who err.

To me, if the American label has to be used, I would say that the youths who speak with the true voice of America are those who joined the moratoria against the Vietnam War. The shrill tones of Spiro Agnew's demagogy cannot drown them out.

Spiro Agnew, George Wallace, Joseph McCarthy, Huey Long, and so on are as American as Uncle Sam. Anti-intellectualism has been a permanent feature of American history except, perhaps, in the remarkable age of the Founding Fathers. In times of stress (Joe McCarthy was a response to the Korean War and the hysterical anti-Communism of the cold war) the right-wing demagogue has a field day. He becomes politically valuable; he attracts votes. An Agnew is egged on by a Nixon; a McCarthy intimidates an Eisenhower.

American democracy is not as shaky as it seems in periods like the present one. When candidates have nothing but their super-patriotic, right-wing extremism to offer, they are treated as Barry Goldwater and George Wallace were treated. The harm these Agnew-type demagogues do—and they are very harmful —is temporary. As Benedetto Croce said of Fascism in Italy, their peculiar form of "Americanism" is a *morbo*, an illness, from which the body politic will soon recover.

"Americans, for the time being, are moving toward the right, which means away from the American belief," Gunnar Myrdal said in the interview I have already cited. "You might say that America is a conservative country, but what you have conserved very often are liberal ideals, and now you have been moving away from them. You are dissatisfied, frustrated. I believe this is temporary. This is the reason I am not pessimistic about America."

The real task, as he said, is "to enlighten the people"—and this is where I return to my journalism. What *raison d'être* does journalism have except to inform and enlighten the people? What I have written here I would have written in different forms for *The New York Times* if I were still on the paper. I am not out of tune with what my successors are writing for the editorial pages as another decade begins. I have never been more proud of *The Times* than when they began to publish, and to defend their right to publish, the secret Vietnam report in June 1971.

The revolt of youth, poverty, integration, Vietnam, Nixon, Agnew, the role of the United States in the contemporary world —on these and similar basic American problems, I am happy to see that *The New York Times'* editorial policies almost always express ideas that I also hold. This is a truly enormous satisfaction. I do not know whether *The Times* has, without my realizing it, shaped my ideas or whether, in a small way, I have helped to build the image that the paper now presents to its readers. Perhaps it was a two-way street.

The New York Times has been an American institution ever since the days of Adolph S. Ochs. He created a mould into which hundreds of us have been pouring what we have of energy, brains, and heart. The changes that have occurred, and are occurring, are notable, but the basic structure is the same. *The Times* is itself. There is no other newspaper like it, but fortunately, within its familiar edifice, a man can put something different, something special, particular, individual, which gives a personal touch, perhaps a fleeting one, or perhaps a mark that endures. A newspaper lasts a day, but there are some days that are not easily forgotten.

I envy those who will be writing about the 1970's. As I said, I believe we are entering a new age—new for the world and therefore for the United States, and within the United States, for *The New York Times.* Nothing could be more obvious than that another, younger generation of newspapermen should do the writing.

Chapter 12

CHANGING *TIMES*

The institution that Adolph S. Ochs created—compact, paternal, familiar, personal, the most powerful journalistic instrument that had ever been forged in the free world—is no more. It is still, in my opinion, the greatest of all newspapers, but it is not the one I joined in 1922 and worked on for forty-five years. The beautifully simple structure, which Ochs built and Arthur Sulzberger and Orvil Dryfoos preserved, is being tampered with. The diversification of interests; the impersonalism; the transformation of an institution into a big business; new directors; spreading ownership; editors without roots in the old paper—these mean change, not continuity.

I do not think that the huge new organization—the word one must use now instead of institution—is sustaining the quality that the paper possessed in the years that now seem to me to have been the heyday of *The New York Times*. It was this quality, along with its high moral and professional standards, that made *The Times* unique. It is becoming a newspaper like a number of others, just bigger, with incomparable resources and prestige.

But I am prejudiced. I know that there had to be changes. *The New York Times* could not stand still in a revolutionary world. I count myself lucky that my career spanned a period when I could share its harmonious greatness, and still be myself.

There are no vacuums in history, and therefore none in journalism. The events of my career—the world wars, Abyssinia, Spain, Korea, Cuba, Vietnam, the politics of many countries, and all the incredible technological developments—had long gestations, but their cumulative effect, as I have written, has been to transform the world of 1900 into which I was born. Journalism, by definition, also has to be transformed, not only in its techniques, but in the more important fields of understanding and interpretation.

"The greater my experience," Georges Sorel wrote, "the more I have recognized that in the study of historical questions a passion for truth is worth more than the most learned methodologies; it enables one to break through conventional wrappings to penetrate to the foundation of things, and to grasp reality."

I like Sorel's use of the word "passion." Any newspaperman worth his salt has passion; he brings zest and concern to his work, if he be writing about petty larceny in a street corner shop or a world war.

Times like these are exciting and fruitful for journalists. In the United States a dissenter is kicked around, but no authority can prevent him from dissenting. There is fanaticism, bigotry, and intolerant ignorance in the American atmosphere, but there is freedom, too.

Many newspapermen write as their publishers want them to, even though they may feel contempt, amusement, or cynicism about their own work. I never felt critical of such colleagues. They were craftsmen, pursuing a trade. I would have been ashamed to work for a Hearst newspaper in my day, but this was because I had certain beliefs and feelings which would have made pandering to the Hearst press a degrading process. Others did not care and simply did a job for the money and fame that were involved. Only a few believed the nonsense they had to write, as Karl Wiegand seemed to do.

Editorial writing is not a craft or a knack that anyone can learn.

It has one feature that startled me when I joined the Editorial Board toward the end of 1949. I decided that I never before in my career really had to think, and I realized that most people go through life without thinking. I also decided that there is nothing harder to do—and nothing so disturbing.

I could never agree with an only too common belief among newspapermen that they can, and should, be able to write about anything. This is something one cannot get away with in *New York Times'* editorials. Ignorance cannot be disguised from those who know a subject. They may sometimes be few, but they are the ones who count, at least by my standards. At best the result of writing from ignorance is superficial.

Of course, even a large editorial staff like *The Times*—about a dozen writers—has to spread itself thin. I developed some authority on Latin America, but I could hardly hope to follow closely the politics and economics of twenty different countries, aside from having to write about Canada, Western Europe, the Vatican, Vietnam, sometimes the Middle East and Africa, plus obituary and literary editorials. Like the teacher who keeps a step ahead of his pupils, I was often just trying to keep a step ahead of our readers.

Judgment was merciless and swift when an error was made. However esoteric the subject, there was always some reader—or several of them—who would spot a mistake and write a letter to the editor which we would be obliged to print. Such letters had to be borne as just punishment. The annoying ones were from authorities who disputed points which could not by their nature be proved, but which one knew to be true—a priest with more faith than realism, a Cuban with more emotions than facts, an ambassador with diplomatic lies.

There were editorials that I wish I had not written. I felt critical (as did Arthur Sulzberger, Charles Merz, and others on *The Times*, and Secretary of State Dulles in Washington) of Jawaharlal Nehru's policy of neutrality in the cold war. We felt that in India's position, with her dependence on the West and her democratic system, she should be pro-West and anti-Communist. I wrote an editorial headlined "The Lost Leader," which

(416)

created a mild sensation and, as I learned later, hurt and embittered Nehru very much. I realized, too late, that it was a foolish and stupid editorial. Even if Nehru, with the Russians and Chinese on top of India, had a choice—which was doubtful—neutrality was the sensible policy for India at that moment.

"I am fully aware," the British historian E. H. Carr said in one of his lectures on *What is History?* "that if anyone took the trouble to peruse some of the things I wrote before, during and after the [Second World] War, he would have no difficulty at all in convicting me of contradictions and inconsistencies at least as glaring as any I have detected in others. Indeed, I am not sure that I should envy any historian who could honestly claim to have lived through the earth-shaking events of the past fifty years without some radical modifications of his outlook."

How true this is of the journalist as well as the historian! Carr, be it noted, is referring to "outlook," or opinion, or judgments. This does not invalidate my contention that if a journalist gets his facts right on any given day, they will always be right.

Professor Carr is on much more contentious ground in asserting that, "It is scarcely necessary today to argue that the historian is not required to pass moral judgment on the private life of the characters in his story." One contemporary who disagrees with him is Arnold Toynbee. "The intellectual's greatest temptation and worst treason," he wrote, "is to try to contract out of his social responsibility as a human being and a citizen on the pretext that as a scholar he is debarred from making moral and political judgments and from taking action."

Lord Acton, who has been an inexhaustible and incredibly rich source of historic knowledge to me throughout my career, believed that moral judgment is the highest function of the historian. He would surely have said the same of the journalist. I felt as the school of moralists did for many years, but I no longer do so. I think that their attitude introduces a bias that can distort the truth and that, anyway, is unrealistic to me. Bias is the trickiest of all features of journalistic work, as it is in history.

(417)

There is no escaping bias, since we are all human beings, not computers coming up with perfect answers to correctly fed problems.

An advantage of growing old is that one is given time to see the other side of a question, to recognize other feelings, and to acquire some intellectual—not moral—objectivity, while still retaining one's own contemporary bias and feelings. A historian should not apply the moral standards of today in judging, for instance, how the Romans treated Carthage and the Samnite tribes; how the Vikings and Danes acted on forays into Britain; or how the colonists treated the American Indians. We cannot get emotional over Genghis Khan, Tamerlane, or Ivan the Terrible, but we who have lived with them cannot humanly avoid moral condemnation of a Hitler, a Stalin, and other monstrous contemporaries. These are the exceptional cases. Those who attack us newspapermen for favoring or condemning the more normal giants of our time—Roosevelt, Churchill, Johnson, Nixon, De Gaulle, and so on—should stop to think that important historic figures are especially complicated. Only psychopaths and saints are all of a piece. Great men, like lesser ones, are good *and* bad.

"It would be strange to demand clarity from people at a time like ours," Dostoevsky wrote a century ago—but this is even more true today. Perhaps it is imagination or the distortion of too close a view, but the world seems so much more chaotic, anarchic, irrational, and complicated today than it was a hundred years ago. I can understand a deeply religious person being dogmatic. I agree that a statesman or politician should feel sure that his policies are right, or even if he isn't, that he should make believe he is. I would feel sorry for any army whose generals were doubtful about their strategy.

But I do believe that an editor should have a goodly dose of humility, especially if he is writing for *The New York Times*, which has such a powerful impact on Washington and other capitals. This is a different theory from Adolph Ochs' "Good Grey Times" policy. He banned cartoons because they could present only one viewpoint. Editorials that say "on the one hand but on the other hand" are wastes of space. A newspaper can take a positive and critical stand that the government, for reasons of state, must avoid. Many of my editorials attacking Latin American dictators were heartily approved at the State Department at times when official American policies favored the dictators. "What is merit in the writer may well be a vice in the statesman," De Tocqueville wrote—and vice versa.

I naturally had my qualms on many occasions. I often thought that we editorial writers had it too easy; we could tell the government what to do, but had no responsibility for the policies being carried out. It is a commonplace that a man or woman who would not dream of telling the corner grocer how to run his shop has no hesitation in telling the U.S. Secretary of State how to run the foreign affairs of the greatest country on earth. For an editorial writer there is, at times, the gnawing worry that he is doing much the same thing. However, it is also a fact that well-informed newspapermen often do know as much—and even more—of a given subject than the men who make the government's policies. We often have personal contacts which officials must shun. It is ten years since any U.S. government official has talked to Fidel Castro, for instance.

The price to be paid for inside knowledge is worth what it costs. It is true that when one gets on terms of friendship with leading figures (in my case, for instance, Juan Negrín, Rómulo Betancourt of Venezuela, Fidel Castro, José Figueres of Costa Rica, Pietro Nenni), detachment becomes impossible. In such cases the choice is between impartial ignorance and biased knowledge. I have no doubt which is preferable; there is no value in journalism or history built on a vacuum.

To be an intellectual is a handicap. One sees the other fellow's point of view. It is impossible to be dogmatic. There is a loss of authoritativeness. One cannot be sure of the answers. Along with so many of my contemporaries, I have lost a sense of certainty, but I do not resent it, as Orwell did, or anguish over it like Sartre. I long ago stopped quarreling with history.

I believe in journalism by empathy, as I have said before. One cannot understand a man, a people, or a country except by somehow putting oneself, or trying to, in their place, feeling like them, seeing their point of view, trying to understand why they act as they do. Living in a country is most valuable, but it is not necessarily a solution. I encountered many an Englishman in India when it was a colony who had no idea how the Indians felt or why; many an American businessman in Latin America as ignorant of the peoples' ideas and aspirations as a farmer in the Middle West. It was extraordinary to me how correspondents who had been in Cuba for many years failed in 1959 to grasp the fact that a thoroughgoing social revolution was taking place and transforming the island. It could be argued that going from country to country and identifying oneself with each as one goes along is a chameleonlike process. However, the chameleon—in this case, the journalist—only adapts his color; he is always the same animal. Show me a man who does not like *past'asciutta,* and I will say that he does not know Italy. If you cannot tell a Chateau Haut Brion from a Beaujolais, you do not know France. If you cannot speak Spanish, Spain and Latin America will always be closed books.

Despite its pitfalls, there is no substitute for going to the spot and seeing with one's own eyes what is happening. Sensible Samuel Johnson provided what should be a motto for all newspapermen: "Trust as little as you can to report; examine all you can by your own senses."

Every experience helps a journalist to understand. I have been in prison—when the Fascists arrested me in Rome after Pearl Harbor. I have watched men die, men killed in war and men executed. I have seen much violence. One gets hardened, but not emotionally indifferent or objective.

In my stretch on *The Times,* I could work alone, as generations of American correspondents had done before me since the War between the States. There is much less scope for the individual today, *The New York Times* of recent years being a good example of the trend. The big stories are covered by groups in a collective operation. Centralized editorial control in New York by a panel of news editors decides what is wanted, what should be done, and what orders to give so that the far-flung correspondents can provide designated pieces of the mosaic that will make up tomorrow morning's picture.

I believe that *The Times*—and this is generally true for American journalism as a whole—has lost something precious in collectivizing and toning down its news coverage. Objectively and quantitatively, something is gained, but my school of journalism aims more for the subjective truth. We may miss our aim at times, but when we strike the target there is something invaluable and incomparable in the columns of the newspaper. That is the sort of journalism that lives for longer than a day.

I do not mean to say that personalized journalism is a thing of the past and will never return. The tradition is too old and too well established. Tacitus was a good war correspondent. The personal witness, the man on the spot, is in a position to provide the only reliable account of an event. He may possess merely a tiny segment of the truth, but it is worth reams of official communiques, government handouts, and the constructions of historians.

This is why, as a war correspondent, I always went to the front to see what I could see. My stories would almost always be buried inside the paper, while the rewriting of the official communiques by correspondents at headquarters would get the front pages. Those communiques were late, inadequate, and slanted. It would be a foolish historian who relied on them. But an account by an honest and competent correspondent who saw something of the action—even a little something—is the true material of history.

"Lo, this only I have found, that God hath made man upright; but they have sought out many inventions." We have done so in my time in more ways than the Teacher intended with his pregnant word, "inventions." Radio, television, transoceanic cables and telephones, satellites, computers, jet planes, interviews with astronauts on the moon—a great and wonderful flowering of mass communication has made important technical differences since I began my career. But the essence of newspaper work is no different today from what it was when Herodotus wandered around what we know as the Middle East, gathering information at firsthand for his histories.

I am not in tune with our exceptionally irrational age. Reason, rationality, logic, common sense, eighteenth-century Enlightenment, nineteenth-century liberalism—these appeal to me intellectually. They are what I would like but know I cannot get. If I have had any guiding philosophy for most of my career, it is the liberalism of all time, which makes the individual the center of society and of the functioning of government, economics, and politics. This led me at times—the latter years of foreign corresponding and the first years of editorial writing—to the seemingly logical conclusion of desiring to see liberal democracy more or less imposed on all nations. This has been American government policy for a great many years, even—despite favoritism to military dictators—in Latin America. I am glad that I played the role that I did in unseating the dictators in Argentina, Colombia, Venezuela, and Cuba, but I have lost my crusading zeal for liberalism. Perón, Rojas Pinilla, Pérez Jiménez, and Batista were bad for much more than ideological reasons.

If Salvador Allende proves to be a poor President of Chile, it will be for much more than the fact that he is a left-wing Socialist with Communist support. His economic policies may prove as unworkable in Chile as Fidel Castro's have thus far in Cuba, but this is a technical, not a moral, issue. I was sorry to see Communism introduced into Cuba, and I am sorry to see Marxism introduced into Chile. I do not think they will work in an efficient manner. Latin America is still to achieve José Martí's dream of an economic and political system uniquely suited to its special needs. If that day comes, the system will probably be some form of social democracy, centralized and authoritative but, I hope, liberal.

The weakness of my old-fashioned type of liberalism, if it be swallowed whole, and its vulnerability to the attacks of the younger generations today, is that in aspiring to the good, one ignores an abiding reality—the bad. Liberals tend to forget that good and evil coexist. The liberalism of my younger days contained too strong an element of the Enlightenment and the school of John Stuart Mill. We had too much faith in progress, reason, and the happy future of mankind. There was too much emphasis on evil as the product of bad economic and material conditions and not enough on some degree of innate human depravity, vileness, ignorance, and stupidity. The philosophers of the Enlightenment thought that man could create a society in which wars, plagues, famines, and tyranny would disappear. Who can have such faith today? Yet I still like the idea that man can achieve a good and satisfying life on earth and does not have to wait until after death. I cannot imagine when that ideal state will come, but for an agnostic like myself who does not believe in immortality, the idea is comforting.

At my birth, and during my upbringing, liberalism was the instrument of revolution. This is how Lord Acton understood the term. Liberalism was dynamic; it worked for social change. True liberalism still does, even though today it is classed as a variation of conservatism. It is unpopular and even ridiculed as a hypocritical part of the Establishment, a relic of the past. For the British historian Geoffrey Barraclough the challenge to liberalism is "the outstanding feature of contemporary history on the plane of ideas." It is a battle that will not be lost.

The New York Times has been fighting that battle valiantly, especially since John Oakes became editor of the editorial page. This is one way, I am happy to see, in which the newspaper has not changed since I retired.

As I have mentioned before in this book, a great many readers learned to identify my editorials, usually because they would know that I wrote about certain subjects—Latin America, Spain, Canada, Italy, for instance—and sometimes because of my way of writing, or style. Within practical limits, I agreed with *Times'* policy that editorials were anonymous expressions of the newspaper's policies. However, individual editors had to be given much latitude in their specialties, and to that extent the editor who wrote could decide on, or influence, the policy.

My editorials became a part of *The Times'* record, and they were expressions of *Times* policies, but they were *my* editorials. I always thought that John Oakes, after he became editor of the editorial page, went too far in his rigid defense of the page's anonymity. When Meyer Berger wrote *The Story of the New York Times, 1851–1951,* for our centenary, names of the writers of editorials were freely given. Perhaps there should be a statute of limitations. I do not see why the fact that I have written certain editorials must be kept secret now that I am no longer on the Editorial Board and years have passed.

Sometimes an editorial is so sensational that word quickly gets about. Gay Talese mentions some of them in his book on *The Times, The Kingdom and the Power,* including one of mine on Vietnam in my last year as an editor. It referred to the newspaper of November 28, 1966.

"When Punch Sulzberger received his *Times* early edition at home that night and read the editorial, which had been written by Herbert L. Matthews, he called Oakes at home and said that he felt it should be killed. Sulzberger felt that the editorial was too emotional. Oakes, who had been off that day, it being Sunday—his place being taken by his deputy, A. H. Raskin, the former labor specialist—read the editorial, agreed that it was too emotional, but thought that killing it would be too obvious. Oakes convinced Sulzberger that it should be merely toned down, and Oakes did the editing himself in time for the second edition that night, eliminating Herbert Matthews' opening paragraph and starting the editorial with Matthews' second paragraph.

"The emotional version drew a great number of approving letters from readers around the country, while the second received a few; but hardly anyone outside *The Times* organization noticed these changes that morning. . . ."

Talese was wrong, for the episode created a mild sensation in New York and Washington, and in journalistic circles everywhere. As a result, the editorial as I wrote it made an impact far beyond what would have happened if attention had not been so clumsily called to it. I could never figure out why two intelligent men like Punch Sulzberger and John Oakes did not realize that it was too late to make a change. The first edition is the one that goes to Washington, and therefore *my* editorial was the one read by the State Department staff, congressmen and the diplomatic corps, among others. Most of these people also got last editions and saw the difference. Anyway, *The Times'* staffs in Washington and New York were buzzing with the story, including the fact that I had written the editorial.

More than the first paragraph had been omitted and some passages had been rewritten by Oakes. For the historic record, and also as a lesson in journalism, I am giving the editorial as I wrote it. The passages omitted are in italics.

"Truce in the Midst of War"

"Kill and maim as many as you can up to 6 o'clock in the morning of December 24 and start killing again on the morning of December 26. Do your damndest until 6 a.m. December 31 and again after January 1, 1967, when it will be all right to slay, to bomb, to burn, to destroy crops and houses and the works of man until 6 o'clock on the morning of December 24, 1967.

" 'Glory to God in the highest, and on earth peace, good will toward men.'

"By all means, let there be peace for 96 hours, which is that much better than uninterrupted war. Ever since the medieval institution—the truce of God—was invented by the Roman Catholic Church for private wars, the pause that comes in the midst of fighting is a blessed surcease.

"Except for criminals, men do not kill each other for pleasure or material gain. Many millions still alive, who were on the battlefields in the two World Wars, will remember the wonder and heartache that came with the brief silence at Christmas time.

"So, for a few days, we will all be spared those dismal communiques about how many Vietcong have been killed and wounded compared to the casualties on the American and South Vietnamese side.

"The different Gods in which each believes will be thanked. What about the statesmen and the generals on both sides? How much thanks are they

due? The time can be used by all concerned to be prepared to kill that many more when the fighting starts up again. Some young men and some Vietnamese women and children too, will live a few days longer than if there were no truce.

"It is not enough. However, it is being made clear in statements on both sides that this is all there will be. *The holiday truce will be a prelude to another full year of war. Washington, Hanoi and Peking want it that way.* There will be no extended halt of the bombing or the infiltration, no advance toward the peace table."

[The above paragraph was rewritten and Oakes then inserted this passage:

["This is the real irony of the truce. How much more meaningful it would be if it were permitted to lead to a diminution in the process of war, to a continued cessation of the bombing, to action by one or both sides that would give this truce some substance."]

"There will be a peaceful Christmas and a peaceful New Year," my editorial continued, "but neither truce will bring hope as things look now. Neither will create a new situation nor break the automated progress of the war. *Secretary of State Rusk has already rejected 'the idea of a general pause, such as we had a year ago' or, it seems, a cessation of the bombing like last year's.* There will be four days of peace—but not a moment of 'good will on earth.' "

(Aside from the omission about Rusk, Oakes had rewritten the ending to read like this: "There will be a peaceful Christmas and a peaceful New Year, but the truce can hardly bring hope under present circumstances. Nor will it create a new situation or break the automated progress of the war. All wars have to end including this one, but for the moment it looks as though there will be four days of peace—but not one of 'good will on earth.' ")

What upset Punch Sulzberger was the strength of the emotions shown in the editorial as I wrote it. A little emotion would have been all right. The subject was a touchy one. I wrote an emotional obituary editorial on Winston Churchill, for instance, but this was a safe subject. I always felt that the more feeling one could get into an editorial—or, for that matter, a news despatch —the better.

It was no secret that Kennedy, Johnson, and now Nixon were unhappy about the editorial page of *The New York Times*. With Kennedy it was domestic policies; with Johnson, Vietnam. Nixon came after my time, but on the basis of the editorials I have seen, I am pleased and I am sure that Nixon is not. Eisenhower would not have fared so well at the hands of *The Times* if, first, he had not been a personal friend of Arthur Hays Sulzberger who admired and liked him and, second, if the editor had been John Oakes and not Charles Merz.

On April 25, 1964, I had a long and stormy talk with McGeorge Bundy who was then a White House assistant to President Johnson, as he had been to Kennedy. He was sarcastic and bitterly critical of *The Times'* editorials on foreign affairs. "Kennedy," he said, "had a very low opinion of the editorials in *The New York Times;* I don't think there is a shade of difference between the way Johnson feels." We were always attacking the Johnson administration, he complained, "writing editorials on the fringe and never on the heart of subjects, and that was why *The Times* editorials did not have anything like the impact and importance they should have."

The military *coup* overthrowing President João Goulart of Brazil had just taken place. Bundy was furious because we had criticized the Johnson administration for applauding too swiftly and openly, although we, too, were glad to see Goulart go. "The important thing was to get rid of Goulart, and this is what you should have concentrated on," Bundy said. That was his opinion. He did not know enough to realize that the Brazilian generals needed no help from us, and that by rushing in—as Undersecretary George Ball had conceded to me the day before —"the world would be suspicious and critical of us."

Bundy's sharpest criticisms, in fact, were for our editorials on Latin America, which he must have known I wrote. After talking to Bundy, I went upstairs to the press room and ran into Max Frankel, who was then our White House correspondent. When

I told him that Bundy had said that Kennedy, like Johnson, had a very low opinion of *New York Times'* editorials, Max asked: "But did you hear what Kennedy said about you?" I replied, "No." Max said that in talking to Punch Sulzberger—his last talk as it happened—Kennedy asked Punch: "Who is it who does your Latin American editorials, Herb Matthews?" When Sulzberger said, "Yes," Kennedy replied that he did not like *The Times'* editorials, but that the editorials on Latin America were very good. So I felt better.

The news and editorial coverage of the Vietnam War has been more courageous than our coverage of the Spanish Civil War when it was felt necessary to "balance" my despatches from the Loyalist side with stories by William P. Carney from the Franco side. Arthur Hays Sulzberger would never have defied the U.S. government by printing the secret report on Vietnam.

It is rarer now for an individual to make his mark and, in a manner of speaking, become larger than the paper. Harrison Salisbury is virtually alone in this respect on the present staff and he, like myself, has embarrassed *The Times* by unpopular and controversial coverage. But the paper publishes his stories— even from a place like Hanoi—and it is a better newspaper for doing so.

On the editorial side, the nearest thing to the voice of *The New York Times* is the very distinguished column of James R. (Scotty) Reston. I confess that for me, the greatest of American columnists and the wisest, soundest, most thoughtful of American newspapermen in my time has been Walter Lippmann. I always regretted that he did not come to work for *The Times.* When I wrote him (and also did an editorial for *The Times*) to congratulate him on his seventieth birthday (I being almost sixty), I said how comforting it was to see that in his case the older he got the better he wrote. Now he has passed his eightieth birthday, and while he is writing little, the wise old thoughtful brain works as well as ever. He is my ideal of the newspaper commentator.

The Times, which has had Anne O'Hare McCormick, Scotty Reston, Tom Wicker, and (on the informational side) Cyrus Sulzberger, is well provided with good columnists. One should add the superb and charming nature editorials at the bottom of the Sunday second column, which (it is no secret, with due respect to John Oakes) are written by Hal Borland.

I often envied the columnists for their ability to express personal opinions in *The New York Times*, and at one moment I might have become the successor to Anne McCormick when she died in 1954. I was very much in the running, but lost out to Cy Sulzberger, which was just as well, as I doubt that I would have done very well at it. I would have been more controversial. One of the most useful functions of a newspaperman is to disturb the peace, to speed humanity on its endless road of conflict and contradiction, to challenge accepted ideas and principles if they seem outworn or unsuited. The press defends the right of its readers to know—against advertisers and business managers as well as governments. No newspaper has a more honorable record in that respect than *The New York Times.*

We newspapermen, better than actors, hold the mirror up to nature. When the image is sometimes an ugly one, the newspaperman is blamed. If the press had not written about the My Lai massacre in Vietnam, it would not, in popular terms, have occurred. If northern newspaper liberals had not written about the atrocious treatment of Negro demonstrators in Mississippi and Alabama all, it seems, would have been well. Even worse—the brutality of Mayor Daley's police in Chicago during the Democratic convention of 1968 was applauded by a great majority of Americans, who actually resented being told the truth by reporters. It is not that Americans approve of brutality; they do not want to admit that there has been police brutality, or that American soldiers can massacre civilians and rape and kill Vietnamese girls, with no feeling that they are dealing with human beings. Too many readers will not look in the mirror. If they do, as with the Lady of Shalott, it is the mirror that is shattered.

The temptation for a newspaperman is to conform, to go along with the crowd, wave the American flag, applaud a Governor Reagan or a Vice-President Agnew, and stay on the side of the angels. I suppose a majority of newspapermen do go with the crowd—and with their publishers; they have to, if they want to earn a living. But I think too highly of my profession to believe that newspapermen want to conform to what they do not believe.

It is, to be sure, frightening to stand alone. There was a period in the Cuban Revolution when I felt like Horatio at the bridge, and was accused of being like the private with whom the company is out of step.

"This is such a difficult moment to live in, one cannot help getting gloomy and also a bit rattled, and perhaps short-sighted," as E. M. Forster wrote in "Two Cheers for Democracy." However, "difficult moments" are the best ones for the journalist. Peace is not news; war is. The Italian sociologist Gaetano Mosca complained fifty years ago about "how exasperatingly slow history is in moving, at least as compared with the brevity of human life"—but the complaint today is of the dizzy pace of history, which certainly did not move slowly during my time. A career like mine rams home what should be the obvious fact, that change, not stability, is the essence of history.

The praise that journalists prize most and the criticism that cuts deepest, as I have said before, come from fellow newspapermen and from people who have a special competence and hence speak with authority. Those who understand the technical problems that are faced, and those who have the knowledge and authority to say: "This is right (or wrong)"—these are the judges who count. I would rather have the respect of other journalists than the applause of a million readers. There is no higher tribute a journalist can receive than for it to be said: "He is a newspaperman's newspaperman."

I have had my share of praise and blame, of course, and I suppose I got what was coming to me in both respects. Yet it would be sour grapes and stupidity to say that, not having won a Pulitzer Prize, I did not want to win one and that I did not think there were years when it could have been given to me for foreign corresponding, war corresponding, or editorial writing. I had a long run of sourness when it came to *The Times* and Pulitzer Prizes. It is one of the very few touches of bitterness that I took with me into retirement.

(430)

Earlier I have described the generally poor corresponding done by Arnaldo Cortesi both in Italy and Argentina. His despatches reflected in their inacurracy and bias his unwillingness to talk to the right people and to become familiar with the countries he was covering. In spite of this, *The Times* arranged to get him a Pulitzer Prize. This was still the period when Arthur Krock, *The Times'* Washington correspondent, was all-powerful on the Pulitzer Committee. *The Times* and the Associated Press pretty well alternated in giving each other prizes for foreign corresponding.

I am just about certain that my paper never tried to get me a Pulitzer Prize while I was a foreign and war correspondent, although I am not alone in believing there were some excellent and obvious chances. In 1957 and 1958 *The Times* refused to nominate me for the Fidel Castro Sierra Maestra interview, although at that time Castro was still a hero. Other members of the Pulitzer Committee were shocked enough to put up my name, but without support from one's own newspaper there is no hope. The only year for which *The Times* named me was 1965, when John B. Oakes submitted a number of editorials on Vietnam that I had written, attacking the Johnson policy of escalation and also on the Dominican intervention. The Pulitzer Committee always avoids controversial subjects, so it was a forlorn hope. As it happened, my editorials on Vietnam in 1965, 1966, and 1967 put forward ideas and arguments that were to become government policy in 1968 and 1969. So I won other journalistic prizes, but not the Pulitzer award.

Timidity, favoritism, conservatism, avoidance of controversy, the effort or lack of effort made by one's own newspaper, the desire to play safe, the always considerable number of possibilities to choose from, personalities—these factors operate every year on Pulitzer Committees. But let me hasten to add that the foreign journalism prize usually goes to someone who deserves an award. It follows that the prize sometimes goes to one who does not deserve it. There is, therefore, an element of disrepute about the Pulitzer prizes on the whole—which does not mean that any newspaperman is not happy to get it when it comes his way.

When the prizes were given in 1939 at the end of the Spanish Civil War, I had a professional satisfaction which touched me— the kind of tribute that I always cherished. Heywood Broun, writing about the Pulitzer awards in his column in the *World Telegraph*, "It Seems to Me," on May 3, 1939, said:

"In the field of journalism I think that Matthews should have received the prize for the dispatches which he sent from Spain, and my judgment is based wholly on the quality of his writing and the accuracy of his material without regard to any suspicions which some leveled against his sympathies. It is only fair to point out that this same traveling reporter was quite a Mussolini enthusiast in Ethiopia and that his present assignment is in Italy, and so I see no justice in the occasional accusation that he wrote from Spain according to his personal political or economic motivation."

I have treasured this tribute chiefly because I realized in 1939, and I can repeat it more than thirty years later, that I did my best work as a correspondent in the Spanish Civil War. It was this work that led to one of the tributes that I have prized most in my career. It came from Ernest Hemingway, whom I respected and liked so much, and at the great time in both our lives when we were covering the Spanish Civil War. In 1938, when my book on the Abyssinian and Spanish conflicts was published in the United States (*Two Wars and More to Come*), Ernest offered to write an introduction to it, but I preferred to have the book stand or fall on its own merits and not profit by being a "Hemingway item" for future collectors. However, when the publishers asked Hemingway for a few words to use on the dust cover, he cabled them the following message:

Herbert Matthews is the straightest, the ablest and the bravest war correspondent writing today stop He has seen the truth where it was very dangerous to see and in this book he brings that rarest commodity to you stop In a world where faking now is far more successful than the truth he stands like a gaunt lighthouse of honesty stop And when the fakers are all dead they will read Matthews in the schools to find out what really happened stop I hope his office will keep some uncut copies of his despatches in case he dies.

Ernest Hemingway

The last sentence was discreetly omitted in the blurb on the cover of the book, but the rest was reproduced then and on other occasions—which is an excuse for the vanity of publishing it once more.

Chapter 13

VALEDICTION

On the eve of retiring in 1967, I wrote a series of four editorial columns for *The New York Times*. This is how I ended the last of them:

"The revolutionary, the reformer, the dissenter have never had easy roads to travel. Guerrilla fighter, political agitator, journalist—something is risked, whether it be life, freedom, or the respect of the Establishment and of the majority.

"Looking back over the kaleidoscopic changes in the world during these 45 years, and passing in review the men and women who made the history of our times, is a process that leaves some pride, some humility—and a sense of helplessness. There is, at least, a residue of satisfaction in thinking that one did not always go the way of the crowd.

"A newspaperman walks with the great of many lands, but he must go his own way—right to the end of the road."

Some years ago, it occurred to Arthur Hays Sulzberger, then president and publisher, to send "Old Timesers"—those who had been on the paper twenty-five years and more—a novel Christmas card. It was a reduced photographic reproduction of the front page of *The New York Times* for the day on which the employee had joined the paper. Mine was for July 10, 1922.

The world had sounded a minor note the day before. The three-column lead story was on a railway shop strike. There was so little important news that front-page stories were devoted to the octogenarian John D. Rockefeller, Sr., condescending to be photographed and discreetly interviewed by the press; Mrs. Percy Rockefeller's party being marooned by a blizzard on a Yellowstone Peak; and Mrs. Mallory explaining why Suzanne Lenglen beat her in the tennis finals at Wimbledon. The two main foreign stories were about a threatened political crisis in Germany and the fruitless Hague conference over the foreign debts of World War I—written by Edwin L. James, incidentally, who got the only by-line on the page.

Anyone can be a newspaperman, I used to say. George Orwell, in one of his essays, gave four motives for his choice of a writing career: "sheer egoism, aesthetic enthusiasm, historical impulse and political purpose," adding that "by nature. . . . I am a person in whom the first three motives would outweigh the fourth." So am I—plus a primary motive which he left out: it is a way to earn a living, not a very good living, but satisfactory. A newspaperman with a steady job will never be rich or poor. Circumstances, Orwell wrote, forced him "into becoming a sort of pamphleteer." They forced me into becoming a chronicler and editor, and accidental journalist or, as I much prefer to be called, a newspaperman.

There is a time for everything, and the time came for me to retire. I chose a period when I knew that I was still useful and would be missed, and when I could count on some years ahead to write books.

"In the winter of 1967," Gay Talese wrote in his book about *The New York Times, The Kingdom and the Power*, "Herbert L. Matthews sat rather forlornly in Room 1048 along a corridor of editorial writers on the tenth floor. Nothing would please him less than to be described as forlorn, a man doing penance in an ivory tower because he had embarrassed *The Times* years ago in Cuba."

After telling of my problems with the office over Cuba, Talese went back to 1949 when I joined the Editorial Board.

"Matthews was then a favorite son of the institution, enjoying a warm relationship with the owners of *The Times;* Iphigene Sulzberger was the godmother to Matthews' only son. But now, in 1967, after forty-five years, he was preparing to leave *The Times,* planning to devote himself to his books and to his belief that history will finally absolve him."

Actually, the "warm relationship" which Talese mentioned never did and never will end. My difficulties with *The Times* over Cuba were professional, as I have said, not personal. Before I left, Arthur Sulzberger, then far gone in his last illness, asked me to come up to his office to say goodbye. I knew that it would be a final farewell and it was, for me, a moving experience. We had worked together for forty of my forty-five years on the paper, during which he had been a friend as well as a boss. So had Iphigene Sulzberger. My wife and I knew Punch since he was a child, and saw the three daughters often in the Sulzberger homes before they were married. *The Times* was so much more to me than a place to work, or a great institution.

I planned to quit at the end of May 1967, but John Oakes seemed so dismayed at the idea of my leaving that I agreed to stay on until the end of September. I had written him this notification on January 9:

> Dear Johnnie:
>
> I will be telling you this in person, but I also thought it best for you to have it on record.
>
> This is a regretful notification that I must resign. If it is all right for you, I would stop work on May 1. Since I presume I would have an annual vacation coming to me, I will start it on that day, using the month of May to clear out my office and—what is infinitely more complicated—for Nancie and me to liquidate our belongings and get out of our apartment by subleasing it. I will arrange to have compensatory time, if necessary, so that technically I will be on the payroll until May 31. [This became September 30.] . . .

I hope I am giving you enough time to find a replacement. In any event, I have no illusions of indispensability. It has been a long run—45 years by the time I leave —and there has to be an end to everything. I shall be 67 years old tomorrow. I want to leave while I can still work. I have a contract for the biography of Fidel Castro for Penguin, and I have another book in mind. I am no longer strong enough to do a day's work and write books on the side. I am quite tired nowadays when I finish a day at the office. . . .

I do not need to tell you or Arthur or Punch how I feel. One does not lightly make a decision like this, but it had to be made.

Please—as with Bill Ogdon [a recently resigned editor]—let me steal silently away, by which I mean no fuss, no farewell party, no silver trays with everybody's name on it, no nothing. Let Nature take its course.

I should add, in case my crotchetinesses give you the slightest doubt, that I have enjoyed working with you more than I can say. You are doing a grand job, and it is a truly great satisfaction to end my career on *The Times* with someone I respect as much as I like.

Oakes wrote a charming farewell piece about me for our house organ, *Times Talk,* September 1967. It contained another of the nicest tributes I had in my career: "Stubborn individualist, gloomy prophet, and dour observer that he is, Herbert's contribution both to the editorial page and to *The Times* as a whole has been immeasurable."

Arthur Hays Sulzberger died on December 11, 1968, while I was on a visit to New York. The newspaper is the same but, as I said, it is different, too. It was clear from the beginning that Punch Sulzberger would not be happy until he was surrounded by men of his own age. Except for John Oakes (who is only ten years older) he achieved this aim by the end of 1969. It is not a happy paper any longer for most of the old-timers in the news departments. I would feel like a poor relation if I were still on

The Times, an object of tolerant affection from a past generation.

My favorite passage from *Tristram Shandy*, ever since I first read it more than a half-century ago, and long before I knew it was so famous, is sadly, drolly serious and sentimental for one of the funniest books in the English language:

"Time wastes too fast; every letter I trace tells me with what rapidity Life follows my pen; the days and hours of it, more precious, my dear Jenny! than the rubies about thy neck, are flying over our heads like light clouds of a windy day, never to return more—every thing presses on—whilst thou art twisting that lock,—see! it grows grey; and every time I kiss thy hand to bid adieu, and every absence which follows it, are preludes to that eternal separation which we are shortly to make.—

"Heaven have mercy on us both!"

Laurence Sterne was being wistful and nostalgic, not really sad, and not saying good-bye to life and work, any more than I do on passing seventy. For Nancie and me it has been a long journey through many lands, in good times and bad—youth, children, middle age, grandchildren, old age—the familiar, eternal progression that was yet so different for us than for others. Now, as 1971 moves on and this book ends, we are back in Cannes, France, in sunshine, among people we like, in a country we have always loved and where our children were born.

Benedetto Croce, then 79, said to me in Naples: "The lights of the world are now garish; they are not good for old eyes." I do not feel so—at least, not yet.

On September 30, 1967, I walked quietly out of my office in *The New York Times* and went home to finish packing for a journey that is yet to end. As I had written Johnny Oakes, I wanted no farewell party. I would have felt as if I were attending the wake at my own funeral.

APPENDIX

On February 24, 25, and 26, 1957, The New York Times *published three articles, the first containing my interview with Fidel Castro in the Sierra Maestra on February 17, and the other two reports on the prerevolutionary situation in Batista's Cuba. A condensation of these articles follows. Two features deserve special attention in the light of later developments and knowledge. Castro then professed—and in my opinion sincerely intended—to make a revolution in a liberal democratic framework. The Cuban Communists were sabotaging him at the time. The other factor is that Castro led me to believe that his forces were larger and stronger than they really were.*

FEBRUARY 24, 1957

"Fidel Castro, the rebel leader of Cuba's youth, is alive and fighting hard and successfully in the rugged, almost impenetrable fastnesses of the Sierra Maestra at the southern tip of the island.

"President Fulgencio Batista has the cream of his Army around the area, but the Army men are fighting a thus-far losing battle to destroy the most dangerous enemy General Batista has yet faced in a long and adventurous career as a Cuban leader and dictator.

"This is the first sure news that Fidel Castro is still alive and still in Cuba. No one connected with the outside world, let alone with the press, has seen Señor Castro except this writer. No one in Havana, not even at the United States Embassy with all its resources for getting information, will know until this report is published that Fidel Castro is really in the Sierra Maestra.

"This account, among other things, will break the tightest censorship in the history of the Cuban Republic. . . . Havana does not and cannot know that thousands of men and women are heart and soul with Fidel Castro and the new deal for which they think he stands."

The article goes on to describe the formidable nature of the opposition to Batista of which Castro and his 26th of July Movement were "the flaming symbol." I pointed out that Fidel headed "a revolutionary movement that calls itself socialistic."

"The program is vague and couched in generalities, but it amounts

(439)

to a new deal for Cuba, radical, democratic and therefore anti-Communist. . . .

"To arrange for me to penetrate the Sierra Maestra and meet Fidel Castro, dozens of men and women in Havana and Oriente Province ran a truly terrible risk. . . .

"From the looks of things, General Batista cannot possibly hope to suppress the Castro revolt."

At this point I gave some details of Fidel's family background and adventurous career, through the mad attack on the Moncada Barracks on July 26, 1953, to the disastrous landing with 82 comrades from Mexico on December 2, 1956, in which only Castro and a dozen companions survived to make a stand in the jungles of the Sierra Maestra. The Havana government was saying that Castro was dead. In a despatch widely disseminated throughout the United States and Latin America, the United Press International had told how he was killed in the December 2nd landing.

"Only those fighting with him," I wrote, "and those who had faith and hope, knew or thought he was alive—and those who knew were very few and in the utmost peril of their lives if their knowledge was traced. This was the situation when the writer got to Havana on February 9 to try to find out what was really happening."

I described how Fidel sent word to a trusted source in Havana to contact a foreign correspondent who could be taken to him and later fly out to write the story. After six days of organization, the come-on signal was received from the Sierra to meet Castro two days later. This meant driving 500 miles all night to the jumping-off point, which was Manzanillo.

"The plan worked out to get through the Army road blocks in Oriente was as simple as it was effective," I wrote. "We took my wife along in the car as 'camouflage.' Cuba is at the height of the tourist season and nothing could have looked more innocent than a middle-aged couple of American tourists driving down to Cuba's most beautiful and fertile province with some young friends [Faustino Pérez, Javier Pazos, and Liliam Mesa]. The guards would take one look at my wife, hesitate a second, and wave us on with friendly smiles. . . .

"In that way we reached the house of a sympathizer of Fidel Castro outside the Sierra. There my wife was to stay amid warm hospitality, and no questions asked. I got into the clothes I had purchased in Havana 'for a fishing trip,' warm for the cold night air of the mountains and dark for camouflage. After nightfall I was taken to a certain house. . . . A courier who owned an open, army-type jeep joined us."

The courier's news was bad and he at first balked at driving the four of us, who were going in, to the foot of the Sierra from where we were to climb up to meet Castro and his band. An army patrol was blocking the road we had to take, the courier said, and anyway, heavy rains had turned all the roads into mud. However, he reluctantly agreed to go by a circuitous route where only one stretch was heavily patroled by Batista's troops. Some guards stopped us on the main road before we turned in to the hills, but we had a good cover story, and although they seemed dubious, they let us through. The jeep bogged down hopelessly before it reached its destination, but we slithered through the mud on foot to a marked spot, turned off the road, and waded through a muddy, bitterly cold stream almost up to our knees. Fifty yards up the slope was our meeting place with scouts whom Castro was supposed to send down to guide us, but they were not there. After a frustrating two-hour wait, sitting on the muddy, chill ground, under the shelter of some bushes to hide from the full moon's light, and eaten up by mosquitoes, one of our party located a rebel scout and brought him down to us.

"The scout was a squatter from the hills," I wrote, "and he needed to know every inch of the land to take us as he did, swiftly and unerringly across fields, up steep hills, floundering in the mud."

He had led us to a grove, dense with vegetation, dripping with wet leaves and boughs. Fidel was encamped some distance away and sent word that he would join us at daybreak. (Incidentally, Che Guevara was with him but did not come down, and I was not to meet him until he entered Havana.) Someone lent me a blanket and I had two hours blessed sleep.

"With the light I could see how young they all were," I continued. "The captain of this troop was a stocky Negro with a black beard and mustache, a ready, brilliant smile and a willingness for publicity. Of all the men I met, only he wanted his name mentioned—Juan Almeida. [He was to become commander-in-chief of the Cuban army.]

"Raúl Castro, Fidel's younger brother, slight and pleasant, came into the camp with others of the staff, and a few minutes later Fidel himself strode in. Taking him, as one would at first, by physique and personality, this was quite a man—a powerful six-footer, olive-skinned, full-faced, with a straggly beard. He was dressed in an olive grey fatigue uniform and carried a rifle with a telescopic sight, of which he was very proud."

We went to my blanket and sat down. Someone brought ham sandwiches and coffee; Fidel broached a box of cigars, and for three uninterrupted hours we conversed.

"No one could talk above a whisper at any time," my story went on.

"There were columns of Government troops all around us, Señor Castro said, and their one hope was to catch him and his band.

"The personality of the man is overpowering. It was easy to see that his men adored him and also to see why he has caught the imagination of the youth of Cuba all over the island. Here was an educated, dedicated fanatic, a man of ideals, of courage and of remarkable qualities of leadership.

"As the story unfolded . . . one got a feeling that he is now invincible. Perhaps he isn't, but that is the faith he inspires in his followers. . . .

"Castro is a great talker. His brown eyes flash; his intense face is pushed close to the listener and the whispering voice, as in a stage play, lends a vivid sense of drama.

" 'We have been fighting for seventy-nine days now and are stronger than ever,' Señor Castro said. 'The soldiers are fighting badly; their morale is low and ours could not be higher. . . . The Cuban people hear on the radio all about Algeria, but they never hear a word about us or read a word, thanks to the censorship. You will be the first to tell them. I have followers all over the island. All the best elements, especially all the youth, are with us. The Cuban people will stand anything but oppression.' "

He complained about the fact that the well-equipped government troops fighting him were using American arms.

"His is a political mind rather than a military one," I went on to say. "He has strong ideas of liberty, democracy, social justice, the need to restore the Constitution, to hold elections. He has strong ideas on economy, too, but an economist would consider them weak. . . .

" 'Batista has 3,000 men in the field against us [he said]. I will not tell you how many we have, for obvious reasons. . . . It is a battle against time, and time is on our side. . . .

" 'They never know where we are,' he said as the group rose to say goodbye, 'but we always know where they are. You have taken quite a risk in coming here, but we have the whole area covered, and we will get you out safely.' "

"They did. We ploughed our way back through the muddy undergrowth in broad daylight, but always keeping under cover. . . . There was one road block to get through with an Army guard so suspicious our hearts sank, but he let us through.

"After that, washed, shaved and looking once again like an American tourist, with my wife as 'camouflage,' we had no trouble driving back to safety [in Santiago de Cuba] and then on to Havana. So far as anyone knew, we had been away fishing for the weekend, and no one bothered us as we took the plane to New York."

FEBRUARY 25, 1957

"President Fulgencio Batista of Cuba is fighting off a revolutionary offensive. As of today, he has the upper hand, and with any luck he can hang on until his Presidential term ends in February, 1959. The economy is good and most workers are contented. There are profitable sugar, coffee and tobacco crops. Tourism has been satisfactory. Investments from the United States are high and General Batista has been made to feel he has the United States behind him. The upper echelons of the Army and the police are his men and they give him his power.

"Yet the President needs luck, for Cubans are a violent, unpredictable people, and the forces lined up against General Batista are strong and getting stronger every day."

I went on to say now unpopular Batista was and how he had lost the young generation of whom the group of rebels led by Fidel Castro was dramatic proof.

"Señor Castro's men; the student leaders who are on the run from the police; the people who are bombing and sabotaging, are fighting blindly, rashly, perhaps foolishly. But they are giving their lives for an ideal and for their hopes of a clean, democratic Cuba. The extent of the violence and the counter-terrorism of the Army and the police are among the things that have been hidden by the censorship."

The rest of the article was taken up with a description of the hitherto concealed, brutal, and "desperate" counterterrorism of the Cuban authorities. I also pointed out that at that time Communism had "little to do with the opposition to the regime" either in the cities or in the Sierra Maestra.

"It is universally agreed," I continued, "that there is more corruption than ever under the Batista regime, and this is saying a great deal in Cuba. The enormous peculations, in which President Batista is said by everyone to take a large share, is more concentrated now, being mostly in the hands of Army generals and public works contractors. There is smuggling on a great scale and Havana is becoming a wide open city for gambling. . . .

"The Cubans are a volatile, tough and brave people. Their anger and disappointment have been rising steadily. It is being said in Cuba that because of this, the future looks more hopeful."

FEBRUARY 26, 1957

"The old, corrupt order in Cuba is being threatened for the first time since the Cuban Republic was proclaimed early in the century. An internal struggle is now taking place that is more than an effort by the outs to get in and enjoy the enormous spoils of office that have been the reward of political victory. . . .

"The best elements in Cuban life are bitterly or sadly anti-United States. . . . The opposition says there is an infinitely harder problem because Washington is backing President Batista and many 'proofs' are offered. The first is the public cordiality and admiration for General Batista expressed on frequent occasions by United States Ambassador Arthur Gardner. Another is the friendliness of the United States investors and businessmen who, despite their misgivings, naturally want to protect their investments and businesses. 'We all pray every day that nothing happens to Batista,' one of the most prominent directors said to me. They fear that the alternative would be much worse, at least in the beginning, perhaps a military junta, perhaps a radical swing to the left, perhaps chaos.

"There is also bitter criticism in Cuba. . . . over the sale of United States arms. While I was there, seven tanks were delivered in a ceremony headed by Ambassador Gardner."

I described the civic resistance movements in Santiago de Cuba and Havana, and then discussed the powerful student opposition against Batista.

"The directorate of the Federation of University Students," I wrote, "has been on the run from the police for many weeks, thus far successfully. The authorities accuse them of complicity with Fidel Castro, with whom they signed a pact in Mexico City, but they say they are fighting a parallel, separate fight for the same goals. . . .

"Through underground connections I was able secretly to see five members of the student directorate, including their leader, José Antonio Echevarría, whom the police want most of all, and who therefore has considerable fame in Cuba at the moment. . . .

"Senor Echevarría said the students were active in the present resistance, which may or may not have meant they were taking part in the bombings and sabotage. The students, he said, would get behind a respected civic resistance movement, but meanwhile they are waiting their chance to get into the streets and join a revolution if there is one. . . .

"Their talk was studded with phrases such as these: 'Cuban students were never afraid to die,' and 'We are accustomed to clandistine struggle.' This is true.

"So one sees three elements lining up against President Batista today—the youth of Cuba led by the fighting rebel, Fidel Castro, who are against the President to a man; a civic resistance formed of respected political, business and professional groups, and an honest, patriotic component of the Army, which is ashamed of the actions of the Government generals. Together these elements form the hope of Cuba and the threat to General Fulgencio Batista."

(On March 15, 1957, students attacked the Presidential Palace in Havana in an attempt to kill Batista. José Antonio Echevarría and another of the students were killed. One of the five to whom I spoke—Faure Chomón—survived to become a cabinet minister in the Castro government.)

INDEX